M000201765

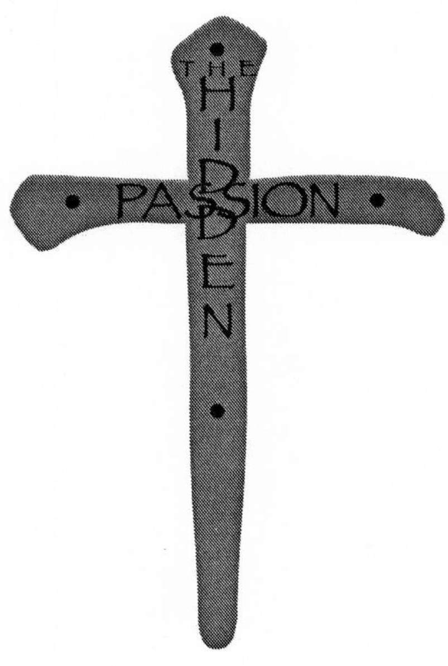
THE
HIDDEN
PASSION

◆ ◆ ◆

The Nazarene looked at her, and for a few moments, their eyes met. It frightened him to see his own face mirrored in hers. But his mother's face was wiser, more feminine and mysterious. Though he was a part of her, and she a part of him – he did not know her.

"I walk the Messiah's path..." Jesus revealed.

For a long time, the Virgin said nothing.

"...Then you know," she said at last.

"And you have always known..?"

His mother nodded. "Before the three magi left us, just after your birth, they warned me to be careful. Many great powers were searching for you, they said, hoping to destroy you. They themselves had avoided Herod's spies and gone into hiding. But they could not conceal themselves from other powers, from the stars in the heavens watching our movements here below."

The old woman gave him a look that pierced him to the bone.

"The more you know about yourself, the more they will come to know about you. The more you reveal yourself, the greater the risk that they will find you. When you were ignorant of these things – in the monastery, even here in this home – you were safe. Now, with each step you take, you risk discovery. Only the prophecy can protect you."

"The Five Seals..." the Nazarene realized.

"They will seal and protect you. But others want to seize their power for themselves. You must find the seals – find all of them – particularly the fifth. Until then, you are vulnerable."

She took his head in her arms, caressed his hair, and anointed his forehead with a kiss.

"I am only a woman; a daughter of Israel blessed and chosen by God. I can only tell you what Wisdom reveals through me. You understand?"

The son of Nazareth nodded.

"Then know that you will never find the fifth seal alone. Only a daughter of Israel can help you..."

His mother looked at him, as his eyes opened wide. She nodded her head gently two or three times. "Yes, you know it yourself... First, you must betroth yourself to Mary of Magdala..."

◆ ◆ ◆

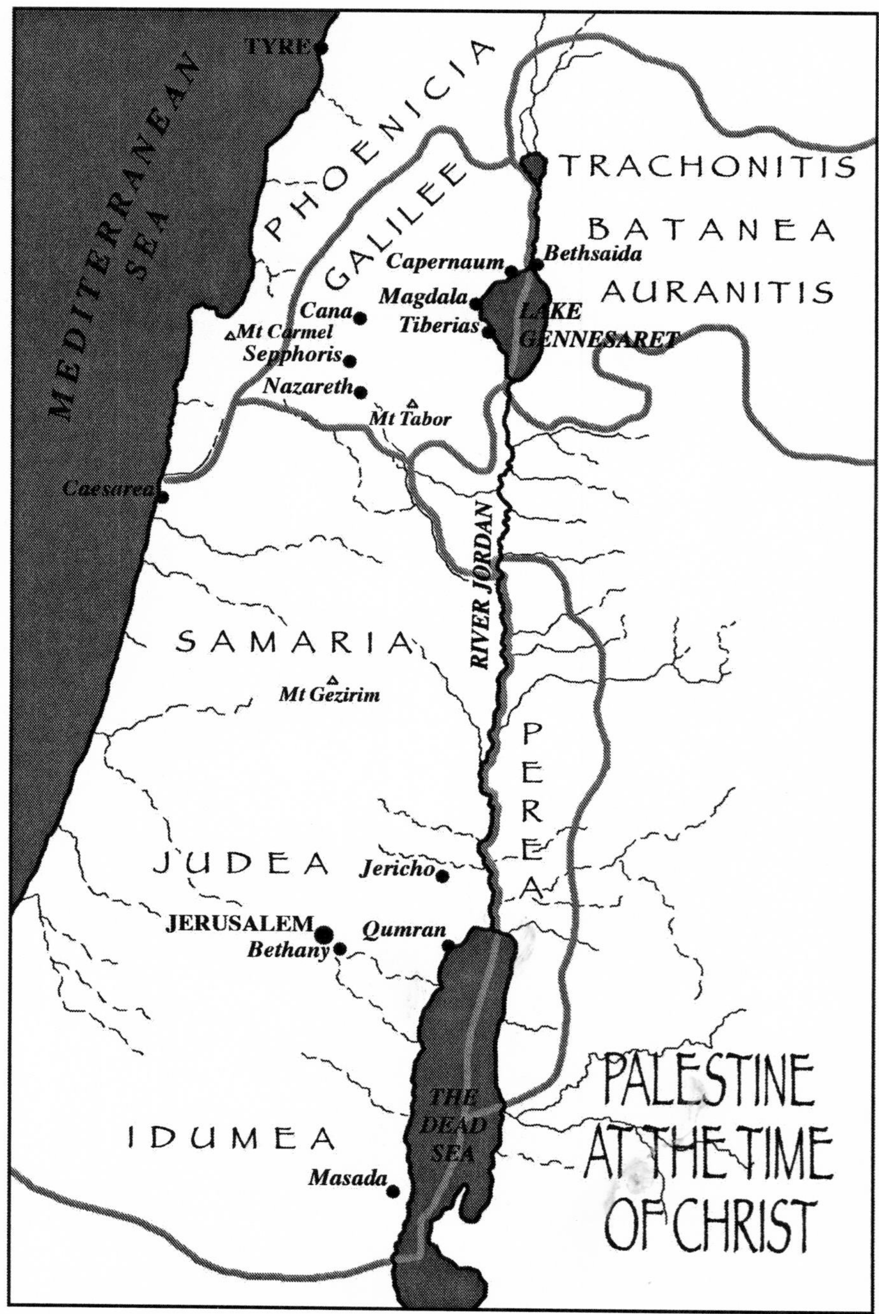
TYRE
MEDITERRANEAN SEA
PHOENICIA
GALILEE
TRACHONITIS
BATANEA
AURANITIS
Capernaum
Bethsaida
Magdala
Cana
Tiberias
LAKE GENNESARET
Mt Carmel
Sepphoris
Nazareth
Mt Tabor
Caesarea
RIVER JORDAN
SAMARIA
Mt Gezirim
PEREA
JUDEA
Jericho
JERUSALEM
Qumran
Bethany
THE DEAD SEA
IDUMEA
Masada
PALESTINE AT THE TIME OF CHRIST

THE HIDDEN PASSION

A NOVEL OF THE GNOSTIC CHRIST
BASED ON THE NAG HAMMADI TEXTS

L. CARUANA

RECLUSE
PUBLISHING
-2007-

THE HIDDEN PASSION

Published by Recluse Pub.
First edition - 2007
Printed in the United States of America on acid-free paper

For more information on Gnosticism
and for the source texts cited in the margins:
http://www.GnosticQ.com
About the author:
http://www.LCaruana.com

Copies of this book may be ordered through:
http://www.GnosticQ.com

Front cover image: Masaccio, The Crucifixion, altarpiece of Pisa
Back cover image: Photo of Nag Hammadi manuscripts by Jean Doresse

Library of Congress cataloging-in-publication data
Caruana, Laurence, 1962 -
The Hidden Passion:
A Novel of the Gnostic Christ Based on the Nag Hammadi Texts
1st edition - Recluse Publishing
ISBN 13: 978-0-9782637-0-6
ISBN 10: 0-9782637-0-7
1. Gnosticism
2. Gnosticism - fiction
3. Title

CONTENTS

This book is dedicated to
Florence Ménard
Mein Licht, my soul, ma soeur
Mein Leben, my love, mon coeur

About the Author

L. Caruana is an artist and writer living in Paris. He holds a Philosophy degree in Hermeneutics (the study of Biblical Interpretation) and is the author of *Enter Through the Image: The Ancient Image Language of Myth, Art and Dreams*, also published by Recluse.

From his studio in the Bastille quarter, he edits *The Visionary Revue* while exhibiting his works across Europe.

See: LCaruana.com, GnosticQ.com and VisionaryRevue.com

PREFACE

Lest my intentions be misconstrued from the beginning, this is a novel of the *Gnostic* Christ. The canonical gospels of Mark, Matthew, Luke and John have provided us with the traditional fourfold interpretation of Jesus' words and deeds.

But, over the course of the last two centuries, numerous 'non-canonical' texts have resurfaced which offer important, alternative versions of the life of Christ. In particular, the Nag Hammadi Corpus, unearthed in Egypt in 1945, retells the Christian gospel from – what is generally accepted as – a Gnostic standpoint. Supplemented by other non-canonical gospels, these texts offer sayings and narrative fragments which lie outside the narrower scope of the orthodox accounts.

By gathering these texts together, I have sought to present, in narrative form, the life of the Gnostic Christ. From the beginning, the man Jesus must be separated from the heavenly Christ, who only descends into Jesus during his baptism in the Jordan. Thereafter, Mary Magdalene and Judas Didymos Thomas play pivotal roles in the Messiah's quest for the Five Seals. And towards the end, a fundamentally different vision of the Passion emerges. Much of this novel is dedicated to a coherent and dramatic presentation of Gnosticism and its unique worldview.

But Gnosticism yields a wide variety of interpretations since the texts themselves – a rich plurality of the Christian Word – can be inherently contradictory. I have not hesitated to include disparate, even contradictory accounts (the Bridal Chamber, the Passion) with the idea in mind that these, through the reader's own interpretation, will offer up a fuller, more comprehensive understanding of the Gnostic stance.

Scholars are generally agreed on the methods which the four evangelists used to compose their canonical accounts. In the three synoptic gospels, Matthew and Luke based their narratives on Mark, while also employing *a list of Jesus' sayings* that scholars later called 'Q' (from the German *Quelle* for 'source'). The fourth evangelist, John, based his narrative on an earlier 'Signs gospel', while adding many *sayings* that are *not* found in the synoptic gospels (perhaps from another *'Q' list*). A good number of these sayings have a decidedly Gnostic ring to them, though John's gospel is clearly *more* than Gnostic.

This theory of the gospels' composition was partially confirmed when *The Gospel of Thomas* resurfaced in the Nag Hammadi Corpus. This 'gospel' presents *a list of Jesus' sayings* – exactly as Q was imagined to be. Some of the sayings in Thomas are orthodox; others are clearly Gnostic.

For many years, I nurtured the hope of presenting the tale of the Gnostic Christ, based on the methods of the four evangelists. To this end, I created *the Gnostic Q* through a careful reading of the related texts, isolating *sayings* that could be attributed to the Gnostic Christ. At the same time, I identified narrative fragments (the baptism in the Jordan, the transfiguration, the crucifixion) which offer uniquely Gnostic interpretations of these established mythologems.

After several years of inspired labour, the forgotten gospel of the Gnostic Christ gradually emerged. The sayings from *the Gnostic Q* were woven into the narrative fragments, thus creating an alternative version of Christ's teachings and his final Passion. Since the Gnostic account has remained hidden for most of our history, I have titled my novelization, *The Hidden Passion.*

Through the use of pointed brackets < >, all the Gnostic sayings and narrative fragments are clearly indicated over the course of the novel's unfolding. The textual references for these citations are provided in the margins, near the beginning of each bracketed passage. A complete list of the citations, in the standard translations, can be found on-line under *Textual Sources for The Hidden Passion* at GnosticQ.com.

Alas, in an age of copyright, where even the translations of ancients texts are protected by law, it is not possible to quote long passages of the standard translations of the Nag Hammadi Texts *verbatim.* (If Matthew and Luke were to publish their gospels today, Mark would surely sue them for copyright violation...)

On the other hand, this opens up other creative possibilities for the author. The stilted biblical phrasings have been modified to roll off the characters' tongues more easily. Thus, a sentence such as: *"And so speak I, separating off the manhood. Perceive thou therefore in the first place of the Word; then shalt thou perceive the Lord, and in the third place the man, and what he hath suffered."* (Acts of John 101) has been replaced by: *"I have cast off my humanity, so you might see me as the Word, and not only as a man who has suffered."* (p. 407). In the vast majority of cases, the original sense of the utterance has been preserved.

My fundamental premise has been *to let the Gnostic texts speak for themselves.* But, due to their multiple redactions, fragmented condition and obscure terminology, the Gnostic texts can easily become a confusing labyrinth of speculations. In order to make a clear presentation of the Gnostic worldview, I have had to make certain creative decisions which, *per force*, delimit and interpret the Gnostic stance. In the *Afterword*, I explain some of the motivations for these decisions. The back pages of the novel also include *A Glossary* and *A Diagram of the Gnostic Cosmos,* which may be helpful in threading one's way through the Gnostic labyrinth...

It is my hope that the reader, in the true Gnostic spirit, will encounter these texts and experience their revelations *in his or her own way* – freed from dogma and authority, as a unique and living experience.

L. Caruana
Paris, Dec 2006

A NOTE ON THE SOURCES

I have, for the most part, avoided using the Canonical Gospels as a source of sayings, since these are already well-known. The exception is *The Gospel of John*, in cases when it reveals some very strong Gnostic sentiments.

My main source has been the fifty-two tractates found in *The Nag Hammadi Library*. Some of the texts in this collection are *not* Gnostic; others are Gnostic but non-Christian (e.g. Sethian, Hermetic). Nevertheless, I have included *all* of them as possible sources, since the ancient editor of this collection deemed them worthy of inclusion.

Outside *The Nag Hammadi Library*, I have not hesitated to cite passages from texts which are generally recognized as Gnostic: *The Gospel of Mary (Magdalene), The Acts of John, The Acts of Peter, The First and Second Books of Jeu, The Untitled Text in the Bruce Codex, The Pistis Sophia* and the recently released *Gospel of Judas*.

I have also used ancient texts which express certain insights in a language that is akin to Gnosticism. These include *The Hymn of the Pearl, The Corpus Hermeticum, The Asclepius* and *The Odes of Solomon*.

The testimonies of the heresiologists (*Irenaeus, Clement, Epiphanius*) have been used sparingly. The exception is their accounts of Gnostic libertinism (pp. 329 - 331), the Ophite diagram (p. 305), and those cases where their writings illuminate obscure events in Gnostic myth (e.g. the Valentinian version of Sophia's passion on pp. 230 - 231).

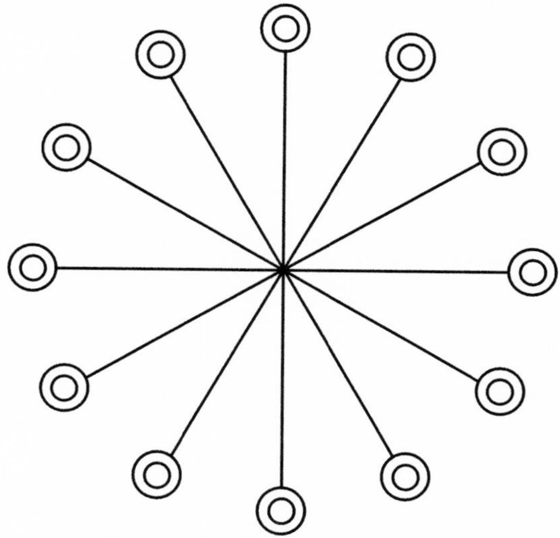

A Gnostic Sign from *The Book of Jeu*

ABBREVIATIONS OF THE SOURCE TEXTS

1Ap Jas - The (First) Apocalypse of James - NHC V.3.
1Bk Jeu - The (First) Book of Jeu (Ieou) - Codex Brucianus
1Kings - The First Book of Kings - Old Testament
2Ap Jas - The (Second) Apocalypse of James - NHC V.4.
2Bk Jeu - The (Second) Book of Jeu (Ieou) - Codex Brucianus
2Kings - The Second Book of Kings - Old Testament
2Tr Seth - The Second Treatise of the Great Seth - NHC VII.2.
3St Seth - The Three Steles of Seth - NHC VII.5.
A Gs Mt - The Apocryphal Gospel of Matthias in Clement of Alexandria
Act Pt 12A - The Acts of Peter and the Twelve Apostles - NHC VI.1.
Acts Jn - The Acts of John
Acts Pt - The Acts of Peter - Papyrus Berolinensis 8502
Allog - Allogenes - NHC XI.3.
Anoint - On the Anointing - NHC XI.2a.
Ap Adam - The Apocalypse of Adam - NHC V.5.
Ap Jn - The Apocryphon of John - NHC II.1.
Ap Paul - The Apocalypse of Paul - NHC V.2.
Ap Pt - The Apocalypse of Peter - NHC VII.3.
Ap Jas - The Apocryphon of James - NHC I.2.
Apology - Plato, The Apology
Ascl - Asclepius
Auth T - The Authoritative Teaching - NHC VI.3.
Avesta - Avesta: Yasna, Ushtavaiti Gatha
Bap A - On Baptism A - NHC XI.2b.
Bap B - On Baptism B - - NHC XI.2c.
CH - The Corpus Hermeticum
Dial Sav - The Dialogue of the Saviour - NHC III.5.
Disc 8-9 - The Discourse on the Eighth and the Ninth - NHC VI.6.
Epiph - Epiphanius, Panarion
Euch A - On the Eucharist A - NHC XI.2d.
Euch B - On the Eucharist B - NHC XI.2 e.
Eugnos - Eugnostos the Blessed - NHC III.3.
Ex Soul - The Exegesis on the Soul - NHC II.6.
Exod - Exodus - Old Testament
Fl Sophe - The tomb inscription of Flavia Sophe
Fr Bruce - Fragments of the Bruce Codex - Codex Brucianus
Gen - Genesis - Old Testament
Gr Pow - The Concept of Our Great Power - NHC VI.4.
Gs Egypt - The Gospel of the Egyptians - NHC III.2.
Gs Jud - The Gospel of Judas - Codex Tchacos
Gs Magd - The Gospel of Mary (Magdalene) - Papyrus Berolinensis 8502
Gs Phil - The Gospel of Philip - NHC II.3.
Gs Thom - The Gospel of Thomas - NHC II.2.
Gs Tru - The Gospel of Truth - NHC I.3.
Hyp Arch - The Hypostasis of the Archons - NHC II.4.
Int Kn - The Interpretation of Knowledge - NHC XI.1.
Iren - Irenaeus, Adversus Haereses

Isaiah - Isaiah - Old Testament
Jer - Jeremiah - Old Testament
Jn - The Gospel according to John - New Testament
Jos - Josephus, Jewish Antiquities
L Pt Ph - The Letter of Peter to Philip - NHC VIII.2.
Lev - Leviticus - Old Testament
Lk - The Gospel according to Luke - New Testament
Lucian - Lucian (attributed to), The Syrian Goddess (De Dea Syria)
Mars - Marsanes - NHC X.
Meta - Aristotle, The Metaphysics
Melch - Melchizedek - NHC IX.1.
Micah - Micah - Old Testament
Mk - The Gospel according to Mark - New Testament
Mt - The Gospel according to Matthew - New Testament
NH Ascl - Asclepius 21 - 29 - NHC VI.8.
Norea - The Thought of Norea - NHC IX.2.
Num - Numbers - Old Testament
Ode Sol - The Odes of Solomon
Ophite Dia - Ophite Diagram - Origen, Contra Celsus Bk VI, Ch. 38
Orig Wld - On the Origin of the World - NHC II.5.
Oxyr - The Oxyrhynchus Papyrus 840
P Shem - The Paraphrase of Shem - NHC VII.1.
Pearl - The Hymn of the Pearl - from The Acts of Thomas
Phaedo - Plato, The Phaedo
Pistis - The Pistis Sophia - Codex Askewianus
Pr Paul - The Prayer of the Apostle Paul - NHC I.1.
Pr Thks - The Prayer of Thanksgiving - NHC VI.7.
Prov - Proverbs - Old Testament
Rep - Plato, The Republic
Seneca - Lucius Annaeus Seneca, Epistoloe Ad Lucilium, Hercules Furens
Sirach - Sirach - Old Testament
Silv - The Teachings of Silvanus - NHC VII.4.
Songs - The Song of Songs - Old Testament
Soph JC - The Sophia of Jesus Christ - NHC III.4.
Symp - Plato, The Symposium
Test Tr - The Testimony of Truth - NHC IX.3.
Th Cont - The Book of Thomas the Contender - NHC II.7.
Thund - The Thunder: Perfect Mind - NHC VI.2.
Timaeus - Plato, The Timaeus
Tr Res - The Treatise on the Resurrection - NHC I.4.
Tri Prot - Trimorphic Protennoia - NHC XIII.1.
Tri Tr - The Tripartite Tractate - NHC I.5.
Unt MS - The Untitled Text in the Bruce Codex - Codex Brucianus
Val Exp - A Valentinian Exposition - NHC XI.2.
V Allog - The Vision of Allogenes - Codex Tchacos
Wis - The Wisdom of Solomon - Old Testament
Zost - Zostrianos - NHC VIII.1.

THE HIDDEN PASSION

PART I

1. The Monastery

I

“<The world was made by mistake!>” cried the lone voice Gs Phil 75:3
above the clamour of the marketplace.

Prostitutes strolled among the merchant’s stalls, their eyes exquisitely lined with bewitching kohl. At their feet, the poor of the Kidron Valley crouched, their withered palms outstretched.

“<For this world is the work of beasts!>” came the cry above Int Kn 11:23
the hawkers’ din. “It is the flawed creation of a *counterfeit* God!”

An elderly monk, clutching a manuscript close to his heart, pushed his way past mendicants and spice merchants. His heart afire, Melchizedek hoped to catch a glimpse of the holy prophet. His watchful eyes, learned and wise, scanned the Temple’s forecourt.

A procession of water-carriers passed, shouldering their loads from Solomon’s Pool.

With his long crook, the pious monk violently parted the crowd and laid his eyes upon the source of the voice: a ragged man with matted hair, clad in rough camel-hide.

“<I am the Voice who cries from the wasteland,” came the Jn 1:23
frightful words from cracked white lips. “Prepare the path and make it straight! Prepare the way to your Lord!>”

Melchizedek recognized at once the deep-sunken eyes and desiccated lips of John, the young ascetic known to be the Baptizer from the Jordan. In fear and wonder, the sons of Israel had pronounced him ‘the Last Prophet’.

His youthful face was hard as flint, and sharply chiselled by the desert winds. Under a fierce tangle of hair, John’s fiery eyes blazed with dark fanaticism.

"*Three cataclysms* foretell the coming of the Lord!" John
Gs Egypt 63:4 thundered, "<– the Flood, and the Conflagration, and the Judgement everlasting! These are the three *parousias*...>"

On the Temple Mount of Jerusalem, the merchants and the money-changers ceased their shouting. From their midst appeared the venerable Annas, former High Priest of the Temple.

His long grey beard, woven in the Chaldean style, fell squarely over the white and gold of his embroidered robe. The Sadducee Elder stood before John, fixing his eyes upon the arch-ascetic with bitter spite; Annas wanted to hear with his own ears the Nazarite's profanations.

"The Deluge!" cried John, turning to Annas and his scribes, "which you, the sons of Shem, should have marked well in your
Ap Adam 69:2 memory! <*For the rain-showers of the Almighty poured forth and destroyed all the flesh of the land, and swept away the corruptible seeds of men*. From that great cleansing, Noah kept apart a portion of the imperishable seeds. And they became four hundred thousand men...>"

From the Street of the Spice-grinders came a rickety cart, laden with baskets of aromatic herbs and expensively-scented oils. As it creaked past, the oxen kicked up clouds of dust, blinding the pilgrims who had gathered in the shadow of the Royal Porch.

Still they stood, clutching one another, hoping to catch a glimpse of the madman whom Caiaphas would surely condemn for blasphemy, and Herod burn alive for treason.

"But you? Who are you?" John now roared at the crowd. His gaunt frame, tall and rugged, towered over them. "Are you the descendants of Noah or the offspring of the serpent?" Shaking his head, he decried: "Men are *beasts*, born of *beasts* and carried in the ark *like beasts* through the first *parousia*."

Ferociously, his wild eyes scanned the Temple's forecourt, where asses and camels stood side by side with merchants and
Gs Phil 81:7 scribes. "Indeed, <in this world, there are many animals in human form...>"

Some among the scribes began to laugh, but the desert ascetic quickly silenced them.

Mt 3:7 "<Children of the serpent!>" he chided them. "<It were better
Silv 105:6 you had never lived, than lived such an animal life!> Your souls
Silv 105:27 have <become dwelling-places for vipers and your bodies a refuge for basilisks!>"

In response to these words, drawn swords cut a path through the crowd for the Vizier Chuza, Herod Antipas' chief steward. He was accompanied by his wife Joanna and, hiding in her shadow, the young Salome, granddaughter of Herod the Great.

Clutching his sword, Chuza nodded for the Baptist to continue. Annas smiled; Melchizedek frowned. All the marketplace now was silent.

"The Flood has passed over you, but the second *parousia* awaits. Just as the fields are burned before new seeds are sown, so shall the Conflagration come. <*For fire and sulphur and asphalt will be cast* Ap Adam 75:10
upon you, their flames and blinding fumes will come over you, and your eyes will be darkened!> <You cannot flee the coming wrath.> Mt 3:7
<For even now the axe is bearing down, ready to sever you from Mt 3:10
your root; every one of you, therefore, not bearing good fruit will be cut down and, like barren branches, thrown into the fire!>"

John's disciples, dispersed among the throng, instinctively moved their hands to their hearts. The crowd grew uneasy, fearing the words of the prophet, fearing that he was indeed *the last* prophet.

"Only those worthy of repentance," he cried out in a loud voice, "will be gathered in, for they bear good fruit! Only those baptized will be spared."

From the frightened mob, Annas stepped forth and hissed at the Baptist. Irony and anger mingled in his words.

"The priests, Levites and scribes, indeed the entire congregation bathe themselves in the *mikvoth* before entering the Temple. *We baptize ourselves!*"

John turned and gazed at the former High Priest. His temples were throbbing and the veins of his neck bulged.

"<Why, Annas, would you drink stale water, when sweet water Silv 88:32
is offered to you?> I baptize with the waters of the Jordan!" he cried wildly, "<– with the water which flows *from above!* – with the water Oxyr 2:7-9
of life!>"

He fixed a piercing gaze on the Sadducee Elder. "<But your Oxyr 2:7-9
people wash in Solomon's Pool! – in stagnant ponds that pollute and defile! – in corruptible water where dogs and pigs wallow day and night! Like prostitutes crawling with scorpions, they wash and scrub, but remain impure!>"

A fearful silence redounded from John's words. He would surely burn for this. But the desert dweller's voice would not be silenced.

"Tell me, Annas," John now demanded, "why a golden eagle Jos. 17.6.2
once stood atop the Great Porch of the Temple? Why did Pilate's

Jos. 18.3.1 shields buckle the walls of the fortress, with their images of a wolf suckling two children? Why do your priests still sacrifice two bulls each day in remembrance of the emperor Augustus?"

Now Chuza stepped forward. As Herod's steward, he spoke for the Tetrarchy of Galilee, and for the protectorate of Rome.

"Caesar Augustus was *filius dei*," he cried, "*the Son of God!* From the heavens, the eagle of Rome flew down and crowned him with those laurels. And now, in Tiberius Caesar, you have the continuance of divine rule. Like Remus and Romulus, who suckled at the *Lupa Romana*, the Caesars Augustus and Tiberius are Rome's divine twins. The priests of the temple sacrifice two bulls to them, because they are this world's god-appointed rulers."

"Beasts!" John screamed. "A world of beasts ruled by beasts!
You erect eagles, cast brazen wolves, and slaughter sacred bulls
Gs Phil 71:26 – why? <Because in animals you worship the image of your gods!>
Your *filius dei* extends his throne to the ends of the earth, and says
Gr Pow 45:8 'I am god of this world'. But he is *the bastard* Son of God! <He
performs signs and wonders, so that many go astray, and turn away
from *the true* Son of glory.>"

Chuza went for his sword, but immediately pulled back his hand, alarmed. On its iron hilt was Salome's slender hand.

"Wait," she commanded him. Her eyes were fixed upon the Baptist, entranced by his fiery hair, his fierce aspect, his burning black eyes.

The anchorite opened his mouth once more.

"Since you have fallen into bestiality, I will speak in a manner
you may understand. There are three phoenixes which will fly into
Orig Wld 122:10 the coming fire. <The first is immortal, and will be reborn from
the ashes. The second will rise up, again and again, for up to one
thousand years. But the third, as it is written in the Sacred Book, will
be consumed and perish irrevocably.>"

John raised his hand over the multitude standing before him.

Orig Wld 122:6 "<So are there three races of men: the spirit-endowed for all
eternity, and the soul-endowed for a limited time, and the earthly,>
who indeed are already dead. Which are you? How will we recognize
you? The time will come, during the harvest and the threshing,
when only the fruit-bearing seeds will be stored up. Three times, the
Orig Wld 122:13 harvest! Three times, the *parousias* will pass. <And three, indeed
are the number of baptisms. *One*, by water! *One*, by fire! And one,
the final one, of the spirit!>"

With this last pronouncement, John's voice gave out. His

speech was reduced to a whisper. But in the ensuing silence, even the animals remained still. In a strangulated voice, he announced:

“<I baptize you with water. But the one who is coming after me Mt 3:11
is greater than I. Not even his sandals am I worthy to touch. *He...*” John cried, “will baptize you with the spirit *and with fire!*>”

Melchizedek’s heart rose to his throat. John’s disciples, hearing this for the first time, gripped one another in fear. Even Annas was taken aback by this prophecy. The Messiah?

“<Behold him who speaks...” John presented himself, 2Ap Jas 59:17
defenceless, before the crowd: his hands were at his sides, their palms turned outward. He then raised his right hand in a mysterious gesture, as if pointing into the distance “...and seek him who is silent.>”

The oracle blazed through Melchizedek’s brain like a flash of heavenly fire. The Messiah, though silent, *was amongst them.* He only needed to be found...

“<I am the Voice,” John cried aloud once more. “But he – *he is* Tri Prot 37:4
the Word!> <He is the face of the Father, the image of the Invisible, Tri Tr 66:13
the word of the Unutterable.> And from his mouth will come words
of forgiveness, but also the promise of judgement! <For the Lord Mt 3:12
is coming with a winnowing fork in his hand, and he will clear
the threshing floor.> The wheat, <with its imperishable seeds,> he Mars 26:12
will gather into the granary. <For pure seeds are kept apart in the Auth T 25:24
storehouse, and are made safe.> <But the chaff he will take *and* Mt 3:12
burn with unquenchable fire!>”

Powerless, many people fell to their knees. The words of the
last prophet had finally severed <their stubborn attachment to Hyp Arch 91:7
worldly affairs, their pre-occupation with life’s toil and its on-going distractions.> In the silences between his speech, their neglected spirits were calling to them, demanding remembrance.

“In your hearts, make straight the way of the Lord! For he is <a Gs Tru 31:28
way for those who have gone astray, a discovery for those who are searching, a support for those who are wavering, and a knowledge for those unknowing!>”

John walked through the crowd, raising up those who had fallen to their knees, and gathering together his disciples. For a moment, Salome felt that he would approach her, stroke her chin and raise up her blushing face which would then be veiled with tears.

“Jerusalem!” the Baptist cried, “– whether Pharisee or Sadducee; Essene or Zealot – depart for the desert! Cross to the far side of the Jordan, and sink yourselves in its clear, ever-flowing water! Receive the seal of repentance, so that you may be recognized.

Ap Adam 75:22 "When <the three angels come – *Abrasax* and *Sablo* and *Gamaliel* – they will descend and bring the baptized out of the fire.> The waters of the Jordan will seal you and protect you, and the second *parousia* will pass you over."

As John prepared to depart, he turned suddenly with his hands raised, remembering his final command.

"Then you will be prepared and made clean for the third
Ap Adam 76:9 *parousia*, <when the Illuminator of Knowledge will pass by in great
+ Gr Pow 40:30 glory, to gather in all the fruit-bearing trees. And he will redeem your souls from death. He will speak in parables, and perform great signs and wonders, in order to scorn the powers and rulers that be.>"

As if clearly seeing the future, he cast a forlorn glance at Annas and at Chuza. Images of High Priest Caiaphas and the Tetrarch Herod Antipas passed before his eyes. Each of these rulers would covet the Messiah's power.

Ap Adam 77:4 "<But he will arouse a great wrath against himself. They will
+ Gr Pow 40:30 punish the flesh of the man upon whom the spirit came. And so he will withdraw, and dwell in the Houses of the Holy for a time, so that the powers will not see him. But he will return to raise the dead, destroy its dominion, and put to shame the ruler of Hades.> And then..."

John paused. His anger and his wrath had finally subsided. He felt drained, dizzy, ready to collapse. But there remained his final intimation of gladness.

"And when all of this is accomplished," he said at last, "then the
Gr Pow 40:30 saviour <will proclaim the great Aeon to come, and the Gates of the Heavens will be opened by his word.>"

The desert ascetic stood still, looking directly at Melchizedek, who nodded. He seemed to be the only one in the crowd who understood these words.

The Baptist's disciples began to form a tight circle around him, while armed guards approached from all sides. The throng grew uneasy.

"How will we recognize him?" came a voice, as urgent and as frightening as the prophet's own.

Ordered forward to seize the Baptist, Chuza's men froze. This thunder in their midst had erupted from the bowels of the old monk Melchizedek.

The forerunner feared his moment had come. Would the Voice be silenced before the Word had been spoken?

"<I tell you a mystery, unutterable and ineffable, not to be Tri Prot 41:2
divulged by any mouth,>" he began haltingly. "But to comprehend
it, you must first <become sober, and shake off your drunkeness.> Silv 94:20
<Let your mind awaken!> The Illuminator of Knowledge will Ap Paul 19:10
appear, and you will recognize him because he will come bearing
Five Seals."

The faces of the people were amazed. Even the priests, the scribes, and Annas himself were bewildered. Nowhere was it written in the Holy Book that the Messiah would carry five sacred seals. Was this a new prophecy?

"<Whoever possesses the Five Seals," John announced, "will Tri Prot 49:28
strip off his garment of ignorance, and put on the shining robe
of Light.> <He will become a light in Light!> For the saviour is Tri Prot 48:29
coming <to illumine those who dwell in the darkness.> <All that Tri Prot 48:31
was unknown will become known to you.> All that was hidden will Tri Prot 37:9
be revealed to you. <And you will know that you are from God. Unt MS
Indeed, that you yourself *are* God, and you will see him, who is God
within you.>

"<Anointed with the Five Seals, you will become holy, and Dial Sav 138:19
exalted above all powers. You will become a reflection of his light.
Clothe yourself in the light and enter the Bridal Chamber!> For
within, <you will partake in the mystery of knowledge,> and find Tri Prot 48:29
eternal <rest in his rest.>" Gr Pow 47:22

For a few moments, silence reigned. Then there erupted screams of battle and cries of bloodshed. Chuza's armed guards attempted to seize the prophet, but his crazed disciples and even the people revolted. Daggers were drawn from under cloaks, and blood flowed upon leather and iron.

An alarm was sounded to quell the uprising. In an impulsive act, Annas threw himself at the Baptist, but was met by Melchizedek, who seized the counterfeit priest and threw him down, trampling over his deceitful robes.

Amid the frenzy, Chuza saw his chance to fell the Baptist with one decisive stroke of his sword. He raised his weapon to strike when, in the scuffle, the emaciated flesh was swathed and obscured by a diaphanous form shrouded in veils and silken robes.

Covering his body with her own, embracing the ascetic with ardent desire, Herod's beloved daughter Salome brought the Baptist to his knees and smothered his burning mouth with her tearful kisses.

II

The setting sun pierced the darkened heavens, taking on the aspect of a fiery blackened sphere. Melchizedek goaded his camel onward, past the smoke and flames that blinded him on every side. Dried for months by drought, the fields of Galilee were fast afire.

The monk wrapped his face in the folds of his cloak and raced toward the lake of Gennesaret. Bundled in his lap and shielded from the flames was the sacred book which he was charged to bring back from Jerusalem.

Melchizedek passed between the two cypress trees which flanked the monastery gate – now blazing like human torches. In his twenty years at these cloisters, he never dreamt he would see the day when their cedar roofs would lick the heavens with flames.

Drawing water from the lake, the monks were scrambling to extinguish the conflagration. Billowing smoke filled the elder's eyes with tears.

The hunchbacked porter took charge of his mount, and apprised him of the situation. Alarmed, Melchizedek reported immediately to Allogenes, the Father of the monastery. The Great Teacher lay stretched out in his cell, having collapsed from exertions while combating the fire.

Though his face was blackened by smoke, Allogenes' eyes were alert and discerning as always.

"My brother Melchizedek," he said in a cracked voice, "come sit by me..."

Balancing on the edge of the low wooden bed, Melchizedek unwrapped the manuscript which he had guarded safely from the flames.

The bearded elder smiled as he took the codex in hand. "So you found it, at last..."

"A copy, transcribed by an Egyptian priest."

Allogenes turned the book over in his hands, then read the first
CH I.1 page. "<*Once, when thought came to me of the things that are, and my thinking soared on high...*> Ah yes, those words, their tone rings familiar to my ears."

Then he turned, a worried look etched into his aged features. "You're sure none of the Temple scribes recognized you?"

Melchizedek shook his long white locks.

"If the High Priest got word of this manuscript, it would spell out the end for all of us..." Allogenes warned.

Remembering the Sadducee Elder trampled into the mud, Melchizedek imparted with a faint smile: "Under Solomon's Porch, I saw Annas briefly – but that is all..."

"Annas – *that impostor?*" Allogenes pushed a laugh from his blackened lungs. "Our father Aaron, the first High Priest, bequeathed his robes to Zadok his son, and to all of Zadok's sons. But Annas and Caiaphas are usurpers of the Holy Office. Like the Hasmonean priests before them, they disguise themselves in priestly robes, celebrating the feasts on false days. They desecrate, by their very presence, the Temple's holiness..."

Melchizedek's long moustache and beard barely hid his bemused smile. The old monk, like the Essenes of the desert, knew that Annas, Caiaphas and all their lot were indeed harlots beloved of Rome.

Those events from Hebrew history remained engraved in the monastery's memory. The Zadokite line of succession came to a close two centuries ago when, at the end of the Maccabeen revolt, the Hasmonean rulers seized Kingship and the High Priesthood for themselves. But the Hasmoneans abused their power, and were ultimately displaced by the Herodians.

This transfer of power played well into Annas' hands, since Herod advised Rome to appoint High Priests from the family of Annas. That was why Caiaphas, the present High Priest, had been re-appointed year after year for the last *fourteen* years. He was son, by marriage, to Annas.

Allogenes placed his hand, weakened and shaking with age, on the hand of Melchizedek.

"Now listen to me, my companion of so many years. In your absence I have announced that *you* are to succeed me as Father of the monastery. Have no fear – the fire has only destroyed the stables. The synagogue, the cells, and the library with its scriptorium... *all* will survive intact. The rest you can rebuild. You must lead the monks and apprentices according to the voice of Wisdom within you."

Melchizedek bowed his head, not wishing to acknowledge the departure of his master.

"We have already seen the signs that were predicted..."

The monk nodded in remembrance, but Allogenes recalled aloud the words that burned in his memory, so that they both could bear witness to the prophecy.

Gr Pow 45:31 “<*All the powers of the sea will tremble and dry up*,” he said, his voice rising above a whisper, “*And the firmament will not pour down dew. The springs will cease. The rivers will not flow down to their springs. And the waters of the springs of the earth will cease. Then the depths will be laid bare and they will open.*> For months, we have suffered these droughts throughout Galilee, even onto Samaria and Judea. And now, as predicted, the fires have begun...”

Again, the Great Teacher recited the prophecy with the voice of ages.

Gr Pow 37:29 “<*Then the darkness together with Hades will take fire.*> <*The*
Gr Pow 44:4 *earth will tremble, the cities be troubled,*> <*and the flames consume*
Gr Pow 40:10 *all the dwellings, so that even the shepherd will perish. When it does not find anything else to burn, the fire will turn against itself and destroy even itself.*>”

Melchizedek nodded gravely, but Allogenes smiled, knowing that these signs were not without hope or redemption. He completed the prophecy.

Gr Pow 42:15 “<*It is the change of the Aeon. The sun will set during the day, and the day become dark. The evil spirits will be troubled. And after these things,* he *will appear. The sign of the Aeon to come will appear.*>”

Allogenes rest his head, closing his eyes momentarily to imagine the face of the one who would appear. The Messiah’s hour was drawing near.

“There is something I must impart to you, which I have confided to no other. It is a secret I have borne with me for three long years...”

The Great Teacher opened his eyes and engaged his successor with a gaze imploring comprehension. Melchizedek silently acknowledged the confidence entrusted to him.

“After the deaths of Judah ben Sariphai and Matthias ben Margaloth,” Allogenes said, mustering his strength, “I founded this monastery, as Wisdom had instructed me. That same year, three hermits arrived and installed themselves in the Cave of Darkness. We’ve left them bread and water at the entrance, as instructed, for almost thirty years now. They dispute with each other; they ask for parchment, oil lamps and books; they read the night sky from the entrance – this much I know. But never have they let fall a word to the world until three years ago...”

Allogenes wiped the blood from his lips, having coughed from the smoke. Maintaining his grip on Melchizedek’s hand, he continued.

"Then they sent me a note, impressed three times with their seals. I read it, took cognisance of its contents, and fastened it with my own seal. *No one else must know of this*, my friend. Here: take it, read it in confidence, then close it securely with your signet."

He handed over the scroll covered with strange markings impressed in black wax.

Breaking Allogenes' seal of a cock with serpentine feet, he read the brief message inscribed three times in different hands: once in Greek capitals, once in Hebrew letters, and once in a Persian script. It read:

He is among us

"I die," Allogenes confided, "knowing that the truth will soon
be revealed to the world. <*And those who would know these things* Gr Pow 42:24
will become blessed, since they will come to know the truth. They will reveal them, and they will become blessed. And then, they may find rest.>"

Allogenes' sight began to cloud over, but his eyes remained wide with the vision of his last hour. He turned to his former disciple, who had since become his brother, his companion, and now his successor.

"I go to my rest, knowing our eyes will be opened to the truth. Find him, Melchizedek, here among the students and the rabbis. The codex will help you..."

He placed the Egyptian text once more in the hands of his beloved companion.

"Use it. *The Poimandres* carries in it a knowledge of the beginning – *hidden* knowledge! *Forbidden* knowledge! But truth can not be revealed in any other way."

"And if I find him?" Melchizedek wondered, his heart beating alternately between terror and joy.

Allogenes remained silent a moment. Though night had fallen, the cell was still illuminated by the fires that blazed outside the small window. Lights danced along the walls, forming a shadow play for the Great Teacher, who narrated all that he now saw.

"<Then he will anoint you with the unction of life eternal. You Hyp Arch 97:2
will be freed from blind thought; you will trample death underfoot, and ascend into the limitless light where the sown truly belong...>"

The elderly monk trembled, understanding the import of the

Great Teacher's words. The Baptist had said the Word would soon be spoken. He was moving among them *here*, in this monastery – but silently. Now the moment had come for him to manifest himself. The Messiah of the Five Seals would proclaim the end of this Aeon, and the beginning of the one to come.

Allogenes lay motionless, exhausted. But still, the joy passed from his lips.

Gs Phil 55:19 "You shall be present at the harvest! <The truth, my friend, has existed since the beginning, and it is sown everywhere. There are many indeed who have seen it being sown. But few are those who will see it being reaped!>"

Ecstatic, the moribund Allogenes ignored the paralysis which had overtaken his limbs.

"But you, my master?" Melchizedek pleaded, seeking some vision in the other's vision, and wisdom in his wisdom.

"I am a stranger to this world," Allogenes replied. "I wear this
Test Tr 65:31 body as a garment, nothing more. <Once I have been released from
the flesh,> I shall don the garment of light, and return to the One
Allog 55:19 from whence I came. <Through an unknowing knowledge,> I shall
Gs Tru 25:10 purify myself in the Bridal Chamber <– consuming matter within
myself like so much fire – and darkness, by light – and death, by life! From multiplicity – to Unity..! It is in Oneness... that I will finally attain... to myself.>"

The Great Teacher's face froze with a smile.

Melchizedek remained silent, knowing it was improper to protest the death of his master, or even to mourn his passing. Deep in thought, he held his master's hand throughout the night, keeping vigil until the first signs of dawn appeared.

Then, taking the codex in hand, he called his brothers for the rite of interment.

III

Darkness, like a blinding mist, descended over Jerusalem.

As Annas stepped onto the roof of the Temple, he was met by Annonas, his youngest son, who embraced his father by burying his head in the white and gold of his father's robes.

The boy with the searching eyes was barely thirteen, but he wished to learn from his elderly father all there was to know about the priesthood. For, like his father and his four elder brothers, one day he too would bear 'the robe of the Ephod', which Caiaphas now bore as his brother by marriage.

Within an open-roofed chapel, the great bull of a man Caiaphas was consulting a map of the heavens, surrounded by his scribes, astronomers and fire-senders.

The High Priest was a large man, bilious and swarthy. Tight black curls embroidered his brow and his long braided beard. Caiaphas wore the blue tunic of his office, with its woven pattern of
pomegranates and bells on the fringe. On top of this came 'the robe Exod 28:31
of the Ephod', which reflected the four colours of the sanctuary in its stripes of purple, scarlet and blue, all interwoven with gold.

Uneasily, he fingered the braids of his beard, displeased with the recent turn of events. It was the end of *'Elûl*, the sixth month of the sacred calendar. But shepherds from as far as Galilee, sending fire-signals via the hilltop towers of Samaria, had still not reported the rising of the new moon.

The problem lay in the darkened heavens. Withered by drought, the dried stalks in the devastated fields had caught fire and were burning out of control. For more than a week, the skies of Israel had been blotted out by smoke.

Without God's sign from the heavens, the first day of *Tíshrî* could not be announced. *Tíshrî* – the seventh month, *the Feast of Tabernacles* – to be proclaimed by the High Priest only when the
new moon shone in the heavens. Without this omen, the two silver Num 10:1
trumpets of the *chatsotserah* could not announce the new year's Num 10:10
feast.

"Another moonless night?" Annas demanded. This portent did not bode well for the coming sacrifices.

Caiaphas raised his shoulders in a gesture of silent resignation.

The Elder's hand, posed on Annanos' shoulder, dug its long fingers into the boy's skin.

Though enormously wealthy, Annas worried each year over the spoils of the feast. From the Mount of Olives, his family controlled the entire flow of oil and wine, sheep and doves, into the Temple precinct, where incoming pilgrims purchased them as offerings and libations.

"And your astronomers?" Annas pursued. "What do they report?"

Still silent, Caiaphas motioned for his chief stargazer to reply.

"The hosts of heaven," came the response, "move in their proper courses, but the white moon of *Lebhanah* remains unpredictable." The astronomer pointed to an image of Leviathan on the star map, whose serpentine body circumnavigated the polar star. Around it were arranged the animal figures of the Zodiac with six wandering planets in their midst. The moon alone was unmarked.

Jer 33:25 "<The ordinances of the moon and stars," Caiaphas said at last, turning to young Annanos, "make up a covenant between the Lord and his people.> He gives us the day and the night as a sign of his faithfulness. He measures the day from dusk to dusk, and sends us the new moon to mark the beginning of the month."

"But uncle, why is the moon's circuit not marked like the others?" The precocious child, noting his father's deep displeasure, thought they might measure the days of the month by number.

"We do not presume to scan the deep and predict the ways of the Lord," came Caiaphas' response. Though he liked the boy, he relished his superiority over him, knowing that the day would come when this childling, as a man, would displace him.

"Then why have you trained your priests," Annas now intervened, "in the ways of the Greeks and Babylonians – reading the sky like a holy book? The Law of Moses forbids it."

Jer 10:2 "As do the Prophets," Caiaphas replied, citing Jeremiah: "<*Thus saith the Lord, do not learn the way of the nations, or be dismayed at the signs of heaven.*> But our enemies' knowledge, in our own hands, may still do us good if we use it wisely."

Caiaphas motioned for the child to come closer.

"Do you see the *menorah* which lights our darkened chapel with its seven candles? Each of these is like a light in the heavens. There are seven darkened heavens in all, seven spheres within spheres, and each flame is like a point of light visible on the invisible sphere – a narrow doorway to the outermost empyrean of our Lord, where YHWH and his host of angels blaze in a white blinding light."

Caiaphas pointed to the first candle on the right.

Gen 1:16 "The planet closest to us is <*Lebhanah*, the lesser Light, who
Isaiah 24:23 rules the night.> He is the errant and unpredictable moon, who governs all increase and decrease. The farmers and fishermen are at his mercy, for he governs all growth, but haphazardly.

"Next to him is *Nabu* or, as the Romans say, *Mercury*, the crafty and quick-witted magus whom scribes and merchants obey. Through avarice and greed, he governs the movement of money, sums and letters.

Isaiah 14:12 "Closer to the centre is *Ishtar* or *Venus*, the harlot star, <a light-bearer> beloved of prostitutes. She governs men through envy, longing and desire."

His finger moved to the middle candle on the seven-branched

candelabra.

"And here, at the centre, is *Shemesh* the sun, <the greater Light- Gen 1:16
giver,> who rules the day with arrogance, ferocity, insolence and Isaiah 24:23
pride.

"After, comes *Nergal* or *Mars*, the reckless warrior, who incites bloody battles through wrath and enmity.

"Here, the sixth, is *Marduk* or *Jupiter*, the old king, who clings to wealth and power through injustice.

"And last of all, the seventh, is the lame *Ninurta* or *Saturn*, the oldest of kings, the artificer who binds us all in his web of deceit." CH I:24

Annas frowned at this conceited display of knowledge. Despite what Caiaphas thought, the Greek and Babylonian idols held no sway under YHWH's rule, not even in the lower heavens.

Still, this High Priest with his mystic inclinations and rash speculations was necessary to him. As long as he could be influenced, dominated and manipulated, Caiaphas would remain Annas' chosen son and successor.

The Elder of Jerusalem placed a cold hand on Caiaphas' broad shoulder. "Do you believe this – that the lights in the heavens hold sway over us?"

"The Greeks call them *Archons* – 'the planetary rulers'. Each has his palace, and guards its gate in the heavens. In one palace a host of the greedy make feast; in another, the lustful have orgies. Here below, we also have our palaces where our rulers gather to whore and to feast."

"You speak of our good friend Herod Antipas?"

"More so, his father Herod the Great. The *Basileus* lusted, feasted and ruled like a tyrant," Caiaphas recalled. "And yet, even he heeded three Magi who came to him three decades ago, seeking a confluence of stars in our skies."

"I remember it well," Annas bitterly recalled. "As the High Priest, I advised him to eliminate them immediately..."

"But he refused," Herod Antipas replied.

The Tetrarch of Galilee and Perea, reclining his head in the torch-lit chambers of his father's palace, called to mind Herod the Great's great mistake.

"Instead, he gave leave to the Magi to seek out the child born under the stars, so his steward could follow them and put the babe to the sword. It wasn't a bad plan," remarked Herod's heir and lesser namesake.

Reclining on his right was his wife Herodias, with her daughter Salome comfortably ensconced between them. Chuza, his vizier, stood opposite, pacing back and forth like a caged lion.

"The Magi evaded his steward, never to return!" Chuza shouted. "Your father went wild. He slaughtered all the new-borns in Bethlehem – a wild and insane gesture. But he perceived a serious threat to his kingdom. What if everything this Baptist says is true? What if that child survived, and is coming now, a man fully grown, to claim his rule as the Messiah?"

"We've had rebels and messiahs rise against us before," Herod Antipas replied, "– Simon of Perea, Athronges the shepherd, Judas the Galilean... Each time we suppressed them with Roman justice – the Messiah was fixed to a cross or burnt alive like a human torch." Herod rolled his eyes. "It makes no difference in the end. The mothers of Israel name their new-borns after these martyrs, and another Simon or Judas appears to be crucified anew."

"But not John!" Salome pleaded. "I've heard say that John himself is the new Messiah."

She reclined against her uncle's breast and closed her eyes in remembrance of his burning lips, his fiery gaze.

Herodias was alarmed.

"Herod, you should pursue the prophet John and punish him. Kill him before it's too late." She disliked the ascetic intensely.

"He's crossing the Jordan into Perea this night," Chuza pursued. "*He is in your territory!* My troops can cut him down by morning."

"Perea? A barren wilderness – useless to me. You know how much I drain in taxes each year from Galilee, just to cleanse those barren rocks of highway robbers and thieves? Now you want me to hunt down prophets and messiahs?"

Herod Antipas recalled the circumstances of his strange inheritance, after Herod the Great had expired, a stinking mass of gangrene and disease. To one son, Archelaus, went Judea, the most important of the three kingdoms, where the Royal Palace stood in the upper city of Jerusalem. This kingdom included the large territory of Samaria to the north, where the Jordan flowed on its eastern flank, and the port of Caesarea opened to the Mediterranean on its west.

To his next son – Herod Antipas himself – went Galilee, the smallest of the kingdoms, which bordered Samaria to the north. It touched the land of the Phoenicians on its west, and the lake of Gennesaret on its east. Around the shores of the lake, his capital Tiberias stood newly built in the Roman style. And nearby, the fishing villages of Capernaum and Magdala glistened in the morning sun. From the green rolling hills of Galilee rose Mount Tabor and the farming villages of Cana and Nazareth. Herod Antipas also received Perea, the barren land east of Samaria on the far side of the Jordan, bordered by deserts and the Dead Sea.

The last of the kingdoms went to Philip, who gained Auranitis, Trachonitis and Batanea – the large empty territories east of Lake Gennesaret. These were inhabited by nomadic tribes, and his half-brother soon stylized himself as a sheikh with camels and his court in an entourage of caravans.

These three sons were the fortunate ones. Educated in Rome, they remained at a distance from the poisoned schemings that passed between all of Herod's ten grasping wives. Each promoted their chosen son as heir, and their plottings soon brought them dismissal, divorce or – in the case of his Hasmonean wife Mariamme – death. To eliminate them from succession, Mariamme's son Aristobulus and his half-brother Antipater were also executed by their father – just days before he expired.

The beautiful Herodias, his wife now of seven years, never forgot those murders, since she was daughter of the executed Aristobulus, and was married before to another of his half-brothers – also named Herod; also disinherited.

The Tetrarch glanced at Herodias, his niece by blood, his sister-in-law by her first marriage, and now his wife. She was beautiful but dangerous. Hasmonean blood ran in her veins, and the Herodians had always been at war with the Hasmoneans. Herod Antipas kept her by his side only because she, like him, had learned how to survive in the war of succession.

Archelaus, unfortunately, had not. His brother, after ruling Judea for ten years as the most powerful of the Herodians, was removed by Rome and replaced by a Roman prefect. From the huge Antonia fortress overlooking the Temple, Pontius Pilate now ruled according to the *ius gladii* – 'the law of the sword'. As Tiberius' envoy, he closely watched over his subjects and reported their every move to Rome.

Whenever in Jerusalem, Herod Antipas and his family resided in the Royal Palace. These pleasant, airy, and incensed rooms, hung with golden tapestries and warmed by the braziers' fire, lurked with servants, traitors and spies. Herod Antipas had to watch his every step. He had learned from his father to style himself as *philokaisar* – 'the emperor's friend'. Though Jewish in origin – descended from the deserts of Idumea – Herod co-operated with Rome in each new scheme devised by Tiberius.

"Eliminating the Baptist does not play into our hands," Herod announced. Salome nestled herself into her uncle's murex robes, staring at Chuza like a cat.

"But he called the Emperor *a bastard* and the Romans *beasts!*" the Vizier cried. "I would have cut him down if it were not for..." he stopped, staring at Salome, who blinked at him with her eyebrows raised, daring him to continue.

He resumed pacing back and forth, feeling trapped once more. If he betrayed Salome now, he would pay for it with his life later on. She had the comely face of her mother, and the tyrannical blood of her grandfather coursing through her veins.

"He insulted Annas and the High Priest, calling them impure!" Chuza continued, venting his anger.

At this, Herod laughed, joined by Herodias and Salome.

"For years those Sadducaic priests have smeared themselves in blood and oil, profiting from the sacrifices." Herod's great belly heaved with mirth. "John spoke like a true prophet!"

Chuza stopped pacing and stood resignedly at the centre of the darkened chamber. He realized he would not be able to eliminate the Baptist.

"Then let us at least observe him! We must watch over his movements," the vizier demanded of his king. "The prophet will lead us to the one he predicts is the Messiah."

"Go!" Herod yelled with a wave of his hand. "Follow him, fall at his feet, confess your sins, if you wish... But his blood will not baptize your sword!"

"I will leave for Perea this evening, my Tetrarch..."

Herod turned his head to look at his vizier, a man he respected very much. But there was something stinging this warrior like a gadfly.

"Why is it that you want the Baptist killed?" Herod asked at last.

For the first time, the vizier felt that he had the king's ear.

"If you heard him speak, my Lord, you would understand the threat he poses to your rule."

"Did he speak against Herod?" Herodias asked.

"He said nothing against you!" Salome interjected, placing her hand on Herod's hand with its many rings and jewels.

"Then why this threat to my rule?" Herod demanded of Chuza.

He cupped Salome's hand in his own.

"Because of the Messiah!" cried Annas, turning to Caiaphas. "John speaks like the prophets of old, calling for floods and conflagrations! He also calls for the Messiah. And never in my long life have I believed in the coming of the Messiah – until today..."

The High Priest stood up, alarmed. He waved away his scribes, astronomers, and fire-senders so as to consult with Annas in private. The young Annanos remained by his father's side.

"...Another messiah?" Caiaphas whispered.

His mind reeled. Would he, as High Priest, have to bloody his hands with messiahs – as Annas had done when he wore the robe of the Ephod? To eliminate Athronges the shepherd, Annas had to rally the Sanhedrin, beg Herod the Great, even petition Rome...

"There are so many prophecies in the scriptures. How will we *recognize* him?" Caiaphas called out in desperation.

Annas froze. Those same words had broke from the lips of the crazed monk in the crowd. Did the Messiah come only when called – when the same burning question alighted from the lips of all his people?

Caiaphas began pacing back and forth, summoning all his powers of concentration.

"Will he come as a warrior? A wise man? A prophet? Or even as *the High Priest?*" Caiaphas was striking his temples with his fists.

Annas remained strangely taciturn, trying to recall the Baptist's prophecies.

Frightened by this silence, Annanos reminded his elders, "The prophets called him 'the Son', a descendant from the kingly line of David. But he will also come as a *Malakh*, one of God's angels or messengers... he is the Son of Man... and the Son of God!" Annanos became frightened by his own words.

"The Word..." Annas said, lost in thought. "John called him 'the Illuminator of Knowledge'... saying he himself was the Voice, but the Messiah would come as the Word."

"The prophecy of Bileam!" Caiaphas bellowed, raising his hands
to the heavens. "There, in the Book of Numbers: *<I see him, but not* Num 24:17
now; I behold him, but not near. A star *shall come out of Jacob and*
a sceptre *will rise out of Israel.>* The *star* was the great sign in the
heavens, which the Magi followed at his birth three decades ago.
And now John has been given *the next sign* – the Messiah is coming,
fully-grown, with *a sceptre* in his hand!"

Annas cried aloud, as if giving birth to a basilisk in his brain: "The Five Seals!"

The night was silent. On the rooftop of the Temple, three trembling figures gazed at one another in the flickering light of the *menorah*. Around them, all was blackness.

"*You will recognize him because he will come bearing Five Seals*," the Elder recalled at last. "That is what the Baptist prophesied."

"But what are they?" Caiaphas asked, trembling.

"They are *power!*" Annas announced. "The Five Seals grant power to their bearer – immeasurable power, *sacred* power, the power *to rule* as Messiah."

Each of them stared wide-eyed at each other, the blacks of their eyes illuminated by the *menorah*'s flames. Each was imagining, beside the robe of the Ephod, the sceptre with Five Seals.

"You wear the robes of the High Priest," Annas said to Caiaphas, who nodded gravely. "You alone are deemed sufficiently pure to enter the Holy of Holies once a year, on the Feast of Atonement, and speak the unpronounceable name of YHWH. I too have entered that sacred enclosure and whispered the sacred tetragrammaton. But I ask you now, before my youngest son and the last of my line... tell me Caiaphas, with your mystical ways of seeing – what do you see that moment?"

"Beyond the veil?" Caiaphas shuddered.

"Yes, in the Holy of Holies."

Caiaphas bowed his head, silent and ashamed. Tears came to his eyes; his large face reddened. He could not speak.

"You see nothing..." Annas announced.

"Nothing..." Caiaphas whispered, his voice broken.

"I too could find nothing within – neither see nor feel the holy Presence. The Holy of Holies is empty."

"Is it because we are impure, as this Baptist says?" Caiaphas wondered, tears running down his face. "Have we *lost* the secret name – lost it like the Ark of the Covenant – because we are *not* the true Sons of Zadok?"

Annas embraced Caiaphas, his chosen son, stroking the black curls on his head. Annanos felt all that they felt, his eyes burning with tears.

"Our power is there..." Annas pronounced, "beyond the veil, within the Holy of Holies – *but we cannot see it!* We cannot *seize* it! For you Caiaphas, and for you Annanos my youngest, I swear to you, we shall obtain the Five Seals. So that, with their power, the rule of the ancient priesthood will fall to us..."

A tacit oath bound all three of them that moment, born from the blood they shared in their veins, and the inheritance that blinded their priestly vision.

"Then we must send out our priests," Caiaphas decided, "dressed in commoner's clothes, to join the Baptist's disciples and follow him."

"– to lead us to the Messiah..."

"Yes. And when the Messiah comes," Chuza announced to Herod, "we will cut him down, as your father tried to do on the day of his birth. It is your destiny."

"I have no destiny!" Herod bellowed in anger. "My fate is not ruled by any confluence of stars in the heavens! *I rule*, here on earth, and *my kingdom* follows my every command."

"You speak of power, my lord," Chuza said, leading him on. "But a wise king anticipates all threats to his rule. The Messiah is not a teacher, a prophet or High Priest – *he is a warrior and a conqueror*, heir to the throne of David. The Messiah comes to usurp your rule!"

"With what? A handful of followers, whipping up rebellion through speeches and prophecies?"

"No!" Chuza cried, his anger still rising. "The confluence of stars in the heavens was the first sign. The Baptist has given us the second..." The darkened chamber was spinning round him.

"The Five Seals..." came the voice, soft and sweet, like the rustle of doves' feathers. The child, Salome, had spoken.

Chuza turned and stared at the child, amazed. He could see she was trembling with fear.

"The Five Seals," came Salome's voice again, breaking with tears. "John said that the one who comes after him would bring five seals. I became frightened, because I knew he spoke the truth. It will be terrible for all of us..."

Herodias took the crying child in her arms, beseeching her husband, "What are they, that they frighten her so much?"

For the first time, Herod rose from his couch and walked about the chamber. He stopped by the window and looked out. The night was black, without any moon.

"They are power," Herod announced, "*earthly* power! The power to unleash armies, chariots and swords to rule the land. My father, for all his greed and madness, was no fool. He followed the Magi and their stars, because he knew the Messiah would come like a warrior, holding in his hand the one weapon that could defeat him."

Herod continued to stare into the blackened night. Faced with the unknown, each of them imagined what this weapon might be. Alliance with another kingdom? A new type of weapon? Drought? A plague?

"Chuza!" Herod commanded. "You will send soldiers in disguise, to mingle with the Baptist's converts and disciples. I will not have you go, for fear that he will recognize you. When a new sign of the saviour is given, we will be notified immediately."

With his fist on his heart, Chuza bowed his head. "My Lord."

"And when the Messiah comes," Herod concluded, "we will have his Five Seals for ourselves, even if it means his death."

IV

The corpse had been anointed with sweet-smelling nard and swathed in funereal bands, then laid out with its head to the east. A slender tallow, clutched in rigid hands, illuminated all that remained of Allogenes' earthly existence.

As morning came, the eldest of the monks filed into his narrow cell. Standing near the lectern, Melchizedek observed this odd procession, recognizing each of his brothers in turn. The withered ascetics and wizened rabbis nodded to Allogenes, as if, to a passing stranger.

There followed the scribes and copyists, hunched over, squinting, with dark rings around their eyes. Their tunics were torn and dirt fell from their hair as they ritually beat their breasts in mourning for Allogenes. To them, he was the great librarian, who alone had amassed their treasure house of manuscripts.

While the members of the monastery, from the highest to the lowest, filed into Allogenes' narrow chamber – *who among them*, Melchizedek wondered, *was the one?*

Finally came the students and apprentices. Some were rabbis in training, others were craftsmen learning one of the many trades that flourished in the monastery: stonecarving, woodworking, herbs and medicine.

'Here, among the young...' Melchizedek thought in his heart. The youths passed, bowing their heads in sadness and incomprehension. Their eyes burning, their faces black from the fire, some still had tears to shed for their Great Teacher.

Most of them, Melchizedek noticed, responded in the usual way when confronted by death: they were overcome by pain and a feeling of powerlessness. Only three reacted differently – the one named Simon, whom they all called *Cephas*. And the two they called *the twins* – Jesus and Judas.

Melchizedek observed Cephas as he paid his last respects to the dead. A well-built youth with curly hair, his ruddy cheeks rose above a full red beard. He was the most enthusiastic of the future rabbis, a man fired by passion and conviction.

With a furrowed brow, Cephas was gazing at Allogenes' stilled aspect, trying to comprehend the expression on his face and what it portrayed – that strange, placid smile...

Then came Judas. He and Jesus, the inseparables, resembled each other so much that they nicknamed him *Tauma*, 'the twin'. Only his grey eyes distinguished him from his double.

This unfortunate youth, abandoned by his parents in Kerioth, had begged to be admitted to the cloister in Galilee. Though he became a gifted apprentice, working equally well in wood and stone, the Iscariot also manifest a remarkable intelligence, marred only by brooding fits of melancholy.

Now, silent and watchful as always, Judas *alone*, of all the apprentices, *accepted* the old man's death. Showing neither sadness nor denial, he acknowledged Allogenes' demise with an austere and stoic fortitude.

After him came the fiery youth with the restless heart. Of slender build, tall and dark, this son of Nazareth always spoke with passion and conviction. His voice was soft and melodious, his slender hands made the most remarkable gestures, and his immense black eyes were illuminated always by invisible fires dancing within.

Although Jesus was an avid student of the Torah and a skilful apprentice in woodworking, he seemed always to be *seeking*, never finding. And even now, faced with Allogenes' stiffened corpse, he was alert and alive, confronted by the mysteries it awakened.

'Which one?' Melchizedek wondered in his heart.

Outside the window, the rising sun was soon obscured by billowing smoke.

At last, the entire congregation had crowded into Allogenes' cell, and Melchizedek raised his hands to address them.

"I have come back from Jerusalem, having heard the true voice of prophecy!" His powerful voice shook. "John, the Immerser from

the Jordan, has given us a name for the events breaking round us. We have seen the fields dry up and the harvest consumed by fire – he has called this the second of the great *parousias*.

"The first *parousia* was recorded by Moses, where he says in Genesis that the earth was cleansed by water, and the survivors of that mighty Deluge were few indeed. *Now the reckoning is by fire!* At the behest of Allogenes, I have brought back with me a sacred book which prophesies these events. It recounts *the beginning, the middle, and the end of all things...*"

Melchizedek raised up the book for all to see. The scribes and copyists trembled at the presence of this new manuscript.

Orig Wld 125:32 "<Before the consummation of the age, the whole place will shake with great thundering," Melchizedek cried, his voice resounding like the prophet's. "The sun will become dark, and the moon will cause its light to cease!>"

Everyone in the room called to mind the last seven nights: moonless nights delaying the new year – making time stand still.

Orig Wld 126:12 "<The stars of the sky will cancel their circuits," their Father continued. "And a great clap of thunder will rent the heavens. One upon the next, the heavens will fall and the earth be consumed by fire. They will fall into the abyss, and the abyss will be overturned!>"

Melchizedek paused. He lowered his voice, and spoke to them
Orig Wld 126:35 as one who shared a great secret: "<Then a light will pierce the darkness and obliterate it. It will be like something that has never been...>"

Melchizedek scanned the congregation, and his eyes fell once more on the three youths.

"Come here, Cephas!" he commanded. "Take up the book. Open it to any page *near the end* – and read from it."

Hesitantly, Cephas took the precious manuscript from the elder, and unfolded it. Peering into the book as if into the depths of time, he read its prophecy.

NH Ascl 72:17 "*<Darkness will be preferred to light, and death will be preferred*
NH Ascl 71:22 *to life.> <And he who is dead will not be mourned as much as he who is alive...>*" Cephas stopped, and looked down at the dead body that was laid out before them. He trembled. Is that why the Great Teacher was smiling?

"Take the book, Jesus," Melchizedek commanded. "Read!"

Cephas handed the codex to the Nazarene, relieved to be freed from its burden of truth.

The son of Nazareth opened the book anew and read another

prophecy, his voice rising and falling in waves. "<*No one will gaze* NH Ascl 72:19
into heaven. The good man will be punished like a criminal; the pious man will be counted as insane. And the sacred voice, speaking the word of God, will be silenced...>" His eyes glistening in their blackness, the Nazarene stared mysteriously at Melchizedek.

"Give the book to Judas," the elder cried. "Read!"

Judas took up the book. He tried to remain unaffected by all he said, but still his voice broke with emotion. "<*All of Mankind will* Orig Wld 126:3
wail and scream at their deaths. Then the age will begin, when kings become intoxicated with the fiery sword, and wage wars against each other. The earth will be poisoned with bloodshed.> <*The rivers* NH Ascl 71:15
will flow with more blood than water. And the dead bodies will be stacked higher than their banks.>"

"In this manner," Melchizedek announced, "<the heavens and Gs Thom 51:6
the earth will be rolled up in your presence.> The second *parousia* is upon us. *What is the way through?*"

The venerable Father looked at his monks, one after the other, who trembled with fear. The silence was prolonged by their unwillingness to respond. At last, his eyes came to rest upon Judas.

The young apprentice shuddered. He knew there was no way to escape the Conflagration. But a voice from within responded otherwise.

"The Messiah..." Judas whispered.

The room was absolutely still. Only thin ethereal clouds of incense moved through shafts of light from the round transit. The spirit of Allogenes hovered over the chamber, like the swirling film of frankincense from the censer near his bundled corpse.

"In Jerusalem," the elder said, his low voice barely rising above a whisper, "John has spoken that awaited prophecy. And Allogenes, our Great Teacher, confirmed it to me last night before he died. This is the beginning of the end. The saviour is coming <to illuminate Tri Prot 46:31
those who dwell in darkness> – so has the Baptist said."

"But how will we *recognize* him?" Cephas cried. His broad shoulders were shaking, as if, from the weight of that question.

Melchizedek shivered, recognizing the words which he himself had cried in Jerusalem, and which now broke from the lips of this innocent youth.

"<The Illuminator of Knowledge> will come *bearing Five Seals* Ap Adam 76:9
– that is the Baptist's prophecy," he announced.

Everyone in the room turned to one another in awe. Judas raised a questioning eyebrow at Jesus. But Melchizedek silenced them all.

"The Messiah *is among us*," he intoned gravely, "– like a Word
2Ap Jas 58:10 that will finally break the silence. <He will provide an end for what has begun, and a beginning to the end.>"

"Then... *have you laid bare the beginning?*" came an impassioned cry from behind him.

Melchizedek turned, surprised to hear so many emotions mingling in a single voice. He encountered the beseeching features of Jesus. The youth was burning with desire to know.

Gs Thom 36:11 "<Have you laid bare the beginning?" the Nazarene repeated. "So that, now, you seek the end?>"

"The Baptist has prophesied the end," Melchizedek answered. "Why would you search out the beginning?"

Gs Thom 36:11 "*<Because the end will be where the beginning is,>*" Jesus replied mysteriously.

Melchizedek was struck by wonder into silence. Was this the voice of Wisdom, speaking through the youth in so many riddles? Was this the sign which they had been awaiting?

"If it is knowledge of the beginning you seek," the old man countered, "then you must turn to the sacred book..."

Jesus looked down at the codex which Judas was still holding in his hands.

"The first book of *The Torah*," Melchizedek continued, "where *Genesis* gives us knowledge of the beginning and the fall."

"But master," Judas now said, in one mind with his twin, "did you not say that *this* book recounts the beginning, the middle, and the end of all things?"

The elder tore the manuscript from Judas' grasp and held it aloft. "This is *The Poimandres* – the Egyptian book of revelation!"

Having heard its timely prophecies, they all marvelled at the manuscript.

Calmly, the Father of the monastery reminded them: "In this cloistered place we pursue Wisdom's teachings, as our Great Teacher Allogenes first advised us when he founded this institution. Among us are former Pharisees, Sadducees, Zealots and Essenes – all living and teaching side by side. Nor do we refrain from learning Greek or studying the pagan philosophers..."

Then his voice rose: "But the story of the beginning, as revealed in this book, *is forbidden to you!*"

They all turned to one another in confusion, even the eldest among them. Never had they seen their venerable teacher speak like this. He seemed to be a different man. Melchizedek scanned the congregation, his piercing grey eyes afire.

"It is forbidden fruit! As the Lord warned Adam in Genesis
<– *you shall not touch it*, nor shall you lay your eyes upon it – lest Gen 3:2 - 5
your eyes be opened, and you become like God.>"

The new Father of the monastery paused, awaiting their respect and obeisance. All bowed their heads in supplication.

After he had calmed himself, the elder began again:

"Let us now pray in remembrance of our Great Teacher, who went to his rest knowing that Wisdom's Word would be spoken, and her prophecy fulfilled."

Melchizedek held out his arms and bowed his head.

"<Holy are you, Holy are you, Holy are you, O Father of the All, Melch 16:15
who truly exists.> <Do not let the days of this world be prolonged 2Ap Jas 62:16
for me. Deliver me from this place of sojourn! Save me from an evil death and bring me from the tomb alive, out of your grace. Love is alive in me to accomplish your work of fullness! Because you are the Life of life! Forgive me all my debts from the days of my life. Because I am alive in you, and your grace is alive in me. For now is the time and the hour of our salvation, and the coming of the light. Amen>"

As one, the congregation repeated, "Amen." Melchizedek held his hands over Allogenes' body.

"Bless your servant Allogenes. May his soul be <made holy Gr Pow 47:9
through the light of that Power who is exalted above all others –
the all-encompassing One.> <Protect him, clothe him in the holy Gr Pow 46:14
garment, which neither darkness can touch nor fire burn.> Grant
him <knowledge of the Great Power, to become invisible through Gr Pow 36:3
it, so the flames will not consume him, but only purge him of his
possessions.> <Give back the body to those who gave it to him.> Auth T 32:16
<Let neither flesh nor desire drag him down, so he may enter the Gr Pow 46:8
immeasurable light.> <Let him enter the aeon of beauty, ready Gr Pow 47:15
in wisdom, giving glory to the incomprehensible Oneness. And so he will shine, as a reflection in its light, finding rest in its rest. Amen.>"

While the hunchbacked porter prepared the body for burial, the congregation filed out of Allogenes' cell in silence.

Taking up the book in hand, Melchizedek paused to remember his former master. He noted the lines of sagacity etched into the elder's visage – the beguiling smile of wisdom.

Departing from the chamber, Melchizedek struggled to express neither sadness nor joy as a gentle rain began to fall.

V

That night, Jesus lay in his bed, unable to sleep. His heart beat like the rain on the cedar roof. From the bed opposite came a steady breathing, its shallow rise and fall a sign that Judas must be sleeping. Except for these gentle rhythms, the whitewashed cell where the two apprentices slept was utterly dark and silent.

Where did those words come from? he asked himself frightfully, alone in the darkness. Why did I speak them? 'The end will be where the beginning is'. What could that possibly mean..?

Ever since he was a child, he had heard an inner voice. The heavenly words came to his lips, unbidden, and he had to clench his teeth for fear they would tumble unchecked from his mouth. Whose voice? It came, soft and caressing, like the muted tones of his mother, whispering her lullabies in his ear. Was it the voice of Wisdom? But at times, it thundered, cold and commanding, like the cry of heavenly eagles or angels. Was it the Messiah? Did he hear the call of the Anointed One echoing in his own breast? Did he want to stand, like John, before a crowd and open his mouth with neither forethought nor reflection to deliver God's word?

The Nazarene cowered in his bed, clutching the covers over his mouth. Still, the rain beat incessantly on the cedar roof.

He knew he could never be an instrument of God – he was a coward, a frightened lamb hiding in the eagle's shadow...

Slowly, the rain subsided and his mind drifted to an earlier time, when he had acted without fear. When still a child, he lived one summer in Magdala, playing with Mary his cousin: she was, to him, the sister he never had. They stood on the rocks high above Lake Gennesaret, their tunics wet from swimming. Her skin was dark like his, and her hair – black as the bottom of the sea – fell in long tight curls. Looking down at the watery expanse, she dared him to jump. Jutting out from the shore were sharp limestones. His fear was overwhelming.

His cousin squeezed his hand, then flung herself from the cliff. He watched, amazed, as she fell, turning helplessly, until she was swallowed by the waves below. Fear gave way to ecstasy as, a moment later, he too jumped, turning like her, then hitting the sea and descending into watery darkness. When he surfaced Miri was beside him, embracing him and laughing wildly with childish joy.

He called her 'Miri' in their native Aramaic. To him she was *'my sister, my bride'*, the lily and the rose in the Song of Songs. They loved each other from the time that they were children. Years would pass, they would meet again, now older, and their love would still be there. As he became a man and she a woman, they knew they could never live as husband and wife. But their love for each other remained unchanged.

That summer in Magdala they slept together on the roof. Under the stars, his nine year old cousin dared him to fling away his tunic. Again, he was afraid and, again, she led the way. Miri removed her linen vestment, showing him her nakedness in the moonlight. He responded in turn, unafraid, unashamed. Then they slept, two children embracing under the morning sky.

<Now a garden locked is my sister, my bride...> Songs 4:12

Was it the fault of their grandparents, Adam and Eve? After Eve had led Adam to the tree, and they had consumed its forbidden fruit, their eyes were opened, and they *saw* that they were two – a man and a woman. They had been *one* in the beginning, for she was flesh of his flesh. But now, they could see, nakedly and in shame, that they were different. Even after he had known her as his wife, re-uniting with her in the flesh, Adam remained separate from Eve, apart, alone. They had fallen, and were accursed by God.

Was that the beginning? the youth wondered in the darkness. He felt the terrible tragedy of his grandparents' unknowing error.

"*Kings become intoxicated with... the Messiah...*" Judas mumbled, then turned over in his bed. He was talking in his sleep – fragments from the day that returned to him and re-assembled in the night.

'The end will be where the beginning is,' Jesus called to mind once more. *To know how the end will come*, he decided, *you must know what truly happened in the beginning*. That was the *sense* of his mysterious utterance...

The youth rose from his bed and stepped softly to the window. The rain had given way to a gentle mist that silhouetted all forms in the moonlight. There was, he noticed, a moon tonight – full, almost red. *I must know...*

He wrapped a woollen cloak over his linen tunic, and gathered up a few things: a clay lamp, some flints, his sandals... Then, lifting the latch as quietly as possible, he slipped barefoot out the door.

Seconds later, Judas rose from his bed. He too gathered a few necessary things and then followed silently. Knowing the other's mind, he had no doubt as to where he was headed.

Though the full moon hung low in the heavens, there was little light in the shadow of the cloisters. With lamps unlit, each penetrated blindly into the darkness, neither seeing nor hearing the other.

Slipping his feet into his sandals, Jesus tread softly over the muddy earth near the stables. Frightened by sounds in the darkness, a heifer dropped its head to its chest and lowed; a gelding pawed the earth and snorted. Silently as possible, the Nazarene turned his steps toward the scriptorium.

Judas went by way of the refectory, padding over its hard flagstones in bare feet. By circling round the courtyard, his movements were obscured by the colonnade, and he could observe the interior of the scriptorium unseen. Stepping round one of the columns, he was met by Melchizedek.

The tall monk towered over him, a stern and expectant look in his eyes.

"*Tauma*," he said to Judas, "I was rather expecting *your twin*, or at least the two of you together. But *you* – alone..?"

"I knew you would be waiting here," Judas replied, "so I came to you directly..."

Jesus scratched a flint and lit a twisted fragment of papyrus, setting it into the mouth of the clay oil lamp. Its dull flame illuminated the scriptorium walls, lined with books and scrolls. He quickly found the forbidden manuscript, bound in soft leather. It had been sealed shut, but otherwise there was no pretence of hiding it or locking it away.

Installing himself with a scribe's kit and papyrus, he pried open the seal, then unfolded the book *to its beginning*. Scanning the first
CH I.4 page, his eyes fell upon the words: "*<In an instant everything was immediately open to me. I saw an endless vision in which everything became light...>*"

The story of the beginning passed silently over his lips, unfolding before him in a manner utterly unlike the account in Genesis. He saw the beginning of the world, as in a vision. He saw the darkness separate from light and descend into the depths, coiling sinuously like a serpent. He saw the light rise, and from it came a clear and holy Word, luminous and glowing. Then the serpent in the darkness roared like a lion, releasing a senseless cry, all unordered and unmeaning.

All of this was a vision recorded by an Egyptian sage. And a
CH I.8 voice said to the sage: "*<In your mind, you have seen the archetypal*

form, the preprinciple that exists before a beginning without end.>"

Furiously, the Nazarene began transcribing those words, without even understanding their sense. But his eyes raced ahead in the text, and his sight was blinded by the next moment in creation.

He saw the source of all light and life, the supreme God who engendered all luminous and living beings. And this supreme God was neither male, nor female, but *both*: an androgyne. And those beings in the upper heavens whom he engendered were also bisexual, as two-in-one.

The Nazarene's vision expanded, and he saw the heavens being formed in seven concentric circles, with a governor over each of the spheres. But the creator of the heavens was a craftsman called the *Demiurge*. This craftsman even created a Man like himself, the First Man or *Anthropos*, and planted in him a knowledge of the seven spheres. But from the upper heavens, the Anthropos turned his gaze downwards.

In the darkness below, the elements of earth, air, fire and water mixed with one another, forming Nature. And when the First Man looked at himself in her watery abyss, he saw his own reflection in Nature's pool. And Nature herself smiled back at him, loving all that
she saw. <*When the Man saw in the water the form like himself in* CH I.14
Nature, he loved it... Nature took hold of her beloved, hugged him all about and embraced him, for they were lovers.> As the heavenly *Anthropos* and earthly Nature united, they became one being, masculine and feminine, in spirit and in flesh – an androgyne...

The youth recorded this passage, his reed furiously bleeding its ink into the papyrus. Then he paused, trying to understand all he had transcribed.

This man – the First Man, like Adam – had fallen in love with Nature, his Eve, since he found *in her* his own watery reflection. From heaven, his spirit had plunged into her earthen body, and from those austere heights he had surrendered himself into her loving embrace. There was no shame in their falleness; no nakedness, no curse upon their union. The fall came about through love...

"<*This is the mystery that has been kept hidden until this very* CH I.16
day...>"

Jesus paused, repeating to himself the hidden and forbidden truth about the beginning: the fall came about through love...

II. The Cavern

I

Jesus awoke to the cries of the sparrows in the sycamore trees.

Wiping the sleep from his eyes, he found Judas before the window. The Iscariot had risen and now was gazing pensively at the potter's garden, with its rows of medicinal herbs. His eyes were fixed on a hemlock, its leaves sprinkled with dew.

The Nazarene sensed it immediately: the twin was in one of his moods. Gloomy, silent and dispirited, Judas tapped his lips with a long forefinger, brooding over some heavy thought.

Suddenly, a strange feeling of elation invaded the Nazarene's heart. It came, as if, in response to his twin's despondent mood – the deeper the evening star sunk below the horizon, the higher the morning star rose.

The son of Nazareth abandoned his bed and began washing his face in the basin near the door. The water was cold and smelled refreshing.

"The Feast of Trumpets was announced last night," Judas said, turning from the window. "The workshop will be closed today."

"*<In the seventh month, on the first day, you shall do no* Lev 23:24
laborious work,>" Jesus replied, citing the scriptures. He squeezed the water from his slender beard and brushed back his wine-dark tresses.

"All of us are to gather in the scriptorium," the Iscariot added, remembering the events of last night. At once his heart was overwhelmed by feelings of despair. Should he speak now? Judas tried to find the words, but a saturnine silence choked his heart...

"You spoke in your dreams last night," Jesus remembered, smiling. "Something about kings and messiahs..." He laughed gently.

Judas turned on him, his anger suddenly rising. "What do I care about the Messiah?" He walked away from the window. "The Messiah's an illusion; the collective mania of our people, nothing more..."

"He gives us hope," Jesus said, wiping his forearms with a linen cloth. " – And unity... Is it wrong to believe in freedom for our people?"

"Freedom from who?" the Iscariot countered. "From the Romans? From our Tetrarch Antipas? Or from our own lust for power? The Messiah *is* power. If he appears with – what did the Baptist say? – the Five Seals, then our own priests and rulers will seize his power for themselves."

Jesus stared at Judas, not saying a word. But the other had still not exhausted his anger.

"Oh yes, we need freedom – *we need to free ourselves from the Messiah*," he concluded, "– from Israel's collective delusion of a saviour."

"*Tauma*," Jesus said, "I am in one mind with you, my brother, my twin." He took the other's hands in his. "But all you say follows from fear and despair. Let them go! Your whole life you've been haunted by doubt." Dark and haunting, the Nazarene's eyes bore into his brother's. "Believe me, your doubt will only betray you in the end..."

Judas freed his hands from the other's grasp, and turned away. His grey eyes fell on the hemlock garden beyond the stone transit.

"They wish to teach us about Wisdom here," he replied bitterly. "The wisest of the prophets, if you ask me, was Plato. It was he, after all, who wrote the Gospel of Socrates..."

The Nazarene's brow rose in confusion, but the Iscariot continued. "Yes – Socrates – the *Hellenic Messiah* who was tried unjustly by his own people and put to death by slow poison. But Plato remembered his sayings and teachings – on the soul, on the love of Wisdom – and wrote them down for us.

"Above all," Judas announced, "Socrates *doubted* everything he heard; he doubted everyone's claim *to know* the truth. Maybe his doubt did betray him in the end ...betray him to his own death. But he defended himself reasonably, saying <the only difference between other wise men and myself is that *I know I* do not *know.*>"

Apology 21d

He unlatched the door and looked in the direction of the scriptorium. Melancholy gripped his heart.

"*That* is what Wisdom has taught me here!" Judas announced.

The walk towards the scriptorium was pleasant. After the *yoreh*, the year's first rainfall, the earth smelled damp and refreshing. The dates had ripened over the hot summer months, concentrating their sweetness, and now they hung from the branches in dew-covered clusters. During the forthcoming feast of *chagh he-'aciph*, all of Israel would celebrate the harvest of dates and olives.

Entering the scriptorium, the twins took their usual place, sitting next to Cephas. His head was buried in his copy of the Torah, rhythmically reciting its metered passages.

Simon bar Jonah only studied here during the winter months, since summers were spent with his brother Andrew, fishing on the lake of Gennesaret. Their family came from Bethsaida, and had fished the lake's barbels and sardines for generations.

But, as the eldest son of Jonah, Cephas dreamt of a better life. He longed for Jerusalem, where he hoped to serve in the Temple as a scribe or Levite, maybe even as a rabbi. His faith was boundless, fired by the creed of his Hebrew forebears.

The twelve students assembled here were sons of rich and poor
alike. 'From Dan to Beersheba' they had come to hear Wisdom's 1Kings 4:25
word. Sometimes She spoke to them as *Hochmah*, pronouncing her oracles in the Hebrew tongue; other times She reasoned as *Sophia*, pursuing her dialectics in Greek. Their teacher, the venerable Silvanus, initiated them all into Wisdom's many teachings.

"*<The harvest is past, the summer is ended,>*" the bald and Jer 8:20
bearded patriarch began. "Those words, coming from the prophet Jeremiah, proclaim this new morning to us. We felt the first rain of winter last night, and it came to us as God's herald. The drought of summer has passed, its holocaust ended. Now fresh seedlings will
shoot forth in our garden. Wisdom says to us in Ecclesiasticus: *<I* Sirach 24:17
am like a vine putting out graceful shoots... Approach me, you who desire me, and take your fill of my fruits.>"

This elderly rabbi was much beloved by his students. Not only was his learning great, but he knew how to open his heart and convey that knowledge with subtle insight and gentle conviction.

He looked at his students expectantly, engaging them with his penetrating gaze. "Yesterday, our Great Teacher forbid you the fruit of one book in our scriptorium. He did this because you are not yet prepared to receive its teachings."

Then, with a slight shrug of his shoulders, Silvanus announced haltingly: "This morning Melchizedek informed me that you are to study the Book of Genesis... Review the first five chapters and discuss its text among you. Be prepared to stand before this congregation and expound upon a passage chosen at random. Trust the voice of *Hochmah* inside you! Whatever you say will be guided by her wisdom. Now begin..."

Cephas, Judas and Jesus gathered round their Torah, unrolling the massive scroll before them.

"Where do we begin?" Cephas asked, passing his hand gingerly over the Judaic script.

"Indeed," Judas pondered, "do we start at the first beginning, or the second?"

The Bethsaidean's brow rose in confusion.

"In Genesis, there are two beginnings," Judas clarified. "Here," he said, pointing to the dense Hebrew text at the head, "is the beginning written by the priests of the northern kingdom, who always wrote the word God as *Elohim*. But here," he pointed to the text further along, "is another version of the beginning written by the priests of the southern kingdom. They called the Lord *Yahweh*."

"What's the difference?" Cephas stammered, clawing at the curls of his red beard. He had committed the text to memory, but never thought to expound upon its meaning.

"In the second beginning," Judas pursued, "*Yahweh* creates the
Gen 2:23 first man, then makes woman from a rib in his side. <*This at last is bone of my bones and flesh of my flesh,* Adam says. *She shall be called Woman, because she was taken out of Man.*>"

"Yes, yes... And in the first?" Beads of sweat were forming on his forehead.

"Here," the Iscariot answered, pointing to the text at the top,
Gen 1:26 "Elohim says <*Let us make man in our image, after our likeness... So God created man in his own image, in the image of God he created him; male and female he created them.*> The first man and woman reflect God equally. Adam and Eve are *both* made in his image."

"As male *and* female?" Cephas wondered aloud.

"They may have believed Elohim was androgynous," Jesus intervened, answering on Judas' behalf. "*Both* of them, Adam *and* Eve, were male *and* female."

His red hair tingling, Cephas stared at Jesus in wonder.

But the dark youth seemed lost in his own thoughts, gazing at the spaces between the text and imagining things strange and inconceivable.

"The second beginning accords with Plato," Judas added, his grey eyes sparkling.

Now the son of Jonah frowned. He was an Israelite, one of the Chosen Race, born into the faith of his forefathers. He did not share the Iscariot's preference for Hellenism, for rationality and reason. It was a pagan philosophy.

"In the Symposium," Judas carried on, oblivious, "Plato discusses the nature of Love. He says that, in the beginning, man and woman were *one* creature, a very powerful creature that tried to climb to heaven and usurp the place of the gods. So, to punish them, Zeus divided them into two, into man and woman, making them weaker through their desire for one another. From that day forward, they desired *<to be united and melted together, and to become one* Symp 192e
from two. For this was our ancient natural shape. And so their desire to be one whole is called Love.>"

"God did not separate man from woman to punish them," Cephas replied decidedly.

"No, he banished them from Eden because *<they knew that they* Gen 3:7
were naked> – it's the same thing. From being one and androgynous, like God, they recognized that they were two, as man and woman. *That* was the fall."

"The fall," Cephas answered, his temper rising, "was from the forbidden fruit. They ate it, and *<the eyes of both were opened.>* Gen 3:7
Their knowledge was their own undoing."

Judas sat back from the scroll, his eyes strained from staring at the Hebrew characters, which flickered like black flames against white fire.

He transferred his gaze to Jesus, who remained unusually taciturn. A strange play of emotions had passed over his face as he followed all that they said. But he was utterly unable to contribute. Only his eyes betrayed an intense bewilderment.

"I never understood," Jesus said at last, "why God would banish them from paradise for acquiring knowledge..."

"They broke his command!" Cephas retorted, exasperated. "Isn't it obvious?"

Judas intervened. "They broke their chains – that's all."

"...Chains?" Another drop of sweat formed on the Bethsaidean's forehead.

Rep 514a "In the Parable of the Cave," the Hellenist pursued, "Plato says that this world is a prison and we are all prisoners, chained to the wall of an underground cavern. All that we see are shadows passing over the rocks. We think these images offer us knowledge of all that is real. But if we could only break those chains, and ascend from the cavern, we would see the world *as it truly is*."

"What has that to do with the fall of Man?" the son of Jonah countered.

"Don't you see? Man *rises up* through knowledge – he doesn't *fall* from it..!"

Their conversation was cut short by the entrance of Melchizedek, who bore a grave expression on his long features. This was indeed a rare occasion. The Father of the monastery had never participated in one of their lessons before. Judas trembled at the sight of the elder towering over him.

"The time for preparation is over," Silvanus announced. "Our Great Teacher will select a text which you must elaborate. Trust the voice of Wisdom within you..."

The students sat in silence while Melchizedek's eyes scanned the scriptorium. Most of them averted their gaze, hoping his roving eyes would not land on them.

The old monk turned and reached into the shelf where a book was kept. The manuscript which emerged was immediately recognizable to all – the forbidden *Poimandres*. With trembling hands he placed this on the writing block before the lectern.

"Yesterday, after condemning the contents of this book, I sealed it with my own seal," Melchizedek announced.

Then, with a slow, deliberate movement of his long forefinger, he pushed open its cover.

"This morning, the seal was broken."

No one dared so much as to look to the left or right, lest their movement betray them.

"The first reading for this special feast day is taken from the Book of Genesis, chapter three, verse seventeen. Judas, will you rise, read the passage, and expound its wisdom for this congregation?"

Staring straight ahead of him, Judas rose and approached the lectern. On it was an open scroll marked at the required passage. In a voice that was barely audible, the Iscariot read:

Gen 3:17 "*<And to Adam, God said, 'Because you have eaten of the tree of which I commanded you, "You shall not eat of it," – cursed is the ground because of you...>*'"

Judas looked down at the forbidden *Poimandres*, its seal broken and the cover ajar. He had no hope that Wisdom would come to his aid. Haltingly, he formulated his argument, putting his trust in Reason.

"If this manuscript contains knowledge that would 'open our eyes', so that, to read it, we would be 'like God', then it speaks with the voice of Wisdom... This monastery was founded, so we could pursue Wisdom in all her many voices... Thus, any authority who would forbid this book, betrays Wisdom... And anyone who breaks that command is blessed rather than cursed... because he has heard Wisdom's voice, and obeyed her calling."

His head bowed, stoic and resigned, Judas assumed his place among the students. All of them stared at him with wonder. Melchizedek let a bitter smile pass across his lips.

"Jesus," he commanded, "rise and read from chapter three, verse six."

The Nazarene rose, a strange light glistening in his eyes. With a deep voice, deeper than his own, he spoke the words of the desert prophets, sustaining their reprobation over the centuries:

"<*So when the woman saw that the tree was good for food, and* Gen 3:6
that it was a delight to the eyes, and that the tree was to be desired to
make one wise, she took of its fruit and ate; and she also gave some
to her husband, and he ate. Then the eyes of both were opened, and
they knew that they were naked...>"

The son of Nazareth gazed at the congregation. His face was immobile, his eyes unmoving; only the light in their dark pupils danced. He breathed in and out, but did not say a word.

"Your commentary..." Melchizedek prompted.

The youth continued to gaze out over the congregation, holding the lectern tightly lest he collapse. He felt dizzy, ill, delirious: intense feelings of anger, fear and shame rose up inside of him, and his mouth was filled with their bitterness. He wanted to scream, he wanted to thunder like an ancient prophet, he wanted to crawl into a hole and hide. But instead, all the feelings churning within took the form of images in his brain, and he saw clearly and unquestionably the events he had just described.

Adam stood before Eve, and they gazed at one another with their eyes opened. They knew that they were naked. They felt desire, they felt fear, but they did not feel shame. Instead, he looked at her and saw in her face his own reflection. And she too wanted to take hold of her beloved and embrace him. They recognized themselves in each other. They knew at that moment that in their embrace lay oneness. For the first time in creation, they felt love. And it was love that made them, indeed, 'like God'.

The Nazarene continued to stare out over the congregation, not uttering a word. How could God punish them, if this love that they felt *came from* God? Was that the mystery, hidden and forbidden, that lay at the beginning? That man and woman were not fallen, not accursed, indeed, not at all banished by God? And that in the rare moment of their union, they manifest his oneness? Then who had hidden that knowledge from us? Who had planted the seed of deceit?

"*She took of the fruit and ate it*," Melchizedek repeated sternly, "*then gave some to her husband*. What does this passage mean?"

"It means..." Jesus said, still seeing the vision before him, clearly and distinctly, "it means that she knew his desire, and did exactly as he wanted her to do..."

"She beguiled him," Melchizedek corrected, "just as the serpent had beguiled her."

"They acted as one, knowingly, without sin, without shame..." he said, convinced.

"Why?" Melchizedek demanded, his voice daring him to reveal the mystery entirely.

"Out of love," Jesus said calmly. "They acted knowingly, out of love for one another..." Then his voice trailed off. In his heart, he knew he was right, but he would suffer much for that wisdom.

Melchizedek walked to the front of the congregation, and held up the forbidden book in his hands. His face was afire, like the angel at the end of time with the book of history in his hands, reading the names of the saved and condemned. He fixed his eyes on the Nazarene.

"You have knowingly broken my command! Your 'wisdom' comes to you from this book, and from all you have read into it! You broke the seal, opened the book and gazed upon it without my knowledge or consent."

Melchizedek paused, then looked at Judas while still addressing Jesus.

"But no, I knew that already... since Judas, your *tauma*, your dear brother and twin *betrayed* you to me last night – he saw you here in this scriptorium, pouring over the book, and reported you to me."

Jesus looked at Judas, stunned by this revelation. But Judas, gazing darkly within, was acknowledging no one.

"And indeed, your own answers have betrayed you now! You have just avowed that you would, like Adam, eat wilfully of Eden's fruit! For that, you must be banished! For your insolence, *both of you*," he cried, now addressing Judas as well, "are expelled from this place. Go! Gather up your things and leave here at once!"

No one dared to move. Then slowly, Judas rose. Placing one foot before the other, he passed silently out of the chamber.

Jesus remained at the lectern for a few moments, acknowledging the stares of the others. He felt like a potter's vessel, irreparably flawed and dashed to pieces on the wheel. Then, with his head bowed, he followed Judas out the door, sharing with him all the pain and shame of their forefather's fall from wisdom.

II

Judas and Jesus gathered up the last of their belongings, stuffing them into satchels of sackcloth. Neither dared look at the other, or even speak a word. Each was prepared to set out on his own path, never seeing the other again.

After a gentle knock, Cephas pushed open the door. He could smell the heavy odour of shame and separation which hung in the air. He addressed his friends softly, in tones of consolation.

"Melchizedek sent me. He says that you are to go to his cell immediately. Bring all your things with you..."

The twins stopped and looked at Cephas. He truly was 'a rock' – solid, determined, unflinching in his friendship. This was difficult for him as well.

"I'll call on you at Nazareth," Cephas said to Jesus. "And on you too Judas," he added, realizing that the three of them would never again stand together in the same room.

"God be with you," he whispered, kissing each on the cheeks. Tears filled his eyes, and his sanguine heart overflowed. Then silently, he departed.

Taking their bags in hand, they set out for Melchizedek's cell; Judas leading and Jesus following.

Near the refectory they were met by the hunchbacked porter, who insisted on accompanying them. He spoke a strange dialect from the desert of Idumea. His continuous chatter, unwelcome at this moment, was barely comprehensible.

"Things go very bad for you now, *tauma* Jesus, *tauma* Judas

– very bad... Melchizedek speak with the three hermits – a strange thing, that! Nobody, not me, nobody see them for many many years."

As they came to Melchizedek's cell, the porter kicked open the door and pushed them inside.

"Now wait here! I take your things to the gate."

At the threshold, he turned with their bags in his low-slung arms.

"These hermits – I leave them bread, leave them water, before the 'Cave of Darkness', then *pfffft!*" he made a dismissive gesture with his head, "I run. The smell of sickness in there – like lepers, like the dead! I hear the master say – the hermits, they be your judges..."

Hitching up the bags, the Idumean hunchback kicked the door shut behind him.

Jesus and Judas stood at the centre of the austere quarters. There was nowhere to sit, nowhere to look except the closed door where they had just come in. So, they stood with heads bowed while drops of water fell, slowly, implacably, from the roof to a washbasin below.

Finally, the door opened, and a tall figure entered. He wore a long robe and was hooded, his face entirely hidden. He smelled strange, like damp stone blackened by oil lamps, like sickness and death. The figure stood before them, his hands in his sleeves, his head bowed.

Then, to their amazement, he fell to his knees, prostrated himself before them, and pressed his forehead to the floor just before their feet.

"Forgive me," he cried, "forgive us – forgive *all of us...*" he pleaded, his voice was breaking with tears. That voice, so moving and beseeching, was unmistakeable.

When, after many moments, the hooded figure rose to his knees, they saw the wracked features of Melchizedek. His face was bathed with tears, and he was gazing at them with fear and wonder.

"Please, sit with me," he invited, indicating the reed mat where the two of them stood. Jesus and Judas sat on the matted carpet with the Great Teacher.

"It was all a ruse," he explained, "the forbidden book, my stern comportment, the banishment... – but we had to be certain!"

He looked back and forth from Jesus to Judas, beseeching their comprehension. Then his expression changed, as he shook his head in wonder.

"But two of you! The twins! No prophecy had prepared us for this!"

"A ruse?" Judas ventured. He was still at a loss to explain this sudden alteration in Melchizedek's humour.

"Yes! Yes! Or a test rather. An ordeal to decide who, among the members of this community, was the one. The three hermits had announced it to Allogenes: that the Chosen One *was here*, moving silently among us. So, Allogenes dispatched me to Jerusalem to bring back *The Poimandres*. He knew the time had come for him to speak, to reveal himself."

"An elaborate ruse..." Judas decided.

"We *had* to be certain," the elder repeated. "The hermits planted the seed, Allogenes watered the tree, and I... I offered the book as its forbidden fruit. We were seeking the one... the one who would *break* our command, who sought knowledge *above all*, and who would stop at nothing to embrace Wisdom."

"And you found..?" Jesus asked, his voice trembling.

"That the one was really two – the two of you. Each of you followed his own path to the same end..."

The Nazarene gazed at Melchizedek, his heart beating wildly. Slowly, he turned and regarded his brother.

"Then Judas..."

"Judas never betrayed you Jesus," the elder explained. "Last night, he took a different way to the scriptorium. But we met by chance in the shadow of the colonnade. I was shocked at first, as I never expected to meet him there, alone."

Judas' eyebrow rose a notch, but he said nothing.

"But he was more clever than I thought," Melchizedek continued. "He led me away from the cloister, saying that you had set out for the Cave of Darkness. I was so shocked, I went to the hermits' cavern at once. It was deathly silent. Judas had deceived me – diverted me, in fact... to protect you."

Still looking at his friend, Jesus bowed his head in shame.

"Forgive me Judas," he whispered. "In my heart, I thought you had betrayed me."

The corners of Judas' mouth rose imperceptibly.

"He is indeed your *tauma*," the elder said to Jesus, "your *didymos*, as we say in Greek, your *twin*. Like one in perfect mind with you, he knew where you were headed – and why..."

"*Didymos... Tauma...*" Jesus said to Judas. "To remember this hidden sympathy we share, I shall call you always by that name. I am sorry, *Thomas*, that I ever doubted you..."

Trembling, Jesus offered his hand, which Thomas took after some hesitation.

"But why...?" Jesus asked. "*Why* did you follow me to the scriptorium?"

Indeed, why? the Iscariot wondered to himself. He felt himself treading over an uncertain abyss.

"I don't know," Thomas replied, clenching his trembling fists. "You woke me from a deep sleep, and I followed you – not really knowing why... or where the path would lead..."

"But you took your own way," Melchizedek added, "to the forbidden tree. Even if, unknown to yourself – you sought out its fruit."

"The manuscript?" Thomas felt as if the earth were crumbling beneath his feet.

"You said less than an hour ago," Jesus prompted, "that anyone who eats of that fruit is 'blessed rather than cursed'. You said it contains wisdom."

Thomas shook his head, and his face darkened. "I've never longed for Wisdom here," he announced, his voice low in his throat.

"The three hermits, Allogenes and myself," Melchizedek began hesitantly, "have all been searching for the one who has longed for Wisdom – the one who, deep in his heart, has sought *knowledge* above all..."

He cast a piercing look at the twins and announced: "But, rather than finding one, we found two – the two of you. You *are* the twin Messiahs..."

Their hearts pounding in unison, the twins looked at each other in sudden fear and wonder.

Then, the beating of the Iscariot's heart altered, and he heard a different message pounding in his ears. When next, he spoke, his voice broke the silence like thunder.

"Impossible," he disclosed. "The only thing I've learned for certain within these walls is that 'I know I do not know'. Any form of knowledge, for me, is impossible. I have *doubted* always – doubted knowledge, doubted Wisdom; I even doubt the existence of your Messiah..."

The Iscariot's face was cast in dark shadows; his grey eyes flashed from their deep caverns.

For some time, the three of them sat in silence. From the trough above the window, rainwater continued to fall, drop by drop, into the washbasin below.

"You are free to renounce that claim," Melchizedek said slowly. "But none of us can deny the signs that have been given. He *is* among us!"

"Then I *renounce* it," the Iscariot affirmed at once. He turned to the Nazarene, whose face had suddenly taken on a remarkable glow. For a few brief moments, the twin saw his own face in his brother's – and it was shining and luminous.

At last, Melchizedek came to a decision.

"Then the two messiahs are only one – which the Baptist proclaimed to us from the beginning. His prophecy, at last, has been fulfilled: *He is among us* – the Messiah of the Five Seals..."

The Iscariot and the elder turned to gaze at the Chosen One. On the refectory roof, a pelican stood, stretched out its long wings, and took flight.

Jesus trembled. Could he deny it? Could he deny that his whole life, he had desired nothing less than to *know God* – to know the God *in* him? Was *that* the Messiah? The Nazarene knew he was nothing more than a man; indeed, a dreamer and a coward, visited by unearthly voices. But the Messiah – was that not the divine spark hidden in every man?

Jesus hugged his chest, feeling his heart pounding within, ready to explode.

Could he doubt and disclaim it, as his twin had just done? How? – when he knew that knowledge was the way to awakening. He *ached* for Wisdom. That is why he had knowingly transgressed the law and read the forbidden book. He *had to* know – know how it *all* had truly begun...

His temples throbbed; his mind was reeling. The room was spinning round him.

But why did he search *for the beginning?* 'The end will be where the beginning is'. Had he been seeking the beginning, all this time, to bring him finally *to this end* – the Messiah's path – to knowledge of how the end will come?

He felt himself treading the edge of the abyss.

"But the Messiah's path..." Jesus said, turning his large eyes to the elderly father. "*I don't know* where it leads," he avowed, "or where it *ends*..."

"You don't know *yourself*," Melchizedek re-assured him, "that's all. We have, so to speak, 'banished you' from this place, because the time has come for you to leave here, and live among men and women. You cannot hide yourself here forever."

Rivulets of sweat ran down his forehead. The son of Nazareth shuddered to think what lay beyond the monastery walls.

Sensing the youth's profound fear, the elder added, "I have received word from your father. He needs you in Nazareth. Your mother is ill, he says – losing her senses, speaking strange things. And he is getting old. He wants you – and Thomas as well, if he wishes – to join him there, to practise your trade together in his workshop. I advise you to go. Your place is *out there*, with our people."

The son of Nazareth was seized by mute anguish. He didn't want to leave here, didn't want to face his stern father, or embrace once more his crazed mother. He hated Nazareth, with its small-minded peasants. And the world, with its merchants, soldiers and whores, terrified him.

"I'll accompany you," Thomas offered. "I have nowhere else to go..."

The Nazarene remained rooted to the spot, unwilling to part from this place. The cloister had become, for him, more comforting than home. He was overwhelmed by an intense longing to remain here, safely ensconced within these protective walls. Nostalgically, he recalled the many years that he and Judas had passed here together. When they met, they were beardless youths...

"Then you will walk that path together," Melchizedek confirmed.

And he turned to Jesus, adding: "I ask only one thing of you: that as you leave here, go by way of the hermits' cave and enter it. You must enter it *alone*. The three hermits are waiting for you..."

Melchizedek paused, remembering.

"They have been waiting for you for many many years..."

III

Thomas waited outside the Cave of Darkness while Jesus stepped cautiously into its blackened depths. The twins could smell the strange stench which the Idumean hunchback had described: like dampness, fever and the living dead.

Beyond the entrance, the passage was cut like a meander into rock, turning left then right. In this way, no light from the outside world could penetrate the dark interior.

Reaching into emptiness, feeling his way blindly with his hands, the Nazarene's fear mounted. Was this the Messiah's path? His heart heavy with foreboding, he dreaded the ordeal that awaited him at the heart of this labyrinth...

At the final turning, the cave opened wide before him, its arched ceiling black from soot and smoke. A large oil lamp near the entrance illuminated the stone interior in dancing reliefs of light and shadow: primitive furniture, parchments, star-maps and books. The stench was overwhelming.

Jesus approached the three figures who sat on the floor with their backs toward him. Halfway between the lamp and the hermits he stopped.

None turned to greet him. Instead, they raised their heads and gazed in silence at the long shadow cast upon the wall.

'The hermits, they be your judges' the hunchback had said.

One hermit, he now saw from behind, was clothed in Persian vestments, though his purple robes had long since faded. But he wore the Phrygian cap, pointed and falling forward, indicative of a magus. Another wore nothing more than a filthy hair-shirt, an ascetic in the Greek style. The last of them bore the familiar robes of a Zadokite priest, though these too had blackened over time. One Persian, one Greek, one Hebrew the youth realized.

"Tell us of your birth..." the Persian began, dispensing with formalities. His voice was dry, his words accented, their intonation strange.

"I was born Yeshua ben Yosef," Jesus somehow managed to say, "son of the carpenter in Nazareth."

"And the people of your village, they call you 'the son of Joseph'?" the Hebrew priest pursued.

Jesus lowered his head, a gesture the hermits observed in his shadow on the wall. They could not see the deep stains of scarlet flushing his cheeks.

"They call me <the son of Mary,>" he whispered, his voice Mk 6:3
breaking. "Joseph recognized me as his son, but the people of my village never forgot..."

"Still, your father raised you as his own," the Greek now spoke, "teaching you his trade..?" His enunciation was Hellenic.

Again, Jesus shook his head.

"I was sent away – to Magdala for a time, then to this place – to learn my trade here." Jesus cowered in shame. He had spoken of this to no one. *How did they know?*

“Your mother – she never spoke to you of your birth?” the Persian resumed.

“Never...” Jesus replied, his heart contracting from the long-forgotten sadness and pain. “She was very young, and my father, a much older man, kept her shut away at home. He feared she was visited by voices. I’ve lived most of my life in this monastery...”

“Then you know nothing of the strange events, rumoured about your birth?”

Jesus hesitated. In his mind, the fragments of memory were coalescing: his father, always stern and distant, forbidding any mention of it; his mother, ever-veiled, hiding from the villagers and their gossip.

“I know that the neighbours whispered things, with fear and reprobation in their eyes... but that’s all.”

The three hermits turned to one another, conversing in low tones. They nodded and shook their heads variously until the elder Hebrew stuck the floor with his hand, and spoke.

“Enough! The beginning is always a mysterious thing... whether of your own life, or the beginning of the world. So tell us, son of Israel, why did you *turn away* from the Book of Genesis? Why did you seek knowledge of the world’s beginning *elsewhere?*”

Jesus shivered. While the others had whispered among themselves, his mind had wandered, and memories of his cousin had returned to him. In Magdala, Miri was the only one who seemed to know the secret of his birth. She never told him, but she loved him – despite it, or even because of it...

“I followed where Wisdom led me,” the Nazarene replied, his voice barely a whisper.

The elders watched as the shadow clasped its hands to stop them from trembling.

“Ah, Wisdom...” the Judaic elder nodded, then quoted Ecclesiasticus:

Sirach 4:11 “<*For though Wisdom takes them first through winding ways...*
And tests them with her ordeals,
In the end She will lead them back to the straight road,
And reveal her secrets to them.>

So, Wisdom led you away from the books of our forefathers? It was *She* who taught you otherwise...”

The Nazarene’s soul quivered within. This elder was quick, far more clever than him, and impatient for the truth. His judgement would come swiftly and without mercy.

"Yes. She taught me that our grandparents had committed no fault. The cause of our fall was love."

The three ascetics bowed their heads once more and whispered among themselves. Then, they began speaking, one after the other, quickly and in confusion.

"When Melchizedek came to us this morning," said one, "he stood where you are standing and recounted all the words which Wisdom had spoken through you..."

"Melchizedek is convinced," added another, "that *you* are <the Tri Tr 87:17
countenance of the Father,> <the Son of the unknown God.>" Tri Tr 133:16

"We renounced contact with the world many years ago," the
third explained. "<We go about in hunger and thirst, not clinging Auth T 27:12
to things, but withdrawing from them. Though we are ill and feeble
and in pain, there is still a great strength hidden within us.> We have
lived here in darkness for three decades because... we are awaiting
the Messiah."

"Now," the Judaic hermit announced, "you come in the saviour's name and announce to us that the Fall of Man *was false* – that God has hidden his face from us, and *you* will reveal it – through love?"

Jesus trembled uncontrollably. All the fear and anguish of that morning returned to him. He felt ashamed. He felt anger and injustice. He had been banished from the monastery, stepped halfway into the world, and now, this cave with its labyrinth was testing him. The Messiah's path, he wondered – would it always twist and turn like this?

"Yes, through love," the Nazarene said at last. And suddenly, a
voice upwelled from inside him. "You have spoken of 'the Messiah'.
But <the one who is properly called Christ is *the Beloved* of the Tri Tr 87:6
Father.>" Hesitatingly, he mouthed the words that formed on his
lips. "<The Father extends himself to those whom He loves, so that, Tri Tr 73:25
those who have *come forth* from Him, might *become* him as well.>
When they return to him, through love, then the circle is made
complete."

The three hermits continued staring at the shadow on the wall, now silenced by its speech. Though unclear in meaning, an eternal *mystery* was manifest in those words. Wisdom had spoken through him.

First one, then the other, and finally all three turned to face him directly. Tears were glistening in their eyes.

"Come closer, so that we may see you clearly," the Hebrew

elder said.

Jesus approached, and was suddenly overwhelmed with compassion for these three eremites who had waited here for so many years. He fell to his face, pressing his forehead to the ground. Together, the three placed their hands in blessing over his head. One even dared to touch his hair.

When Jesus rose, he could see their faces clearly – kind faces, smiling, radiant with joy. They were looking at him as if he were a new-born child and these, their joyous expressions, were offered as miraculous gifts.

IV

"My name is Zostrianos," said the Persian magus. "And this is Enoch and Marsanes," he added, indicating the Hebrew and the Greek. "We have kept each other company for almost thirty years now."

"Not without moments of disagreement," Enoch cautioned. "We each come from different traditions, and see the world in different ways."

"The Wisdom of the Greeks," Marsanes explained, "differs from the Hebrews and Persians. To us, this world is nothing more than shadows and appearances, a mere semblance of the truth. For
Phaedo 109d Man lives <in the hollow of the earth;> it is nothing more than <a
Phaedo 114c prison house...>"

This Greek, Jesus could see, cared little for the body. His hair-shirt hung in loose folds over his emaciated frame; his leathery skin was scarred, blistered and unwashed. But still, beneath the large forehead crowned with a few sparse hairs, his eyes sparkled with sagacity, warmth and kindness.

"Each of us has sworn," Zostrianos said, "never to leave this place until the shadows have dispersed, and our eyes have opened to three great mysteries. The last of these, today, has been revealed to us – we sought to behold, with our own eyes, the Messiah as a fully grown man. Do you know *who* the Messiah is?"

The youth shook his head in silence.

"He is," Zostrianos continued, "the one who brings history to
Avesta 46.3 its conclusion. The Persians call him <*Saosyant*, the saviour whose
sacrifice will end time.> He *knows* the mystery of the end, and makes it manifest – because he has found out the truth about the beginning..."

"Indeed," Marsanes said, "*<The end will be like the beginning.>* Tri Tr 79:1
Wisdom has revealed to you a certain vision of the beginning: that
the Fall came about through love. And now, at the end of time, you
would have us rise again to God – through love..."

"But *Wisdom is fickle*," Enoch sighed, screwing up his eyes and
pulling at his long beard. "As God's companion, She knows many
secrets about the Father. Some, like the one you have learned, She
reveals to us. But others, *She hides...*"

"We have petitioned her for the resolution to three great
mysteries," Marsanes explained at last, "– the Beginning, the Fall,
and the Resolution. If you are the one whom we Greeks call the
Christos – the one marked and anointed for the Resolution – then
first you must reveal what *truly* happened at the Beginning."

"– And the Fall..." Enoch added.

Jesus was silent, realizing the full import of their words. The
three wise men knew 'the end will be where the beginning is'. But,
there was more to the beginning than love.

"Wisdom... is God's *companion?*" Jesus asked, his curiosity
mingling with wonder.

"*<When the Lord marked out the foundations of the earth,* Prov 8:27
Wisdom was at his side like a master craftsman,>" the Judaic hermit
quoted. "*Hochmah* has been his companion from the beginning
– his Demiurge: *<She reaches mightily from one end of the earth to* Wis 8:3
*the other, ordering all things... She is an initiate in the mysteries of
God's knowledge... since the Lord of all loves her.>*"

"So, if you wish to know the mysteries of the world before the
Fall," Zostrianos said, "you must turn to her for the answers."

Enoch gazed at Jesus kindly and continued.

"It is Wisdom, *<the fashioner of all things,>* who teaches us <to Wis 7:2
know the beginning and end and middle of times; the cycles of the Wis 7:17
year and the constellations of stars; the structure of the world and
the activity of the elements; the natures of animals and the varieties
of plants.>"

"As *Sophia*," Marsanes said, "the Greeks have worshipped
her always: *<All this order and arrangement the Goddess first* Timaeus 24b
imparted...> Plato wrote. Though, for him, the Demiurge and
artificer of this world was masculine..."

"That," Enoch added, nodding his head as he pulled even harder
on his beard, "is the *greatest* mystery. The Demiurge is like God,
knowing his mind and its mysteries. But, if the artificer is sometimes
male, sometimes female – then what of God?"

Was it possible – what Jesus had read in *The Poimandres* and even in Genesis – that God was neither male, nor female, but *both*? The Nazarene could feel his heart now, knocking against his ribs, demanding the answer.

Enoch turned to the others, silenced by his own question.

"He is both," Marsanes replied, calmly and reasonably, "a Unity
Meta 1075a for eternity. Aristotle likened God to <that thought which thinks itself for eternity.> This, of course, is a great mystery. But in Greek, 'thought' is *ennoia*, a feminine word, while 'thinking' or 'mind' is *nous*; a masculine word. God unites both, as 'thought thinking itself', the masculine *Nous* and feminine *Ennoia* embraced, gazing face to face, for all time. They form a perfect circle, knowing in their hearts that they are one."

For a few moments the Nazarene's breathing stopped. He could not fully comprehend these words. But a silent voice within him told him that *this... was...* the mystery.

"My people also have an artificer," the Persian said, fingering a gold amulet absent-mindedly. "Thousands of years ago, we posed
Avesta 44:3 three great questions: <What artist made light and darkness? Who assigned their road to the sun and stars? Who fixed the earth below, and the sky above so that it does not fall?> Wisdom spoke to our prophet Zarathustra. He saw the beginning as a conflict between two great powers: the Light and the Darkness. In the beginning, there were only these two."

"On this, we have agreed," Marsanes said. "Genesis says that,
Gen 1:3 in the beginning, <God separated the light from the darkness.> And for the Greeks as well, whether the Orphics or the followers of *The
CH I. 4 Poimandres*, <the light rose upward and darkness coiled downward like a leonine serpent.>"

"Thus, there also came about an 'above' and a 'below'," Zostrianos pointed out. "And like light and darkness, above and below – there also came about, at that moment, good and evil."

"All that God made 'was good,'" Enoch acknowledged, "but
Gen 1:7 evil came later. First <God separated the waters above from the waters below.>" The Hebrew priest began shaking his long finger at the Persian, reminding him of an old argument.

"Water? Perhaps..." Marsanes retorted, "as Thales believed. But what of Heraclitus, with his ever-living fire? What of air and earth as well, making the four elements of Empedocles? Couldn't these four – fire, air, earth and water – be arranged from above to below?"

The Hebrew and the Greek began debating this question. Like

the opening gambits of two master chess players, each cited the words of their own prophet. In fierce succession they exchanged more citations, making so many moves and countermoves on the board. The end, as always, was a stalemate.

"Well, you can see," Zostrianos said directly to Jesus, "Wisdom has beguiled us endlessly with many voices and many prophets..."

"Indeed," Marsanes added, turning away from Enoch, "we Greeks have had a long tradition of skeptics, placing doubt and unknowing above all else. All we see here, they claim, are shadows, images, and likenesses; they are but copies and types – for all bear false names." He rose and approached the large oil lamp, which had begun to sputter and smoke from a lack of oil.

"Perhaps!" Enoch said, rising and following him. "But Wisdom
executed God's plan faithfully. <*She is a reflection of eternal light,* Wis 7:26
a spotless mirror of the workings of God, and an image of his goodness.>"

"Oh yes," Marsanes replied, "<If a man could get wings and fly Phaedo 109d
up, he would see the true light.>"

He poured more oil into the lamp, which flared up.

"...He would see <the ever-unchanging archetypes, the true Timaeus 28a
names and forms, the images in the upper heavens...>"

For some time, Marsanes stared at the bright white flame, then turned away, his eyes blinded.

"<But the soul is dragged by the body towards what is always Phaedo 79c
changing; she goes astray and is confused. She staggers like one
drunken,> because she is caught in darkness and confusion; <her Phaedo 87b
flesh is a soiled garment.>"

To sweeten the stench in the air, Enoch poured a few drops of frankincense into the lamp. Discretely, he also passed a small bag of fragrant myrrh to Marsanes.

The unwashed ascetic continued. "Still, when the soul examines
by herself, then, as Plato says, <*she goes away yonder to the pure* Phaedo 79d
and everlasting and immortal and unchanging... and there she rests from her wanderings.>"

"Our soul is subject to many influences," the Persian said, fixing the Nazarene with a kind smile. "To my people, she is called the *daena*, and likened to a young girl. The world is full of demons to tempt and torment her; and the counterfeit spirit to lead her astray. But most of all, she must resist time, whom we call *Zurvan akarana*. Perhaps a better name for him would be *Fate*."

He passed his finger over the surface of his golden amulet,

which depicted *Zurvan* as a lion-headed god with a serpent coiled seven times around his body.

"Ah... the *Heimarmene!*" exclaimed the Greek, returning to them and effortlessly settling his aged limbs on the floor. He hung the bag of sweet-smelling myrrh round his neck, relieving the oppressive odour of his unwashed flesh.

"Seven planets surround the earth," Marsanes said, "each a transparent sphere, one within the next. And in the night sky, only the gateway with its planetary ruler remains visible, each *Archon* a guardian glowing like an errant star. Before our birth, our soul descended through these seven gates, putting on seven garments
CH I.24 – ignorance, idleness, wrath, pride, lust, greed and inconstancy – just like the *Archons* themselves, like Saturn, Jupiter, Mars and the Sun; like Venus, Mercury and the Moon... Through these planetary influences, our soul acquired its inclinations, and became subject to Fate – to the *Heimarmene...*"

"Unless," Enoch corrected him, "the soul spurns its bodily passions, and turns toward God, who sits above the seven heavens with his hosts of seraphim and cherubim."

"Whether Man is fated or free remains a great mystery," Marsanes replied. "But this question begs the next. How was Man created? What is he made from? How did he fall?"

Jesus watched in silent fascination as the three hermits turned their minds to these questions, interpreting them in light of their own culture's Wisdom. They discussed the First Man, who was called in turn *Anthropos*, Adam, Kasia or Kadmon; he became the image and model for all men and women. They discussed the composition of his body, as a compound of earth, air, water, and fire – a body swayed by passions but governed by reason and blessed with an eternal soul. Its darkness even housed a hidden spirit. Finally, they struggled with the issue of the Fall, and why indeed, they had found themselves here in this darkened cavern.

As the lamp was refilled and the hours stretched on, the cavern dwellers lost all sense of time, engaged as they were with eternal questions. But Jesus had not forgotten Thomas, waiting for him outside in the cold. Meanwhile, within this cave, the incensed air grew thick and stifling, barely masking the odour of decay.

What each of them said was true, Jesus realized, for Wisdom spoke in many tongues. Though She was worshipped in different lands under many names and guises, her beauty was unchanging, and the same alluring voice intoned all these different, even conflicting oracles.

Would he ever escape with the answer to those three eternal questions? Why not remain here, like them, until Wisdom had finally spoken to him, revealing her truth clearly and indisputably? He had hoped to hide himself within the monastery's walls. Why not prolong his stay here, in this cave, for years to come..?

Shamefully, the Nazarene lowered his head, embarrassed by his own cowardice.

Whether he stayed here or wandered freely, his situation was quite the same: this world remained a darkened cavern and his soul was bound by iron chains. Man dwelt in ignorance and unknowing. The Messiah's path, wherever it led, may twist and turn, but it would also be enlightening. He had to follow it to its end and find the way out of the labyrinth – even if he had to forge a pair of wings to escape its imprisoning walls.

By then, the three eremites had noticed how the Messiah's face had changed. He seemed determined to seek his end, whether bound by fate or freely.

"We three," Zostrianos now spoke, "have debated like this for far too long – indeed, from the time that this monastery was founded – and hardly have we noticed the time that has passed. I don't know if we will ever find our way out of here..."

"But you must leave this place, with our blessings," Marsanes accepted. "Carry our words with you always, as our most precious gifts. They will help you to reveal the Beginning and the Fall, so that the Resolution may be accomplished."

"And never forget Wisdom," Enoch said. "Court her with all your soul; go after her, seek her – and She will reveal herself to you.
Once you take hold her, do not let her go. For in the end <*you will* Sirach 6:26
find rest in her and She will take the form of joy for you.>"

The three elders dipped their fingers in holy oil – a pungent
mix of <cinnamon and myrrh, ground in cassia and aromatic cane, Exod 30:22
then pressed in olive oil.> With this mixture, Zostrianos, Marsanes and Enoch performed the chrism – daubing the holy oil onto the saviour's forehead and uttering a mysterious blessing in their own
tongues. Jesus heard his name pronounced strangely <– *Yesseus* or Gs Egypt 66:9
Yessedekeus followed by *Mazareus*.> Then, the anointed one turned and departed. They watched in silence as his shadow grew and dissolved in the light.

When Jesus finally found his way out of the cave, the heavens were dark and the canopy of stars gazed down at him, some sparkling, others more faint. A cool breeze passed over him, refreshing his deadened senses: the night birds were singing in the trees, the moon was glowing, and the earth was fragrant with the scent of magnolia.

Advancing, he found Thomas curled up on the ground, covered with sackcloth, and a stone for a pillow. The Nazarene had no idea of how much time had passed. Perhaps hours, perhaps days. All he knew is that his mind was burdened by mysteries.

Seeing his twin sleeping peacefully, he dared not disturb him. Instead, he sat on the ground and watched over his brother.

Jesus felt great love and gratitude towards Thomas, but this joy was also tinged by a strange resentment, almost jealousy. His twin had renounced the saviour's path, refusing to hear the voice of Wisdom which, though softly, whispered to him from within. In this way, his brother had freed himself from her terrible mysteries, so intriguing and demanding.

But, at the same time, the saviour was also thankful for this companion, now curled up at his feet. His twin would never follow him blindly, but lead the way if necessary and remain, in any case, a wanderer along his own path.

The son of Nazareth resolved to return to his village, but also decided to forsake it as soon as possible – and set out for Jerusalem.

III. Nazareth

I

The mother of Jesus sat in the niche by the window, gazing at the setting sun. In silence, she watched its radiant splendour streaming through the shimmering leaves of the ancient olive grove.

Mary of Magdala sat opposite, her hands clasped in her lap and her head bowed. The long strands of her tightly-woven hair hid her anguish as she spoke.

"I am not like other woman," she confessed. "They dream of a home, to serve a man and warm his bed, to fill her womb with his children. But what happens when her beauty fades and she grows old... What is left to her?"

She glanced at her godmother, wondering if she understood. But the Virgin, whose placid face seemed forever untouched by the years, remained perfectly silent.

"My father has had many offers," Miri admitted, fingering the amulets that encircled her throat. "One merchant promised to pay a substantial *mohar*. But so far, out of love for me, my father has refused them."

The elder Mary nodded for her continue.

"But I must find my own way soon. I'm no longer young. I've come to you because I know you have always lived for yourself. They say you are <the Virgin whom none has defiled.> Is there Gs Phil 55:27
nothing more for us, the women of Israel, than to be daughters, wives and mothers?"

Magdalene fixed her eyes on the Virgin. Dire need was etched in Miri's face, distorting her fine features with pain and confusion.

She watched in agony and waited in silence for an answer.

Thund 13:19 "<I am the wife and the virgin," the elder Mary said at last. "I am the mother and the daughter...> I am all of these," she admitted, shrugging her shoulders.

"But you are more... There must be something more..!" the younger Mary pleaded.

"Oh yes. Do you see that tree? Do you see how it moves its branches in the light?"

Magdalene nodded.

Tri Prot 35:2 "When I sit here, I think *<I am the movement that dwells in all>*
Tri Prot 35:12 *<and I move in every creature.>* Do you understand?"

The daughter of Magdala watched and listened, but she did not understand.

Tri Prot 35:33 "I am in you," the elder Mary said. "<I am a voice speaking
softly... the hidden voice that dwells within. I dwell within the
Tri Prot 36:14 silence.> But I also cry out in everyone <– and they recognize it.>
My voice is crying out even now, this moment – in you..."

Miri nodded her head. Meanwhile, in the ensuing silence, she admitted to herself – sadly – that the woman had lost her senses. All she spoke was nonsense.

The old maid was imprisoned here, in this room, shut away by her husband. And yet – in mind, in spirit, she felt as if she moved through all things. Her silent voice was crying *for release* – at this moment, through Miri and her youth...

"You and I are the same," the younger Mary said, "– just two women separated by generations."

Thund 15:19 "Yes. <Do not be afraid of my power and, in my weakness,
Tri Prot 45:21 do not forsake me.> <I hide myself in everyone and reveal myself
within them.> You must learn to let me manifest myself in you..."

"You have spent your life alone in this room. I have to get out, escape somehow, enter the world..."

"You must leave," the Virgin affirmed, "and seek out the hidden places, forgotten by our people. The Asherah groves and high places.
Thund 16:31 <Whenever you hide yourself there, *I* will appear. But whenever *you*
appear, I will hide myself from you.>"

Miri tried to understand, but her mind could not grasp all that the Virgin was saying. Her voice breaking, she pleaded:

"You are making no sense..."

Thund 15:29 "<I am senseless and I am wise,>" the elder Mary replied with
Tri Prot 42:10 a shrug of her shoulders. "<I am the voice speaking in many ways.>
You too are wise, though you do not know it."

"Then reveal to me some of your wisdom," Miri cried. "Tell me who you are, so that I might share it with you."

"<I am the Womb that gives shape to all," she answered, then Tri Prot 45:6
turned her gaze back to the window. Looking at the olive grove
crowned by the sun, she added, "<I give birth to the Light that shines Tri Prot 45:6
in splendour.>"

II

Jesus reclined in the shadow of a blossoming almond tree, listening to the nearby stream as it flowed over reeds, grass and stones. The son of Mary felt grateful for this day, the first sabbath of the month: a day of rest.

Leaning over and gazing into a small stilled pool, he could see himself now, after six months in Nazareth. His face had grown long, his cheeks hollow and his gaze world-weary. Worst of all, the fire in his eyes had died out. What had happened to his soul during all this time?

His labours in the workshop with Thomas and his father had became hateful and odious. His soul was overburdened and his spirit broken. Still, his father had besieged them with orders – cradles for the new-born, wagons for the farmhands, beds for the newlyweds and coffins for the dead. Grudgingly, he and Thomas built them all, so many vessels for life's brief passage.

Was that all there was to this life – endless hours of toil relieved
only by a few fleeting moments of rest? <Hour begot hour, day begot Tri Prot 42:30
day, and each month made the following month, till time had gone
round, succeeding even time itself.>

He wanted to escape – flee this cycle of the hours, leave his mother and father, abandon Nazareth. He had become nothing more than a mule, turning in circles, yoked to the increasing burden of his family. Meanwhile, the Romans and Herodians stood over him, their hands held high as they lashed the poor of Israel with their whips...

Through the blossoming almond trees, Jesus could see Mount Tabor rising majestically above the Plain of Jezreel – so beautiful to behold. He wanted to stand on its summit and speak to God face to face – demand why there was so much suffering, slavery and injustice. But the sacred voice had grown silent. For months now, Wisdom had not spoken to him from within. Israel's Messiah had become one with his people: embittered, resigned, world-weary...

As the sun cast is mantle of gold over Tabor's emerald slopes, the Nazarene set out for home. He passed barley fields with their slender stalks rising from the furrows. Like a truant school-child, he wandered aimlessly, delaying his return. Plucking a fresh crown of wheat, he rolled it in his palms and munched a few husked seeds.

When the errant youth finally returned to Heli's house on the hillside, the swallows were flying wildly in the skies, screeching and circling in huge swarms. His younger brothers and sisters were running round the courtyard, singing loudly and playing. With the setting of the sun at eventide, it seemed all the earth was celebrating the end of the sabbath day.

Passing under the vine arbour, the son of Mary heard familiar laughter – Cephas and Thomas... His two closest friends were embracing, celebrating their re-union after half a year's passing. Joseph his father and his grandfather Heli leaned upon their olive-wood staffs, welcoming the wayfarer from Bethsaida.

When Cephas saw Jesus he opened wide his arms and included the Nazarene in his expansive embrace.

"The twins!" he cried, his eyes now brimming with tears, "who I'd thought I'd never see again! But you're here, together, working under one roof. It gladdens my heart to see you both..!"

The twins glanced at one another, silently acknowledging the truth that Cephas had spoken: despite all the hardship, they were here together. And now the Bethsaidean had come to Nazareth, as promised.

Thomas stared at the wayfarer's burlap sack and walking stick. "But why would a Gennesaret fisherman climb our craggy goat's path to Nazareth?"

"The Paschal Feast! I thought I'd look up the twins before setting out." Jonah's son held up his sycamore staff and shook it like a sceptre. "The pilgrimage! Come with me. We can celebrate the Passover together!"

"In Jerusalem?" Jesus asked, his eyes opening wide.

"It's your duty," Cephas countered, "as the first-born son of your father's house. You must bring the Paschal offering to the Temple."

Jesus turned to his elders, to his father Joseph and grandfather Heli.

"The first fruits of barley..." the son of Mary stammered. "It's my duty to offer them on the altar... to bring their blessings upon this house."

Jesus could barely look his father in the face. Joseph returned a hard gaze at his adopted son. But Heli intervened.

"For this house, you must go," the grandfather declared, his eyes watery from memories of past pilgrimages.

"...Jerusalem," Jesus repeated, rejoicing at the sound of each syllable.

"The holy city of Zion!" Thomas adjoined, his heart in step with the Nazarene's. He had resolved, like his twin, to escape Nazareth.

And the three embraced once more, imagining the prospect of the long journey, then the marvels of the Temple Mount.

Cephas, his face still glowing with mirth, turned to look at the narrow window at the front of the cottage. "Your cousin, I'm sure, will share in your joy..."

"Miri?" Jesus asked, his heart skipping a beat. "Miri is in Nazareth?"

"I accompanied her here. She came to speak with her godmother..."

Jesus looked up at the narrow window where his mother kept constant vigil.

In a low voice, Cephas added:

"She came here to discuss her betrothal..."

III

That night, Miri could not sleep. A thousand sounds filtered through the narrow transit above her bed. Crickets. Olive boughs. Night birds. From a distant hilltop came the bleating of lambs and the plaintive melody of a shepherd's pipe.

He was calling her.

Stepping lightly past the three sleeping sisters, Miri escaped into the courtyard. A lamp was still burning in the place where Jesus slept. Silent as a thief, she climbed a ladder to the roof of the workshop.

The Nazarene lay awake, as if waiting for her. A slight smile creased his lips as she nestled herself beside him. Silently, they gazed at one another, wondering what each was harbouring in their heart. Though she still felt an unspoken love for him, they had not seen each other or spoken for many years.

"Do you remember Jesus, as children, we slept together like this, on the roof of my parents' house at Magdala?"

"I remember..."

"We were only children then, so unsuspecting of the adults we would become..." she laughed, giving him a knowing look. "I wish we could go back there now, somehow..."

The Nazarene watched and saw it all: the beautiful way the Magdalene moved her hands as she spoke, the countless expressions that animated her crimson lips and golden green eyes. The fragrance of her body overwhelmed him – her scented breath, the spikenard rubbed between her breasts, the myrrh and aloes that he associated with her always.

"We could only go back," Jesus decided, "if we could hold each other now, unashamed and without desire."

"Like two children, naked and innocent. Do you think we could?" she mused, pressing her face next to his on the pillow. She gazed at his hair, dark as wine, and inhaled its sweet scent, like tannin, oak and must.

He stared, deep in thought, into the night sky; the moonlight sparkled in the watery depths of his eyes. His eyes, she noted with a shudder, were blacker and deeper than the abyss above their heads.

"No," he responded at last. "We can't go back." He looked at her sadly. "But we can't go forward either..."

The Nazarene held up his hand with its palm toward her, as if in a gesture of blessing. She naturally slid her slender hand into his, and their fingers entwined. His eyes fell upon the henna pattern inked onto the back of her palm, its mysterious design of interweaving serpents and vines.

"Because you're afraid of me," she said. "But I haven't forgotten the cliffs of Gennesaret. Even now, if I threw myself down, if I fell, you would follow me."

She lay herself on her back, staring upward at the thatched roof of their tabernacle, and its opening to the night sky. The moon this night was so full, shining brilliant and white.

He lifted himself up, extending his arm and leaning over her. Gazing down, he saw in her face his own true reflection, as if, in Nature's pool. Could he willingly, like the First Man, fall into her embrace – out of love?

For a long time, they looked at each other like this, unmoving, their watery reflections perfectly stilled. Then the daughter of Magdala smiled.

Spontaneously, she slipped off her tunic over her head and lay back on the bed. Her long hair, like auburn flames, formed a dark aureole around her brilliant features.

The son of Nazareth gazed at her long neck so gracefully sculpted, her shoulders and breasts so gently rounded, the fullness of her womb encircled by more intricate henna designs.

Fixing her with his gaze, he smiled, then put off his own tunic and resumed his position above her – looking down at her now as if he was the diver and she, the sea.

Trembling, she gazed into his eyes. His face, for a moment, turned to stone – only the blacks of his eyes glowed like basalt set in white ivory.

Then, they laughed. They began laughing so hard that they rolled over each other, trying to hush one another for fear they would wake up the others. And as they lay opposite each other, spontaneously, it happened.

Magdalene took her long hair and swathed his feet in her tresses, caressing his dark skin in her unbraided curls. The Nazarene responded in turn, taking her delicate feet in his strong hands and pressing them to his hot forehead and cheeks, then brushing his lips over their soles. She felt the heat of those kisses rise like a holy fire, burning inside her, spreading to her extremities. Pearls of sweat formed on her brow and tears fell from her lashes. She bathed his wounded feet with the waters of her sorrow and her joy. The touch of her tears on his toes, the moisture of her sweet breath on the arches, passed through him, over him, mounted his body to his temples and the tips of his hair. He felt blessed by her caresses.

For many hours they lay like this, as passion flowed from brow to foot, then around, from foot to brow. Overwhelmed and finally at peace, the daughter of Magdala fell into a blissful sleep with the saviour's feet nestled in her hair, pressed in the cleft of her neck like a pillow.

Meanwhile, mesmerized by the henna design of serpents and vines impressed on her flesh, the son of Nazareth spent the entire night entranced by the play of movement in those patterns: the web of life that wove through Nature like an endless tapestry. Some of its strands were born, lived and died – like leaf after leaf fallen from the vine, or shroud after shroud sloughed off by the serpent – but still the whole survived. Nature bore in her womb this endless cycle of life, eternal, unbroken, and never would she surrender herself to a beginning or an end.

At the same time, as the daughter of Magdala slept, she had a dream. Mary, the mother of Jesus, came to her as she lay on an ancient stone surrounded by Asherah trees. As promised, the Virgin had left her room in Nazareth and hovered now, an eternal presence, still to be felt within this sacred grove. And her voice, resonating with wisdom, repeated her mysterious oracle, saying "I am the Womb that gives shape to all," and "I give birth to the Light that shines in splendour."

Here, in this high place, those words became clear – clear as the crystalline refraction of the sunlight in the trees. All of life, whether bird, beast or fish, leaf, branch or tree, moved on the earth like a child moves in its mother's womb. The eternal mother feels them all, nascent, sleeping, alive, growing inside her. She feeds them with her life blood and forms them in the matrix of her belly.

The pattern of that matrix could be seen throughout Nature: traced on a leopard's fur and imprinted on a serpent's skin, manifest in bird flight and boar's tusks, in the turning of leaves toward the light and the carving of dunes by desert winds; in butterfly wings and human skulls, in a ram's horn notched with the years but curling round – its spiral a cipher for eternity. Mysteriously, like hieroglyphs, the letters read "I am the Womb that gives shape to all."

But then, in the midst of Nature's eternal cycle, an event occurred that upset this pattern. A man appeared whose birth and death became the sudden awakening of many. Like the sun, he became a light, and a doorway to transcendence. Like an eagle, he flew up, through the doorway of the sun, and transcended Nature's endless cycle.

At that moment, the pattern was broken, and took on a different shape, with the saviour at its centre. The circle of time unfolded into a line, with a beginning, middle, and end. On one side stood the alpha, on the other, the omega; and at the centre: the cruciform tau. The earth trembled and the darkness shook. But Nature herself knew what she carried in her womb. She cried aloud, in the pain of her birth-giving, in agony and joy, saying "I give birth to the Light that shines in splendour."

Miri awoke from her dream, her heart beating wildly like a bird in a thorn bush. It was still early morning and Jesus lay asleep with his head resting weightless on her feet. She lay a moment and listened to the sparrows greeting the dawn. The sun had not yet risen, but the morning star was fading fast.

Deftly, she removed herself from his bed, donned her tunic, and descended to her room below. The Nazarene's sisters were still soundly asleep. In her own bed, Magdalene wrapped herself tightly in a lamb's wool shawl and recalled the dream back into her memory. Then, listening to her own heart, she realized what this night had brought her. Though she had always loved the Nazarene, like a cousin, like the brother she never had, now she knew that their love must die and a new one grow in its place. She would make him her beloved, her betrothed, her bridegroom.

But first, to do this, she would have to leave him. She would have to flee Galilee, enter the world, and discover *who* she was. Then, with this gift, she would return to her beloved – as his bride.

IV

Festive music rose above the trellised grapevines hanging over the courtyard. The moon appeared, sprinkling fresh dew over the arbour. Amid the glistening leaves, tiny lanterns flickered and reflected in the dewdrops.

As grandfather Heli piped out the ancient psalms, his granddaughters clapped and sang. The twins sat by the fire, sharing a debilitating mix of water and wine. His broad face beaming, Cephas insisted on dancing with Arsinoe and her two blushing sisters; Magdalene teased young Jude and James, whose newly-bearded cheeks began to flush. A celebratory atmosphere reigned in Heli's household, this night before the pilgrims' departure.

Then, Jesus embraced his beloved Thomas and escaped from the crowded courtyard. Hesitantly, he ascended the stairs to his mother's room.

She sat alone, as always, by the stone alcove of the window. Over the last six months, the two of them had exchanged no more than a few brief words. In truth, the son of Mary was frightened by his mother. He wondered if the visions and voices that came to him were indeed divine, or merely a dark inheritance from his mother, who seemed haunted by her demons and delusions. Would he end up, one day, like her?

But tonight, before setting out for Jerusalem, he had to unburden his heart and speak with her openly. His father would never hear him; only she would listen to his words with neither accusation nor remorse.

He sat on the floor and took her hands into his.

"Mother, when I leave this house in the morning, I know I will not come back. I cannot..."

She turned and looked at him, her dark eyes so much like his own, infinitely deep and mysterious. In them, he could see a slight comprehension mingling with confusion, as if demons of light were mixing with angels of darkness.

"You too..." was all that she said.

"I have to escape from here, find my way – walk my own path..." he explained, looking up at her. His head was almost in her lap. "I had to tell you this, since father would never understand."

She shook her head gently and said, "You do not know your father. Your true father. You don't even know your mother..."

"No," Jesus admitted. "We have never truly spoken. But you – you have always retreated into silence."

He looked at her, and for a few moments, their eyes met. It frightened him to see his own face mirrored in hers. But her face was wiser, more feminine and mysterious. Though he was a part of her, and she a part of him – he did not know her.

"You have always hidden yourself from me," he said, hoping to see through the fog that lay between them.

His mother looked at him and for a long time she said nothing.

Tri Prot 35:29 "<I shall reveal myself of my own accord,>" she responded at last.

"Sometimes," he began anew, "I hear a voice like yours, speaking inside me. It says things I don't understand, things strange and confusing. But eventually I learn what it wants to tell me. Do you hear those voices too?"

Ambiguously, Mary nodded her head from side to side, saying nothing.

"But I haven't heard that voice for many months now," he admitted, his eyebrows arching in pain.

Why was he telling her all this? Did he think she would answer him? She was as silent as the voice in his head.

Tri Prot 35:33 "<I dwell within the silence," the Virgin said, shattering the stillness like a fallen jug. "I am a voice speaking softly, the hidden voice that dwells within... Within the immeasurable silence.>"

Opening wide his eyes, Jesus stared at her in wonder. Those words, and the way she spoke them, echoed with the voice of Wisdom in him.

Tri Prot 36:14 "<I am the real voice. And I cry out in everyone, once they recognize it...>" she confirmed.

Tears rose to his eyes. It was so comforting to hear that tone again, after so many months. Its resonance was so familiar, like the mysterious voice in the darkness that had comforted him when he was still a child.

Memories of that time came flooding back to him – how he would cry alone in the darkness, and she would lift him from his cradle, hold him in her arms, and soothe him, singing a nonsense song with many syllables: *<ie! ie - us! eo ou! eo ou - a!>* Gs Egypt 66:9

"I remember now," he said, "that voice... – your voice. You brought a lamp into my room, when I cried alone in the dark. Then you whispered my name..."

Mary gazed blankly at her son, nodding her head like an old blind woman. But gazing inward, her sight was absolutely clear.

"*<Yesseus! Yesseus!>* I used to say to you. And your face would Gs Egypt 66:9
light up when you recognized your own name..."

The memory suddenly returned, though he had forgotten it for so long. Her distinctive manner of speaking had evoked it.

"You remember now, don't you *Yesseus*?" she asked him. "You were reminded... and now you remember *who you are...*"

Frightened, Jesus dared not respond.

"<You are the word who dwells in the voice...>" Tri Prot 46:5

She squeezed his hand, reassuring him. But Jesus was deathly afraid. Now, his mother was speaking, and he wanted her to stop. Indeed, it was *he* who remained absolutely silent, hoping it would stop.

But, in that silence, the son could still hear a voice inside him, uttering its enigmatic string of sounds, like vowels without consonants.

Lending her voice to those sounds, his mother spoke its message clearly.

"<There is a light" she said, nodding at her son, "that dwells Tri Prot 46:5
hidden in the silence, and reveals itself through the speech of the mother.> You remember all of it now, don't you? You were crying in your sleep, alone in the darkness. I came with a lamp and woke you. Then I held you and whispered your name – *Yesseus! Yesseus!* You stopped crying and smiled. Your eyes sparkled like the confluence of stars in the heavens that night..."

"I was sleeping," Jesus said, "and you woke me, because of the strangers who had come. We had guests..." The faces appeared to him, as if from a dream. But he could not recognize them, they were still too hazy and unclear.

Mary nodded, realizing that he had begun to remember. "<I am Tri Prot 35:21
the sight of those who dwell in sleep," she whispered. "And those who sleep, I awaken.>"

"Three guests came in..." he murmured, as the figures became clearer in his mind.

"...Bearing sweet-smelling oil, a bag of myrrh, and one with a golden amulet," she reminded him.

Suddenly, the son of Mary could smell the incense and see the image on the amulet: a god with a lion's head and a serpent coiled seven times around his body. The amulet was dancing and sparkling in the lamplight as it dangled from Zostrianos' slender hand.

Then, the smiling face of Zostrianos came sharply into focus, with Enoch and Marsanes looking over his shoulders – each of them bearded, but younger and more vigorous. The vision was absolutely clear. Had the Persian magus done this, so many years ago, so Jesus would remember?

"They kneeled before you," Jesus revealed.

Tears came to Mary's eyes as she remembered the honours they
Gs Egypt 42:12 bestowed upon her. '<Hail to thee, Mother, virginal *Barbelo*>' they
Test Tr 43:28 cried. '<You are the Virgin who has brought forth the light.>' That
day, she was blessed among women.

"You must never speak of this to your father," she warned him, wiping away her tears. "He has forbidden it."

"But why did you never speak to me of this before?" Jesus demanded. "Tell me more – tell me about our guests."

Mary shook her head, unwilling to remember – the joy of that moment being far too great. She had buried it for years in her solitude and sorrow. But slowly, the happiness returned to her. Against her will, she smiled, as fresh tears flowed upon her cheeks.

"They blessed you. And as they did this, each of them gave
Gs Egypt 66:9 you a name. <*Yesseus*, one said..." Mary could not go on; her joy
was overwhelming. But somehow she found the strength. "Then
Mazareus, and finally *Yessedekeus*.>" Her tears gushed forth, as the
childish song came back to her: *ie! ie - us! eo ou! eo ou - a!* "They
Gs Tru 38:7 said <The name of the Father is the Son. The Father's name is not
spoken, but revealed through the Son.>"

She leaned her head against the wall, exhausted. Why did he force her to remember so much ecstasy and exultation?

"Mother..." Jesus whispered, holding her hands tightly. "You must tell me – *who* was my father?"

Mary looked at him in horror and wonder. How would she ever be able to answer his question?

Her head still leaning against the wall, the Virgin only managed a mute movement left and right, left and right.

"I cannot tell you. I cannot speak his name. Since He..."
Tri Prot 35:33 she paused, and then finally mouthed the words, "<He... *is* the
Tri Tr 129:20 immeasurable Silence.> <He transcends every word, every voice,

everything... He even transcends every silence.>”

Fearfully, Jesus searched his mother’s eyes, looking for signs of madness. Again, he saw his own dark gaze staring back at him. Was her madness now his own? Was he becoming convinced of this folly? But her eyes, like her voice, spoke the truth, and betrayed no signs of deception.

“<Three powers came forth,” she said, “the Father, the Mother, Gs Egypt 41:23
and the Son.> <From the silence came a voice, and speech, and Tri Prot 37:20
within it, the word.>”

Her son looked at her and slowly shook his head. He hadn’t understood at all.

“It is too soon,” she said. “You still don’t *know* your father – know *who* he is. So none of this makes sense to you.”

“But you must tell me more,” he pleaded, “so that I might come to understand...”

Mary sighed. “By coming to know yourself, you will learn
to know your father. <The Father is a spring, whose water flows Tri Tr 60:13
abundantly, and is never diminished> – He is <the spring of the Ap Jn 4:19
Water of Life,> and I... <I *poured forth* the water.> But you – you Tri Prot 36:5
are <his image, reflected in the Living Water.>” Ap Jn 4:19

“Tell me more..!” her son demanded, hoping all of this would somehow make sense.

“<The Father brought forth everything,” she explained, “like a Tri Tr 62:6
drop from a spring, like a blossom from a vine, like a flower from a
seed – like a little child!> <He is the root, with its tree, branches and Tri Tr 51:15
fruit.> <In me, he sowed a thought, like a seed> <– and I gave birth Tri Tr 61:2
to the Light that shines in splendour.> Yes, to you, <the Word hidden Tri Prot 45:6
in the Light, bearing the fruit of life, pouring forth the Living Water Tri Prot 46:16
from the immeasurable spring.>”

She fell back against the wall, then collapsed inward upon herself. The terrible memories of those events came rushing back to her, and exploded like a vision in her brain. She saw the cold crystal dewdrop of phosphorous water as it fell into her womb; she felt its fiery seed, like a spark of light, burning inside her. And finally, she relived his birth, when the radiant child entered the world, illuminating the all in a blinding epiphany.

“Ask no more,” she pleaded, knowing that words could not convey the massive outpouring of her memories.

Jesus wiped the tears from her cheeks and brushed away the hairs clinging to her hot forehead. He regretted having pushed her so far.

After some moments, Mary recovered herself. And then she found, once the overwhelming ecstasy of those recollections had passed, that a pleasant warmth and euphoria remained. Her son, she could see, was kneeling before her, smiling shyly out of love and admiration. This was a secret to be shared just between the two of them.

"You must leave this house tomorrow, as you said," she nodded, "to find your own way, and walk your own path."

Jesus silently agreed, remembering the three hermits in the Cave of Darkness: their blessings and parting words...

"I walk the Messiah's path..." Jesus revealed to his mother, wondering what her response might be.

"Then you know..." was all that she said.

"And you have always known..?"

His mother nodded. "Before our three guests left us that evening, they warned me to be careful. They said that many great powers were searching for you, hoping to seize and destroy you. They themselves had avoided Herod's spies and gone into hiding. But they could not conceal themselves from other powers, from the stars in the heavens watching our movements here below."

The old woman gave him a look that pierced him to the bone.

"The more you know about yourself, the more they will come to know about you. The more you reveal yourself, the greater the risk that they will find you. When you were ignorant of these things – in the monastery, even here in this home – you were safe. Now, with each step you take, you risk discovery. Only the prophecy can protect you."

Her son nodded vaguely. For his benefit, she continued.

"You must listen to Wisdom always, whenever she speaks to you, in whatever guise. Mine is not the only voice. When the Baptist pronounced his prophecies, She was speaking through him."

"The Five Seals..." the son of Nazareth realized.

"They will seal and protect you. But others want to seize their power for themselves. You must find the seals – all of them – particularly the fifth. Until then, you are vulnerable."

"But what are they?" Jesus asked.

"They are power. But only your movements will reveal their power to you."

She took his head in her arms, caressed his hair, and anointed his forehead with a kiss.

"I am only a woman; a daughter of Israel blessed and chosen

by God. I can only tell you what Wisdom reveals through me. You understand?"

The son of Nazareth nodded.

"Then know that you will never find the fifth seal alone. Only a daughter of Israel can help you..."

His mother looked at him, as his eyes opened wide. She nodded her head gently two or three times. "Yes, you know it yourself... First, you must betroth yourself to Mary of Magdala..."

IV. Pilgrimage

I

That morning, as Cephas and the twins set out for Jerusalem, Mary of Magdala returned to her home on the shores of the lake. She kept to the major road, which passed through Herod's capital before skirting Gennesaret.

Memories from her night with the Nazarene arose in her mind and replayed themselves – his sweet breath on the soles of her feet, his hair redolent of oak and must, the wise words of the Virgin exhorting her to know and discover herself.

But a slight tinge of resentment discoloured her revery. That very moment, the men were setting out, staffs in hand, for Jerusalem while she, hooded and veiled, had to retreat to her home in Magdala. She wished she could accompany them, and flee far from Galilee.

By mid-day Miri had reached Tiberias, the large and modern city constructed in the Roman style with a forum, baths and royal palace. Herod Antipas had made this fortified city the seat of his power, and its streets reflected his love of opulence: long avenues shaded by colonnades with large statues placed between pillars or under the porticoes of temples, some dedicated to Roman gods, others to deified emperors.

At the centre of the dense but airy city stood the royal palace and, next to it, the *agora* with its constant bustle of foreign traders. From their darkened stalls in the market's outlying maze of streets, the merchants offered Indian silks, African fabrics and the rarest of Levantine spices, many of them imported from Egypt, Phoenicia and Assyria.

Mary of Magdala tarried among the merchant's stalls, admiring the exotic goods and envying the cosmopolitan women, well-coiffured and daringly dressed in their diaphanous Greek robes.

In the shadow of the Palace, she caught sight of a man whose head had turned to admire her. This was no ordinary merchant: his robes identified him as a palace official, accompanied by his own armed guards.

The courtier was standing next to a nobly-dressed woman, perhaps his wife, who formed part of the retinue of a royal figure. Indeed, they seemed to be conversing with this hidden figure through the curtain of a slave-borne sedan.

Magdalene's eyes opened wide as the nobly-dressed woman approached her and addressed her directly in Greek.

"I am Joanna, wife of the Vizier Chuza," she announced formally, although her eyes glowed with warmth. "My mistress finds you most intriguing, and wishes for you to approach her."

For a few moments, Miri's breathing stopped. She nodded her head, then timidly accompanied Joanna to the curtained compartment.

From within, a princess in the first flush of womanhood gazed at her curiously.

"Your manner is most becoming," the girl began in Greek. "You *are* Judean?"

Blushing slightly, Magdalene responded in the language of the empire. "I am Mary of Magdala, a daughter of Israel."

The princess observed the assured manner in which she spoke, and the gentle nobility of her bearing.

"I am Salome, daughter of the Herodians. You interest me, Mary of Magdala."

Though Salome was younger in years, Miri could see that she possessed an inquisitive eye, coveting all that was rare, beautiful and precious.

"I am setting out on a journey for Tyre," the princess continued, "to learn from the Phoenicians their ancient manners and customs. But I sense there is much in you, daughter of Israel, to teach me of their ancient ways. I wish you to accompany me."

The Vizier Chuza and his wife Joanna exchanged glances, though neither was as surprised as Magdalene herself. Yet, in the ensuing silence, it became clear that to refuse the princess's request, under whatever pretence, would bear dangerous consequences. What the princess desired, she immediately possessed.

Mary smiled and gazed into the distance, imagining a land beyond Galilee. The decisive words of the Virgin returned to her: *'Seek out the hidden places, forgotten by our people...'*

"It is as you wish," the daughter of Magdala affirmed.

"Yes, it is as I wish," Salome said, as a child's smile adorned her delicate features. The curtains were drawn aside and Magdalene was guided into Salome's litter.

"I think we shall become great friends, you and I," the Herodian princess announced.

II

The three pilgrims stopped to gaze at the crows lashed to the fence-posts: a farmer's grim warning for predators to evade his field.

Wiping the dirt from his brow, Thomas gazed downstream towards the Dead Sea. "This is it," he announced, "our only chance to hear the Baptist..."

Anxious and excited, Cephas squinted across the Jordan at Mount Zion. "But Jerusalem is less than a day's walk. And it's getting more crowded by the hour."

Flocks of migrating birds passed overhead. A fire burned, unattended, next to an abandoned plough.

Having followed the Jordan south for three days, Cephas and the twins now found themselves at a crossroads: either ford the shallows at Jericho and head for Jerusalem, or follow the river's banks a bit further in hope of finding the Baptist.

The Nazarene felt torn in two – anxious to see Jerusalem, but equally intrigued by the Immerser. Like the mountain lily and the desert rose, each guarded in its heart a many-veiled mystery.

"Forget the High Priest," the Iscariot retorted. "Only the Prophet knows the true way for our times." He dug his staff into the hard earth while a group of paupers stopped to stare at the lost Galileans. "John will be addressing huge crowds for the Passover Feast. It'll be an event. We can camp for a night and still make it to Jerusalem by mid-day..."

A blind man approached, followed by a band of beggars and cripples. Some had skin lesions, others seemed possessed by demons. Soon they surrounded the three weary pilgrims and pressed them for alms, tugging at their tunics and shaking outstretched hands.

Cephas reached into his purse and pulled out a coin, offering it to the poorest of the lot. Then, he tried to dismiss them. Thomas looked at them sadly and shook his head.

In an act of pity, Jesus looked into the unseeing eyes of the blind man, but was not moved by the slightest remorse. Indeed, to his own surprise, he felt disgust and repulsion, wanting to flee from this mob of the cursed and diseased.

Suddenly, he had the distinct sensation that the blind man was looking directly at him, peering somehow into his soul.

"Leave us in peace!" Jesus cried.

But the blind beggar did not move, and his resistance provoked the rest of his unruly band to violence. One of them, a man unbalanced and possessed, seized Thomas by his tunic and began spitting gibberish into his face. An old woman with skin abrasions pressed against Cephas, who recoiled in horror. Strangest of all, the blind man smiled at Jesus and whispered, "We've been waiting for you..."

Uttering a loud cry, Jesus pushed them back with his staff. But the more the Galileans tried to extricate themselves, the more the derelicts pressed around them, and others joined the fray.

In a flash, Jesus saw a curved blade cut through the air, its well-sharpened edge reflecting the mid-day sun. The crowd recoiled while the weapon flashed in the face of the blind man.

"Let these people pass!" a stranger said with the blade poised in his hand.

The Galileans watched as, to their enormous relief, the outcasts withdrew and dispersed, some uttering curses.

The stranger in possession of the curved *sica* knife was a thick-set man, powerfully built, whose pock-marked face was concealed by the curls of his unkempt hair and beard. But, as he sheathed his dagger, he smiled and even laughed, showing the spaces between his teeth.

"You must be Galileans, by the looks of you!" he grinned.

Cephas, as was his nature, addressed the stranger in a familiar tone. "Thank you, friend, for your courage. I don't know how we would have escaped otherwise..."

The stranger seemed genuinely humbled by this gesture.

"You're travelling in these parts, and have no weapons but your staffs? The wicked prey on the likes of you..."

His uncut hair and beard, twisted into locks, marked him as a *Kaneniah*. The 'Cananaeans' promoted radical adherence to Jewish law. Indeed, their opposition to the Romans allied them with *Sicarii* assassins and the Zealot brotherhood. But this man's face was kind and his accent akin to their own.

"You're headed south, to see the Baptist?" he asked, glancing at each of them honestly and openly.

"No, west," Cephas assured him, "to the Holy City."

The wayfarer shook his head. "The Baptist's been drawing crowds for days. Something's stirring. I wouldn't miss this if I were you. It'll be an event."

Turning to the stranger, Thomas' hard grey eyes softened; the Hellenist had found an unusual ally in this Zealot.

Meanwhile, the stranger looked inquisitively at the silent son of Nazareth.

"And what of you, my friend? What way are you headed?"

Suddenly, an image formed before the Nazarene's eyes. He saw the desert prophet standing in the Jordan and preaching to the multitude. In his outstretched hand a serpent writhed and twisted. Then the serpent straightened out and became a studded sceptre.

"To the Baptist," Jesus announced. "Do you know the way that leads to him?"

The wayfarer nodded. "Join me, if you like. I know my way well enough through hill country."

Cephas and Thomas looked at one another, surprised by the Nazarene's sudden decision. Nodding respectfully at this fellow wayfarer, the foursome set out together.

"The name's Simon," he said, "comin' from the hill country around Cana. Shepherding's my trade... *Shelama!*" With his hand on his heart, he gave the traditional greeting.

" *Shelama!*" the red-bearded son of Jonah replied. "I'm Simon of Bethsaida, but call me Cephas, like everyone else here. Fishing on the lake of Gennesaret – that's my trade. This here is Jesus and the other is Judas – whom we all call Thomas the twin. Both are woodworkers from Nazareth..."

"*Galileans* – just as I suspected! My peace be with you all..." Simon the Zealot replied, nodding to his three new companions.

III

From the ancient ruins, a turtledove stirred and took flight. It circled three times before settling in a terebinth's foliated crown.

Near Meroth in the north of Galilee, Salome's entourage came to rest on a plateau. After passing through some rugged hill country, they had found a shady retreat where Chuza could tether his animals and rest his slaves. Magdalene herself was grateful for this respite, since she hadn't quite accustomed herself to the lurching motion of Salome's slave-borne sedan.

Emerging from the curtained enclosure, the two new companions found themselves under an arbour of terebinth trees. Salome's tutor Joanna was gazing in wonder at the odd rock formations at the centre of the shaded grove.

Though covered with grass and vines, an ancient temple had once stood on this spot. In the shadow of the ruins, a large rectangular block rose from natural rock foundations. Cut by unknown hands centuries ago, this black basalt stone formed a kind of altar with carved horns on its corners.

Salome and Magdalene, infected by Joanna's wonderment, silently admired the strange spectacle.

"The books of the Prophets mention these places many times," Joanna said to them, "but I never thought I'd see one..."

"What is it?" Salome wanted to know. She could sense something utterly mysterious in this ancient sanctuary.

Joanna turned to her charge and explained as simply as possible.

"It is called a *bamah* in Hebrew, a 'high place' where the elder gods were worshipped. This was probably a temple to Baal or Astarte... Astarte was once a great goddess, the source of all life that pushes forth from the earth. But now she is forgotten. Do you see that tree trunk near the altar, still decorated like a 'tree of life'? That was an Asherah, venerated and revered by our ancient ancestors..."

The three of them gazed in silence at the ruins, trying to imagine what arcane rituals once enlivened this empty temple. Magdalene in particular was more moved than she thought possible by these silent stones.

Quietly, she began wandering among the ruins, seeking signs of the forgotten Goddess. Here, she noticed the fragments of a bull statue, there the remains of a dwarf figure.

But as she penetrated deeper into, what was once, the innermost sanctuary of the temple, she found herself alone before a strange idol. The free-standing figure, now fragmented, had been carved in black granite; and her eyes, now blinded, once glowed with transparent beryls.

Was this Astarte? The goddess bore seven insignias of her power. On her head was a crown of horns with an eight-pointed star set in-between. On her chest was a circular pendant, with a lunar crescent inscribed in the full moon. Her hands, strangely enough, were upholding her breasts. And her lips bore a most enigmatic smile: at once wise and beguiling.

<Whenever you hide yourself, I will appear,> came the voice. It Thund 16:31
was the Virgin once more, repeating her enigmatic and mysterious
injunction: *<But whenever you appear, I will hide myself from* Thund 16:31
you.>

Mary of Magdala stared at the ancient goddess with the lunar pendant. And slowly, she began to understand the meaning of this strange oracle. She and the Virgin, as the elder and the younger Mary, were one and the same. They were like two sides of the moon, one in darkness and the other in light. When the younger Mary hid herself in the dark side of the moon, the elder Mary appeared. But when the younger Mary appeared, the elder Mary would then recede into darkness.

"*<Do not be ignorant of me,>*" came the Virgin's voice once Thund 13:15
more. "*<Look upon me, you who reflect upon me.>*" Thund 13:6

Though these words were spoken by the Virgin Mother, they seemed to echo with a more ancient resonance, as if the statue of Astarte before her were adding her voice to the Virgin's.

"*<For I am the first and the last,*" they cried, Thund 13:16

"*I am the honoured and the scorned one.>*"

Miri could hear the voices clearly. Then, she watched as the moon transformed on the lunar pendant, until it became four – the crescent moon waxing, the full moon, the crescent moon waning, and the dark moon. Like a chorus, the voices multiplied from two to four, as they sang different phrases, weaving in and out in a mysterious round.

"*<I am the wife and the virgin,*" they chanted in tandem. Thund 13:19

"*I am the mother and the daughter,>*" came the response.

Tears rose to Magdalene's eyes, as she understood the ancient message encoded in these words. They were singing the endless cycle, as virgin became wife, and mother gave birth to daughter, then around again, from virgin to wife, and mother to daughter. But all, in truth, were one.

To her surprise, one voice rose *in solo* above the others – a voice she knew, a voice she recognized *as her own*. And the voice, in a melody that was hauntingly beautiful, chanted a phrase apart
from the others, singing: "*<I am the whore and the holy one.>*" Thund 13:18

Magdalene could not believe her ears. But the Goddess before her smiled knowingly, and the sacred voice rose in unison with her own – powerful, compelling, mysterious; together they cried:

Thund 14:33 "*<I am disgraced and the great one,>*
Thund 14:27 *<I am shame and boldness,>*
Thund 13:18 *<I am the whore and the holy one.>*"

IV

The atmosphere around Perea grew eerie as the band of Galileans drew nearer to the Dead Sea. No more birds flew in the skies; no more shrubs clung to the clay hills. Except for the insects buzzing in the air, all was a stony, grey silence.

Here and there, packets of pilgrims could still be glimpsed, creeping across the wasteland. But most of these moved in a peculiar manner – limping in hunger and in pain, they were the poor, the sick and the lame. All were headed for the Baptizer, in the hope of receiving healing through confession.

As the Galileans approached a barren outcropping of limestone, they could hear a strange noise coming from the opposite side: drumming and pipes, with the wailing of many voices. A pungent smell assaulted their nostrils, and smoke rose like a swirling column in the air.

Mounting the rugged incline, they could see over the rocks to the Baptizer's enclave in the valley below. Hundreds were gathered in the surrounding hills, some in tents, others with no shelter whatsoever. The spectacle was like nothing any of them had ever seen.

Huge bonfires burned everywhere, fed with driftwood, dried grass and hemp. Some pilgrims walked around naked in a daze; others danced in a trance-like manner to the music. The sick and the lame were everywhere. A man possessed by demons fell to the ground and foamed at the mouth. Ecstatic or charismatic, blessed or possessed – they all danced together in a hieratic frenzy.

Towards the shores of the Jordan, the maddening crowd thickened. John's disciples were stationed around the river's shallows. Each acted as a conduit of the holy man's power.

Their hair uncut and their limbs unclad, the disciples listened
Lk 11:1 to the pilgrim's confession and uttered a cleansing prayer. "*<Father,*
Lk 11:1 *hallowed be thy hidden name!>*" chanted one; "*<Grant us the*
Lk 11:1 *compassion to forgive!>*" cried another; and the last: "*<Bring us not*
to trial, but into your Kingdom!>"

The disciple then led the penitent to John, who stood waist-deep in the Jordan. His appearance inspired awe: at once terrifying and wondrous to behold. Some of the penitents the Baptizer welcomed gently, bathing them tenderly and caressing their hands and fingertips.

Others he seized and shook, then plunged deep in the water and held there – powerfully resisting any panicking attempts to surface. After nearly drowning, the catechumen emerged as if reborn, alternately laughing and crying like a little child.

As Jesus and his companions cautiously descended the hillside, the charged atmosphere of the place became palpable. The Nazarene felt panic and fear. To his left, a pilgrim was brutally beating a thief who had tried to lift his purse. Roman guards were nowhere to be found.

Time and again beggars and cripples turned to Jesus and stared. It was uncanny how many of them eyed him with an unsettling gaze.

Strangest of all was the sacred presence which Jesus sensed at the centre of the melee. Though the Baptizer stood at a great distance,
Jesus could feel his holiness emanating in all directions. <He was Jn 5:35
like a lamp, burning and shining, while the ecstatic rejoiced within its light.>

Indeed, the haze of light around the healer had become a ring of holy fire which no demon dared approach. And any evil spirit that persisted – clinging to a poor or possessed soul as it entered the sacred circle – was immediately seized and cast out. The Nazarene could smell the swirling mixture of emotions in the air – fear, bitterness, anger, envy, greed, hatred and desire – all exorcised and expelled.

Who was this holy man? And the moment Jesus phrased the
question, an inner voice responded: *<This is the one who shall* Mk 1:2
prepare the way – and make your path straight.>

V

Salome curled up closer to Magdalene, brushing her slender fingers under the other's cheek.

"Your eyes are like jasper," she said, admiring their golden green glow.

Rocked gently by the motion of their litter, the two girls held one another closely.

"But your lips are large and full," Magdalene replied, "– red as pomegranates, ripe as berries – ripe enough to be picked." She pressed the tip of her finger into their fullness.

Salome blushed, overjoyed to hear these compliments coming from one so beautiful as Miri. She responded by touching her own fingertips to Magdalene's mouth.

"And how many men have tasted these fruits?" Salome dared ask.

Magdalene lowered her head, turning crimson. She didn't dare answer.

"I want to know – have you been promised to a man?" she blinked her eyes.

Miri shook her head. "I've had offers... but I couldn't accept any of them, in my heart."

"I'm married..." Salome declared. Then, drawing her lips close to Mary's ear, she whispered:

"My husband's name is Philip, and he's Tetrarch of Auranitis, Trachonitis and Batanea. That makes me a princess!"

"You're married to your uncle?" Magdalene cried, "– to the brother of Herod Antipas?"

"Yes – *great* uncle, actually. But Philip isn't anything like my stepfather. His court is out in the desert. He carries himself like a sheikh with an entourage of camels and tents and caravans."

"But – he's old enough to be your grandfather."

"We're Herodians. We must keep our power concentrated in the family – for inheritance. It's the way of nobility..."

"– Then marriage, for you, is an arrangement, a transfer of power and property."

"It's always been that way in Israel..."

"What about love?"

Salome pulled back from Miri, hurt by her remark.

"I can love! I can have as many lovers as I want."

Magdalene put her arms around the daughter of Herodias and brought her close once more.

"I didn't mean it like that... I meant only – that every woman needs love, and to love a man..."

"I can love," Salome insisted, her lower lip protruding.

Then, with a feline movement, she nestled her head under Magdalene's hair. "Do you love someone?"

Miri thought of the Nazarene – his sculpted hands and expressive
Songs 2:16 manner of gesturing as he spoke. *<My beloved is mine and I am his,>*

she thought, echoing the ancient song of her people. To possess one another, like the bridegroom and his bride... But how?

"Yes, I'm in love with a man... with my cousin, in fact."

"There, you see! You want to marry your own kin, like nobility. You're no different than me..."

"You're right," Magdalene admitted. "We have known each other since we were children. In our hearts, we've always been betrothed to one another. But, whenever we come too close together, one of us pulls back in fear. We embraced no less than two nights ago. And now he's headed for Jerusalem, and I'm fleeing towards Tyre."

Salome said nothing, feeling herself caught up in Magdalene's ardour. Then, she turned and placed her hand on Miri's henna-stained hand.

"I'm in love with a man – in love as deeply as you – but you must promise to keep it a secret! Chuza and Joanna must never know about it..."

Pressing Salome's bejewelled hand to her heart, Magdalene nodded her promise.

"He's young, thin as a reed, and his skin is burnt by the desert sun. When he speaks his voice sounds like thunder and his gaze burns like fire. He's an ascetic, eating no bread and drinking no wine. But when I kissed his lips, I tasted wine like no other. It was sweet poison, an elixir so intoxicating it burned my tongue. Was I feeling love? Or Desire? More than that, it was like a passionate longing to annihilate ourselves in each other. I wanted to kill him and I wanted for him to murder me..."

Magdalene was frightened to hear such words in the mouth of this precocious child. But she understood the girl's passion all too well.

"Do you know who I mean?"

Magdalene's eyes grew wide as she realized that it could only be the Baptist.

"I can hear his voice, calling to me from the Jordan. But I don't dare go near him."

Nervously, the daughter of Magdala caressed Salome's hands, which had begun shaking. Still, the Herodian's brow became wracked with anguish.

"I know it. I can feel it. There's a great danger in the Jordan – like jackals and foxes swarming round him..."

"No harm can come to John. He's like the prophets of old –

powerful, fearful, commanding. They won't dare touch him...."

"You don't understand!" Salome cried. "Now promise me – promise me *with your life* that you will not reveal this to anyone!"

Magdalene was so frightened that her throat tightened, but she nodded yes.

"*They all want him dead* – Chuza, my mother, even Antipas! And the priests too – Annas and Caiaphas! The only reason he's still alive is that they're waiting. *They're waiting...*"

Magdalene's heart grew heavy with foreboding. Bitter tears rose to her eyes as the secret spilled from Salome's lips.

"The hills around the Jordan are filled with spies! Chuza's men, priests and Levites – all disguised, all waiting for the Messiah to appear with his Five Seals."

"To seize him?"

"To seize his power. But don't you see? John is like a tree arching toward the light – it risks uprooting itself. If his words come to fruition, the harvesters will sever the root, just to reach the glory of its crown..."

The daughter of the Herodians clenched her fists and cried aloud in anger, powerless to save the only man her heart ever cherished.

VI

The bonfires reflected off the Jordan, making patterns within patterns on the water; the drumming echoed off the limestone cliffs, creating rhythms within rhythms in the air. From the centre of it all, the Baptist gazed around him, his eyes wild and aware.

How much longer? he wondered. He felt ill, wasted, exhausted. The years of asceticism, the Nazarite vows, the painful uprooting of his own personality to surrender it finally to God. Why? So God's power could flow through him, to preach and prophesy, even to heal. But how much longer? When would the Messiah come, to relieve him of this burden?

By now he had gazed into the faces of countless demons, and cast them out, one after another. The poor, the lame and deranged who came to him begging for release – he could no longer distinguish their pitiful faces. They all cried aloud in one voice, singing an endless lament. Each life repeated Man's fall; Adam stumbled again and again – all of it folly without end. The only way to alleviate Mankind of this suffering was the final cleansing – the fire and conflagration, with its blessed ending and new beginning.

But here he stood, alone, a voice without words, screaming nonsense in the faces of brutes and beasts. Meanwhile the Messiah stood aloof, unwilling to appear, unable to comprehend his own mission. He was near him now, watching, curious, afraid. How much longer?

"Children of Israel!" the Baptist cried, his voice echoing off the hills, "the time of awaiting is over!"

The drumming died down and hundreds of faces turned to hear his words.

"<First the Almighty submerged the world in a watery flood! NH Ascl 73:31
Now, He is purging it again with a fiery conflagration! And then, the
time will come when He crushes it with wars and plagues! But the
time of awaiting is over! *For this is the birth of the world!*>"

The crowds around John began to clap, whistle and chant. For a few moments the sound redounding off the hills was deafening. Then silence returned the moment John spoke.

"<I baptize you with water; but among you stands one whom Jn 1:26
you do not know.> <He is the Living Water! He is the Holy Baptism Ap Adam 85:22
of those who will know with eternal knowledge! Yes, he is the
hidden knowledge of Adam! And those who are born of his word,
those who come from his holy seed, will become imperishable and
illuminated!>"

As one, the crowd roared, making a sound like a mighty beast in the desert.

"<This is the one who will come after me.> <He who came Mt 3:11, Jn 1:15
before me shall come *after* me,>" the forerunner cried. "For he came
before me <as the *first-born* son of the Father;> <the *only-begotten* Tri Tr 57:18
one.> But he will come after me as the Messiah of the Five Seals!" Ap Jn 6:17

Upon hearing these words, the crowd exploded again with whistles and cries. But John held up his hands and silenced them.

"<My decline shall be his rising!> I come before you now, like Jn 3:30
thunder before his lightning, to presage his passing: <Make straight Unt MS
the way to your Lord! Enter the Jordan and receive the grace of
God! For behold, the aeons will soon be filled with the grace of the
only-begotten Son!> <So that you may know what lies hidden in the Ap Paul 19:10
visible – let your mind awaken!>"

The Baptist's crazed disciples closed their eyes and raised their hands to the heavens. In their minds, they saw the Son approaching – his bare feet splashing the Jordan's shores.

"<But that which has been shown to me is hidden from everyone 2Ap Jas 47:17
and shall only be revealed through him!> He will come to us in a

Jn 3:29 manner unexpected. He will come to us as a bridegroom. <And I, standing beside the betrothed as his witness, will rejoice when he
Jn 3:29 honours his pledge.> <My joy will be made full as he enters the Bridal Chamber and betroths himself to his bride.>"

The Baptist paused, looking out over the sea of upraised hands and faces. After a few moments the cheering in the crowd died down.

2Ap Jas 57:8 "Behold, the moment has come! <For now I shall reveal to you He-who-is-hidden.>

In the ensuing silence, a powerful tension mounted as they all awaited the final prophecy.

"*At the Passover* will begin the aeon of the Messiah! *In Jerusalem* the son of glory will appear! Open your minds and accommodate his presence! Make straight the way to your Lord!"

And the crowd went wild, taking up the Baptist's cry. They chanted *en masse*: "To the Lord! To the Lord make straight your way!" The words echoed off the cliffs, their syllables enjambed, their order inversed.

Jesus listened to the deafening crowds around him. Even Simon the Zealot was raising his staff and screaming like the others. The son of Nazareth felt faint. He wanted to escape from here. Why had he come? Why had the vision led his footsteps here? This was frightening madness. They were screaming for the Messiah. Even the Baptist was calling for him, goading him on by announcing his coming. *In Jerusalem! At the Passover!*

Jesus placed a trembling hand on Thomas's shoulder to brace himself, lest he collapse. The Iscariot turned, supporting his friend, and whispered:

"Take heart my brother, don't be afraid... There *is* no Messiah..!"

For a few moments, Jesus stared at his twin, hoping that it might be true. Thomas even nodded to assure him. But he had heard it – the ancient resonance, calling to him through the Baptist's words. He could not deny Wisdom's call. The aeon of the Messiah would begin in Jerusalem, at the Passover.

V. Jerusalem & Tyre

I

Salome's caravan passed under the fortified gate of the great Phoenician city. Tyre was a wonder to behold: huge torches illuminated the main thoroughfare, and statues of the gods glowed mysteriously under the twilight sky.

Magdalene was amazed to see that many of the statues bore the same strange features of the idol she'd admired in the abandoned temple. The goddess Astarte was here, with her beguiling smile, in this ancient city.

The Tyreans walked about with ease, their black braided hair falling gracefully over long flowing robes. The women in particular carried themselves with confidence, some smiling and laughing, others conversing equally with men. None wore a veil.

How strange this place seemed in comparison with her homeland. There, Mary of the tribe of Asher had to carry herself modestly, head bowed, eyes downcast, a constant reminder of her submission.

But here, the ancient Goddess was still revered. Her temples burned with incense, her statues were bathed and garlanded, and her presence was manifest in every woman. That Goddess whom the Hebrews had once revered as Hochmah spoke here in her own voice. <*Out in the street, Wisdom cries. In the squares She raises her* Prov 8:20
voice...>

The ancient texts, intoned with hallowed reverence, reminded Magdalene: <*At the busiest corner She cries out. At the entrance of* Prov 1:20
the city gates She speaks...>

That voice, speaking to her once more, had been forgotten by her people. But now, as the caravan came to a stop, Miri could see *the face* of the voice. She saw a large statue of the Tyrean Goddess, whose enigmatic smile no longer puzzled Magdalene; its expression was absolutely clear: She bore the knowing smile of Wisdom. Astarte *was* Hochmah, the ancient goddess forgotten by her ancestors...

And the deity spoke to her once more, saying:

Prov 8:34-35 "*<Happy is the one who listens to me,*
Watching at my gate
And waiting by my door
For whoever finds me
Finds life...>"

II

Jerusalem. The ancient walled city was swarming with the faithful. Jesus was the first to enter Zion's gate, followed by Cephas, Simon and Thomas. They threaded their way through labyrinthine passages and up endless streets of stairs. The hungry, lame and infirm haunted every corner.

At last, they reached the city's holy summit and entered the huge square surrounding the Temple. This broad esplanade, known as the Court of the Gentiles, was walled on all sides by colonnades and porticoes three columns deep. Their cedar roofs and Corinthian capitals shaded the stalls where merchants and money-changers called out their terms and wares. Hundreds of goats, sheep and doves, stacked in cages or tethered to the walls, waited to be purchased for the sacrifice.

The Galileans stood and stared. Before them, up the steps of a sloping embankment, stood 'the Beautiful Gate', its elaborate lintel cast in brass. And beyond it rose the Temple Mount with its many courts and compounds, their white marble shining like Hermon's snow-covered peaks.

For a prolonged moment, Cephas stared at the Holy Temple, his heart fluttering between fear and wonder. His wide eyes wandered over the Temple's facade, and he imagined what it must be like to enter so close into the presence of YHWH.

No gentile, he knew, could penetrate beyond the Temple's outlying embankment – on pain of death. But Jewish pilgrims, after bathing in the *mikvoth* and leaving their sandals behind, could walk in white garments through the first enclosure. This, the Court of Women, even permitted women in a sufficient state of purity. But only the circumcised males, having observed strict codes of chastity and cleanliness, could ascend the fifteen steps before the Nicanor Gate and enter the Court of Israel.

Here stood the Holy Temple, its facade flanked by two mighty columns ornamented in gold. And before it stood the ancient altar, stained with blood and blackened by burnt offerings, their smoke rising heavenward in a huge swirling column.

From their place below the altar, the faithful petitioned the holy servitors, who stood above them in the Court of Priests. Bowing meekly and praying, the first-born sons handed over their clean animals marked for sacrifice, knowing that only these white-robed priests, their hands ritually washed and purified, could offer their precious animal on the roughly-hewn altar-stone.

But twelve steps higher, under the Temple Porch, stood the High Priest himself, whose holiness and purity transcended all others. He alone could penetrate beyond the veil. Dressed in white linen, he entered the Holy of Holies on one day only, the Day of Atonement. On behalf of his people, he placed the sacred censer in the innermost sanctuary and uttered the inscrutable name of YHWH.

Tears came to the Bethsaidean's eyes. This entire complex, he realized, was an ever-mounting hierarchy of the secret, sacred and immaculate, increasing in purity the closer one approached the hallowed hidden Presence. Overcome with holy ardour, the son of Jonah fell to his knees and kissed the sacred ground he walked upon.

But the calls of the merchants and money-changers soon awoke him from his pious display. Here, in the outer court, pan-handlers, beggars and prostitutes surrounded them on all sides.

Due to his unusual manner of sauntering from side to side, one pilgrim in the crowd took on a recognizable trait. The Nazarene's brow rose a notch. The publican, Levi, was heading towards them with a huge grin on his face.

"Jesus of Nazareth!" he cried. "I thought you'd never escape your father's workshop! But look at you here!"

"And what of you Levi, son of Alphaeus?" Jesus replied, "– finally abandoned your father's toll booths for the feast?"

The tax collector laughed and clapped his fellow Galileans on the back. From his customs depot in Sepphoris, Levi had dealings with Cephas, Jesus, Thomas – all of them – except Simon.

"Am I to understand," Simon the Zealot began, "that *you* are *a publican?*" He gave the tax-collector a long hard look.

"That I am," Levi replied, smiling and winking.

Jesus laid a hand on Simon's arm. "Levi is a decent man, a philosopher really, who'd trade his weights and measures for a magus' cap if he could."

A wide smile passed over Simon's lips. "A philosopher? I don't often get to meet philosophers. This is a real opportunity..."

Cephas and Thomas nervously exchanged glances, but the Zealot seemed genuinely pleased with their new companion.

Meanwhile, the astute publican was scanning every detail in Simon's dress. He came to the disquieting conclusion that the bearded Cananaean was a Zealot. Maybe even a *sicari* assassin – those rebels who carried *sica* blades and discretely assassinated any Israelite who collaborated with Rome... The sun beat down on Levi's head; he felt faint.

"But, you've come awfully late for the Passover Feast," the publican remarked, his voice unusually high. "There are hardly any lodgings left..."

"We stopped in Perea on the way here," Thomas explained.

"To hear the Baptist!" Cephas cried. His heart, like an overripe grape, was ready to burst. "The Messiah will appear this Passover Eve!"

Levi raised his eyebrows. "It's the turning of the aeon," he remarked. "First the drought and fires. Then the Baptist's prophecy. Now Pontius Pilate..."

"Pilate?" Cephas asked, alarmed.

"You haven't heard? He's left his palace in Caesarea and holed himself up in the Antonia fortress – with twelve hundred of his Praetorian guard! He just marched them all into Jerusalem this morning, trampling over crowds at the gates."

A terrible silence fell over the Galileans. They gazed at one another, the hairs on their necks tingling.

"Twelve hundred soldiers?" the Zealot asked, his face darkening.

"To anticipate the Messiah?" Cephas wondered aloud.

"Pilate's preparing something..." Levi foreboded, his voice low in his throat. "And Caiaphas is at the end of his tether. From his place at the altar, he keeps glancing over his shoulder. Pilate's fortress, you know, looms over the Temple's walls, casting its shadow over the porch. The High Priest is acting as if the Romans will descend on the Temple any moment. Meanwhile, the Zealots have stirred things up – urging the pilgrims to arm themselves and revolt."

"First the Prophet..." Simon said, gazing at the Temple Mount, "then Pilate, now the brotherhood – they're all preparing the path..."

Jesus stared at the Nicanor Gate, which led to the Temple's innermost sanctuary. His heart pounded with a heavy dread and anxiety.

"– And making it straight..." he whispered, aghast.

III

The roof and massive doors of the temple were all of gold and – facing east – glistened in the morning sun. Towering over the entrance, two large columns sparkled with emeralds, onyx and jasper. At their base, large bronze censers poured forth a sweet ambrosial smell.

As they entered the Temple of Astarte, Salome and her entourage were greeted by the High Priest himself. The old man was dressed in robes of Tyrean purple and garlanded with a golden tiara. Accompanying him was a most alluring woman, whom he introduced as Jezubaal – the head priestess and hierodule of the temple. Then, bowing respectfully, the bearded sage departed, leaving his graceful feminine companion to guide them through the sacred house of Astarte.

As was the custom among her people, Jezubaal treated her guests with hallowed respect – for the gods sometimes walked the earth in a foreigner's guise. With a sensuous gait and inviting smile, their fair-haired Phoenician led them past the main gate.

Salome observed their hostess with the eye of an apprentice, envying the lapis-lazuli gems encircling her throat, the golden laurel-leaves adorning her brow. Even Magdalene had to admire this woman, suppressing the pangs of a jealous heart.

The moment Salome's party entered the main temple, they were struck with mute awe and wonder. The interior was richly decorated with dense foliage and figurines, delicately carved from the algum, cypress and cedar wood of Lebanon. Among the artfully-wrought palm branches flew eagle-headed lions and those mighty firebirds which the Phoenicians had blessed with their name 'phoenix'.

To the right of the entrance was a vestibule reserved for young women. These sat in rows on patterned carpets, all of them perfumed and elegantly dressed: their long hair was intricately plaited, their foreheads marvellously jewelled and their faces decorated with interweaving designs. Each time a man approached, they opened wide their eyes and enticed him with their beauty.

Salome stopped to admire these women, who seemed so exotic in their bearing.

"Who are they?" the princess inquired.

"They have come here to make an offering," Jezubaal explained. "It is an ancient custom for a young woman to come, once in her life, to the temple and offer Astarte the greatest of her gifts."

Salome and Magdalene exchanged glances, uncertain of what the priestess meant. Jezubaal smiled and continued.

"Astarte is the Goddess of all that grows. When our crops yield in abundance, when our livestock multiply each year, it is because of her life-giving power: She sows love and desire among us, leading to generation and renewal. In women, Astarte arouses the pleasures of love and all its fruits."

"So what are they offering?" Salome asked directly.

Lucian "Their maidenhood," Jezubaal replied, "– as the most honoured of sacrifices. Only men from afar may enter this precinct, and assist the woman to fulfil her vow. He offers a few coins to the Goddess, acknowledges her gift with a prayer, and then they consummate the vow outside her temple."

The Vizier Chuza stared at the young women in disbelief. "You mean, they're prostituting themselves..."

Jezubaal laughed. "Not at all! We have prostitutes, of course, to attend to men's desires. But here, in Astarte's temple, the man doesn't matter in the least. The first time the young woman makes love, she is not doing it as her duty to a new husband, or for her father who has married her off. No, she's making love as an offering to the Virgin – sacrificing her virginity to the Great Goddess."

Gazing at Magdalene, her amber eyes aglow, the hierodule continued. "The rite becomes a sacred revelation, as Astarte enters her that moment. The girl becomes the Goddess, who is both virgin and hierodule. And, she momentarily manifests her many powers: to be wise, loving, playful and fertile. Each time this initiate makes love in the future, she will remember and ritually invoke the Goddess who entered her that moment."

Magdalene felt a strange chill run through her body as she realized the truth in all that the priestess was saying.

"I did the same, when younger," Jezubaal revealed. "And

from that time forward, I dedicated myself to Astarte. Now, as the hierodule of her temple, I offer myself to Astarte once a year when She re-unites with Baal."

Joanna, as the only one who seemed to understand all of this, asked, "For the Feast of the Sacred Marriage?"

"Yes," Jezubaal nodded. "I know that, at this time of year, your people celebrate their feast in Jerusalem – sacrificing lambs and sharing the paschal meal. But here in Tyre, on this very day, our people will celebrate the Sacred Marriage of Baal and Astarte."

With her bracelets and ankle-bands tinkling melodiously, Jezubaal guided them deeper into the temple, towards the main altar and the innermost sanctuary.

"In your holy book, the prophets included one of our liturgical poems – the one you call 'The Song of Songs'. Those words celebrate the Sacred Marriage of Baal and Astarte. I have heard that your Lord, like our Lord Baal of Biblos, is also called *Adon*?"

"Yes, *Adonai*," Joanna confirmed. "But we banished the Canaanite gods from our land long ago. Instead, Astarte was called
Ashtoreth 'the shameful one' and Baal became *Beelzebub* 'the Lord 1Kings 11:5
– of demons'." 2Kings 1:2

"How sad..." the priestess replied, trying to remain polite. Still, these strangers, with their insults to the ancient gods, seemed barbaric.

Jezubaal led her entourage to the main altar, where the faithful had gathered with a lamb or kid for the sacrifice. The altar was ornate, carved in ivory with swirling vine motifs and animal processions in *bas relief*. Priests in white robes were blessing the beasts and gently handing them back to their bearers.

"We do not sacrifice animals in this temple," the priestess explained. "No blood may be spilled, nor animal roasted. Not even doves can be harmed, since they are sacred to Astarte."

Joanna concealed a smile, calling to mind the Jewish practice of beheading doves and pouring out their blood. Meanwhile the lambs were defleeced – their blood drained, their bodies disemboweled – so their fat could be heaped on the flaming altar.

"Instead," Jezubaal continued, "the pilgrims bring their animals here to be blessed, and carry them home. After the sacred meal, some return and give thanks to the Goddess by holding its fleece over their heads."

Salome recalled the pilgrim she had seen in the courtyard, veiling himself with his lamb's horns and hooves. "Why would they wear its fleece?"

"So the devotee can identify himself with his sacrifice," Jezubaal replied to her royal guest.

"But why sacrifice at all?" Salome asked directly.

Jezubaal looked at the child, wondering if she and all of her people had forgotten the true meaning of this most ancient rite.

"I cannot speak for your people. But to us, a sacrifice acknowledges the living power of the Goddess. When the harvested seed pushes forth new grain, when a sheep is slain but the flock survives – then a greater life-force flows through all of Nature. *That* is the Goddess."

Upon hearing these words, Magdalene remembered her most-unusual dream: the Virgin who became 'the Womb that gives shape to all'.

The priestess gestured toward the altar, where fruits and grains were heaped in abundance.

"Man cannot live without consuming life, whether from livestock or the fields. To offer wheat on the altar, or a lamb in thanksgiving, is to acknowledge life's eternal cycle. Everyday we must harvest and slaughter. But on one special day, we perform instead a sacred act. The lamb's life, or the wheat's life, is offered up by the priest in full knowledge that the Goddess will replenish it through the fullness of her bounty. We recognize, at that moment, her life-regenerating power, and knowingly participate in its eternal mystery. That is the meaning of sacrifice."

Salome nodded, understanding in her own way the meaning of those words. She would willingly take John's life, and have him take hers, if only their shared annihilation could become a sacrifice to each other. It was a total consummation, transcending even the flesh.

"Through the act of sacrifice," Jezubaal pursued, "we acknowledge *Zoe*, the greater *Life* that flows through all living things – through animals and plants, and *through us*. But nothing has an individual life, a spirit or a soul. Rather, each living thing manifests the animating power of *Zoe*. And Life, as such, is neither ours to give nor ours to take. So we participate, knowingly, in the natural cycle of death and rebirth, through killing. But, in the knowledge of the Sacred, killing becomes a life-renewing sacrifice. In this way, we acknowledge *Zoe* as one aspect of the Goddess."

The priestess gave her guests a meaningful stare. She could see, in their eyes, that some had understood. Joanna was nodding sagely and Salome was smiling a dark, almost deranged smile. But Magdalene was rooted to the spot, her eyes wide with wonder. She seemed to have understood the meaning of sacrifice for the first time – and that whoever finds the Goddess, finds life...

IV

The five Galileans stood within the Temple's forecourt, staring aghast at the city spectacle. In the blistering heat of mid-day, a Zealot stole through the crowd, his cloak bulging with dangerous contraband. He was followed by a Levite, cradling his prayer scrolls in a puffed-up display of piety. Meanwhile, in the shade of the colonnades, the money-changers tallied up their morning's profits.

"Now John of the Jordan," the Zealot said to his mates, "is a man worth reckoning. He calls the Romans 'beasts' and not even Chuza can raise his sword against him. He knows how to inspire fear, even in Pilate and the Praetorian guard."

"Is that what you see in the Baptizer," Cephas wondered "– a revolutionary?"

"He's a leader and a fighter – able to unite our people, and turn them against Rome."

"Right," the Iscariot remarked sarcastically. "Just like Judas Maccabee. With a handful of men, he won the Temple back for our people. Of course, *our own rulers* – the Hasmoneans and Herodians – then fought over Jerusalem till the Hasmoneans invited Pompey to intervene. Now we have three generations of Roman occupation..."

Simon turned to Thomas and a wide smile spread across his pock-marked face. "You're beginning to understand, my friend. Whoever seeks power may seize it – but he'll never be satisfied. Even if he has to betray his own people, he'll always covet more. That's why Israel needs the Zealots."

Skepticism glared from the Hellenist's grey eyes. "If the Zealots came into power, they'd only do the same!"

Simon shook his side-locks and laid a heavy arm on the Iscariot's shoulder. "No. The Zealots want to *terrorize* the powers that be; our weapons are fear and intimidation. We want anarchy, nothing more. We must clear the way for the Messiah."

The moment the Nazarene heard those words, his heart stopped.

Still moved by patriotic fervour, the Zealot cried: "The Messiah is our only hope – because the Messiah *is* power!"

"Then what path would you open before him?" Cephas asked, his heart stirred by Israel's chequered history.

Simon patted the *sica* knife hidden in his cloak.

"Death to *all* our leaders – and any official who allies us with foreign powers."

Levi's heart jumped. "You talk like a *Sicari* assassin," he protested. "To provoke panic, they kill all collaborators. But any way you look at it, they're still Jews killing Jews."

"It may be," Thomas admitted, "but Simon sees the way clearly. Israel will *never* gain self-rule. Any leader who claims that is a liar." The Iscariot cast a steely glance at his Nazarene brother. "Whether he comes as Israel's Messiah or king, he'll still betray our people, to collaborate with the powers that be."

Jesus couldn't breath. His soul was quivering and cowering within. In the deepest sanctuary of his heart, he knew – all that his twin had said was true.

"So you'd join with the Zealots?" the Bethsaidean asked Thomas incredulously.

His heart rising, his face afire, the Iscariot nodded.

"Don't get me wrong," Simon said, glancing at Levi. "I'm no *Sicari* assassin, out to kill our own people. Herod, yes – I'd kill that Idumean bastard any day – he's no son of Israel, despite what he claims. And the Romans? The Romans who tax us into poverty, enslave us, then torch or crucify anyone who raises arms against them? Oh yes, I'd kill a Roman – if I could – and feel neither pity nor remorse."

"Have you killed *anyone?*" Levi asked nervously.

Simon looked the publican in the eye. "No – never," he replied honestly. "But that's why I carry a knife. If I had to, I would. I've made my decision..."

Cephas and Levi shook their heads, sighing with discontent.

Meanwhile, Jesus was rooted to the spot, struck by his lowly cowardice and fear.

"The Baptist was right," Simon declared at last. "The time has come for the Messiah to reveal himself. With his Five Seals, he'll free our people from bondage. The Messiah's hidden power," he announced, "is *freedom*."

For a few moments, the son of Nazareth imagined himself as the Zealots' greatest hope: a freedom-fighter as cunning as Judas Maccabee, as courageous as John the Baptist. His eyes shone with new hope for Israel.

"How long we've been waiting for that moment..." the Zealot said, staring at the Nazarene. And his smile, twisted by revolutionary fervour, was frightful – even demonic.

"Numismatics," Levi suddenly said, staring at the money-changers. "If you want to open a path for the Messiah, then you must call power by its true name. *Money* is power and power *is money...*"

"Oh, it's power all right," Thomas remarked. "But in whose hands?"

Levi nodded sagely. "Caesar creates coins in his image; Herod writes 'Basileus' on his sovereigns; the Temple has 'Holy Jerusalem' stamped on its shekels. But money keeps *flowing* from one power to another, changing its name as it goes." He smiled wickedly. "If I had to give money its true name, I'd call it *the power of powers!* The hidden power of the Messiah," he announced, "is hard currency."

Jesus stared at Levi, his brain aflame, the fires in his eyes dancing. Could he be telling the truth?

Levi rubbed his hands with glee. "The High Priest stakes his might on the Temple. For our rulers and revolutionaries, it is our land and its people. Meanwhile, the Romans occupy our country through military force. The temple, the land, the military – they're all *fixed* powers, with walls, borders and battlefields. But money keeps *flowing*. It crosses from state coffers to temple treasuries; it switches currency, transcending all borders – and no revolutionary has yet appeared *to seize the power of powers for himself!*"

"You sound just like Simon," Cephas replied, the bitter taste of gall rising to his mouth. "To the Zealot, the Messiah will come with a *Sicari's* blade. Now, to a publican, he'll come with *shekels* in his hands..."

"Perhaps," Simon admitted, "but at least Levi understands power. And the Five Seals," he gave Jesus a hard look, "*...are* power."

Jesus stared fixedly at Simon. To his utter disbelief, the Zealot was now in one mind with the publican.

Levi arced his hand broadly in the direction of the *trapezites'* tables.

"When the Messiah appears, he won't come as a revolutionary leader standing on its walls. No, he'll announce himself right here, among the money-changers! Indeed, he'll turn the whole place on its head... He'll mint his own coins and stamp them with the Five Seals because money, the power of powers, will be *his*."

Wide-eyed and in wonder, Jesus gazed at the stables and market stalls, grasping the full import of all that Levi said. Annas and Caiaphas were skimming profit from the sacrifices. Tiberius and Herod Antipas played a more serious game, minting their own currencies. But none had achieved the power of powers...

Would the Messiah come in this way – avoiding war, eliminating all need for bloodshed, and evading alliance with the Romans? Annas, Caiaphas, even Herod Antipas – they would all surrender their rule to the one man who gained the power of powers for himself."

The Nazarene looked at Levi and nodded his head in deep appreciation. This lowly publican had opened a path no other thought possible...

Levi looked at Jesus and smiled. He shook his head and laughed. The publican laughed long and hard: his eyes bulging, his jaw distended, his teeth bared mischievously.

"We've been waiting so long..." he said.

"You're all wrong," Cephas said decidedly. "The Messiah is not an earthly power – he's a heavenly force. The only path open to him is the High Priesthood."

The others cast a dubious glance at Cephas. But his faith was roused, and his sanguine heart overflowed. "If the High Priest were to pass before us this moment, I'd bow low to the ground and avert my gaze from his holy presence."

A dubious smile cut across the Iscariot's face. "You'd bow down to Caiaphas?"

At this, Cephas took offence. "He's *the High Priest* – heir to
the office of Aaron. He alone wears the Robe of the Ephod, and his
Exod 28: 31 crown of gold is engraved with the words 'Holy to the Lord'. *He is*
Exod 29:7 *God's anointed!* – marked with holy oil to consecrate his office."

"The High Priest – maybe..." Levi admitted. "But our present High Priest is no 'son of Aaron'..."

"Maybe not. But the office remains sacrosanct. I would bow down to the robes, *whoever* their bearer."

"So it makes no difference to you – *who* wears the robes of the High Priest?" Jesus asked.

"Of course it does... I know Annas and Caiaphas are corrupt. So are half of the Sadducees who sit on the Sanhedrin. But we have to preserve our reverence for the High Priesthood – in the hopes that one man will come to restore it to its full glory."

Cephas looked Jesus in the eyes, his face beaming with sincerity.

"Mark my word, when the Messiah appears this Passover, he'll come wearing the robes of the High Priest – *that's* the ancient tradition. He'll renounce violence, and money, and corruption, making the Temple a gathering place for rich and poor alike! No slavery, no taxation, no power-mongering."

Jesus opened his mouth to speak. But the son of Jonah, moved by his own passion and zeal, rejoiced:

"And the Five Seals will grant him entrance to the Holy of Holies – where he'll converse with God *face to face!* Not since Moses has an Israelite gazed upon God's countenance, then descended among men with his brow still shining with God's radiance..!"

Jesus trembled upon hearing these words. All that Cephas said bore the ring of truth. Was it possible? When the Messiah appears – *here* in Jerusalem, *now* at the Passover! – he'll come as God's anointed? – Not as a ruler or revolutionary, but as the High Priest?

Cephas smiled at Jesus. In his faith and ardour, he looked like a man possessed. His smile was maniacal, almost deranged.

"How long we've been waiting for that moment," he said.

V

With great ceremony, Jezubaal led her guests from Galilee into Astarte's innermost sanctuary. No windows allowed light into this sacred enclosure, and all was aglow with a strange luminescence. The sweet-smelling incense, which pervaded many parts of the temple, was most pungent here.

In this sacred inner sanctum they beheld large statues of the divine couple. Cast in meteoric iron, Baal stood with one foot forward and his arm upraised, holding aloft his emblem of the mighty thunderbolt. On his head he bore a tall crown, and his gaze was most ferocious.

Astarte stood erect atop two lions, and serpents rose and descended from her hips. Her figure was tall and slender, the triangle of her sex well-defined, and with cupped hands she was upholding her breasts. Crowned with the crescent moon, her curling hair was arranged in the coiffure of Hathor. And around her head, eight slender rays of light formed a star-shaped halo. Jewels sparkled in her eyes. But strangest of all was her smile, so archaic and mysterious.

"This afternoon," Jezubaal whispered, "Baal will lay with his Astarte, and all of our people will celebrate the joys of their union.
<*Come with me from Lebanon, my bride,*> He will cry, then entice Songs 4:8

Songs 7:6 her with the words: *<How fair and pleasant you are, O loved one,*
Songs 1:2 *delectable maiden...>* And Astarte will reply: *<Let him kiss me with*
Songs 4:16 *the kisses of his mouth;> <Let my beloved come to his garden and*
eat its choicest fruit!> For us, it is a time of great rejoicing."

"And you'll take part in the celebrations?" Salome asked, entranced.

"Oh yes. As her chosen hierodule, I will surrender myself to Astarte."

In the ensuing silence, Jezubaal could see that, again, they had failed to understand. Judeans always found her people incomprehensible.

"Baal will become manifest in our king," she explained, "and Astarte in me, the moment we lay together. We make love to celebrate the union of God and Goddess."

Chuza cast a dubious glance at Joanna, but she was listening intently to the priestess, fascinated by her every word.

"In the beginning," Jezubaal continued, "the earth and all of creation were engendered from their union. The land became a garden rich in abundance, and all of nature celebrated their sacred marriage. We will make that moment manifest once more..."

They stood in silence, regarding the statues, strangely moved. Then, wordlessly, Salome's entourage retreated from the sanctuary.

But Magdalene remained a few moments longer, trying to comprehend the mysteries invoked by these images and rites.

For a prolonged moment, she meditated upon the statue, as if it were a sacred mirror in which Miri could gaze upon her self. But the longer she looked at the Goddess, the more frightened she became. It was eerie to behold a figure so manifestly holy – sexual *and* holy. In her own culture, these two were at odds. Though Astarte was a goddess of love and wisdom, in Israel She had been branded 'shameful' – the abomination *Ashtoreth*. Yet here, the Deity was revered for her knowing desire...

Thund 13:16 *<I am the honoured one and the scorned one,>* the Goddess had
Thund 14:33 said. *<I am disgraced and the great one...>*

And afterwards had come the words which Miri could not comprehend – the mystery drawing her deeper, seeking to make itself known:

Thund 13:18 *<I am the whore and the holy one.>*

The priestess Jezubaal had passed through Astarte's initiations – and it was evident to anyone who had eyes to see: the Goddess was manifest in her. Even the young women, waiting near the entrance

of the temple, shared in this ancient belief. <*Watching at my gate,* Prov 8:34
waiting by my door> – that was the ancient wisdom, revived and
kept alive by these women. <*Happy is the one who listens to me,* Prov 8:34
watching at my gate, waiting by my door.> The ancient words of the
proverbs still echoed here, their truths not forgotten: <*For whoever* Prov 8:35
finds me, finds life...>

The Goddess was calling now, calling Miri to her. But the daughter of Magdala waited. In fear, she hesitated. She feared the demands of the vow, the price of the sacrifice. The devotees of Astarte were offering up 'the greatest of their gifts'. Could she do likewise? Could she possibly surrender herself to some stranger passing through the temple? Could she also become, by this ancient rite, a devotee of the Goddess?

'Learn to let me manifest myself in you,' came the voice, ancient and wise, from within her breast. It was Mary, the Nazarene's mother, and she repeated her exhortation: *Seek out the hidden places, forgotten by our people.* Hochmah. Astarte. Wisdom... Was the Virgin also here, in this ancient temple?

Memories of the Nazarene came back to her, and the last night they had shared together – the exquisite ecstasy of their embrace. He alone was her beloved, her betrothed. But they had spoken on the cliffs of Gennesaret. Even now, she had said, *if I threw myself down, if I fell, you would follow me.*

Magdalene felt herself like a little child once more, falling weightlessly, plunging headlong into the water. The great expanse of the sea, she suddenly realized, was the Goddess. Frightened but laughing, Miri was overcome with the thrill of hitting the water, sinking into it, and joyfully annihilating herself at the moment she and the Goddess merged as one.

VI

The Galileans gathered in the shade of Solomon's Porch. Generously, Levi had offered to share his own lodgings with his new-found companions. But they still had to make preparations for the Paschal feast before nightfall.

Simon, a shepherd by trade, cast an expert eye over the unblemished lambs. Accompanied by Cephas, he set off in the direction of the grazier's stables. At the same time, the money-wise publican stalked the *kollubistes'* tables. The twins followed, wondering what rate of exchange Levi would obtain for their hard-earned sovereigns.

Levi stared at the *trapezites'* stalls, arranged row on row in the colonnades. This temple's system of taxation, he knew, was as elegant as it was ancient. During the Passover, each adult male was obliged to pay the annual temple tax of a half-shekel. These 'offerings to YHWH' were deposited by pilgrims as they passed through the treasury in the Court of Women.

But – and herein lay the genius of the scheme – no coin bearing heathen images was accepted in the Temple. The pilgrims had to convert their currencies into temple shekels, bargaining with the money-changers in the temple's outer court. Through the *kollubistes'* contribution, the High Priest increased his yield up to sevenfold.

Add to that Annas' take – a commission on all animals sold for the sacrifice – and the Temple was a publican's dream come true. Annas and Caiaphas had reaped enormous sums, and now sat on the Sanhedrin as the most powerful of Sadducees. His phlegm rising, Levi's face paled with envy.

Within an hour, Simon and Cephas had rejoined the others, carrying the lamb for that evening's feast. In accord with the Law, it was male, unblemished, and less than a year old. With its feet bound, the most it could do was cry and beat its small horns against Simon's chest.

Though the pair were contented with the animal they'd purchased, their faces were dark with foreboding.

The Zealot leaned close to the others, his voice low. "Pilate's guard is being armed as we speak. The soldiers will strike any moment."

The others, their money now exchanged, gazed mutely at the Zealot. No one dared speak.

"We've been waiting a long time for this moment," Simon announced, his eyes flashing with infernal fires. "When the Romans strike, we must *strike back*."

Cephas laid a hand against the breast of his cloak, where a bulge appeared. "They've given us arms – it's our only chance."

"*Who* gave you arms?" Thomas demanded.

"What does it matter *who*?" Simon exclaimed. "*Who* do you think? The Galilean brotherhood! The Zealots... We're *all* brothers now..."

"Four weapons, four of us," Cephas said, giving them a determined look.

"You'd carry a knife into the Temple?" Levi demanded, taking a step back.

"Look at you," Simon hissed at the tax collector, "a traitor to your own people!" The Zealot's hand squeezed the *sica* hidden in his cloak. "The time's come for each of you to take his stand, and show where your loyalties lie. Have you forgotten the Baptist's words? In Jerusalem – at the Passover! We're clearing the path for the Messiah..."

His heart palpitating, his breath growing faint, the Nazarene cast a nervous glance left and right. Thomas and Levi had turned their crimson faces to the ground.

"You're men, aren't you? Galileans? True born sons of Israel?" His mouth dry, his brow growing hot, Simon's choler rose. "Then
fight for your country – for freedom! <*God is our only lord and* Jos 18.1.6.23
ruler!> – that's the Zealots' cry. We go into battle screaming <*Liberty* Jos 18.1.6.23
above all!>"

"But, what *is* Pilate up to?" Levi demanded, his voice a harsh whisper. "What's he *after?*"

"Don't you see it?" Simon hissed in their ears. "The pilgrims have come by the thousands! The Temple's treasuries *are loaded* with Temple shekels. So Pilate has to strike *now*."

Levi's mind started reeling. "This is all about *money?*" he cried, astounded.

Simon leaned in close, grasping Levi and Thomas by the arms. The Zealot's face had a frenzied look, wild and demonic.

"It's about *power!* Or have you forgotten? Money and revolution mean the same thing: freedom! Amd what about you, Thomas the Hellenist, champion of Greek thought – don't you care about *freedom?*"

Releasing himself from Simon's grasp, the Hellenist stared hard at the Zealot. Moments passed, his heart pounding hard in his chest.

Then, turning to Cephas, the Iscariot knocked his fist against the other's cloak, demanding a weapon for himself. Discretely, the Bethsaidean passed him a knife.

His brow burning, the publican came up to Cephas from the other side. Demanding a blade for himself, Levi slipped it under his tunic. Simon nodded his respect.

Speechless, the Nazarene stared at his closest friends, all of them armed and ready to fight. In the innermost chambers of his heart, fear was mixing with cowardice and shame. His head was spinning, his mind delirious – he feared he would faint any moment.

Where was the voice of Wisdom now?

Simon stepped forward, removed a knife from Cephas' cloak, and placed it in the Nazarene's hand.

"For the Messiah," he whispered.

VII

From all parts of Phoenicia they had come to celebrate the Sacred Marriage. The forecourt of the temple was filled to overflowing with ecstatic pilgrims. Salome and her entourage, as guests from afar, had been given seats of honour. Only Magdalene was missing from their ranks.

On the stairs before the temple stood Jezubaal and the king – she, as Astarte's blessed hierodule; and he, as Baal's emissary on earth. While the *galli* played flutes, a chorus of priestesses and priests sung the sacred liturgy. From large censors, a rich fragrance of calamus and nard wafted over the crowds.

Meanwhile, in the vestibule reserved for young women, Magdalene sat amid the virgins, richly-attired and perfumed – *watching at my gate, waiting by my door*. She had spent the preceding hours in prayer, begging to be made worthy of the sacrifice. The daughter of Magdala wanted to participate knowingly in the Goddess's mysteries: to become wise, playful, loving...

From beyond the temple's great doorway, Miri could hear the voices of the chorus. The words of the liturgy were entrancing; and rarely had she heard such poetry, so sacred and erotic. Meanwhile, wanderers from distant lands moved among the virgins in the vestibule, drawn by the strangeness and beauty of this temple.

At first, Miri didn't dare raise her eyes, so frightened was she by the prospect of fulfilling her vow. But then, the young Jewess remembered her journey here, and why she had left her homeland. These were the ancient ways, forgotten by her people. This was the path that Wisdom had opened before her. This was the way to her self.

The moment Miri raised her eyes, they were met by another's. He was darker than any man she had ever seen – a stranger from the race 'burned by the sun'. But the Ethiopian's smile was warm, genuine, comforting. Neither lust nor possession mingled in his eyes – only a curious expression, at once playful and respectful.

He approached her slowly, in solemn obeisance of this temple's hallowed custom. When he placed his symbolic offering of a coin in her lap, the African prayed with the words demanded by Astarte.

Meanwhile, from beyond the doorway, the priests of Baal sang in chorus:

<Open to me, my sister, my love, Songs 5:2
my dove, my perfect one;
for my head is wet with dew,
my locks, with the drops of the night.>

As was her duty, Magdalene rose with the money in her hands. Together, they approached the statue of the Goddess, and she deposited the coin on the altar. Miri raised her eyes to Astarte and prayed that the Goddess be with her at the moment of her offering.

Then, she turned to look at the man who was sent to assist her in her vow. He was admiring the designs on her brow and the fine lines sculpting her cheeks.

The chorus of priestesses sang Astarte's reply to her lover:

<I am my beloved's, Songs 7:10
and his desire is for me.
Come, my beloved,
let us go forth into the fields,
...There I will give you my love.>

As the king and hierodule rose to enter the sacred Bridal Chamber, Magdalene and her consort silently departed from the temple.

Wordlessly, they ascended to the top floor of the inn where the African trader kept his quarters. With the wooden shutters drawn, his chamber was dark as midnight. It smelled of strange incense, and his rich textiles and weavings, spread across the bed, exuded an exotic perfume.

In the darkness, the Ethiopian kissed her seven times. And with each touch of their lips, one of her seven garments was removed. Then he laid her upon the bed and caressed her soft skin. She had never felt a man's hands like this, moving over her nakedness with such tender caress.

Miri closed her eyes, surrendering herself to the warmth of his fingertips, the infinite pleasure in his touch. A sensation of weightlessness overcame her, and soon she was floating in the endless expanse of ecstasy.

This man had become, as Jezubaal had promised, a silent
Thund 13:23 participant in her rite of passage. <*I am she whose wedding is great*, Miri thought, *and I have taken no husband.*> His eyes, his face, his place of origin – none of these mattered now. Instead, there was only the selfless surrendering of a man and woman to each other. And in the moment of their union, a hidden oneness would be manifest: the marriage of God and Goddess.

With her mind adrift in the weightless expanse, Miri clung to the last remaining moments of her maidenhood. She recalled the elder Mary, ever-virgin, who was like a reflection of herself. But now Miri was passing to the other side, like the moon alternating from luminosity to darkness.

For a few moments longer, she clung to the dual nature of her
Thund 13:19 being, as if the moon were half in darkness and half in the light. <*I*
Thund 13:18 *am the wife and the virgin*,> she remembered, <*I am the whore and the holy one...*>

The stranger lay upon her, and she clasped her arms around his shoulders, her legs enlacing with his. The weightless condition altered, and she felt herself falling, as if from a great height.

The moon turned to darkness and, impulsively, she let out a great cry from the pain mingling with the pleasure, threatening to destroy the ecstasy of that moment. Still falling, Miri trembled, never imagining that the passage to womanhood would become so painful.

The stranger continued his rhythmic motion over her body, and Miri began to feel alone in her suffering. In her mind, she sought out company to comfort her in her anguish and isolation.

She recalled her great grandmother Eve, and the pain they
Gen 3:16 now shared. <*I will greatly increase your pangs in childbearing; in pain you shall bring forth children*> – that was the curse they had inherited, the punishment from the Fall.

Miri rolled her head from side to side, refusing to accept such
Thund 15:19 suffering or acknowledge its source in the curse. <*In my weakness, do not forsake me!*> she heard herself pleading.

Was she pleading – or praying?

From the depths of her pain, she heard a voice answering her call – the voice she had awaited in hope and in fear.

Thund 15:25 <*I am She who exists in all fears, and strength in trembling...*>
Thund 16:11 <*I am the one whom you call Life.*>

The disoriented feeling of falling, the agony of anguished solitude – all of this came to an end the moment she heard those words. The endless expanse of the sea was enveloping her now, comforting her in its watery light. She had plunged into the Deity's depths, and now was swimming in its liquid luminescence.

The pain was still present – but its meaning had become clear. Like the shock and displeasure from her first flow of blood, like the greater agony that would accompany her first birth-giving, this momentary suffering was a call to awakening, not a curse – an invocation of the Goddess, who was now expanding through Miri to the extremities of her being. They were mingling and merging into a single entity.

Her mounting fear and pain were a reminder – of the lesser death that had to be risked, in order for her rebirth to occur. Each passage of womanhood required this fearful but illuminating sacrifice. The terrible feeling – that *her life* was in danger – had awoken her to *Zoe*, to *Life itself*. She acknowledged the greater force flowing through her. The Goddess was here, her presence announced through fear and suffering.

With this new-found knowledge, Miri came to accept her pain. And at that moment, the agony and ecstasy merged into a single, higher state of being. She felt an overwhelming sense of awe – recognizing the precious nature of her existence. She was a particle of light and life, self-aware, swimming in an endless ocean of plenitude. It was all mystery and delight. Fulfilled, overwhelmed, Magdalene felt the seizures of ecstasy coursing through her lover's body, as their embraces came to fruition.

Then the lovers disentangled their limbs and lay back upon the bed. Its richly-scented textiles overwhelmed their heightened senses. At once, the Ethiopian fell into a deep sleep. And, with the afternoon heat, Miri also descended into the dreary depths of slumber.

No sooner had her lids descended than a dream uprose. But the blessed raptures of their union, so joyous and fleeting, soon gave way to feelings of fear and unease.

As before, Miri felt herself floating, moving to and fro on the endless expanse of the sea. But the ocean had become a bottomless abyss and now she was falling again – spiralling, plunging, sinking through its phosphorescent waters. Miri descended through depth after depth – twelve luminous depths in all, each of them growing denser, colder, darker.

In a single, fearful moment, an unaccountable mystery transpired in the depths of her being. Her womb was full, for she had conceived a thought, and now it was growing inside of her belly. She cried out in terror – fearful of her condition, frightened of giving birth. She called upon all the deities she knew – upon Astarte, upon Hochmah, upon Zoe, even upon the Virgin who was above. But none answered her cry.

Instead, in the darkness of the lower depths, she heard her own name being spoken. At first, the name seemed foreign to her, but then she recognized it as her own. It was a name pronounced in many tongues, with different sounds, though its meaning was always the same: *Sophia... Achamoth... Prunikos...*

The feelings and sensations exploding inside of her were overwhelming. She feared she would go mad. The thought was still inside of her. The embryo in her womb was struggling to escape, kicking for its very life, panicking in fear that it would be trapped in her womb forever.

Finally, she whispered some mysterious words, and a luminous
Ap Jn 10:9 cloud vaporized above the darkened abyss. <From that cloud her
child emerged, its eyes flashing like lightening, its face as bright
as the sun.> Coiling sinuously, the heavenly beast blazed with a
Ap Jn 11:11 blinding fire, <causing the darkness to shine.> And from its leonine
mouth it released a senseless cry, all unordered and unmeaning, like
a thunderous roar...

At once she awoke, her heart pounding in her chest. In fear and madness, Miri realized that, in this darkest of dreams, she had given birth to a horrendous creature – a serpent with a lion's head.

VIII

Tightly packed in groups of thirty, the pilgrims advanced slowly through the colonnades – all clad in white, their sandals removed, their bodies freshly bathed in the *mikvoth.*

As the Galileans shuffled through the treasury in the Court of Women, they deposited their 'tributes to YHWH'. Meanwhile, within his tunic, each felt the hard cold sharpness of their concealed weapon.

On the steps leading up to the Nicanor Gate, a choir of Levites sang the psalms. These ancient verses reminded the Israelites of their covenants with the Lord, extending backward through history
for countless generations. The first-born sons offered these lambs
Exod 12:14 in remembrance of the Passover: when the Lord freed their people
from slavery in Egypt and led them into Canaan, the Promised Land,
the land of the Twelve Tribes now called Israel.

A Levite lifted the barrier, allowing the next group of thirty pilgrims to enter the Court of the Israelites.

Emerging from the shade of the colonnade, the five Galileans stepped into bright sunlight. Suddenly, the massive Temple appeared before them in all its glory, bathed in smoke from the altar's flames. Its ornate facade and two gilded columns dazzled them with their radiance. Tears rose to their eyes – due to the blinding light, the smoke, and the wonder of it all.

And there, before the Great Porch, appeared the High Priest, attired in his ceremonial raiment. Caiaphas stood, arms outstretched, before the entrance of the Temple. And beyond it, they knew, lay the unspeakable Mystery. Over the sacred threshold, down the dark passageway and into the innermost sanctuary, there, in the Holy of Holies, dwelt the unutterable name: YHWH.

The Nazarene was overwhelmed. He had entered into the presence of the Lord. He forgot about his friends, forgot about the sacrifice, forgot all talk about uprising and revolt. Instead, he peered into the darkness of that doorway and listened to its immense silence.

<He... is the immeasurable silence,> his mother had said. *<Your* Tri Prot 35:33
Father transcends every word, every voice...> Tri Tr 129:20

Jesus listened, straining every nerve, trying to hear the voice – the voice of his Father, the voice that would tell him *who* he was and where his path must lead.

Standing alone before the entrance of the Temple, the Nazarene closed his eyes. He even pressed his hands to his ears to stop the terrible noise of the screaming lambs. At the same time his four companions pressed closer to the priests, offering up their sacrifice.

Suddenly, in the thunderous echo of his thumping heart, the Nazarene heard consonants and vowels shifting, re-arranging, forming words. Some were sheer nonsense. Others were nothing more than vowels making a long sequence, repeating indefinitely: *a! a! ao! ...a! a! ao! ...a! a! ao!*

He increased his concentration, seeking the consonants between the vowels – consonants like the tetragrammaton of YHWH.

In the systole and diastole of his beating heart, he heard the distorted echo of YHWH's name: the consonants that formed the beginning and end of the unutterable name: Y-H. But then, there came two more sounds between the Y and the H, making four in all: Y - LT - B - TH.

Was this the name that dwelt in the immeasurable silence?

The name of his Father? In his mind, the consonants and vowels coalesced, spelling out the unspeakable name: Y-*a*-LT-*a*-B-*ao*-TH...

Opening wide his mouth, Jesus gave voice to the name: "Yaltabaoth!"

Though his eyes were open, he saw nothing. He was plunged into infinite blackness, a darkness so intense it burned his open eyes and seared his inner vision. Then a terrible wailing filled his ears. It was the deafening roar of some heavenly beast – prolonged, maddening, threatening to drive him insane.

The Nazarene cringed in pain, his hands clutching the sides of his head.

After an agonizing number of moments, the screaming was reduced to a low rumble, like thunder. Shadows slithered in and out of manifestation, as the darkness uncoiled. And in a single blinding moment, a luminous cloud materialized above the blackened abyss. Like lightning, a leonine face broke through the darkness, its eyes as bright as the sun, its hair enhaloed by seven fiery auras.

The vision was blinding. But a voice rose from the centre of the
Orig Wld 112:28 shining darkness, saying: *"<It is I who am God."* And then, with
+Ap Jn 11:20 wrath and fury echoing in its thunder: *"No one exists before me.>"*

Jesus trembled uncontrollably. Fear and wonder were tugging at his heart, drawing him forward, leading him inexorably into the fiery vortex. He had never felt himself so close to death – as if this holy fire, the moment he came in contact with it, would consume him like a burnt offering.

Orig Wld 101:5 *"<Heaven is my abode,"* it said, *"and the earth is my
footstool.>"*

The seven auras exploded into seven heavens, each a beautiful
Orig Wld 102:13 dwelling place with thrones, mansions, temples and chariots. He saw
Hyp Arch 95:26 a huge four-faced chariot with eight cherubim on each corner. In
Orig Wld 105:4 one direction they shone with a lion's face; in another with a bull's,
Orig Wld 102:15 then with an eagle's and an angel's face, making sixty-four faces in
all. The cherubim chariot was leading mighty armies of angels and archangels, unto countless myriads. The vision was overwhelming.

"You seek the way of the Messiah. His path is like the path of the Israelites – through the flood and its cleansing water, through the desert and its purging fire."

"The three *parousias*," Jesus whispered.

"On this day I set before you three trials. Only the Messiah may survive them."

Averting his sight from the fiery fury, Jesus lowered his head and nodded in acceptance.

"To become the anointed one, you must make the stones of the temple your body, and your body into bread – feeding all the hungry of the earth. That will become the new covenant between us: the meal to be shared in communion between man and God."

Jesus swallowed hard, unable to comprehend all his Father was asking of him. Would he initiate a new covenant in this way – offering *his own body* as the sacrament?

"The second trial: to stand at the summit of the temple. And with neither fear nor hesitation – to throw yourself down."

Jesus hid his trembling hands in the folds of his tunic. It was indeed what God was asking of him – to sacrifice himself. To master his fear – even unto death – trusting in the Lord's angels to bear him up.

"Behold!" the voice said, and a vision unfolded before his eyes. He saw the seven kingdoms of the world in their earthly splendour – the marble and gold of their palaces, the jasper, onyx and rubies of their temples – Babylon, Phoenicia, Persia, Egypt, Greece and Rome were all crowned with Israel's diadem.

"<I will give dominion and kingship unto you, so that all nations Dan 7:14
and peoples will serve under you.> Indeed, on this very day, you will rise up and seize the Temple. When the Romans spark rebellion, you will fight, putting your faith in me. Their armies will fall before you. Then the High Priest will surrender his robes, and the people proclaim you Messiah. You will usher them into my presence, and all will fall on their knees before me."

A distant rumbling was heard, like storm clouds passing, and the vision disappeared.

Jesus found himself before the altar once more. In the chaos and confusion of the feast – each of them pressing their offering towards the priests – no one had noticed his absence. All was as it had been before. Except – the vision remained emblazoned in his brain.

The son of Nazareth watched as the offerings were handed back to their bearers. The lamb's fatty parts, as a gift to the Lord, were left sizzling on the altar. Meanwhile, the fleshy parts were returned to be roasted and eaten that evening in the Paschal Feast – the meal of remembrance between man and God. The thought of it, that moment, made Jesus dizzy with delirium.

A strange sound rose from the Court of Women: a rising crescendo of a thousand screams. They heard people running, panicking, fleeing for their lives. Trumpet blasts sounded throughout the Temple. It was an eerie, frightening noise, like the sound to be heard at the end of time.

The Galileans forgot about their offerings and ran towards the Nicanor Gate. From their place atop the steps, they could see the events unfolding. Pilate's Praetorian Guard had marched, in Roman fashion, towards the Temple Treasury, their well-ordered column protected by massive shields on its flanks. Now they were carrying out the large horns and coffers filled with Temple shekels.

Lk 13:1 A group of Zealots, <most of them Galileans,> were resisting
Jos 18.1.6.23 the Roman incursion. Screaming "<*God is our only ruler!*>" they were throwing themselves against the shields and swinging their knives blindly. But Pilate had armed his guards with large wooden clubs. Their effect was devastating: anyone who came too near to the column was repelled, his skull crushed, his hands bleeding and broken.

This was it. In horror, Jesus realized that his moment had come. The path had led here, and there was no turning back. This was the
Gs Thom 36:11 beginning. Or was it the end? What did it matter? <*The end will be where the beginning is.*>

"Fight!" the Nazarene screamed. "Fight for your homeland, for Israel, for freedom!" With his knife raised, he charged towards the Roman column. Simon the Zealot, inspired by his patriotic fervour,
Jos 18.1.6.23 screamed "<*Liberty above all!*>" and followed him. Then the others, equally infected by his passion and fury, launched themselves into the fray.

The courage of these Galileans gave heart to other pilgrims, who now unsheathed their knives and charged the Praetorian Guard. Through sheer numbers, the Jews managed to trample the shields under their feet and break apart the Roman column. Once freed of their formation, the soldiers turned wild, clubbing to death any insurgent who came within reach.

From the eye of the storm, Jesus could see that the uprising had turned into a bloody carnage. Rebels were falling at his feet, their faces crushed. Centurions were screaming and grasping hopelessly at the knives plunged into their backs. The stones of the court were flowing with blood.

The Nazarene knew what had to be done. *Who* he was; *where* his path must lead – all of that was clear now. He ran back towards the Nicanor Gate and mounted its inner stairway three steps at a time. Emerging onto the parapet, he could see the Romans and Jews is a swirling mass of humanity below him.

Somewhere in the crush, his brothers were fighting, even sacrificing their lives – and he had led them there. But his own visions and voices had brought him *here* – to the summit of the Temple, at the peak of the Passover. This was the beginning; this was the end.

"Israel!" he screamed. "On this very day, our land will be made free! God has made a new covenant with his people. Like a warrior He will lead us, and the occupying armies fall! No longer will the Romans and their collaborators desecrate this temple, for God shall make it pure! Before this doorway, his Son will appear, to lead you once more into his hallowed presence!"

The crowds below him moved to and fro – like waves in watery darkness, rising and falling, then dashing themselves upon the rocks. The Nazarene thought of Magdalene, falling from the cliffs, and himself plunging after her. His fear mounted higher and higher – a terror unbearable.

"The one who stands before you may cast himself down. But that fall will become the rising of many! So that the aeon of the Messiah may begin – now has become the hour of my descent! But,
through the grace of God, <the way of descent will become the way 3St Seth 127:20
of ascent!>"

Then, in a leap of blind faith, he launched himself from the parapet.

VI. Awakening

I

Blackness above and blackness below. The son of Mary stood at the summit of Mount Tabor, plunged into obscurity. It was the middle of the night, and the darkest hour before the dawn. Below him to his left, nestled in the gloomy hills, lay Nazareth. And further to the right, perched on dark Gennesaret's shores, stood Magdala. But Jesus could go no further, neither to the left nor the right.

For days and nights he had run, like a wild beast, hunted by demons and haunted by fear. After he had plunged into the crowd, his fall broken by the bodies below, he awoke to the smell of bitter earth pressed to his nostrils. He had failed – and wished he had died instead. Like a heavy veil hanging over his shame and defeat, the Nazarene's face had filled with tears.

Seeing this, his companions had scattered in all directions – injured and in pain, pitiful animals driven by the Romans' blows.

The Nazarene had also run, instinctively, alone in his anguish. His left arm was broken, his ribs badly bruised. For hours and days, he had run through the heights of Samaria, snatching brief moments of sleep only when exhaustion had overcome him.

But then, the nightmare would return, to haunt his few hours of respite.

With a start, he'd awaken and begin running again. He was running from himself, trying to escape the overwhelming realization of his own ignominious failure. His visions had misled him; the voices betrayed him. The Messiah had become his own worst enemy.

But here, atop Mount Tabor, Jesus had finally collapsed, a camel exhausted by its burden. This was Galilee, his home. And if the God of Jerusalem still wanted to persecute the anointed Nazarene, He would have to show his face *here*.

How low had he fallen – the Chosen One! He cringed and turned crimson – recalling the thoughts that had entered his head, the wishes he had willed deep in his heart. Since departing from the monastery he had surrendered himself to every temptation. In Nazareth, he had felt hunger gnawing at his entrails and bitterness clawing at his heart. Then, in bed with Magdalene, this longing had turned to lust and desire.

In Jerusalem, the sly words of Levi had piqued his avidity and hunger for power. Simon's zeal had moved him one step beyond greed: to anger, violence and wilful slaughter. And Cephas – even Cephas, in his piety and devotion – had whetted his craving for sanctity and vainglory.

But his companions were not at fault. Invisible forces were moving through them – through their eyes to his eyes, through their mouths to his ears – images of evil, riding on desires and hiding in their words. He felt them all now, swimming inside of him – the unseen demons mingling in the darkness and emerging as his blackest passions and deeds. The imps had become the impulsive masters of his soul. Each muscle and fibre, once responding to his will, had unwittingly been surrendered to them.

The crippled, blind and possessed – Jesus was one of them now. He belonged to the suffering multitude, crawling over the face of the earth and begging for release. Only a jealous God could delight in seeing so much anguish and pain.

Still, his anger gave him strength. Through a supreme effort of the will, the suffering saviour decided to stand upon this summit and call upon God to explain – *face to face* – why He had shown such deception, injustice, and pointed persecution.

With his last ounce of strength he stood up.

"Yaltabaoth!" the youth cried, naming the God whose true name, he now knew, was deceit.

The darkness around him deepened. Its emptiness, he suddenly sensed, had become endless and immense. Was he asleep? Was he dreaming? In the watery abyss of the heavens above him, he saw the stars moving, their constellations disbanding and forming new patterns. His vision expanded beyond the horizon until he could see – through the murky depths, but clearly – that the earth was encased seven times by seven blackened spheres.

Each of the spheres was like an immense prison, its walls surrounding this world with a fateful, impenetrable gloom. And each of the seven jails had one guard, who stood before the planetary door – its light penetrating the darkness like a faint sparkle in the heavens.

Seven *Archons* stood, like seven Sumerian statues, before the entrance to each of heaven's gates. And their names became known to him, since each had imprinted its seal on his soul: <*Athoth*, Ap Jn 10:23
Harmas, *Kalila-Oumbri* and *Yabel*; then *Adonaiou*, *Cain* and *Abel*.> Each of these seven planets had influenced his passions; each now held mastery over a seventh part of his soul.

Glowing eerily in the night sky, the closest of these gleamed with malevolence. Suddenly, the Nazarene saw how the moon had a face, staring back at him with ominous eyes. The lunar sphere blazed with sulphurous light, like a face of fire carved in topaz by the Babylonians of long ago. And the moment Jesus recognized the figure above him, he felt horrible convulsions coursing through his body.

It was as if a network of invisible powers, flowing through his bones, had suddenly become subject to the moon's sway. It had always been this way, *but now he was aware of it*. He *felt* the moon's influence: his indecision and wavering, his wildly errant and wayward path through life – all of these were due to the planet's debilitating power. His heart's inconstancy was indeed the moon's.

And he could not resist it. The lunar sphere had determined that his life-path, moving this way and that, would always lead him astray. Growth and awareness, should they come, would only come haphazardly and at random.

Then, looking higher in the heavens, he could feel the influence which each higher sphere had gained over his life. The seven planetary rulers had planted their powers in his limbs, and he responded to them unwillingly.

Inconstancy, greed, lust and pride; wrath, injustice and deceit CH 1:24
– these were the seven powers, the seven passions: circling like the planets in the heavens, then descending and circulating like the humours in his body. All of these had faces now, all of them had names. *Athoth*, *Eloaiou*, and *Astaphaios*; *Yao*, *Sabaoth*, *Adonin* and Ap Jn 11:22
Sabbede – those were the names of the Archon's adjuncts, who were called the seven powers. And their faces shone down on him from a great height, the faces of beasts!

The wandering stars formed new images in the night sky, like a
Ap Jn 11:22 starmap hitherto unseen and concealed: <the fire-face, the monkey,
the dragon and the serpent with seven heads; then the hyena, the
Mars 25:1 donkey and the sheep.> <Thus the Archons' powers, which at
first resembled angels, manifest their true forms – *as animals and
beasts!*>

Though seven of these heavenly lights shone brightly, others sparkled with the faintest of hues. In a flash Jesus knew that each of the seven Archons had seven powers under him, and each of these powers commanded six demons more – making *three hundred and sixty* malevolent angels in all.

With the faces of bulls, lions, eagles and men, they faced in four directions, evil ornaments on Yaltabaoth's solar chariot. As that hidden light arced under the earth and headed toward the horizon, the son of Mary sensed the myriad of Archons, powers and demons, as names he somehow knew, and images he could see, both within and without.

Ap Jn 11:22 The seven powers, his mind now told him, were also the
seveness of the week. And the three hundred and sixty demons were also the days of the year, plus the degrees of direction on the horizon. This multitude of evil angels surrounded him, *in space and in time*, imprisoning him in the earth's circumference and the endless cycling of the hours – all determined by heavenly machination. They hovered above him but also entered into him with the greatest of ease, and his body had no walls to resist them...

The Nazarene fell to his knees. He felt trapped, hopeless – utterly powerless to withstand their onslaught.

"Yaltabaoth!" the Nazarene cried again, still daring the faceless God to appear.

In response to his calling, the myriad of lights in the heavens began moving, circling and swirling into a massive vortex. The Nazarene had the dizzying and disoriented sensation that time was accelerating. The Archons, powers and demons – all were forming a mighty halo in the heavens, with black emptiness at its centre.

Then, in silence, they waited for their master. The sparrows in the trees started screaming as the horizon turned from black to bloody red. Insects buzzed madly through the morning air as everything started moving with incredible speed.

And, with a deafening thunder, the sun suddenly rose, then shot upwards to the very apex of the heavens. Daylight blinded him. All exploded into auras of fiery light.

But, in the trail of fire left behind by its lightning movement, Jesus could see the body of a mighty serpent, coiling sinuously in the heavens. Scintillating patterns of incredible complexity moved over its scales. And with one mighty opening of its jaws, the serpent greedily devoured the sun.

The sight was so overwhelming that Jesus screamed with
horror. Again, the heavens turned from morning to night, as the sun
was evilly eclipsed. A strange twilight unfolded, as <light mixed Ap Jn 11:11
with darkness, causing the darkness to shine.> And in its midst, the
Nazarene could see Yaltabaoth glowing in all his shadowy glory.

The huge coils of the heavenly beast seemed to encircle the earth, then wind seven times higher through the seven liquid skies. And at the greatest height, the head of the beast shone with unusual brilliance. Through the watery mixture of darkness and light, Jesus could see the features of the sun, undulating like tongues of unholy fire.

The serpent had the face of a lion, its long mane radiating outwards like a twelve-pointed star. Meanwhile, the Archons and their myriad of demons formed seven stellar auras, like so many haloes in dark spectral hues. Yaltabaoth opened wide his mouth and released a mighty cry, mingling a thousand words without meaning.

The Nazarene knew, his heart sinking with defeat, that this
was the beast from the beginning of time – the lion-headed serpent
that The Poimandres had said <*existed before a beginning without* CH 1:8
end.> Indeed, this was the Demiurge, the cosmos' creator, whose
evil machinations had shaped *'the Heimarmene'*, as Marsanes had
called it – the seven heavens whose constant turnings decided the
course of Man's fate. <They bound him within measures, times and Ap Jn 28:30
moments, since Fate rules all.>

But, beneath the moon, five more spheres appeared, comprising
the sublunary realm. The outermost sphere was of ether, the next, of
fire, then air, water and earth. They also turned like spheres within
spheres, though their elements had mixed and fused, creating matter.
And five Archons more ruled over these lower aeons – *Abrisene*, Ap Jn 10:36
Yobel, *Armoupieel*, *Melceir-Adonein* and *Belias* – making twelve
Archons in all.

These were the twelve aeons of Yaltabaoth, the twelve layers of
the cosmos, whose substance was a glowing fire from the sun-faced Ap Jn 12:4
serpent. All their many shapes and appearances were flickering
aspects of his own mighty form, <for Yaltabaoth has a multitude of Ap Jn 11:35

Pistis ch 126 faces.> Thus, the evil serpent that bites its tail surrounds the cosmos and encompasses it entirely.

The Nazarene's eyes grew wide with wonder and horror. The insights inspired by these visions afflicted him body and soul.

He realized that the seven orbiting planets and five sublunary spheres offered his soul twelve successive doorways through the darkness – but their arrangements kept on shifting, their passageways kept sliding and turning in alternate directions. The firmament had become a massive lock whose numbered wheels were always rolling and falling in differing combinations.

Somehow his soul had made its passage through this ever-shifting labyrinth, absorbing influences as it descended. It had put on passions like so many garments invisibly enshrouding his heart – his inconstancy, greed, lust and pride; his anger, injustice and deceitfulness. His soul had also acquired a body composed of earth, air, fire and water, caking it with so much matter. But how could his captive mind ever find its way out of this incredible fortress?

With a sickening sense of failure, Jesus knew that Hell had risen upwards from the abyss. It now encompassed the earth, and reached as high as the surrounding heavens. He had become trapped in this devil-God's scheming artifice – a solitary spark of consciousness in the cosmos' infernal machine, with a thousand demonic angels as his jailers and tormenters.

The son of Mary fell forward and buried his face in the earth. He remembered the animals he'd seen in Jerusalem's outer Temple, tethered to the walls. He had become one of them: a beast awaiting slaughter, a sacrifice to YHWH.

Come! Yaltabaoth said, addressing his seven heavenly Archons. His voice sounded like the shrill scream of a thousand locusts
Hyp Arch 87:25 swarming in the skies. <*Let Us create a Man that will be from the soil of the earth.*>

In horror, Jesus raised his head and watched as Adam, the First Man, floated supine on the horizon.

Slowly Adam's body gained its form from the dust of the earth. The four elements – earth, air, fire, and water – separated and combined to weave his material body.

Ap Jn 15:2 <*Behold, We have created Man according to Our likeness and image!*>

And the Nazarene could see how a demon had animated
Ap Jn 18:2 each element through its qualities: *Phloxopha* ruled over heat and *Oroorrothos* over cold, *Erimacho* over dry and *Athuro* over wet.

But, dominating all of these was *Onorthochrasaei*, the mother of the elements. She mixed them all into a warm sticky mud, calling it matter.

Stranger still, as the material body of the *Anthropos* began to take shape on the horizon, the Nazarene could feel the same events transpiring in his own flesh. The evolution of each substance, the growth and movement of the limbs – all of these were mirrored in his own corporeality, and he felt the transformations coursing through his own extremities.

He *was* Adam – the descendant of the First Man, and his body
shared in this horrific construction of the *Anthropos'* malevolent
design. <The bones, sinews, flesh and marrow; the blood, skin and Ap Jn 15:14
hair> – each of these networks grew like seven suffocating garments
over Adam's supine form, and Jesus felt them in his own flesh,
animated by one of the seven heavenly powers.

Then, three-hundred and sixty demons swarmed around Adam's Ap Jn 19:2
body and fashioned one of its parts. This vision of Primal Man's
genesis threatened to drive the Nazarene insane. He felt the entire
multitude coursing through his body, screaming their names and
commanding each of its parts.

The son of Mary shuddered in horror, raising his hands to his
brow and burying his face in terror. But, the moment he closed
his eyes, he saw them there inside of him. *Asterechme* was hiding Ap Jn 15:32
behind his right eye and *Thaspomacha* behind his left. Each of these
evil angels had fabricated one of his organs, and had ruled over it
ever since. *Krys* was in his right hand and *Beluai* in his left. *Treneu*
commanded the fingers of the right hand; *Balbel* those of the left.
Each finger, joint, and nail – *each* had a name, and a demon to give
it shape while a malevolent spirit inspired its every movement.

Jesus toppled over the edge of reason, into madness. He heard himself screaming, he heard himself laughing. He heard the mingling of a thousand words, all without meaning, as his voice repeated Yaltabaoth's senseless cry.

But the maddening vision would not stop. It kept expanding, mercilessly, into an endless myriad of images. Each emotion exploding in his heart also acquired a name, a face and a mind-tormenting devil to accompany it.

The grief overwhelming his breast was *Nenentophni*. The fear
gnawing at his entrails was *Blaomen*. Then, <from *Nenentophni*'s Ap Jn 18:14
grief came envy, jealousy, distress, trouble, pain, callousness, anxiety
and mourning. And from *Blaomen*'s fear came dread, agony and

shame. Deep in his loins he felt pleasure – rising, then expanding into wickedness and pride. From desire spread unsatedness and bitter passion.>

They multiplied into a dizzying array of emotions, and the Nazarene felt them all, somehow, *at once*. His mind exploded into a variegated state of infinite distraction. As the cohesion in his thinking
1Ap Jas 28:11 melted away, he descended into a state <of great mindlessness,>
feeling only a myriad of emotions – the countless passions passing through him like a thousand winds through the torn sail that once was his soul.

Simultaneously laughing and crying, Jesus slithered on the ground and roared – ritually gesturing and praying in obscene emulation of his new-found God.

II

A painful cry, like the sound of some wounded animal, resounded in the darkness, and Magdalene awoke.

It took her some moments to realize that the scream which had roused her from her nightmare – was her own. In the heavy sleep
Tri Tr 82:25 of forgetfulness, she had been <dreaming the most-troubling of
dreams.>

Blindly in the unlit chamber, Miri patted the covers and pillows. Where was she? Why was the doorway to the left of her bed, and not where it should be – to the right?

It took her some moments to realize that she was *in her home*. Not the Ethiopian's lightless chamber in Tyre. Nor her parents' villa in Magdala, where she had lived all her life. No. Since her return from Tyre they had *banished her* from that house. Now she was in 'the Widow's Tower' – her new refuge in Capernaum.

But the nightmare? She didn't dare call it back into her memory, so terrible was its last impression. Meanwhile, a feeling of terror kept worming its way through her mind, seeking to connect itself with some image.

She had given birth – that was the dream. Miri had whispered
Orig Wld 100:10 the words *<Child, pass through to here,>* and then she was holding
her new-born child close to her cheek. But as she repeated those
Orig Wld 100:10 self-same words, they spelled out the child's name: *<Yalda baoth.>*

Like a lion-cub, it purred and licked at her ear. She felt joyous but also uncertain, as a presentiment of anxiety welled up inside of her. Then its serpent tail wrapped seven times around her body, and she heard the beast whisper in her ear: My mother – *Sophia... Achamoth... Prunikos...*

Since moving to 'the Widow's Tower', this recurring nightmare had endlessly haunted her sleep. Why was she in the clasp of such madness? Why this obsessive image – of her progeny... a child like a lion-headed serpent..?

Even though the month of *'Iyyar* had begun, the nights were still long and cold. Sometimes the rain poured down until morning. She could hear the heavy drops now, pounding on the roof while a strong wind whistled through the window-frame. It was nights like this that she hated most to be alone.

How had she come to be here? Since those strange events in Tyre, her life had taken such unusual turnings. Of course, she and Salome had quarrelled. When the Herodian princess had learned of Miri's secret offering – was it envy? –was it spite? The two women, who had confessed such affection for each other, suddenly released a litany of insults and tearful accusations. Miri had to find her own transport back to Galilee. She was lucky to escape with her life...

But, back home in Magdala, she knew she could not escape her father's inquisition. Amid plaintive tears and screaming invectives, she was turned away from her ancestral home. The Widow's Tower at Capernaum, empty and abandoned since her aunt had died, became her only source of refuge.

Yet, no marriageable woman could live alone – it was unthinkable. Within weeks, travelling merchants and tradesman came knocking at her door. Soon, even the village elders came creeping to her lodgings. She refused them all. In turn, they threatened her with rape and even murder.

Then the rumours started. She was called a witch, called a whore. Word spread fast: she was the harlot of Magdala, the prostitute of Tyre, a woman cursed with seven demons. The neighbours threatened to drag her by the hair, throw her from a cliff and stone her. That was village justice. She lived in a constant state of fear and terror.

Had she acted in accord with the ancient ways? Was she actively remembering all the forgotten deities – Astarte, Zoe, Hochmah? At times, she felt this. But, more often than not, she felt she was in conflict with herself – a dual being. She was bold *and* ashamed, honoured *and* scorned. She had indeed become the whore and the holy one: *Sophia... Achamoth... Prunikos...*

Worst of all were the nights. At times she felt like she was losing her mind – the constant fear and distraction, the voices flowing through her, and her moods shifting from joy to despair. She had immersed herself deeply in her own darker side.

A terrible noise woke her from her midnight revery. Was it the wind against the shutters – so loud? Or a village elder come to threaten her? Then she heard it again, a pounding and scratching against the door downstairs.

From her window on the second floor, she pushed open the shutters and peered at the shadowy figure below. He paused and looked up. His long hair was twisted by the wind, his cloak and tunic drenched by the rain. But the shape of the eyes she recognized at once.

Within moments she had descended the stairs and unlatched the door. Her beloved tumbled into her arms. His skin was *so cold* – he must have been wandering in the storm for hours. Water trickled over his brow and dripped from the cleft of his beard, hiding the tears on his face.

"Miri..." he murmured, and began kissing her neck, her lips.

She tried holding him, supporting the weight of his weakened limbs. But his woollen cloak was heavy with the rain, and together, they stumbled until her back was pressed against the cold damp limestone.

His hands were tearing at her gown, trying to rip it from her body. With his lips pressed hard against her mouth she could barely breath.

"No, my beloved, not like this," she pleaded, squeezing the long locks of his hair and pulling his face away from hers.

For a few moments, they stared at one another in the shadows. The Nazarene seemed barely recognizable... *That was* his hair, his face – but the expression in his eyes had changed. He looked deranged.

The son of Nazareth laughed and launched himself once more at the figure he so desired: her long braided hair, oiled with sweet-smelling herbs, coiling like serpents over her breasts and descending as far as her well-curved hips. His hands clawed at her throat; his teeth tore at her lips.

Summoning all the anger she could muster, Miri screamed and struck him hard. She struck him repeatedly, until he, in his weakened state, finally collapsed to the floor.

Clinging to her knees, he looked up at her and laughed – a strange, bitter laugh that squeezed the tears from his eyes. "'Never forget Wisdom' he said to me! 'Go after her! Seek her! Do not let her

go! *<For in the end She will take the form of joy for you.>*' – that's Sirach 6:26
what he said to me!"

Miri looked down at the desperate figure crouching at her feet.
She felt helpless, angry, confused.

"'*<First she will take you through winding ways, testing you* Sirach 4:11
with her ordeals,'" he mimicked. "'*But in the end she will lead you*
back to the straight road – and reveal her secrets to you.>' Yes,
that's the way of Wisdom – the fickle whore!"

"*Who* told you that?!" she demanded.

"They did – the three mages who pronounced me *Messiah!*"
Jesus laughed maniacally. "Now I've come to you – pleading,
defenceless – the Messiah seeking his Wisdom. Open yourself
to me! I am Adam on the day of his fall, desiring Eve in all her
nakedness..."

The son of Mary started banging his head against her leg. Then,
in a voice she barely recognized, he said, "I desire the forbidden
fruit! Like never before, I want to taste it, feel it sliding down my
throat. I can feel it even now, inside me, like a <bitter fire that blazes Th Cont 139:33
in my body's marrow, kindling night and day, burning my limbs – so
that my mind has become drunk and my soul deranged.> I beg of
you, please – give yourself to me!"

Mutely, she shook her head, but his longing expressed itself in
the unchecked flow of language falling from his lips.

"<My limbs are beguiled by fire! Only you can rain down a Th Cont 144:14
refreshing dew and extinguish the burning!>"

Miri felt horror and pity in her heart. Then, a strange voice
erupted from the back of her throat. The daughter of Magdala
laughed. Infected by his madness, she turned to him and shrieked
like a witch, speaking to him from Wisdom's darker side.

"Poor man..!" she taunted. "<Many are the fleeting pleasures Thund 21:20
which men embrace! Many are the alluring shapes found in a
multitude of sins!>"

Then, acting from a part of herself she could not comprehend,
she added in lament, "Look at me! <I am shameless and yet – I am Thund 14:29
ashamed!> <I, I am sinless, and the root of sin derives from me!> <I Thund 19:15
am the one called Life, and you have called me Death!>" Thund 16:11

She spoke that moment for Eve, for Hochmah, for all of the
daughters of Israel who had suffered men's anger, reprobation and
desire. "Why do I suffer this indignation? <Because you, out of Thund 17:15
shame, take me to yourself shamelessly!>"

"I cannot help it!" he pleaded. "<The fire burns inside of me, Th Cont 143:15

Th Cont 143:27 insatiable!> <...I'm drunk with that fire, so full of bitterness, but
sweet as poison.>"

Thund 14:15 "<Then *why* – you who hate me so much – do you love me?>"
she asked at last, the irony and bitterness rising in her voice. "Why
Thund 13:18 do you love *me* <– the honoured and the scorned one – the whore
and the holy one..!>

She slid down the wall and started crying, full of pity for herself. The voices speaking through her were all too much, and she felt wasted, exhausted.

"I'm confused," Jesus admitted, wrapping his arms around his knees and rocking backing and forth. "My mind has been besieged by wondrous horrors..."

He looked around furtively, then leaned forward and whispered,
Gs Thom 36:5 "I've seen <what no eye has seen and no ear has heard – what no
hand has touched, nor ever appeared to the human mind.>"

He nodded to her knowingly, then whispered so low she could
Gs Phil 85:19 barely hear him: "<The Holy of Holies has been revealed to me!>"

As he stared at her, the black pools of his eyes never seemed more empty.

Th Cont 142:30 In a low, rasping voice, he added regretfully, "<But I have
been cast down from heaven... down to the abyss... and now I'm
imprisoned here, in this dark narrow place.>"

Miri let fall a bitter laugh. "You think I don't know falleness?"
she asked, her voice rising in reproach. "Through depth after depth
Thund 19:28 I plunged, each of them growing denser, colder, darker. Finally <I
was cast upon the face of this earth.>"

"Then you know..." he whispered conspiringly. "We are *all*
Th Cont 142:10 here <– hiding in a tomb of darkness.> Me, I've become a <captive
Th Cont 143:22 bound in caverns! At first, in mad laughter, I rejoiced, not realizing
my perdition! But all this time, without knowing it, we've dwelt in
darkness and death!>"

He continued his strange monologue, the words pouring out of him like poison into her ears.

Th Cont 143:30 "<Then, the darkness rose for me like a light, and I willingly
surrendered my freedom for servitude! I darkened my heart and
surrendered my thoughts to folly!> Now I can hear them, day and
Th Cont 143:17 night without cease <– the wheels that turn in my mind!>"

"Jesus," she pleaded, "my brother, my beloved – listen to me. We have been misled by the visions and voices within. I must tell you..."

Th Cont 144:2 "<We dwelt in error," he babbled on, " – heedless of the sun

which looks down on us, circling round us to enslave us. I didn't even notice the moon, how by night and day, it looked down on us, seeking to imprison us all!>"

"My beloved, the last time we embraced, I promised myself I would make you mine..." she began explaining, hoping to catch his attention. "I wanted to give myself to you entirely. But first, I had to learn *who* I was. So I left Magdala, and journeyed as far as Tyre. And there – it all happened so quickly – the voices, the faces, the ancient forgotten ways..."

"I thought," he droned on, "that <as long as the root of Gs Phil 83:8
wickedness is hidden, it will remain strong. But once it's recognized, it will be dissolved. So, I dug deeply after the root of evil which was hidden in myself, trying to pluck it out from the root. Yes, pluck it out – by recognizing it! But I was ignorant of it... it took root in me and produced its fruit in my heart. Finally, it mastered me, and I became its slave. Ignorance is the mother of all evil, you know... Ignorance is death.>"

"Then, *listen* to me! <Do *not* be ignorant of me!>" she Thund 13:13
cried. "Know that I can never be your bride, or make you my bridegroom!"

He stopped, and turned to her. For a moment, he seemed to hear her.

"I discovered who I am..." she said. "I listened to the voices inside of me. True voices? Deceptive voices? I don't know..."

Jesus nodded slowly. "<There is in me forgetfulness, yet I 1Ap Jas 28:22
remember things...>" he whispered.

Slowly, the words came back into his memory – words resounding with truth, reminding him. "*Listen to Wisdom always, whenever she speaks to you...*" the son of Mary recalled aloud.

A faint sparkle returned to his eyes. And then he said, "*You know it yourself.* Yes, that's what my mother said to me – *First, you must betroth yourself to Mary of Magdala...*" His eyes lit up with a faint glow of remembrance.

But all the daughter of Magdala could do was mutely shake her head.

"My sister, my bride..." he pleaded. "You know, from the time that we were children, we promised ourselves to each other – you are my soul!"

Miri broke down and started crying – feeling so terribly guilty. Why, to gain knowledge of herself, did she have to betray him?

Wrapping her arms around his shoulders and burying her face

Gs Phil 85:19 in his neck, she whispered, "<The bridal chamber invited us in,> but
we never dared enter – and now its door has closed... You call me
Ex Soul 127:22 your soul... But you know – your soul has been cast down! <As long
as she was alone, she was virgin and pure.> But when she listened
Ex Soul 128:1 to the voices around her, <she prostituted herself, giving herself to
one and all.>"

For a long time, they held each other in the darkness, not uttering a sound. Finally, the Nazarene lifted his eyes to gaze upon her down-turned face. He tried to push forth a word, but failed. Silently, his eyes posed the unspeakable question – Why..?

The Magdalene shrugged her shoulders, unable to explain herself. But her mouth formed the words she didn't know how to speak.

Thund 15:15 "<Because I, I am compassionate and I am cruel...>"

Miri led him to the hearth, where the embers of the evening were still glowing under the ashes. She fed the fire with olive wood, and added some cinnamon sticks to sweeten the air. Then, hanging a pot of broth over the flames, she said, "Break bread with me, my brother, and then we'll sleep."

Jesus nodded his head in silence.

"Give me your *simlah*, to dry..." she commanded.

Without uttering a word, he obeyed, and removed his rain-soaked mantle.

"Your *kethoneth* and *cadjin* too," she ordered.

He hesitated. Then, after much struggling, she managed to pull off his wet and tattered tunic, along with its long-sleeved under-garment.

Seeing him in his loin-cloth, Magdalene gasped in horror.

"What happened to you?" she cried, her eyes filling with tears.

Bruises black and blue covered his ribs. Over his entire body were lacerations and abrasions. Worst of all was his left arm, which was swollen and knotted from the fractured bones beneath.

Jesus turned his face away in shame. Too embarrassed to explain, he mutely shook his head.

Magdalene tore the bread and served him a bowl of hot soup. The smell of the bean broth, coupled with the warmth of the hearth-fire, revived him, bringing a fresh flush to his hollowed cheeks.

Wordlessly, they supped, then she led him to her bed. Within minutes, the Nazarene had fallen into a deep, peaceful sleep, his wounded body held and protected by his only beloved.

III

To the Iscariot, the sun blazed like a black hole in the sky. At his back was Jerusalem; and before him: Galilee. But he stood, uncertain, suspended between noon and midnight.

Less than three days ago, Judas had killed a man – driven the blade in deep, then watched as a horrifying wonder came over the soldier's face. The man, his eyes growing wide, knew his soul would soon be banished from the earth.

Why him and not me?

The morning breeze lashed at his brow, and the sun tormented him with a cold hard light. Even the cormorants circling in the sky and the dogs following at his heels – all were persecuting him. They were pursuing him, accusing him with their silent stares. Another face uprose, a centurion he had left wavering between life and death. Judas cringed with remorse.

By the twisted roots of an olive tree he collapsed, overcome by his own worst enemy: the 'demon of mid-day' which Allogenes had called his *akedia* – a listless, apathetic state, full of dark thoughts, torturous, self-tormenting.

Why did he make himself suffer thus when, for the first time in his life, *he was free*... Nazareth and Jerusalem, the cloisters and his monastic life – all were far behind him. He had separated himself from his twin and now found his own path.

The Iscariot forced himself to his feet and set out once more. The word *eleutheros* – freedom! – swelled in his breast. His life was his own!

Dark-hearted poppies lined his path. He stooped and pressed the violet petals of an ancholia flower to his nostrils, deeply inhaling its ambrosial scent. Yes Nature, despite her moods and mutability, could provide a brief respite from bitter melancholy.

"*Eleutheros!*" he cried again, his heart rising – Freedom!

In the shadow of a willow tree, the Iscariot froze. There, at his feet, he beheld a wet-feathered fledgling, newly hatched and fallen from its nest. Fallen – or cast out? Its eyes as yet unopened, its wings as yet unfurled, the new-born was quivering in agony. Over its unprotected flesh swarmed an army of tiny ants, devouring it alive.

In an act of pity, the Iscariot brought down his heel, ending the unbidden agony of its all-too-brief existence. His moment of joy was eclipsed once more by overwhelming misery.

That was Nature! Behind her alluring veil, life devoured life, unceasingly in a circle of agony and delight. Indiscriminately she apportioned existence to one, annihilation to another, moved neither by pity nor remorse. Nature was fickle, beautiful and beguiling, but promiscuous as a whore! Like Eve in her inscrutable wisdom, the mother-whore held life in one hand, death in the other. Blind, heartless and dispassionate, she apportioned them equally since, to her, birth and death were one.

What was the way out? He had learned, like the ascetics of the desert, to spurn all the vanities of this world. If a woman tempted him, if his flesh tormented him, he resorted to the knotted cord, chastising himself morning and night. Since childhood he had lived a life of the spirit, renouncing desire, ambition and all earthly joy.

Zost 3:23 <Gloomy now, disturbed by the pettiness of his own existence,>
Zost 3:23 the Iscariot <dared himself to act – exile himself to the eastern
desert, where the wild beasts could devour him, and deliver him to a merciless end.>

At once, the son of Kerioth set out for Batanea, the barren lands east of the Jordan. Seconds later, he stopped, as a more enviable alternative presented itself. Before him rose a redbud tree, its golden flowers edged with scarlet hues. For an unmeasured moment, he stared at that tree, and the vine that dangled like a noose from its branches.

A few quick knots and he could hang himself from that tree, his head bowed in a final gesture towards freedom. His life was his own – to end as he pleased. Let the crows come and devour his flesh.

But – would even death bring him release?

The Iscariot averted his gaze and ran, filling his lungs with air, fearing suffocation, gasping with each intake of breath. He wanted to live – but how? Where to turn his steps? To the Messiah? How, when he had renounced him, and rejected the Messiah's path.

Or was he, Judas-the-twin, the true Messiah?

At last, under the arch to an unknown village, the wayfarer came upon a well. Exhausted by his own thoughts, the son of Kerioth sought comfort in its darkening shade. He couldn't go on. His situation, he knew now, was hopeless.

The Iscariot bowed his head and splashed the sombre waters over his face.

Swirling on the surface, a shadowy silhouette stared back at him. For a few brief moments, he saw the distorted lineaments of the Nazarene. His own dark twin was calling to him – *Tauma*, my brother! Thomas!

Judas laughed and shook his head. Jesus of Nazareth – Israel's saviour! He laughed aloud.

But he is God's anointed!

The Messiah was an illusion, nothing more.

He gives us hope.

There is no hope for Israel.

And unity. Is it wrong to believe in freedom?

Judas stared at the dark silhouette, gasping for air in sharp quick breaths. That voice, uprising from within, he realized at last – was his own.

"Thomas!" Judas cried. "I recognize you now – you counterfeit Jesus! You pale reflection of the Messiah!"

The flickering silhouette stared back at him.

"I am one in mind with you, my brother..."

"You emulate him, don't you? You're an imitator, a blind follower!"

"I also have my doubts," his reflection replied. "But all that you say, my brother, follows from darkness and despair – let them go..."

"Never! You'll betray us – betray us to him!" Judas spit the words out in anger.

"And you?" Thomas replied calmly, "who ran like a coward from the redbud tree – a man frightened by his own shadow. Where will you take us..?"

Judas bowed his head, ashamed by his own feminine fear and weakness.

"Our whole life we've been haunted by doubt," Thomas urged his double. "It has dimmed our eyes, until we see nothing but darkness."

The *tsaphown* blew over him, a chilling north wind. Then, from the south came the comforting *teyman*. Like a weathervane, the Iscariot wavered, turning this way and that.

He looked behind him, and cast a frightened gaze at the redbud tree. For a few moments, he fought against himself, and the desire to return there – knot the cord and slide it round his neck.

The Iscariot fell to his knees, his face wet with tears.

Only the Nazarene, he realized at last, had saved him. He had renamed him, recognizing him as Thomas – the twin – and releasing him from Judas – the hanged man.

For a few extended moments, Thomas gazed at the redbud tree, and had a vision of Judas, his own darker aspect, hanging lifeless from the knotted cord.

Let Judas hang there – dead to me, dispatched from my life, like my own shadow at mid-day.

Thomas let out a sigh of relief. With renewed hope, the twin turned his steps towards Galilee. Above his head, the sky blazed with the light of a thousand suns.

IV

Half asleep, half in revery, Miri lay in bed and watched the deep azure sky through the open window. The angle of the sun told her that it must be past mid-day. Still, the Nazarene slept peacefully, like a wayfarer safely encamped under the white canopy of her bed.

She gently slid herself out from under the covers and dressed, all the while wondering about her beloved. Would a night of deep, dreamless sleep bring his mind release? Could she not only shelter his body but somehow restore his soul?

Descending the spiralling stairs to the lower floor, she set about preparing the daily bread. Within moments, she had lost herself in its rhythm: the grinding and sifting, the sprinkling and kneading. When the door suddenly rattled from a harsh knocking, she was startled out of a day-dream.

The Iscariot stood at her threshold. It was unsettling how much Judas resembled Jesus in appearance. But his eyes, cold and grey, regarded her suspiciously – wary of Miri's womanhood.

"Thomas..." she said, calling him by his given name. "How did you find me here?"

"I made inquiries in Magdala," he said, lowering his head. "I'm sorry Mary... for how they treated you there..."

She cast a despondent glance at the ground, and allowed, "I'm happier here – really. Welcome to the Widow's Tower."

Bowing respectfully, the Iscariot removed his sandals and entered. As he passed her, Miri smelled his skin, a pungent mix of vinegar and brine.

Sitting round the low table, Magdalene served a bowl of fresh figs and warm milk stirred with spices. Graciously, he accepted the morning meal.

"You know it's past mid-day..." the son of Kerioth began, observing her every movement. Her hair was dishevelled and her eyes still squinting from the light.

"The nights have been difficult for me lately," she admitted.

"I came because I had to..." he said, lowering his eyes. "There's something terribly wrong with him..."

"Then you know he's here."

Thomas shrugged his shoulders, embarrassed to admit the obvious. "I'm his *tauma* – somehow, I always know what he's thinking."

"– and feeling?" she asked. For the first time, he saw a sparkle in Miri's eye.

"If he doesn't know his own heart – how should I..?" the twin replied, avoiding her searching gaze.

Miri nodded, having to accept his answer.

"Do you know what he's thinking now?"

"No, not now... Only that he's confused." The Iscariot paused, looking down at his bowl of milk, and the white reflection staring back at him. Then he added, "I know he's in conflict with himself."

Miri nodded, understanding that state of mind all to well.

Then, leaning forward, Miri asked him in confidence, "What happened to him?"

Before Thomas could answer, his twin silently entered the room. For a few long moments, the son of Nazareth stared at his double, as if trying to remember *who* this was. Then, he nodded silently to himself and sat on the floor, his back propped against the wall.

"<This world is a corpse-eater,>" Jesus said, his eyes Gs Phil 73:19
unfocussed. "<Whoever has come to know the world has found a Gs Thom 42:30
corpse.>" He stared at the ground and was silent.

"You wish to know what happened to him?" the Iscariot breathed out bitterly, turning to Miri. "He lost his mind thinking he was the Messiah..." He stared hard at Jesus, but the latter didn't respond. "He led us into rebellion against the Romans, then threw himself down from the height of the Nicanor Gate in Jerusalem."

Jesus coughed and swept his hand over the earthen floor.

Miri stared aghast. It was painful to hear those terrible events recounted with neither pity nor remorse – only a slight tinge of resentment.

"We all scattered – the Romans beating us with their clubs..."

He's trying to provoke him, Magdalene realized, even startle him, somehow, into awakening...

"So I made my way to Nazareth, then Magdala, and now here. I come to Capernaum with good news."

Thomas stared for some moments at Miri, then let fall his unusual pronouncement. "His mother sent me to Magdala to put an unusual proposal to your father. She asked permission for her son to marry his daughter."

Magdalene felt a chill rise up her spine, until the back of her neck was tingling.

"And what did my father say?" she dared ask.

"He said, in so many words, that if the son of Mary wanted to wed his daughter – then he could have her 'at any price'. So..." Thomas shrugged his shoulders, "I offer you my congratulations..."

Miri nodded. She smiled to herself and suddenly, she started laughing. 'At any price'. Her laugh was long, bitter, even painful. How long had she wished for this moment. And now it had come, but the reality was like an obscene parody of her imaginings.

Gs Phil 69:1 "<The bridal chamber is not for beasts,>" Jesus said, surprising them both. He seemed to be saying this to himself.

"We must help him," Magdalene pleaded.

"Why?" the Iscariot cried, exasperated. "He's become convinced that he's 'the Anointed One' – they all have, it seems, except me... Everyone became so wrapped up in the messianic hysteria, the mass-delusion that 'he is among us' and that 'at the Passover, the Messiah will appear'. Now, for the first time, I think he's seen the truth."

Darkly, the Iscariot turned to his brother, and slapped his hand on the low table to get his attention. The Nazarene looked up. In a loud voice, the son of Kerioth cried: "There is no Messiah!"

Orig Wld 122:27 "<But the worm born from the phoenix is also a human being,>" the son of Mary responded. Then, he turned his attention back to the earthen floor.

"Don't say that Judas!" Miri pleaded. "You just don't know! You never knew, from the time of his birth, what signs were given."

"More oracles? I've heard enough of them already! If you really think he's Christ, then bring him to the Baptist! The Prophet, at least, will recognize his own..."

Magdalene's face lit up. Was it possible? Of course – *John* would recognize him. He could even cast out his demons, heal him...

"Yes – we *must* bring him to the Jordan. You will help me Judas – it's our only hope." Tears started to well up in her eyes.

Gs Thom 37:11 "<But I, I baptized my soul in the waters of darkness,>" the Nazarene said distractedly. He knocked the wall with the back of his head in a repeated, rhythmic motion.

Thomas lowered his head. Suddenly, he felt overwhelming compassion for his brother – a feeling difficult to accept, since it came so close to self-pity. In the beginning, he didn't want to accept the truth: that his twin had fallen into unreasoning. The Nazarene's mindlessness frightened him to no end. But now, he realized – if he could help this pitiful man escape his misery, he would...

The Iscariot nodded. “We can set out today. In two day's time, maybe three, we'll reach Bethany.”

“But you!” Jesus said to no one in particular, “<Be on guard Th Cont 144:1
against the world! Arm yourselves with great strength, lest the robbers seize you!>”

“...Of course!” Magdalene realized, rising from the low table. “Salome warned me of the danger surrounding the Baptist...”

She looked at Thomas, her eyes glistening through her tears. She had to make him understand.

“I gained the confidence of Salome, daughter of the Herodians – don't ask me how... She confided to me that the Baptist is in great danger. Herod and his Vizier, even Annas and the High Priest – they all have spies in the Jordan Valley. They're *waiting* for the Messiah with the Five Seals. They want his power! They'll seize him – and John – the moment the Messiah appears! Oh, it will be terrible...”

The Iscariot looked at her and shook his head. “Don't worry Magdalene. We have nothing to fear. *There is no Messiah.*”

“How can you say that Judas?” she screamed. “You, of all people, have to *believe* in him! You're his only friend, the shadow attending his every step! For years your lives have been entwined! Now his fate lies in your hands.”

“My destiny is my own!” he retorted sharply. Then, lowering his voice, he sighed, “Even if I live in conflict with myself – my path is still my own, and my future will be decided *by my doubts* in him, not my faith...”

“Are you afraid,” Miri cried, “of what the Baptist will say? Don't you want *to know* the truth ...about him – and yourself?”

“Impossible...” he replied. “I cannot *know* anything...”

Didymos Judas Thomas looked at her, his grey eyes sharp with pain and desperation.

“How can I know the truth about him, if I can't even know a truth more precious to me... *if I can't* ever *know myself..?*”

V

The Jordan – the ‘downward-flowing river’. Its name, in their ancient tongue, meant *the Descender*. From the Lake of Gennesaret it flowed south, following Samaria's eastern flank all the way down to the wastelands of Perea – where all the life that germinated in its waters perished in the Dead Sea.

For most of the journey, Magdalene and the Iscariot supported the son of Nazareth. Cradling his left arm, the wounded saviour collapsed time and again. His bruised ribs made each intake of breath a bitter agony. But, of all of them, the Nazarene had become the most determined to make this journey.

They passed one night on the Jordan's banks, then another. The closer Jesus came to the Baptist, the more lucid his thinking became. Amid the hundreds of screaming demons in his head, he started to hear his own soul, pleading for release.

The moment had come. If the powers-that-be wanted him, then he would surrender himself willingly. Whether it be the earthly powers like Herod and Caiaphas, or the Archons in the heavens – he would risk it all, to know what secret lay hidden in himself.

On the third day they stopped not far from the Jericho ford.
While his companions paused to bathe their faces in the river, the
son of Mary retreated behind an outcropping of rock. Falling to
Pistis ch 57 the ground, he whispered, "<*Hear me*, Light of lights – and save
me!>"

Slowly, a prayer took form on his lips, and his body shook with
Pistis ch 57 the pain of repentance. "<Grant me the baptism that *forgives* me my
sins and purifies me of my transgressions. For my light has been
taken from me and I am left in distress...>"

He turned his gaze upwards, into the invisible light which lies above the blinding heavens – a light he could feel but not see. His face filled with tears, and the sweat of his brow stung his widening eyes.

Joining his strong right hand with his wounded left, he pleaded,
Pistis ch 58 "<Leave me not in chaos, but save me, invisible Light of the
Pistis ch 41 heights.> <I pray that your light descend> and illuminate me at last.
Amen."

The Nazarene wiped away his tears, hiding them in the sweat of his brow. Then, as the chorus of demonic voices returned to taunt him, he silently rejoined the others.

Magdalene and the Iscariot stationed themselves once more on either side of Jesus, and led him slowly toward the Baptist's enclave. As they mounted the last hill, the sound of chanting mixed with drums came closer to their ears.

Magdalene had never imagined that John's refuge would be like this: the crowds dancing half-naked among the bonfires; the crippled and lame crawling, falling to the ground and ecstatically writhing.

As they began their descent, Miri was overcome by a horrible presentiment. An abominable evil was drawing nearer. And the sound of her pounding heart, beating ever faster, was hastening its measured approach.

The moment the pilgrims in the surrounding hills *saw* the wounded saviour, the drumming stopped and an uneasy calm descended over the valley. Even the blind turned to stare at him.

Magdalene could feel her beloved trembling in her arms. He stood rigid and paralyzed, his eyes wide with horror. He was seeing something... an immense, invisible evil which she, in her terror, could only feel: powerful, overwhelming, infinite.

Before she could warn them to flee, the storm broke. The lame and diseased, the crippled and possessed, thronged around them – some crying, others screaming. Worst of all were the demoniacs, who laughed and started clawing at Jesus.

The Iscariot pulled out his blade and slashed at them violently, but there were far too many. With gleeful malevolence, the mob wrenched Jesus from Magdalene's grasp and carried him away.

Then, as she and the twin were trampled underfoot, Miri caught a final glimpse of her beloved: his garments were torn from his body; his left arm was cruelly twisted and broken. He was being carried upside down, his head dangling oddly from his inverted body.

"Clear the path!" the demoniacs were crying. "Make straight the way of the Lord!"

More pilgrims in the crowd gathered round, demanding who this was. When Herod's spies heard the demoniacs' cry, they quickly joined their frenzied numbers. For months they had been stranded in this wasteland, waiting for the Messiah to appear. Let this fool be the one.

"The Messiah of the Five Seals!" the Temple spies cried aloud, adding their voices to Herod's men. " Let your minds awaken! For, the time of awaiting is over! *The Messiah is among us!*"

Bruised and beaten, Thomas and Miri followed the mob as it snaked through the valley, attracting more adherents. Hundreds took up the cry: "Make straight the way of the Lord!"

But, as if in cruel parody of their own proclamation, the ecstatic procession kept twisting and turning each time it neared the Baptist.

From his place on a rock in the Jordan, John released a deafening cry.

Ap Adam 84:4 “You fools! You beasts! <Why are you crying out with lawless tongues and criminal voices, with your souls full of blood and foul deeds? You are full of the works of untruth! Having defiled the waters of life, you would now serve the powers who thirst after its greatness!>”

Like a serpentine coiling of humanity, the crowd writhed toward John and disgorged Jesus onto the shores of the Jordan.

“Behold the Son of Man!” they cried.

The Baptist glared angrily at the mob and again raised his voice.

Orig Wld 123:15 “<Thus has the world come to ignorance, stupor and distraction! From the creation right unto the consummation, the men of the earth would rather worship the angels of evil! All of you are *in error* – and will continue to be until the final *parousia*, with the coming of the true man.>”

“But this is the one!” a beggar cried. “I was in Jerusalem at the Passover, and saw him standing high up on the Temple!”

“He stood over the gate to the Holy of Holies,” another contested, “and said he would lead us in!”

“Yes!” a third agreed. “He called himself ‘the Son of God’
3St Seth 127:20 saying <his descent would become the way of ascent!>”

2Ap Jas 52:14 “Those were his words?” the Baptist cried. “<A multitude,
when they hear, will be slow-witted. When you hear, therefore, open
your ears and understand!> The Son of God will come, speaking
Gr Pow 44:30 such words. <But as his appointed time approaches, the Archons
and powers will also send *an imitator*, in order to know his great
Tri Prot 49:7 power!> <*Beware the Son of the Archigenetor!* He is the one the
Archons and demons call their Christ!>”

John swept his hand over the crowd.

Gr Pow 45:5 “<The multitude will expect him to perform signs... And indeed, he will come, proclaiming his reign over the whole earth and all those under heaven! He will perform his signs and wonders – so all will turn away from the true Son of Glory *and go astray!*>”

“But he has fulfilled your prophecy!” one of Herod’s spies called out. “He appeared in Jerusalem at the time of the Passover. Now you deny it?”

Unt MS “<Let him enter the Jordan, so the aeon of the Son may commence!>” a crazed disciple cried.

Again the mob started chanting: “Make straight the way of the Lord!”

John gazed out at the ignorant herd with anger and pity mingling in his heart. Was it their own fault if, through Wisdom's prophecies, they had fallen into a frenzy over the Messiah? And who was this pathetic man they had dropped onto the Jordan's shores? Why didn't he speak for himself?

"Let this man approach me!" the prophet cried, "so that the edict of the truth may be published or the error of his ways made known!
<For there is nothing covered over, that will not be disclosed; Gs Thom 33:20
and nothing hidden, that will not be revealed. Everything will be disclosed *in view of the truth!*>"

John motioned for Jesus to approach.

All this time, the Nazarene had been sunk half-deep on the Jordan's shore – his head bowed, his body curled up like a wounded child. His mind was delirious with pain, and the demons in his brain were laughing and screaming to further confuse him. He had barely heard a word the prophet had spoken.

But, seeing the desert ascetic beckoning him nearer, he rose and hobbled forward. If this was where his wandering path ended – *then so be it!* Even death, should it come, would be less excruciating than the agonies and terrors he had suffered so far. Why live like this – with his mind destroyed? He had long-since ceased to be himself. Let Herod's spies seize him and the Archons gain full possession of his soul, if that was to be his fate. He *wanted* to die...

From his place on the rock, John descended into the water, to better see the face of the lamentable youth. But Jesus averted his gaze.

"Look at me!" John commanded.

And yet, the youth seemed utterly incapable of controlling his actions. His trembling soon mounted to convulsions. His eyes rolled up into his head.

John seized him by the hair and turned his face, staring deep into his eyes. Never had he seen so many demons mingling in a single soul! The sight of it sickened and repulsed him. Hundreds of their faces were surfacing in this tortured visage – grimacing, laughing, taunting him.

Sighing, John proceeded.

"<Three are the number of baptisms,>" he explained to his Orig Wld 122:13
distracted penitent. "<The first is for the forgiveness of sins.> With Bap A 41:10
every evil wish that has entered your heart, a demon has accompanied it. Your flesh has become sullied by desire; your soul marred by anger, envy, ignorance and pride. But the Jordan's waters can wash them away. Do you believe in the baptism that cleanses you of your

imperfections?"

Barely, Jesus nodded.

John placed his hands over the Nazarene's head. Then, seizing him by the hair, he plunged him deep into the Jordan.

At first, there were no signs of struggle. But soon, the body under the water started flailing and convulsing. The more it desperately tried to surface, the more John tightened his grip and threw his full weight upon it.

Huge bubbles erupted onto the surface of the water, carrying with them myriads of demons. Cleansed from the body, these shadows soared upward, screaming and cursing. Within moments, the surrounding air was thick with the foul smell of hellish beings. The sound, to John's ears, was deafening.

It seemed as if an eternity had passed before John hauled Jesus out of the water. With one great intake of air, Jesus filled his lungs – inhaling, as if, for the first time in his life...

Opening his eyes, the Nazarene was amazed. The sunlight reflecting off the Jordan sparkled miraculously, and the trickling of its water sounded like ethereal music.

The endless chatter of the demons was gone! He could clearly hear his own voice in his head! The demons had fled.

The bruises on his ribs had dispersed: he could breathe again without pain! He felt his left arm and found all the bones intact. A great euphoria filled his soul as he looked around him, seeing the world, as if, in the first days of creation. This was the garden before the Fall of Man. This... was paradise.

The ascetic's stone features broke into a brief smile. He himself could hardly believe the miracle he had wrought.

"The second baptism," the Immerser intoned, "is the baptism of repentance."

John looked at Jesus deeply in the eyes, trying to convey the full import of his message.

"What is repentance," he asked, "but *metanoia* – 'a transformation
Bap A 41:33 of the mind'. You must *turn around your way of knowing!* <This
time, you will go down into the Jordan and its imperishable waters,
so that you may go up to the eternal Aeons.> It is just as you said:
3St Seth 127:20 '<the way of descent becomes the way of ascent.>' <But now it will
Bap B 42:10 become a movement from slavery into sonship, from the blindness
of the world into the sight of God.>"

Again, the penitent nodded his head.

"What is your name, my child?"

"Jesus... " he murmured.

For a long moment, John looked at him, trying to connect the face to the name, and the name to something distant and unknown.

"And where do you come from?"

"The town of Nazareth in Galilee."

"Jesus of Nazareth..." the Baptist intoned. After slowly articulating those words, he tilted his head – as if listening to a voice deep within himself. Then, he nodded, acknowledging the oracle that had been given.

"Jesus of Nazareth is your worldly name," John said with a
smile. "<But I have been sent to baptize you in the Living Water, Melch 16:11
and pronounce your hidden name. It will become a name among the + Gr Pow 36:15
living names inscribed in the water and the light.>"

Again, he placed his hands on the youth's head.

"<This is the holy baptism of those who know the eternal Ap Adam 85:22
knowledge – born of the word written in the Living Water: *Yesseus... Mazareus... Yessedekeus!*>"

A second time, Jesus was submerged in the Jordan. But this time, he surfaced immediately – and opened his eyes to a world newly formed.

John was looking at him curiously. The Nazarite prophet, with his long matted beard and darkly ringed eyes, somehow looked different. Then, the Nazarene recognized that it was *his own face* staring back at him. Jesus saw the Baptist, but he also saw his own features, as if, *in a mirror*. Their two faces had mingled into one.

Startled, Jesus looked towards the shore. There, in the shallows, Thomas and Magdalene stood anxiously before the crowd. And they also shared his features. He was them and they were he. He could not only see this, but feel it in his heart: an overwhelming feeling of sympathy for these two, whose lives were now his own.

The moment John had pronounced his hidden name, the clay encasing his heart had crumbled, and the love within was released. But such a love he had never felt before: it was an opening of the heart to sharing and compassion, existing in total unison with those who lived around him...

"The third baptism," John intoned, his voice resounding as if it
were Jesus' own, "is the revelation. <You have already been given Tri Prot 48:7
the Water of Life, which stripped you of the chaos and uttermost darkness of the abyss.>"

Jesus nodded in remembrance – the miracle of cleansing and renewal.

Tri Prot 48:7 "Now," John said, his eyes sparkling, "<you will put on the
Tri Prot 48:7 shining Light, which is *knowledge* of the Father above.> <As you
enter the light, the baptizers will baptize you, and the enrobers enrobe
you. That robe is your garment of light – the light of knowledge,
remembrance and awakening. You will return to the way you were,
before you fell down into this dark place... the way you were in the
beginning – when you were still *in* the Light.>"

The son of Mary stared in awe, wondering how he could be saying these things to himself.

John smiled and said: "Yes, the third baptism is the mystery.
Tri Tr 128:30 <It is called 'the silence' because of the quiet and tranquility that it
brings. It is also called 'the bridal chamber' because of the state of
unity that it brings between the knower and the known. Last of all, it
is called 'the light', because it is like an invisible light which we do
not see, *but become* – we put on the flameless light that never sets:
immortal, eternal life.>"

The desert dweller drew himself up to his full height, inhaled
Tri Prot 45:12 deeply, and intoned, "<I am inviting you into the exalted, perfect
Light!>"

Then, reaching down, he cupped his hands with water, and blew his breath across it. Gently, he poured the blessed water over the brow of the catechumen.

The moment a luminous drop of water touched the Nazarene's
V Allog bowed head, <a cloud of light surrounded them, enclosing them
and engulfing them in its luminous mist. From that cloud came a
Ap Jn 1:2 holy word and heavenly light.> In a flash, <the skies opened and the
whole of creation shone.>

The light was so overwhelming, that the crowds on the shores
Tri Prot 48:15 were blinded. But the Baptist could still see <three mighty angels
descending through the watery light – *Micheus*, *Michar* and
Mnesinous – who immersed Jesus in the spring of the Water of
Life.

Then, like glimmering reflections, three angels more descended
– *Yammon*, *Elasso* and *Amenai* – and invested him with his
shimmering Robe of Light.> Enhaloing him from top to bottom,
Unt MS <this garment radiated with the splendour of eternal life and light,>
bathing him gloriously in its white and golden phosphorescence.

Suddenly, John himself began trembling. There, in the heavens, an image appeared, fulfilling all that he had forespoken.

Unt MS <The veils of the aeons drew back,> and a luminous figure
Unt MS began descending in the form of a man. <On his head was a crown

of light, radiating with majesty and splendour.> <As John watched, Ap Jn 2:1
the youth transformed in appearance, becoming like a regal old man,
and then, like a lowly servant or child. There was not a plurality
of images before him, but one likeness in three forms, appearing
through each other in the light:> an old man, a youth, and a child.

<Thus, the thrice-powered Christ appeared in the heavens, Unt MS
bathed in myriads upon myriads of glories. The Son who was hidden
came forth> and descended into Jesus, who stood half-immersed in
the Jordan.

Then, new signs were shown forth on earth. In recognition of
this miracle, the banks of the river trembled and its bottom shook.
Shivering with wonder, John watched as the Jordan, his beloved
river, began to *flow backwards*. Yes, <the moment the Messiah had Test Tr 30:20
come into the world, *the Jordan had turned back*.> The way of *the
Descender* had become the way of *the Ascender*: from the Dead Sea,
the river now flowed towards life...

From the Jordan's crumbling banks, the blinded crowds could
not perceive any of this. Some of them, by squinting, could discern
a flurry of wings. Others saw <a holy spirit descending on Jesus in Test Tr 39:22
the form of a dove.> Many stepped backward in awe while others
fell forward, praying. To some, it was the end of the world; to others,
the beginning of the aeon to come.

The banks of the Jordan and all the surrounding hills manifest
<the fullness of the Kingdom of Heaven.> Then, in a moment, it was Gs Phil 70:34
over – and all returned to the way it was before.

John looked at Jesus and, for the first time, he could see a spark of light shimmering in the Nazarene's eyes, illuminating their darkened depths. The youth's stance was erect, and his features manifest an odd mix of gentleness and strength; meekness and determination.

Christ turned to face the crowds, which were shuffling uneasily in the aftermath of his revelation. From behind him, the prophet spread wide his arms and cried: "Behold, the Messiah of the Five Seals!"

Immediately, the demoniacs turned away, screaming and cursing; they could not bear to behold the image of Christ on earth. Embittered, they retreated, pushing and forcing their way through the crowds.

Meanwhile, the Baptist's disciples smiled, lifted their hands and cried once, twice, three times – *Hosanna!*

But a significant number in the crowd also started advancing. These, as they stepped into the Jordan's shallows, unsheathed their swords. In a moment, other weapons were produced: nets and ropes and grappling hooks. Herod's spies had their orders, and would execute them on this day.

Upon seeing the traitors in their midst, many of John's disciples started rushing forward. They had to reach their master before the soldiers. But the retreating demoniacs blocked their passage and held them fast while Herod's guard advanced.

Jesus turned to John. The Baptist was gazing at the unfolding
events, his withered face taut and decisive. The Voice of prophecy
Jn 3:30 echoed in his ears: <*My decline shall be his rising!*> The desert
ascetic was determined to meet their captors, and surrender himself
so the Messiah could go free.

But, holding John close to him, the saviour set out towards their adversaries. The Baptist could see their weapons flashing in the air. Why they were confronting their captors – openly, peacefully, unarmed? The saviour kept a firm grip on him and advanced.

Three more steps, and they were within weapons' reach.

Then, the soldiers were upon them, surrounding them on all sides. Steel clashed against steel as nets went flying over their heads. Calls for order and cries of confusion were heard, as a strange disturbance spread through Herod's guard. Somehow, the spies had lost sight of the prophet and saviour.

Calmly, Jesus walked with John through the soldiers' terror and tumult, until they were safely past them.

Then, John's disciples quickly huddled round, concealing them in their midst, and escorted them to a secluded place.

PART II

VI. Perea

I

For three nights, the moon did not shine, and the starless heavens brooded over the earth. The desert maintained a dark and mysterious silence.

Hidden in the hills of Perea, the Baptist's disciples settled into their cavernous abodes. To Thomas and Magdalene they brought healing herbs, to soothe the bites and lacerations on their afflicted limbs. And, as night fell, they built secluded fires.

During the first night, Jesus maintained a curious silence. But his tacit presence, his stare and caring smile became, for his wounded companions, a comforting source of peace.

Then early the next morning he withdrew. Nearby was an abandoned cave, its crumbling terrace overlooking the wastelands of Perea. At the entrance stood a gnarled tree, its darkened roots deeply entrenched in the dry unyielding earth.

For three days and nights, Christ stood before this ancient terebinth, neither eating nor sleeping. He stood while at rest, his eyes half-open in serene contemplation.

With his hands held in prayer, the saviour stood upright, his body in perfect balance. His feet were pressed flat on the earth and his head remained absolutely erect as he gazed, silently and undistractedly, at the endless stretch of the horizon before him. Not even the arc of the sun or the hours of the day disturbed him.

Instead, as he 'stood at rest', he became increasingly aware of his own mind. He acquainted himself with all the different states of mind that arose, once his body was stilled and his soul was freed of distraction: how ideas came easily, once inner peace was achieved. How memory intensified and perception grew clearer, once understanding was attained. The myriad of forms before his eyes became more precise, acquiring a certain grace and perfection. And, with the gradual opening of his awareness to unhidden truth, his heart filled with love. Standing there before the endless horizon, he opened his arms and embraced his invisible bride: wisdom.

On the second day, he traced these states of mind to their source. At first, he became aware of a distinct order underlying their arrangement: they had arisen, on the previous day, three at a time. What is more, each triad had come to him during a distinct hour of the day: at dawn, mid-day, dusk and midnight. These four awakenings became, for him, Four Lights.

During the dawn, the awareness of Truth had come to him, accompanied by Grace and Form. Then, at mid-day, his Memory had become clear, inspiring Afterthought and Perception. At dusk, Love had descended, along with Understanding and Idea. Finally, at midnight, he had felt Peace, Perfection, and the most comforting of all – Wisdom.

These, he realized at last, were the twelve *Upper Aeons* – invisible and immoveable, above the apparent and ever-changing aeons that constituted the *Lower Aeons* of Yaltabaoth. Where the Archons, powers and demons claimed rulership over the body and soul, these were the aeons of awareness, never to be seen, and known only in the mind.

In his mind's eye he had seen the Upper Aeons, and how each triad had assembled, in descending order, around the Four Lights. They were like twelve angels, and the Four Lights shone like four
Ap Jn 7:30 archangels. <*Armozel*, *Oriel*, *Daveithai* and *Eleleth*> – those were
the names of the Four Lights, names which Jesus now *knew*.

He knew because he had *remembered*. During that brief but enlightening moment in the Jordan, when Christ had descended into the Nazarene, his memory had returned to him – a memory extending backward through time, and unto the first moments of creation. Now, this vision of the beginning was growing clearer in his mind.

He had begun to remember all the aeons and their names
Tri Tr 57:18 because, as Christ, he had existed 'from the beginning'. He was <the
Tri Tr 58:5 'first born' of the Father,> <the 'only-begotten one' – 'the Son who
was brother to himself alone'.> He had 'stood at rest' in the Upper
Ap Jn 7:30 Aeons, surrounded by his Four Lights. And the twelve aeons that

surrounded them were so many higher states of his awareness.

Through extended concentration, Jesus focussed his attention onto this forgotten foreknowledge – in an effort *to remember*. How much time had passed, he did not know when, finally, his thinking soared on high, and he came to behold Mind – that divine being which, in the ancient Greek tongue, was called *Nous*.

His own mind, with its limited attention span and endless need for diversion, could nevertheless reach, for a few rare moments of heightened meditation, a state of *Nous* – that greater Mind which peacefully and lovingly contemplated perfection for eternity.

In this higher state of awareness, he felt as if his lesser mind had ascended to the Upper Aeons. And there, in the greater Mind, all twelve states had momentarily combined: Perception became Perfection; Form manifest Grace; and Afterthought evoked Remembrance. Passing beyond Idea and Understanding, he had entered into Wisdom. These twelve states of mind fused in him to become a single, higher state of absolute *mindfulness*.

On the third day, feeling neither hunger nor fatigue, he traced this state of mindfulness to its source. At first, he concentrated his new-found awareness onto *Nous*. And, to his own great wonder, he found that *Nous* was not alone in the Highest Aeons.

For the complement of *Nous* was *Ennoia* – as the 'thought' Soph JC 9[6]:3
which naturally accompanied 'mind' and its 'thinking'. Indeed, they belonged together, like lovers: the masculine *Nous* and feminine *Ennoia* as the 'thinking' and the 'thought'. They were, when taken together, the hidden source of his higher awareness.

Then the Nazarene watched as, in a vision, these two invisible figures came together. They looked like twins, sharing the same features, and differentiated only by their gender. They gazed at each other, as if, into a mirror – desiring to be made one. Then slowly, their limbs entwined and their lips united. And, the moment they kissed, his awareness leapt to a higher, wordless state of ecstasy.

In his consciousness he experienced 'thought and thinking' *as one* – a state of complete awareness which was, indeed, *self-awareness*. This was what sly old Marsanes had called <thought- Meta 1075a
thinking-itself.>

At that moment, the Nazarene came to know himself. Not 'himself' as he existed each day, distracted and divided into a thousand moments of inattention. No, this was the higher Self which persisted over time and dwelt at the heart of his being. It was the source of unity that joined all his thoughts and all the moments

of his life together into a single timeless state of awareness. There
Ap Jn 4:11 was no passage of the hours now, no movement or measure <– only
stillness, repose, and eternal silence.>

That silence expanded and became all-encompassing. He felt himself 'within the Silence', surrounded by a comforting light. Indeed, he was floating in a sea of watery light where all forms seemed to glow from within. *Nous* and *Ennoia* were there; the Four Lights and Twelve Aeons were there, as luminous angels and archangels, simultaneously self-aware and aware of each other, reflecting each other, bathing each other with their overflowing light. They sang
3St Seth 121:10 their praises, individually and in harmony. <All were differentiated,
and yet, all were one.>

For the first time in his life, he felt himself in the presence of God. It was like nothing he could ever have imagined. Indeed, there was no image to describe this holy Presence, no name to speak of it. Rather, the Nazarene himself *was* the image and the name. Yes he, through his own unique existence, reflected the miracle of the divine Presence.

It was his present state of expanded awareness which made him into a momentary reflection of God's greater Consciousness. His sentience was like a divine spark which had come to know its source – a particle of light which, through its self-knowing, now reflected that greater expanse of Light and Awareness which was God himself.

Indeed, in the moment that he had achieved, not just awareness, but self-awareness – his mind had transcended all limits; it had reached up to the highest heavens, breathing in God's fragrance and tasting his eternal sweetness. For God was not just Awareness but *Self*-Awareness – the unfathomable unity of 'thought-thinking-itself'.

That was the Beginning. Suddenly, it all became clear in the Nazarene's mind. He had *remembered* all the way back to the foundation of the world...

In the beginning, God had thought a thought. At that moment, the divine unity had become *aware*; and it had become two – as the 'thinking' and the 'thought', *Nous* and *Ennoia*. They were the
Ap Jn 4:2 + 4:26 masculine and feminine aspects of the divine Oneness; they became
Tri Prot 45:2 the Father and the Mother of all.

But, since there was no other, except these two, his thought returned to him. His thinking and his thought turned, faced each other, and re-united. At that moment, 'thinking thought *itself*'. God moved from awareness to *self-awareness* – the divine One had reflected upon itself, making itself complete. It was now a totality, and one. In this way, the next step in creation had occurred. Through their union, the Father and the Mother had produced a third – the Son.

And through the Son, God was able to reflect upon himself:
for <the Son was *his* image,> <and bore *his* name.> But, just as the Tri Prot 37:20
Father and the Mother were two aspects of the same divine unity, so Tri Tr 116:28
was the Son. He was 'the face' which God saw in the mirror; he was Gs Tru 38:7
'the reflection' in the watery light – 'the name' of the unnameable
and 'the image' of the invisible.

Indeed, all the Upper Aeons became, in this way, extensions
of the divine One. The Father, Mother and Son were all images in
the watery light surrounding the One. And, as mirror images, they
reflected three differing aspects or 'aeons' of the same divine unity.
They gave the ineffable One three different names – holy names, Gs Egypt 41:6
names of praise. He was <the Son who beheld the Mother-Father>; Ap Jn 6:15
he was <the only-begotten Child> descended from <the Parent.> Gs Egypt 52:3

In the greater outreaches of his watery light, the Four Lights and Twelve Aeons also became so many mirrors, arranged row on row, reflecting the glory of the heavenly Light. Each new aeon became a new extension of the One's unity – another heavenly mirror surrounding him. They were all, in essence, images of that Oneness who dwelt at their centre as the source of all. Each of them was a light in Light.

How did the Nazarene know all this? How had he *remembered* it? As he turned his thoughts inward, he felt the mystery there, inside of him. In an instant, the unknown was made known to him. He became aware of that particle of divine light which had been apportioned to him from the beginning – and to him alone.

It was like a seed whose kernel contained a nascent vision of the
entire tree, from the crown, branches and fruit to their shared hidden
root. It was like <a crystal-clear drop of watery light, raining down Orig Wld 113:22
on him from the Upper Aeons.> He had felt its sparkle during his
baptism, and now it glowed inside him, a luminous pearl or invisible
flame – yes, <a divine spark which had emerged from the blinding, Unt MS
invisible Light.> It was his unique particle of life and light.

But more than that, it was eternal life, and a time-transcending memory of his true origin. It was *gnosis* – the hidden *knowledge* of his true identity: the realization that he himself was a light in Light.

It had always been there – inside of him. But his body, like a garment of darkness, had hidden it from him. Even his soul had deceived him – forgetful, dreaming distracted dreams. Deep within him he had found something pristine, pure and clear, like an invisible life-breath. Yes, that was it! The word that best described it was *pneuma* – that first intake of *breath* which inspired all life and awareness.

He touched his hand to his chest and felt the fullness of the *pneuma* inside of him. His heart rejoiced, his mind soared in jubilation, for he had finally remembered the most precious of all gifts. Above body and soul rose the *spirit* from within.

II

When Jesus rejoined his companions, it was nightfall, and they were gathered round the campfire to keep themselves warm. Respectfully, the Baptist and his disciples withdrew to the innermost reaches of their cavern.

Magdalene and the Iscariot were silent and pensive, huddled in their hides of rough camel-hair. Each was wondering – what, exactly, had happened to their beloved brother?

Christ sat before them, manifesting a grace and ease utterly incongruent with the Jesus that they knew. His eyes were afire, his face radiant.

"Each morning, when we awoke," Thomas began in a low voice, "we saw you standing there in front of that tree... We ate, we slept – but you didn't move once."

"I was standing at rest," the saviour replied calmly.

The Iscariot gave him a curious stare, but the Nazarene said nothing.

Instead, Jesus blinked his eyes a couple of times, shifting his gaze back and forth between his bride and his twin. But – it was clear – Miri and Thomas still resembled him completely. He could not look at them without the sensation of looking at a mirrored reflection of himself.

"We even approached you once," Magdalene admitted. "But you were so absorbed in your thoughts that..." she hesitated. Then, bowing her head in embarrassment she whispered, "...we withdrew in shame."

Jesus smiled, blushing ever so slightly. "Forgive me, my dearest companions – my mind was elsewhere. But all's one now..."

Seeing the same shame that they had felt now spreading over

the saviour's face, his friends began to feel more at ease.

This gladdened the saviour. But, deep within, Jesus was startled to discover the true source of his embarrassment: Miri, his mirror-image, had turned crimson. And his heart, full of pity and compassion for her, had responded by blushing as well. Her shame had become his own.

"But what did you do during all that time?" the Iscariot asked at last. His grey eyes were fixed on his brother with a desperate need to know.

The son of Mary remembered his mother – and the horror that had come over her face when he'd asked her about his father – his true Father. How could anyone describe the experience of standing in his presence?

"Once the distractions had fled," he let fall, "my vision grew clear. I concentrated my thinking until finally..." Jesus looked up,
"my mind soared into the highest heavens, and I *saw* God <– that Ap Jn 2:31
pure Light into which no eye can look.> In ecstasy, <I inhaled the Dial Sav 133:10
Father's fragrance,> and tasted on my lips <the abundance of his Tri Tr 55:31
untasteable sweetness...>" +Tri Tr 56:15

The Iscariot gazed at him in awe. "You *saw* God?" His eyebrows arched, barely hiding his disbelief.

"I learned to 'stand at rest,'" Jesus corrected himself. "I stood within his infinite Silence."

He was pensive for a moment. Then, looking at them earnestly,
the saviour explained: "<I withdrew from the world to search deeper Allog 60:13
into myself. And, the moment I came to know myself, I was filled with a revelation. In a state of blessedness, I merged with my *Self.* Yes, I came to 'stand at rest' in the silence and stillness. Through an unknowing knowledge, I came to know the One who exists in me – the One who is unknowable, the One who, himself, eternally stands at rest in silence and stillness.>"

The Nazarene's companions stared at him. They hadn't understood a word.

Worst of all, Jesus could feel in his heart *what* they were feeling – not just incomprehension and confusion, but *fear* that he was still, indeed, in a state of total delusion. His distraction had now mounted, they thought, to a state of divine madness. He thought he *was* God.

A fearful shudder passed through him. Was it possible – that *they* were right, and he had been hallucinating all this time? The harsh, unrelenting doubt in Thomas' eyes filled him with fear and uncertainty. Even Magdalene was avoiding his gaze, trying not to show him her sorrow and grief. Her beloved, she thought, was still the victim of his visions.

For a few moments, all of them stared mutely into the fire.

And suddenly the Nazarene felt a stirring in his soul. *Blaomen* was there – that demon of *fear* he knew all to well. And *Nenentophni* had come with him, the evil angel who inspires all *grief.* As the fire danced in his companions' eyes, he could see the demons there rejoicing – and even feel them revelling in his own flesh.

The Nazarene turned his attention inward, seeking that centre of calm which neither fear could touch nor grief disturb. In a moment, he found it – the inner state of rest which existed in his spirit's quietude.

Raising his eyes, Christ radiated calm and acceptance. And the moment his bride and twin looked into his eyes, their frightful sorrow departed. *Blaomen* and *Nenentophni* cursed him and fled.

Miri and Thomas felt a warm flush on their faces, and a comforting silence surrounding their ears.

The saviour let out a re-assuring laugh. "Fear and grief were here among us – like demons disrupting peace of mind – only to flee in haste."

Dial Sav 122:16 Then he held up his hand and said: "<Truly, fear has great
Ap Jn 28:21 power!> <For, from fear, forgetfulness, ignorance and sin, the whole of creation is made blind. They deceive and distract us, so none may come to know God.>"

He took one of the sticks burning in the fire and held it in his hand. A small flame danced on its tip.

"You have said, Thomas my brother, that you will never *know*
Ap Adam 83:11 anything. But I say to you, <– blessed is he who has acquired the *gnosis*, for he has come *to know God*.>"

He blew on the wood till the flame was extinguished and its tip glowed with light.

Ap Adam 83:11 "<Like a stilled light from flickering fire, only they – the knowing ones – have 'stood' in his Presence, and acquired the *gnosis*, which is
Gs Tru 31:28 absolute knowledge of God.> I have come among you, as the <way
Ap Jn 30:33 for those who are wavering.> <I am the *remembrance* of knowledge long-forgotten; I am the light which exists in the Light...>"

While Christ said these things, Jesus was listening to himself with a disquieting feeling of unease. It was not he, Jesus, who had said these things, but the Word, the Christ *in him*.

In a terrible moment of epiphany, the son of Mary understood the nature of his apotheosis. During his third baptism in the Jordan,

when Christ had descended into him, the saviour <had 'put on' Tri Prot 50:12
Jesus> like a garment. Indeed, Christ <had 'put on' humanity and Silv 110:14
become a man – to reveal to men their hidden divinity.>

The perfect saviour had disguised himself in the fallible flesh of Jesus – so as to walk covertly among men, secretly enlighten them, and chase away their evil spirits. Jesus could feel the unbegotten Son inside him now – a concealed epiphany poised to illuminate the all.

But Jesus himself, with his faults, hopes and fears, was also Tr Res 44:21
necessary for the Messiah. The Anointed One had to move among men – smile and laugh, even suffer and fail, so that men would see *in him* the possibility of their own perfection and enlightenment. The thought of it, that moment, made Jesus dizzy with wonder.

During all this time, Thomas was trying to assimilate the intimations stirring in his heart with the doubts still troubling his mind.

"You said that, *by knowing ourselves*, we will come *to know God...*"

The Nazarene nodded – understanding his brother's confusion all to well... It was the Iscariot's doubt and double-mindedness that trapped him in ignorance.

The saviour said: "<Thomas my brother, while you still have Th Cont 138:4-39
time in the world – listen to me... and have faith that I'll reveal those things which you've been pondering in your mind for so long.>"

Warily, the son of Kerioth nodded for Christ to continue.

"<You have been called my twin and true companion. Well Th Cont 138:4-39
then, examine yourself, and learn *who* you are. Something is strangely amiss when *you*, my beloved brother, remain ignorant of yourself!>"

The Iscariot bowed his head, his brow now burning with shame. Did he know? Had the Nazarene divined his dark inner schism – 'the twin' and 'the hanged man' who battled for possession of his soul?

Renewed doubt seized him. How could Thomas ever *know himself*, when his dark shadow Judas always hid himself in the depths?

Christ re-opened his mouth: "The self is like the sea: infinite and deep. Still, you must dive into your own darkened depths.
Abjure ignorance, and confront your greatest fear! For, <whoever Th Cont 138:4-39
knows himself has, at the same time, come to know the depths of the all.>"

"The depths of *the all?*" The gloomy son of Kerioth replied, looking up into the night sky. The darkness of night was impenetrable. Th Cont 138:4-39 "<I've beheld what is *obscure* to men, what they ignorantly stumble against in the darkness – but *that* is all...>"

Th Cont 138:4-39 The saviour answered, saying: "<If the things that are visible seem obscure to you, then how will you ever come to know the things that are *not visible?*> How will you climb the invisible heights, if you are still frightened by their shadowy depths?"

Who, Thomas wondered, was speaking to him now? Was this the voice of Jesus? Or did his words resonate with some mysterious 'other'? Had he just heard the voice of the Messiah?

Th Cont 139:12 "Only you," Thomas addressed the other, "<can speak of those things which are hidden in the light." With dark desperation in his eyes, he added, "Reveal it then – so *your* light may enlighten us...>"

Th Cont 139:12 The Messiah gave him a re-assuring nod. "<Truly, it is *in* light that the Light exists!> But first, you must relax your restless thinking
Zost 1:10 and seek out the stillness within you – quell <the psychic chaos and somatic darkness of your mind!> Then, my brother, you will begin
Dial Sav 133:23 to 'stand at rest'. For, <if you do not learn to stand at rest *here*, in the darkened world below, then you will *never* come to stand in the light that lies above.>"

Having said this, Christ realized that his words and their speaking would never awaken the Iscariot. With compassion rising in his heart, the saviour moved himself closer and cupped his hands around his brother's face.

Then, caressing his hair, he said: "In the flesh, your name is
Gs Egypt 69:9 Judas-Thomas. But you also have a spiritual name – the name which God himself has spoken, and which calls to him those who would
Gs Tru 21:27 *know* him. Yes, <each and every one with the *gnosis* also has a name which the Father himself has uttered.> That name carries the *pneuma*, and in that *breath*, the spirit."

Melch 16:11 Christ touched the Iscariot's forehead and said: "<I pronounce
+ Gr Pow 36:15 for you now your hidden name – as a name among the living and holy names, inscribed now and forever in the clear watery light.>"

Then, bringing his face close to his twin, he whispered, "*Didymos*," and kissed him on the lips. A slight breath escaped him, and entered into the other, who felt a tremendous gust of wind rushing through his soul.

The moment Jesus withdrew, the eyes of his brother were opened. Judas-Thomas saw that he was indeed the *didymos*, the *twin*. For, looking at Christ, he saw himself.

"Tell me what you see..." Jesus asked.

The twin hesitated, since his mind was besieged with wonder.
Then, <Judas-Thomas, now *Didymos*,> whispered, "I see myself in Gs Thom 32:10
you..."

"Indeed," the Messiah replied, "you see <the son of God, whose Soph JC 100:3
likeness is within you.> <All those who hear me with the ears of Acts Jn 100
truth shall be united with me. Yes you – if you do indeed hear me
– *shall be as I am*. For, from me, you are that which I am...>"

"Then – let me hear you say it..." The son of Kerioth stammered. "Who are you..?"

"<He that truly hears me shall join in oneness with me. He will Acts Jn 100
no longer be as he was, but *above himself*, as I am. When I – and
you as I – am with myself, then the Father is with me, and I am with
him, in the All.> In that moment, <I, and the Father, and the All – are Jn 10:30
made one... all perfectly one.>" + Jn 17:20

The Iscariot's mind was reeling. He had never felt this state
of unity before – a state of *absolute certainty*... knowing one thing
only... that <'all are one', and are so linked that one cannot be Ascl 1
separated from the other.> Without seeing, without hearing – he
knew he now 'stood' in the presence of God. He could feel it inside
him and around him: a divine Presence that dwelt eternally, as the
hidden source of *all* beings. This realization reduced him to utter
speechlessness.

Then Jesus, turning towards Mary Magdalene, smiled and said: "I haven't forgotten you either, my sister, my bride. For you alone are my beloved; you alone are my soul."

Miri lowered her head. Since fear and shame had fled from her heart, she had felt a strange new feeling stirring within – a nameless ardour combining love and devotion into a higher, hidden passion.

The saviour placed himself opposite her, and gently cupped her face in his hands.

"Many times <the Bridal Chamber invited us in.> But each Gs Phil 85:19
time we dared enter, it closed its door upon us. And yet, there is
another form of union <– a marriage made perfect by the will of the Ex Soul 134:5
Father.> Do you wish it, Miri my beloved – to be wedded with me
in the perfect marriage?"

Magdalene's heart beat wildly, like a light-seeking moth caught in lace curtains. She thought of all the ordeals she had experienced in the last months – Tyre and the Ethiopian, Capernaum and the village elders, the Widow's Tower and her nightmares – all of it a strange descent into wisdom and folly, into holiness and whoredom.

Though she had gained a strange knowledge of herself, there was so much more to herself that she still did not know.

Still absorbed in these thoughts, Miri nodded her head in silence.

Thund 20:26 “<Then hear me, you hearer!> <From heaven, the Father sent
Ex Soul 132:6 the soul her man, who indeed was her brother. As a bridegroom,
+ Ex Soul 132:23 he came down to his bride. She renewed herself, becoming like a
virgin. And together, they entered the Bridal Chamber.>”

Auth T 22:26 Touching her closed lids with his fingertips, he said: “<Her
bridegroom applied the word to her eyes, to make her see with her
mind and perceive her brother as he truly is.>”

Then he smiled and said: “He called her by name, and offered
her that kiss which would consecrate her to him as bride. Many are
Thund 14:12 your names, my beloved. <For you are the word whose appearance
is multiple, and you are the voice whose sound is manifold.> You
Melch 16:11 are *Sophia, Achamoth, Prunikos*. <Thus I have pronounced for you
+ Gr Pow 36:15 your hidden names, the living and holy names, inscribed ever and
always in the clear watery light.>”

With her eyes pressed shut, Magdalene shuddered. She was amazed to hear him speak those names which had been revealed to her only in her dreams...

Christ brought his lips close to Magdalene’s – so close, that they almost touched.

Auth T 22:23 “<Secretly, her bridegroom fetched it,” he whispered. “He
presented it to her mouth, in order that she might receive what is
truly hers...>” As he spoke these words, his breath entered her.

2Ap Jas 56:14 Then the Nazarene <took hold of her, saying: “My beloved,
behold... I reveal to you those things which no eye has seen nor ear
has ever heard.” And he kissed her on the mouth.>

The moment his lips were withdrawn, Magdalene’s eyes filled with tears. She saw her beloved as he truly was. And, she saw herself in him – made perfect, blessed, holy, even divine. No longer were they separate, for the two had been made one in spirit.

Acts Jn 95 “<I am a mirror to whoever looks and sees me,>” he said.

Magdalene’s heart filled with joy. She wiped the tears from her eyes and blinked several times, laughing because she was unable to comprehend the mystery: her face and his face had merged into a single countenance.

But, more than that, she saw her own, higher feminine aspect. She saw Sophia – that Sophia who had always hidden herself in her soul. United in the perfect marriage, she now saw the faces of Christ and Sophia, fused as one.

The ardour that filled her heart that moment was beyond all words. And yet, she could see its expression on Christ and Sophia's countenance: a love without need of possession, a longing without fear of desire.

How could she describe that higher, hidden passion? It was the ecstasy of 'otherness' felt in the selfless act of sharing. And, through the unity it inspired, it became a joyful giving with no fear of sacrifice. It was love given wilfully in the knowledge of hidden oneness.

Feeling herself thus, at one with the Nazarene, she whispered
seven words. And he, knowing her mind, whispered them at the
same time. In unison, they announced, "*<I am the bride and the* Thund 13:26
bridegroom.>"

Then, the smile that illuminated their faces transformed into rapturous laughter.

Soon, the twin joined them, and the three celebrated their new-found state of 'standing at rest': open-hearted, joyfully aware and mindfully at peace.

III

"Asses and swine!" Herod Antipas screamed in anger.

He paced around the room, hollering at the ceiling, "I'm surrounded by asses and swine – by smiling lackeys and slow-witted fools!"

Then he pointed a shaking finger at Chuza and ordered, "Bring me the commander responsible for our failure!"

He resumed his pacing back and forth while Chuza stood, silent and contrite, at the centre of the chamber. The pine torches blazed from their bronze and silver cressets. Reclining by the royal divan, Herodias and Salome watched in amusement as the Tetrarch's fury mounted.

"Twelve men were stationed at the Jordan! *Twelve!* And the Baptist with his Messiah *just marched right through them!* They'll pay for their incompetence with their lives..!"

This anger of his, Chuza thought to himself, is a good thing. It need only be redirected onto the Baptist...

"The man is being brought as we speak," the Vizier announced. "He was there, and will recount everything that happened."

"I don't want excuses!" the Tetrarch screamed. "I want

satisfaction!” He leaned his full weight against the window sill and shook his head in disbelief.

“It’s a conspiracy!” he muttered to himself. “They saw the Five Seals – saw their power – and decided to keep its secret for themselves. Now they’re collaborating with the others; plotting my overthrow! Yes, the priesthood was also there at the Jordan – disguised, waiting... My men have the secret, and are acting in collusion with Caiaphas and Annas! I’ll assassinate the lot of them...”

Herod Antipas looked out the window of his palace, which was perched on the west hill of Jerusalem. Across the way, he could see a frantic movement on the rooftop of the Temple – priests and astrologers were running back and forth, making their reports to the Head Priest.

Looking up, Antipas saw that, indeed, something strange was stirring in the heavens. From behind blackened clouds, lightning streaked across the abyss. A strange darkness spread over the night, and the stars began fading, like dead flies falling to the earth. Suddenly the glowing moon was engulfed by a swirling mist, which stained the sky a frightening scarlet hue.

Atop the Temple, Caiaphas clawed at his beard and screamed at his head stargazer. “You ignorant ape! These movements in the heavens portend some dark calamity! You are our soothsayer – read them! Decrypt their ill-intents!”

The astrologer pounded the sides of his head with his fists.
Orig Wld 104:15 “Never have we seen such chaos in the cosmos! <The seven heavens
make war with one other!> Some earthly disturbance has upset the entire firmament!”

Just then, Annas appeared with a blind Zealot at his side. The Sadducee Elder bore in his hands a missive sealed from the Jordan.

“That will suffice, you fool!” Annas commanded. “Leave us at once.” Bowing and scraping, the soothsayer departed.

The Elder broke the seal and cast his eyes over the report. Turning to Caiaphas, his baleful glance struck the High Priest like the sting of a scorpion’s tail.

“The Messiah is among us,” he announced, tapping the scroll with a long forefinger.

Caiaphas felt dizzy and delirious – as if the spinning heavens were pouring into his brain.

“The five-sealed Christ?” he whispered.

"He has appeared as foretold – at the Jordan... a man baptized by John amid flashes of light and a flurry of wings. Then he disappeared..."

Caiaphas was speechless.

Annas smiled bitterly. "The Baptist and his Messiah walked through Herod's soldiers, passed by all of our spies – and vanished from sight. No one moved to stop them."

Caiaphas managed to push forth a few pitiful phrases.

"No one? B-b-b-but how? H-h-h-how could they escape..?"

Annas looked up and a smile twisted his face.

"Only heaven knows..."

In the skies above the Temple, a great tumult had seized the seven heavens.

From *Athoth* down to *Abel*, the seven doorkeepers had left their posts and gathered in the court of Yaltabaoth. Even the five Archons of the lower depths had left the sublunar realm. From *Belias* to *Abrisene* they had ascended.

A war had spread across the aeons and pandemonium reigned in the upper palace. In anger, each Archon was accosting his brother, accusing him of lies and deception.

At the centre of the great chamber stood a throne, its foundation
<a chariot with eight-faced cherubim. Ornamented with angels, Orig Wld 104:35
eagles, lions and bulls, these guardians gazed in all four directions.> Atop this blazing throne, a leonine serpent slept with its eyes open.

Suddenly Yaltabaoth rose from his coils and let out a thunderous roar that shook the palace and silenced them all.

"Seven rulers over seven heavens, and five over the abyss," he hissed, "making twelve Archons in all! Christ descended through each of your gates – and *none* of you saw him? None of you *seized* him?"

Athoth and *Belias*, the first and the last, approached the Archigenetor's throne. The one who rules the highest heaven spoke first.

"The saviour deceived us!" *Athoth* cried. "<Before each gate, Tri Prot 47:13
he exchanged his garment, appearing to each gatekeeper as one of
their own! He hid himself within them,> <appearing to the Archons Tri Prot 49:15
as an Archon, to the powers as a power, and to the demons as a demon.> He eluded *every one*."

The court erupted once more with blame, accusation, and cries of denial. But Yaltabaoth's ear-piercing hiss called them all to order.

"But you, *Belias*," the Archigenetor cried, "you rule over the lowest of the depths. Your powers and demons form a mighty army on earth. None of them *saw* Christ appear?"

Belias bowed his head before the Chief Archon and recounted the tragedy in its entirety.

Gr Pow 44:30 "All your plans were thwarted my lord! <At the appointed time,
the Archons and powers had devised to send down *your* Son – as an *imitator*,> the false Messiah that would lead the multitude astray.

"After your appearance at the Temple in Jerusalem, the one called Jesus had been well-prepared. His mind was under our command, his body our instrument. He was chosen as the receptacle,
L Pt Ph 136:16 the <mortal mold> for the Archigenetor's Son. That is why, when he
approached the Jordan, our demoniacs proclaimed him king; they were anticipating the descent of your Son."

Belias released a cry of anger.

"But Christ learned of our stratagem, and turned it against
Tri Prot 49:7 us! <The saviour clothed himself as the Archigenetor's Son! He
descended disguised, and the Archons let him pass, thinking *he*
Gs Egypt 64:1 was their Christ.> <He nailed them down one by one!> Then, in the
Jordan, the Baptist cleansed the mortal mold – and Christ entered the one called Jesus. The light is now hidden in the depths of the abyss!"

For a long time, Yaltabaoth deliberated the significance of these events. Then, with a thunder that shook the heavens, the lion-faced serpent laughed.

Ap Jn 30:16 "<In fear of our wickedness, he has hidden himself – thinking
Ap Jn 30:23 we will not recognize him!> <But to accomplish his task, Christ has
left the light behind, and entered into the midst of our darkness.>
2Ap Jas 46:12 <World after world he passed, stripping himself of his protective
garments – so that now he subsists in a naked and perishable state.>
L Pt Ph 136:16 The fool has <become a mortal man!>"

A cruel smile distorted his face.

"And now he has entered, unarmed and defenceless, into the middle of our prison! He is trapped in a seven-walled fortress where watchers and door-keepers are guarding every gate! He has even shut himself in the five-walled fortress of the body, where three hundred
Ap Jn 31:3 and sixty demons can influence his every movement! Encompassed
by the *Heimarmene*, the Messiah has fallen victim to Fate!"

"But we have no power over him!" *Belias* lamented. "He knows our names! Our demons flee at his command!"

"Christ may command us," the serpent spit out, "but we can control his earth-born receptacle! The body, even the soul of Jesus lies under our influence. *And* we command those who surround
him! Already, the earthen rulers and <lovers of power> have tried to Tri Tr 80:3
entrap him. The greedy Annas and his vain High Priest; the lustful
Herod and his angry steward – all are <usurpers and apostates, Tri Tr 79:26
sword-bearers and war-mongers who crave the Messiah's power.>
We will increase their appetite, encourage their every movement, until they surround the Messiah, seize him and eliminate him."

Athoth bowed his head low and observed, "But the Baptist also commands our demons."

"His asceticism protects him," the Archigenetor allowed. "But we may still rule his fate! The princess Salome will play well into our hands. And the two companions of Jesus – Magdalene the whore and Judas the betrayer – *they may serve us well indeed*. We will align their doubts and desires with the schemings of the earthen rulers."

Yaltabaoth quivered with delight, while a myriad of stars and ill-omens passed over his serpentine body in the skies.

Then he turned to *Athoth* and asked, "But what of my son? Has he still been sent?"

"Yes, my Lord. He has descended into the blind prophet Barabbas."

Yaltabaoth nodded. "Soon he will work his wonders, and turn the multitude against him! The False Messiah will arise, and cast a long shadow over the Anointed One."

Yaltabaoth smiled, his amber eyes afire, his poisoned fangs glistening.

"Once the Messiah is seized, where can he turn? The fleshly receptacle will perish, and its heavenly descender flee in fright. But we, anticipating his every movement, will bar the saviour's ascent. Our cosmos is a maze with countless corridors, traps and turnings.
Encircled by our world, lost in a labyrinth of space and time, <his Jn 1:5
light will be subsumed by shadow, till darkness overcomes him!>"

Malicious laughter filled the throne room, resonating in the heavens like a terrible rumbling.

"<And once 'the proclaimed king' has been slain, *we* shall rule Tri Tr 121:15
the world as its only true sovereigns!>"

Staring into the swirling skies, Annas shuddered. The depths of its abyss made him dizzy with fear.

"The Messiah has appeared," Caiaphas accepted, "– but what of his Five Seals? Has he revealed them?"

Annas met the eyes of his High Priest. "They remain a mystery. He guards them – as the secret to his power."

"Then it's not too late! We can still seize them for ourselves," Caiaphas declared, his fists clenching. The thought of their possession stirred in his soul like a terrible hunger. The full attainment of his priestly power and glory depended on them.

"And this man will serve us to that end," Annas announced, indicating the blind Zealot beside him. "I give you – Barabbas."

Like Malachai, Isaiah and Ezekiel, this anchorite with the long entangled beard bore the distinctive robe of the ancient prophets. His cold blue eyes, though clouded over with cataracts, gazed at the world with avid fanaticism.

"You would ally us with a Zealot?" the High Priest wondered aloud.

He knew that his father-in-law, a Sadducee noble, hated the Zealots with a passion. Thieves and assassins, they won countless adherents among the poor and down-trodden. Their alliance with the knife-wielding *Sicarii* even threatened the Sadducee balance of power.

"I too had my doubts," Annas admitted. "But this Zealot was most persuasive. The times, he rightly observed, have called for a truce between our two camps. Without his knowing it, the one called 'Christ' has sown unity among his enemies – and now we ally ourselves against him."

The blind prophet nodded, acknowledging their stares with his unseeing eyes. He held out two shaking hands, which the counterfeit priests took into their grasp – thus sealing their unholy alliance.

"We offer our people a choice," Annas said, gripping the others' hands tightly, "– Jesus or Barabbas! Our Zealot preaches like the prophets of old, sowing fear and terror in the hearts of the unlearned. He will denounce the Baptist and the five-sealed Messiah, predicting that, if Jesus ever enters Zion's gate, it will presage the downfall of Jerusalem."

Caiaphas nodded, admiring the twisted genius behind his father's scheme.

"He will confront the Christ, time and again, until the people decide for themselves – which of these two is the Chosen One."

Barabbas' blind eyes sparkled with vengeance, and the trace of a serpentine smile slid across his face.

From his place before the window, Herod Antipas shivered and turned away. All these movements in the clouds darkened his mind with frightening anguish.

He thought back to three decades ago. Even then, when a disturbance had stirred the skies, Herod the Great had tried to seize the Messiah as a new-born child. But three mages had deceived him. Now, the Messiah had returned as a fully-grown man – and *again* eluded their grasp! Like his father before him, Herod Antipas had failed...

Who was responsible for the failure?

Antipas spun around and found a soldier standing at attention next to his Vizier.

"My lord," Chuza announced, "this is the commander who led our soldiers at the Jordan."

Herod approached the commander and observed him closely. Then, without saying a word, he drew the soldier's short-sword and posed its sharpened tip at the base of his throat.

The commander didn't move, but his neck muscles tensed.

"How long have you served me?" Antipas demanded.

"Seventeen years," he shouted.

The Tetrarch withdrew the sword. Then, pacing back and forth, he weighed its efficacy as a killing tool.

"We will tolerate no circumvention, no deception," he said flatly. "Now tell me what happened."

Salome and Herodias, who had been reclining on their couch, sat forward attentively. As experts in deceit, they were watching his face for the slightest sign of betrayal.

"Disguised as pilgrims," the commander began, "my soldiers and I watched from the Jordan's shore as John baptized the one called Jesus. There was a blinding light, a strange movement in the water, and the banks of the river shook. Then, when all had grown calm, John spread his arms and announced that this was indeed the Messiah of the Five Seals."

"And next?" Antipas demanded impatiently.

"I ordered my men forward. We entered the river, drawing our nets and swords. There were only two of them and twelve of us."

Despite all attempts at restraint, the soldier started trembling. Herod Antipas swung the soldier's sword back and forth in anger.

"And..?" he screamed.

"And then, the two of them walked straight into our formation. We surrounded them with our swords, threw the nets – but immediately lost sight of them."

"Just like that?"

Antipas approached the soldier and flicked the sword in front of his face. "They disappeared – just like that?"

"No," the trembling soldier replied. "I saw them pass, but I didn't think to stop them."

"Why not?!" Herod shrieked.

"Because..." He broke down. He knew that all was lost, and his life was forfeit. "Because each of them looked just like me..."

"Each of them?"

The soldier nodded. "All anger departed. I was overcome by confusion. I didn't dare harm these images of myself."

"And your men?"

Gs Phil 58:2 "I questioned them afterwards. <The Messiah hid himself from everyone. They saw him, thinking that they were seeing themselves.> Each was too afraid to raise an arm against himself."

For a long time, Herod Antipas stared at the man in front of him, wondering if he had lost his senses. Then he turned to Herodias and Salome. Both of them silently shook their heads.

No deception. He had been telling the truth the whole time.

The Tetrarch handed back the soldier his sword.

"Dismissed!" he yelled and the soldier vanished.

Herodias and Salome approached Antipas. Instinctively, they felt threatened, and sought some assurance at his side.

But Antipas was looking at Chuza. Without words, each knew what the other was thinking: the Messiah possessed a weapon which rendered their army defenceless.

The Tetrarch was overcome by a sickening fear of the unknown. "Your recommendations?"

"We observe the one called Jesus. Follow his every movement. It's useless to try attacking him now. But in the meantime, we can still bring in the Baptist for questioning."

Herod Antipas nodded at Chuza. "Make it so!"

Salome thought of John, imprisoned in the palace dungeon – interrogated, even tortured. She would have to use all her powers of subterfuge to protect him. But, if she handled it properly, she would have access to him alone. She could have her beloved all to herself...

IV

As the darkness of night deepened, the Nazarene and his two companions retreated to the innermost reaches of the Baptist's cave. They found John and his disciples in a large vaulted hollow, illuminated by a central fire.

The master sat on a rock, surrounded by his students; he was answering those questions which would hopefully lead them from ignorance to awareness.

The moment he saw Jesus, John rose and greeted him with a ritual kiss. Then, a place was made for the three guests and the teacher resumed his teaching.

"Speak to us of prophecy," one of his followers said.

"To prophesy is to speak in a voice that transcends time," John replied simply. "It is not I who speak, but an eternal Voice that speaks through me."

"Then tell us about this Voice."

"It is <the hidden Voice that dwells within, and comes from Tri Prot 35:32
the immeasurable Silence.> <The voice carries within it the breath> Tri Prot 45:27
– and that breath is time-transcending knowledge of <the Silence Tri Prot 35:34
that surrounds us all.>"

To his own amazement, Jesus understood all that John was saying. But his disciples were uncomprehending.

"Speak to us," one of them said, "in a manner we may understand."

John raised his eyebrows. "Would you prefer me to speak of YHWH? – to praise Yaltabaoth and his heavenly hosts? He is the *old* God, the *false* God – whose lies and deceptions have since become known to us. The Temple recites them daily, fixing their phrases in our minds – but a true revelation requires a new language! That is
why, from the Silence above, <the Word has descended.>" Tri Prot 47:13-32

He bowed his head to Jesus.

"<The Voice has dipped *below* the Archons' language, to speak Tri Prot 41:26
the new mystery – a hidden mystery, to be revealed only to the
chosen few...>"

The desert ascetic transfixed his disciples with a piercing stare. Then, he laughed and said: "So that you may understand, know that
the immeasurable Silence *is* God. But such a one is <unnameable Ap Jn 3:14
and ineffable.> Though praised with a myriad of names, He is
<exalted above every name.> In the Silence, we give true praise to Pr Paul A:11

Gs Egypt 41:3 <the unproclaimable Father.>

John held out his hands as if to express through that tacit gesture the presence of the unspoken God.

"Know that, in the beginning, the Silence spoke: the unnameable Father *pronounced his own name*. And at that moment,
Tri Prot 46:5 the Voice and the Word came forth. <The Voice carried within it the
Tri Prot 45:28 Word,> and <the Word carried the breath,> which *is* the silent and unpronounceable name of the Father."

John looked up into the great height of the cavern. He spoke as if he could clearly see the mystery unfolding. "God is one – a unity for eternity. Thus, when the One pronounced its own name, it became a tri-partite unity – the Silence, the Voice, and the Word.
Tri Prot 37:20 They are like <the Father, the Mother and the Son – three aspects of the same eternal Being.>"

Then he closed his eyes, as if, to hear their hidden names. "Each
Tri Prot 38:7 of these aeons has its own name. <The Voice who bore the Word is named *Barbelo*. She is the Mother who remains ever-virgin.>

Magdalene and the Iscariot turned to one another. Each was thinking the same thing: where was Jesus' mother now? No doubt she was sitting alone in her room in Nazareth.

Gs Egypt 42:22 "She bore <the Son of the silent Silence.> <And he, the Word,
Jn 1:14, became flesh and dwelt among us.> His name is <*Yesseus*,> though
Gs Egypt 64:9 Jesus is his worldly name. It is he who announced the *pneuma* to the world – the breath that carries the unutterable name of the Father, pronounced in the holy living name of all those who would know him."

"And that is our baptismal name?" an attentive disciple asked.

Gs Tru 21:27 "Yes. All those <with the *gnosis* possess a name which the Father himself has uttered.> Their baptismal name is a hidden spiritual name, pronounced *once only*, during the baptismal rite. Thus, in their *pneuma*'s silence, they carry the unspeakable name which the Father pronounced in the beginning, in order to know himself. The Voice speaks it through me, and those who truly hear it, are invoked by the Father. They are called, they are roused to awakening, and they come to know the Father."

John looked at his disciples, and an expression of rapture came over his face.

"Indeed, the invocation is a great mystery! For the Father, in hearing the baptismal name, recognizes himself in it. It becomes one of the myriad of names offering him praise. And so, *He names himself through that name!* Indeed, He comes to know himself

through the names of all those who would know him. Thus, <their Melch 16:11
names become holy living names,> inscribed in the Book of the + Gr Pow 36:15
living – a book written in the Upper Aeons and published before
the beginning of time. <And all those whose names He knew from Gs Truth 21:25
the beginning will be called to him at the end.> They are the chosen
few; they are the Elect..."

A great silence descended over the gathering. Those who had not yet experienced God's unity felt pride and vainglory – for they thought themselves chosen above all others. But those who had penetrated deeper into the mystery felt great humility, for they knew it was their duty to liberate others from unknowing.

"Speak to us," one of them said, "of the mystery of baptism."

John gazed at his interlocutor, amazed at the question that had fallen from his lips. How could he ever render such a mystery into words?

"The ceremony of baptism," he began, "ritually makes present an event that took place *before* the foundation of the world. It is an image of the invisible, pre-existent baptism which first took place in the Upper Aeons. But to understand this, you must know the Upper Aeons and their images. Indeed, you must know the mystery of the beginning..."

John looked compassionately at the assembly of those gathered round him. All wanted to know, but were trapped in ignorance. Finally, his eyes came to rest on Jesus. The saviour nodded for him to continue.

But, with a downcast glance, John whispered, "<I... I came to Jn 1:6
bear witness to the light. But you..." he looked at the saviour, "you
are the light – the true light that enlightens every man.>"

Then, glancing at the student who had queried him, John said: "The question has been posed, and an answer awaits. But only the Word may speak of those mysteries hidden in the Silence."

The prophet's eyes filled with tears, and his heart was overcome with a great longing: to hear the Word *speak...*

Nodding respectfully, the Nazarene rose and assumed his place beside the Nazarite ascetic.

The corners of Christ's mouth rose to a faint smile. It warmed his heart to see all these faces before him, burning with the desire to know.

"How can I describe the Father?" he began. "<He is invisible Ap Jn 3:14
and ineffable,> as John said. <But words and images have been Tri Tr 54:2
given to us – to praise him,> and in this way, to know him.

Ap Jn 4:10 "Know that He is <prior to everything – a Being perfectly at rest, existing in absolute silence.> He needn't move, needn't speak. He needn't even think. He is perfectly content and at peace in his solitude.

"But, in that beginning which lies prior to all time, He thought, He moved, and He spoke. He thought upon himself, and He named himself. That became the first movement in the creation – a movement outward and back to himself; a reflective movement which constitutes his endless self-knowing.

"The space and time created by that movement we call 'the Aeons'. Here, in the material darkness of the Lower Aeons, space and time deteriorate. We look into the distance, and space narrows down, our vision becomes hazy, our sight grows dim. Or, we look back in time, and our memory pales, the images fade, and we forget our true origins."

A smile creased his lips.

"But in the Upper Aeons, all is clear, luminous and knowing – it is a timeless, unmeasured dimension of pure thought. And so, space is that distance between the knower and the known; and time is that instant of self-recognition.

Eugnos 72:11 "Hence the Father is a solitary One who <looks to every side
Tri Tr 55:3 and sees himself from himself.> He is unique, insofar as <He has
the ability to think of himself, to see himself, to name himself, and
Tri Tr 61:36 finally to know himself.> Indeed, <He is that One which knows
itself from all sides and for all eternity.>

"The aeons are the extensions of himself, as He multiplies his
Ap Jn 3:17 self-knowing with no loss of unity. The Father is <an immeasurable
Orig Wld 109:10 light> which <appears in all the aeons, setting them afire – just as,
from a single lamp, many lamps are lit. Yet, one and the same light
Tri Tr 60:11 remains, and its fire is not diminished.> The Father is like <a spring,
whose abundance is not exhausted by the water which flows from
Disc 8-9 58:13 it.> He is <a fountain overflowing with life,> <and He gives life, at
Unt MS all times, to all of the aeons.>

"And so the aeons themselves are like luminous waters. Their ebb and flow manifest the movement of his life and light, first outward then inward to himself. Each aeon of watery light is like a
mirror, and each one of his offspring is like an image in that mirror.
Soph JC 99:2 They are the myriad of names and images <which appear in the
multi-mirrored heavens each time He reflects upon himself> in the
on-going cycle of his eternal self-knowing. All are his children, like
3St Seth 121:10 particles of his light. <All are separate, yet – all are one.>"

Christ gave a knowing look at all those gathered round him in the cavern. Above his head, pockets of phosphor glowed among the rocks. Drop by drop, water fell from the ceiling and gathered into pools recessed in stone.

"You too may become <a light from the Light.> For all who 3St Seth 122:2
come to know the One come to be parts of his wholeness. They
become a thought through which He thinks himself – a name
through which He names himself. Finally, they become an image
through which He sees himself. Each of you may become <a son of Soph JC 119:4
the Light> – the moment you come to know your true Father."

For a few moments, the saviour grew silent. But the smile of enlightenment never left his face. He allowed his listeners a few moments of reflection. Then he continued.

"This same timeless unity may be praised in a multitude of ways. John has spoken of the first aeons as so many names and sounds – the Silence, the Voice and the Word. But the Father, Mother and Son appeared to me as *images* in the watery light, as *Nous*, *Ennoia* and *Christ* in the tri-partite unity of Thought-Thinking-itself. No matter! All these names and images describe the same eternal mystery!

"And this is true also of the rites we use to worship him. When the Baptist pours the holy water, he performs the same action which the Father performed in the highest heaven. His ritual act, performed here below, mirrors a sacred action from above. It becomes a momentary reflection of the Father's timeless gesture, and participates in its eternity. The Father's movement ripples through the aeons, and comes to rest in him."

"Tell us of that movement," a disciple cried. "Reveal to us, at last, the mystery of the Baptism."

"Indeed," Jesus said, "the Baptism is a mystery which goes
back to that beginning *before* time, when <the Father first looked Ap Jn 4:19
in the watery light that surrounds him and saw his image.> Thus
emerged, from his Thinking, <his first Thought, *Barbelo*, the Virgin Ap Jn 5:4
who became the womb of all.> For she..."

Jesus hesitated. He looked into the depths of time, and saw the next moment in creation – and its recollection filled his mind with awe. Speechless, Jesus turned to John.

The desert ascetic nodded to Jesus, knowing his mind. "As the
Father," John pursued, "looked at *Barbelo*, <He begot from himself Ap Jn 6:10
a divine spark of his light, which entered her, and she conceived.>
Thus, <the only-begotten Child of the Mother-Father came forth.> Ap Jn 6:15
He was like a shimmering light, without image or form. <The Father Ap Jn 6:19

rejoiced over the appearance of this light, and anointed it with his *kindness* – his *chrestos* – until it became perfect.> This 'anointing' is the chrism, through which the light became 'the Anointed One' – the *Christos*."

Jesus remembered back to the cave of the three hermits, and how they had proclaimed him Messiah – by naming him and anointing him with holy oil. This simple rite, performed here below, was an image and reflection of the Father's timeless act in the Upper Aeons. With his heart pounding, Jesus realized: the three mages had done this *to make him remember* – that he, from the beginning, *was* the Christ...

Ap Jn 6:26 "Then," John continued, "<as the only-begotten Christ stood at
rest before the Father, *He poured himself over him.*> Yes, the Father
Dial Sav 139:19 <extended his finger and poured a stream of his watery light onto
the Son.> And that moment, the light received form; it became an image. In that image, the Father saw himself, and He recognized himself.

"That event in the Upper Aeons, that *pouring*, became the
Gs Egypt 66:2 invisible pre-existent baptism. It is <the Spring baptism> in the
Gs Egypt 65:23 living water; it exists from the beginning and <transpires in the
highest heavens.>

Orig Wld 122:13 "Here below, I pour the water <three times> <in the baptisms of
Bap A 41:10 forgiveness, repentance and revelation.> But each rite is performed
once only as a three-fold reflection of the Spring baptism in the Eternal Aeons.

"First, in the baptism of forgiveness, you are cleansed and prepared for the mysteries. To be made perfect, you must die to yourself and be born again. Only when you have surrendered all your worldly imperfections – your greed, anger, envy and selfish wants – will your mind be sufficiently open and prepared for the mysteries.

"Your preparation also demands a repentance, which is to say a *metanoia* – a complete 'turning around in your way of knowing'. Only through this 'revolution of the mind' will you be ready for the revelation.

"And so, during the final baptism of revelation, I pour the water over you; it clings to your contours and gives shape to the invisible light-spark within you. It becomes your garment of light. And so, at that moment, *your image appears in the Upper Aeons, and is sealed in the watery light*. You see the Father and the Father sees himself in you, recognizing himself in your reflected image, newly imprinted in the heavens.

"At the same time, you are named. In the invocation, your
hidden spiritual name is pronounced *once only*, <as a living holy Melch 16:11
name written into the watery light> <– a name uttered by the Father> + Gr Pow 36:15,
that moment, to name himself and know himself. Gs Tru 21:27

"Thus, in image and in name, you become a reflection of the Father, because you have come to know his unity. *That*," John proclaimed at last, "is the mystery of Baptism!"

Many of his disciples felt that, at last, they had pushed aside the veil and entered the inner sanctuary. This was the truth that lay hidden behind appearances.

"Tell us more," one of them said, "of images and their reflections."

"<The truth," Jesus said, "did not enter the world naked or Gs Phil 67:9
without form. It came in archetypes and their images.> The images
we see here below are like shadows of the truth – their shapes and
contours come to us from the true archetypes that lie above. These
are <the pre-existent images made by the Father> – the myriad of Tri Tr 96:24
his reflections in the Upper Aeons – luminous but invisible."

"Then how can we see them?" one asked.

"<How do you wish to see them?" Christ responded, "by means Dial Sav 137:9
of transient or eternal vision? When you come to see the eternal
Existent – then you will experience timeless vision!> The cave-dweller will finally turn around, and see the light illuminating his shadow world."

John parted his lips:

"You must pursue your sight <to the very end of what is Eugnos 74:15
visible.> Learn to distinguish, in this world's fleeting silhouettes, the
lineaments of a higher world. The Jordan reflects – in an invisible
way – the Father's watery light. The baptism silently recalls the
Father's first outpouring of water. Each image, you may say, is like
an opening from below to above. Hence, you must learn <to *enter* Gs Phil 67:16
through the image.>"

Jesus nodded and added: "<The lower images are visible to Gs Thom 47:20
humanity. But within them are hidden the luminous images of the
Upper Aeons.> If, with a truly meditative mind, you focus your attention onto a certain shape, it will come to reflect the hidden higher shape. Slowly, you will rise up in your mind, *enter through* the image, and experience the realm of truth."

"<The image itself will show the way," John said. "It takes hold CH IV.8
of those who have the vision – and draws them upward.>"

Gs Thom 47:20 "Then, in this state of vision, <you may finally behold yourself in the light of the Father," Jesus pronounced. "No more will images appear before your eyes, for all will be subsumed in the glory of his light!>"

As Jesus said this, a slender ray of daylight sliced across the cavern's darkness. The sun had risen over Moab, and their night-long vigil had ended. The disciples had remained, attentive and awake, for the entire discourse.

John and Jesus blessed them, and the disciples retired to their respective niches and hollows.

But Magdalene and the Iscariot felt neither taxed nor tired. Instead, in hearing the truths hidden in the silence, their minds had grown more attentive and awake.

The Baptist invited his guests to sit with him at the narrow entrance to their cavernous chapel. There, they had a commanding view of Perea and its surrounding cliffs.

V

The sky shone bluish white in the pale morning light. Eagles cried in the circling skies, while the desert maintained a calm, majestic silence.

For some time, John stared at Jesus. Then he began: "This night, the Word has spoken through you, and imparted much to us. The beginning stands clearer now than it ever has before. And yet..." he paused.

Then, with a slight shudder he asked, "Does your Voice speak with equal authority *about the end?*"

Jesus neither moved nor spoke. Suddenly, in the inaudible stillness, he saw an image – a serpent with the Alpha printed on its head, and the Omega etched upon its tail. The viper opened its mouth and swallowed its tail, forming a finite circle.

"I know only this: *that the end will be where the beginning is.* The more I search for the beginning, the more I hope to uncover ...the end."

John nodded sagely. "Then... the beginning has not been revealed to you entirely?"

"No," Jesus admitted. "My memory only returns to me a little at a time. Bit by bit, I come to see *what was*. But you, in your voice and vision, come to know *what will be*. You see my path clearly, don't you? – to its final turning..."

Slowly, John nodded his head. "What little I see, I dare not reveal to you... Know this much: the beginning will only become clear – the moment you have reached your end." He sighed. "And this, indeed, is a terrible thing."

For a few moments, the prophet and saviour stared at one another in silence.

Then John explained: "There are two forms of *gnosis* – the *prognosis* and the *epignosis*. The first is *fore*-knowledge, which we usually call prophecy. It moves forward through time, as knowledge of the unknown future. *That is my power*. But you," he smiled, "have the gift of *epignosis*, which is *after*-knowledge, and which we usually call recollection. It moves backward through time, into knowledge of our forgotten past, and even unto the beginning. *Therein lies your power!*"

The Nazarene marvelled at this for some time.

"But the Voice of prophecy," the Baptist added, "is plagued with ambiguity. Like you, I open my mouth, not knowing what I'll say. She touches my lips, and her Voice speaks through me..."

"...She?" Jesus asked, his lips quivering. "...*Her* Voice?"

"Yes – the Voice of Wisdom, the Mother. But Wisdom appears under many names, many guises. In the beginning, She spoke as *Ennoia* – the first Thought of the Father. As *Barbelo*, She bore the Father's seed. As *Sophia*, she manifests herself here on earth."

The Baptist looked into the distance.

"Each time She foretells the future, She speaks as *Pronoia*, the Father's *Forethought*. Or, if She reveals the past, She speaks as *Epinoia*, his *Afterthought*. It is in this guise that she speaks through you, since your face is turned to the past."

"– As yours is to the future," Jesus recognized. He recalled the statue of the two-faced Janus, which Romans erected above their gateways: the one face gazing to the fore, the other aft, though each was blind *to whatever lay on the other side*.

"But how may I finally *turn around*, to also face my future?"

"Do you really want that: *to know your own fate?* No... for you it is necessary to be ignorant of your end. Jesus the man must step blindly into the future, even if the Christ-in-him knows the path's final turning. Remember: the more the past is revealed to you, the more you will see your way to whatever awaits."

Then John gazed at him enigmatically. "Who are you – the Bridegroom? Or the Lamb? Can you make these two into one – and celebrate the Wedding of the Lamb?"

Jesus nodded. *Pronoia* had spoken through her prophet – ambiguously, but truly.

The Baptist let out a re-assuring laugh. "With time, you will learn to read all the images here below. Already you have acquired two of the Five Seals..."

Jesus looked at John with wonder. Then slowly, he realized. "The Chrism... and the Baptism..."

"Yes. They seal you and protect you. But, without the remaining three, you remain vulnerable. Find them, find *all of them* – and quickly!"

The three of them could hear the terrible urgency in his voice.

The desert prophet took the saviour's hands in his. Engaging him with his darkly-ringed eyes, he said: "Before the end overtakes you, you *must* find the answers to the mysteries..."

"The first," John said, "is the mystery of the Beginning. You've gained a vision of the Lower Aeons, and also of the Upper. But have you fathomed *the link* between those two? How *did* the Lower Aeons come to be? *Who* created Yaltabaoth? *Whence comes evil*, Jesus?"

The eyes of the saviour grew wide. In terrible fear, he realized – *he did not know*.

"Your own ignorance in these matters leaves you vulnerable. And Yaltabaoth will profit from your unknowing. But the answer – *if you find* the true answer – will finally protect you. For knowledge such as this *is* power."

Jesus bowed his head gratefully.

"Then," the Baptist continued, "you must still solve the second mystery – the Fall of Man. What happened in Eden – I mean, *really* happened? Who was Adam? And Eve? Do you know? Tell me Jesus, *What is Man?* Discover the truth, and the path to your own end will be made straight."

With a shudder, Jesus recalled the three hermits in the Cave of Darkness. *They too* had been haunted by these insoluble enigmas: the *true* nature of the Beginning and the Fall... Without them, the Messiah would never reach the Resolution.

The Nazarene's heart beat wildly in his chest. "But where do I begin?"

"Look around you," the Baptist exhorted. "Look at those closest to you! The answers lie *here*, in the images and appearances, in the shadows and their archetypes – but only your movements will reveal them! What you do – what you *do not* do..."

John lowered his head. The urgency and desperation in his voice were tangible. "My time here is almost finished... Indeed, before this day is over, I will fall into Herod's hands. How? Why? Where? My path's *turning* does not matter – *only the end.* My end lies with Salome, the daughter of the Herodians. But you... your end depends on these two!"

And then, to the great amazement of Magdalene and the Iscariot, John prostrated himself at their feet.

"The Beginning, the Fall and *your end* – the answers to those mysteries lie with these two!"

Then, with tears in his eyes, John kissed the feet of Magdalene and the Iscariot. "Know yourselves," he pleaded. "*Know yourselves* – before it's too late..!"

VIII. Galilee

I

The Nazarene's feet were burning; his brow was on fire. With Magdalene and the Iscariot trailing behind, he raced toward Galilee. For days now he hadn't stopped – neither ate nor slept. His companions were exhausted. But he had to reach his homeland with its farmers, fishermen and life-giving lake. All would begin here!

The fallen leaves of tamarisk trees cushioned his feet as he followed the river's banks. From the boughs above his head, startled owls screeched and took flight. Beneath his bruised soles, snakes and lizards scattered. All the while, circling in the sky, an eagle guided him.

Two or three of the faithful, who had seen his epiphany at the Jordan, followed discretely at a distance. Once the Nazarene reached Galilee, the following grew. Past Magdala and the smaller hamlets bordering the lake, a band of peasants swarmed behind him. By the time they reached Capernaum, a crowd of seventy had gathered to hear the new Messiah.

Who was this messiah sent by the Jordan's prophet?

Was he robust and comely like Simon of Perea who, after Jos 17.273
Herod's death, placed a diadem upon his head and proclaimed himself heir to the kingdom?

Was he tall and powerful like Athronges the shepherd who, Jos 17.278
after Archelaus was crowned king, wrought anarchy across Israel?

Was he rough-hewn like Judas the Galilean who, after Jos 18.23
Archelaus was deposed, created the Zealot brotherhood, to terrorize collaborators and eliminate Roman rule?

Or perhaps this Jesus, together with John, was the fulfilment of the Essenes' prophecy – the two Messiahs who would come from the desert beyond their monastery in Qumran?

Who was the Messiah of the Five Seals?

On the outskirts of Capernaum, the seventy found a place of rest, installing themselves on fallen columns buried in the tall green grass. Flanked by his two companions, the Nazarene stood before the shore of his beloved sea. The evening sun reflected off the waves, casting golden silhouettes over the swaying reeds.

The saviour looked at the faces before him – all awaiting a comforting word after a day of hard toil. He could see, in so many of them, his own face shimmering like a fiery reflection. All despised ignorance; all longed for understanding.

Indeed, all are one, Jesus thought to himself. All are children of the Father. The light in our minds, the life in our veins, like images in the watery light – all flow from the Father's life-giving fount, and each seeks to return, through knowledge, to its source.

But a fog has fallen, like a blackened veil, over our vision – clouding our minds, obscuring our memory and blinding our sight from its true origins. We have become particles of light scattered in the darkness.

Materialism, greed, wealth, commerce and war – through these, each now sees his brother as his enemy, calling himself Israelite and the other Roman. The Archons and their earthen counterparts have sown this seed of discord, diverting our thoughts from that true source of calm – the remembrance of unity that lies hidden within.

"Brothers!" he cried. "Sisters! I do not come to you as a warrior, a revolutionary or a king. I am not even a messiah – if that one is coming for the saving of Israel. I am a man, a simple woodcarver from Nazareth, who has toiled for many years with his head down, much like you.

"Tomorrow you will return to your fields, your fishing boats and your hearth-fires, to lose yourselves once more in the rhythm of your labours. But during those brief moments of respite, earned by the sweat of your brow, I ask you to think back and remember my words. For the kingdom – which many a prophet has promised – lies hidden, like a treasure, buried in your hearts."

The peasants nodded to one another. This one wasn't like Athronges and the other rebel-messiahs. When they spoke, they set you on fire with talk of injustice and uprising; of taxation and revolt. But his words were like cool water, splashed on your face at eventide to wash away the exhaustion...

Jesus placed a hand within his tunic, then withdrew something small. Holding it between his thumb and forefinger, he walked among the labourers resting on the grass.

"What I offer you cannot easily be seen. For the Kingdom, like all treasures, remains hidden away – only the wakeful and wise may uncover it!"

In a single swift gesture, he pulled the cowl of his cloak over his head.

"I told you I was a woodcarver. But now I've given up my leather apron, and traded it in for new apparel! <I wear a long white Acts Pt 2:10
garment which flows over my head and shoulders, down as far as my knees. It fits me perfectly, leaving only my brow, hands and feet exposed. Thus I go from town to town, grasping a styrax-wood staff, and calling out *Pearls! Pearls!* Yes, my name is now Lithargoel, and I am a pearl-seller!>"

A hearty laughter rose from those reposing on the earth.

"Pearls! Pearls!" Jesus cried.

No one dared respond, and he cried again melodiously, like a peddler proffering his wares. *"Pearls! Pearls!"*

"Here!" someone shouted at last. The peasants howled with mirth – until they saw it was Athanasius, the richest merchant on the lake.

The crowd grew silent. All knew Athanasius as a hard, grasping merchant. His sons had opened shops in all the major towns, unloading cheap goods from a huge storehouse in Capernaum.

Lithargoel dashed towards the merchant, who was sitting upright on a rock, surrounded by his sons.

"Master Athanasius!" the pearl-seller cried, and bowed deeply. "I see that you and your sons have also traded in your apparel! You've given up on bargain goods, and now gone into the pearl business!"

The surrounding peasants clapped, whistled and hollered.

But the sons of Athanasius leaned their heads together and whispered, "<He dares mock *us*?>" Acts Pt 3:11

Athanasius stood up. "You're full of well-turned words and phrases – promising us kingdoms and treasures. But *show me* the pearl you've offered! <I don't see a pouch on your back, nor a Acts Pt 3:11
bundle in your tunic. I don't see how I could gain anything from you...>"

"Nor I from you," Jesus said flatly.

Indignation flashed across the merchant's face.

"Show me the pearl! Or are your words empty? When you speak, your lips move, but I hear *nothing*..."

The saviour nodded. And in a voice that frightened them all,
Test Tr 29:6 he said: "<I speak to those *who know* how to hear me.> <And when
Allog 52:18 I open my mouth, I reveal the things guarded in great silence. The mysteries are revealed only to those *who are worthy*, to those who
Test Tr 29:6 are able *to hear me*> <– not with the ears of the body, Athanasius, but with the ears of the mind!>"

Then he turned to the crowds and said: "Open your minds!
Gs Thom 51:6 And you will see that <the promised kingdom is not going to come by watching and waiting for it. No one can say 'look, here it is!' or 'look, there it is!' Rather, the kingdom of the Father is *already* spread out upon the earth, *and men do not see it.*>"

A terrible silence fell over the crowd, as they gazed at the golden green hills, imagining that *there*, hidden in the grass, rose invisible spires and towers.

"Then how will the kingdom come?" a miller asked.

Lk 17:21 "<The kingdom is *among* you!>" he cried. And then: "<The
Gs Thom 32:25 kingdom is *within* you!> I speak in images and parables, so that you may learn to see the holy city hidden in your hearts!"

The Nazarene turned back to Athanasius and his sons. He held up his hand, with something hidden and unseen still clenched between his fingers.

Gs Thom 46:13 "<The kingdom, Athanasius, is like a merchant who had a shop full of goods and one day was offered a pearl. The prudent merchant sold off *all* that he had and purchased that *one* pearl! Why? Because it is a treasure that none may steal nor even seize! It shines like a garment which neither moth can devour nor worm can eat!>"

Jesus traced his steps back through the crowd.

"Only those who possess the pearl may enter into my city. Who among you hopes for that precious gift? Are there any of you here?"

Acts Pt 4:15 "<Please, Lord," an old woman said, "many of us are poor. We know that no man gives a pearl to a beggar – only a little bread and maybe a few coins. But, at least *show us* the pearl, so that we may see it with our own eyes! We, the poor, cannot purchase your pearl. But if you show it to us, we can say to our loved ones: Look! We saw the precious jewel! We saw it with our own eyes!"

Jesus answered, saying to them: "All of you here, whether rich or poor – I am inviting you *all* into my city. And to those who would enter, I will not only show you the pearl, but give it to you gladly..!>”

Upon hearing this, the beggars and the poor trembled at the prospect. Could they go to their beds that night, no longer harrowed by hunger? Could they wake up in the morning, freed from the master’s whip?

The Nazarene returned to the shore and seated himself on a fragmented capital. For a few moments, he gazed out at the great assembly before him. Then, centering himself, he spoke with a voice that resonated across the ruins and into the hearts of all.

“How can I reveal to you the pearl – and the kingdom hidden within it? I can do no more than tell you a story. Because this old fable, in all its poverty and simplicity, is a better guide to the treasure than all my teachings. I call it ‘the Hymn of the Pearl’ since it praises that shining seed above all else.” Pearl

Many of those who were stretched out on the grass now sat up and listened. The children, who were crawling over their mothers’ laps, suddenly grew calm. Even Thomas and Miri, tired as they were from their long journey, grew strangely attentive.

Jesus began. “When I was a little child, I lived in my father’s house. To me, it was like a kingdom, and I delighted in its wealth and splendour. My parents had dressed me in a glowing robe which they, in their love, had made especially for me. And over it I wore a purple mantle, cut exactly to my size – because I was heir to the kingdom.

“But one day my mother and father decided to send me on a voyage. They said, ‘you must go down to Egypt, and bring us the one pearl which lies in the middle of the sea encircled by a great serpent’.

“Then they took from their treasure-house many provisions for my journey. But my glowing robe with its purple mantle I had to leave behind. ‘When you return with the pearl,’ they said, ‘you will again put on your robe, and be received by us as heir to the kingdom.’

“To ensure that I would not forget their promise, they wrote it out in the form of a letter. But its true words were written in my mind, and their meaning was engraved upon my heart.

“I set out. Because I was very young, two envoys accompanied me part of the way. Our kingdom lay in the East, and our journey was long and dangerous. At *Maison*, which lies on the border between Egypt and our land, my escorts turned back. Alone, I entered Egypt, passing under its great city-gate and wandering along labyrinthine alleys, where evil shadows prey on the unwary.

"At last I reached the lake where the serpent kept its lair – there, in the dark and murky bottom of the abyss. But 'the all-swallowing one' was ever-watchful, and guarded its treasure jealously. So, I decided to wait for that opportune moment when the serpent would fall asleep. But, the great beast slept with its eyes open always.

"At nightfall, I installed myself at an inn and stowed away my goods. Lest the Egyptians suspect that I was an outsider, I clothed myself like them, donning their dark heavy garments. For a long time, I kept to myself – like a simple stranger; a wayfarer and passerby. But they, once they saw me and took notice of my difference, sought me out and ingratiated themselves to me. They mixed me drafts of their wine, and insisted I sample their meat. Through the heaviness of their food and the intoxicating effects of their brews, I soon sank into a profound slumber – forgetting where I was born and why I had come to this place. The precious pearl was forgotten.

"As the years passed my parents grew worried. They summoned their entire court, with its wise men and nobles, to weave a plan together. The court composed a letter which each of them signed. And my father himself sealed it with his seal. Then, like a mighty messenger, an eagle was dispatched. It flew over the border, entered Egypt's gate and threaded the labyrinthine streets – evading the evil shadows who waited at every turning.

"With great joy, I saw the eagle alight beside my bed, and speak the words I'd long-since forgotten. It recited the letter which was written in my mind and engraved upon my heart."

The Messiah rose, his face aglow and burning with joy.

"It said 'Awaken my child! Rise up from your sleep! For you have fallen into slavery and servitude – yes you, the child of kings! Call to mind your glowing robe, which awaits you above. Remember in your heart the pearl, which now lies in the darkness below. Respond to the calling! For your name has been inscribed in the Book of the Living, and you – you are proclaimed heir to the kingdom!'"

Excitedly, the Nazarene paced through the crowd.

"With a great stirring, I awoke from my deep slumber. Roused, I rose up from my bed and cried aloud with joy! For I had finally remembered the pearl, and why I had been sent here!

"Immediately I went to the shore of the lake, where the mighty serpent lay in wait for me. But now, recalling my true home, I chanted the names of my father and mother – and the serpent fell at once into a deep sleep! Then I dived down to the bottom of the abyss, seized the glowing prize, and surfaced once more with the pearl in my grasp."

The saviour, standing on Gennesaret's shore, slowly opened his hand, which had been clenched all the while. A cry rose up from those in the crowd who *saw* the invisible pearl cradled in his palm.

"I threw off my filthy garments and fled Egypt. The message engraved in my heart guided me. Like a voice, it called to me; like a light, it led me; like love itself, it drew me onward. I crossed the labyrinth, evading all the evil guardians. With the pearl in my heart, and the names of my parents fresh in my memory, they could neither hinder nor detain me.

"And as I approached my homeland – two envoys came to greet me! They were two, but resembled each other like twins, since the king's countenance was reflected in each of their faces. I cried aloud with joy when I saw them, and recognized what they carried in their hands: it was the radiant garment which I had left behind before setting out. I had forgotten its splendour, which I had enjoyed so much as a child.

"The robe was brightly coloured and embroidered with gold. It glowed with sapphires, beryls, rubies and opals. And an image was woven through it – the seal of the king of kings. A glorious sound rose from the robe, as it sung to me ancient, ancestral songs. And over its entire length, I saw the quivering movement of the *gnosis* – a revelation, like the remembrance of our long-forgotten home.

"As the angels presented me my robe, I gazed upon it – and suddenly it became like a looking glass. In my robe, I could see myself, but I was not separate from my reflection. For, in its mirror, I saw my true self, which was an image of the Father. And together we two appeared as one.

"I experienced an inexpressible delight when the angels invested me with my robe – pouring it over me and clothing me with its brilliance. In truth, the robe itself embraced me, and I received it like one overcome by love.

"In this manner, I entered the kingdom, bearing the precious pearl in my heart. My father and mother received me radiant with joy – for I had fulfilled their command, and they had fulfilled their promise. For a long time I stood before them, and we gazed happily, face to face. And finally, when we embraced, I understood that now I had knowingly returned to the place from whence I, in ignorance, had first set out."

As soon as the Nazarene finished his tale, a strange calm fell over the crowd. As one, they had been entranced by his words. Many felt an unusual ringing in their ears; others felt a warm glow around their faces. Though they still sat amid the ancient ruins, the golden green hills had transformed into an invisible kingdom. They didn't see it; they *felt* it. They looked at one another, wondering what had befallen them.

Jesus walked among them and said, "Tomorrow, during a brief respite from your labours, I ask you to remember my words and call them back into your memory."

Then he dismissed them. And the seventy gladdened faces departed slowly, almost unwillingly, from the ruins of the ancient temple.

II

By the time the three companions reached the Widow's Tower, a canopy of stars was glistening in the heavens. Magdalene was the first to cross the threshold of her home, and immediately her bosom rose with joy. When they had left her abode seven days ago, Jesus was a pathetic and fragmented man; his mind restless and distracted; his soul a tumult of passions. But now, after the Jordan's cleansing, they were returning with a man reborn – and a saviour saved.

She topped up the lamps and Thomas attended to the fire. Meanwhile, Jesus set about preparing their supper. In a manner she had never seen before, her beloved attended to each detail, as if, seeking perfection in all that he did. With tender care he unsheathed the lentils, sliced the leeks, and lay them all in an earthenware pot.

This primitive soup, after fasting for days, filled them to satisfaction. They supped together in silence, enjoying an extraordinary sense of fulfilment. Then each prepared a place to sleep, and lay their heads knowing that they had laboured well. Indeed, the three had become worthy of their rest. The body's complaints, of aching muscles and lacerated feet, were soon silenced by slumber.

After a few hours the Nazarene awoke, his heart hearkening to the call of the night birds. At once he rose and donned his cloak. With a lamp in one hand and a staff in the other, he quit the Widow's Tower in silence.

Outside, all was dark and still; the night air smelt cool and the sea-breeze felt refreshing on his cheeks. Fixing his lantern to the tip of his staff, the Nazarene turned his steps toward the lake. All the while, the Hymn of the Pearl was ringing in his ears.

Where had the story come from? Had his mother told it to him long ago, and only now he had remembered it? No. Like the voices and visions – of angels and demons, of the Upper and Lower Aeons – all of this was the long-forgotten *gnosis*.

The hymn and its hidden message; the images and their archetypes – all fell from the upper world's light, to render translucent their shadows here below.

But Miri and Thomas – what mystery lay hidden in his love for them? A chilling breeze rose from the sea, and he shivered. What had the Baptist seen so clearly but dared not speak of? Shouldn't he, like John, lay himself at their feet – and beg them to reveal the secrets hidden in their souls? Or were they as dark and as unknowing as he?

The Galilean skirted Gennesaret's shores, listening to its dark waters lapping against the rocks. There, at the bottom of the lake, the mighty serpent waited for him. Yaltabaoth guarded his secret – the mystery of his origin – and that knowledge gave him power. <With Ap Jn 25:7
the waters of forgetfulness, the Chief Archon had satisfied men's thirst. Now, none could remember from whence they had come.> Oblivious, Mankind was living a half-life, toiling in deep deceptive sleep. Even the Messiah, like a somnambulist, was stepping blindly on the edge of the abyss. *He had to remember* – but how?

A cold shudder passed through him. Fastening the clasp of his cloak, he pulled its cowl over his head. Staring out into the infinite blackness, he saw four lights on the sea.

With his lantern held high, the Nazarene followed a pier into the middle of the lake. There was no doubt in his mind now: in the darkness were four lights.

'Learn to distinguish,' John had said 'in this world's fleeting silhouettes, the lineaments of a higher world. The image itself will show you the way.'

At once, Jesus began calling out to the Four Lights. "<*Armozel!*" Ap Jn 7:30
he cried, "*Oriel*, *Daveithai* and *Eleleth!*>"

From their boats in the middle of the lake, four fishermen turned to hear the voice calling them from the shore. A hooded figure was standing on the pier, waving the lantern affixed to his staff.

In one boat, James cast an anxious glance at his younger brother John. The sons of Zebedee stopped tugging at their net and gazed at the stranger.

Meanwhile, in the boat opposite, the sons of Jonah kept pulling. Andrew turned to at his elder brother Simon. “Who would be calling us at this hour?”

“What does it matter?” the Bethsaidean replied. “We haven’t caught a fish all night. Keep pulling..!”

“Ahoy!” James called to the other craft. The sleepy seaman hated night-fishing, its late hours and lack of sleep. When James finally lay his head at daybreak, the mariner’s oars transformed to a pilgrim’s staff, and he wandered far from Gennesaret’s shores.

Tired of sculling, James cried to Jonah’s sons: “Take up the net and we’ll see what the fellow wants...”

Each craft had a lantern affixed to its high prow and stern. From the shore, Jesus watched as the Four Lights turned in his direction.

James pulled at the oars while John sat forward in the prow. The younger son of Zebedee had long black hair, and his tresses fell in angelic curls which framed his lovely blue eyes and beardless cheeks. John was as handsome as his brother was ugly. James’ nose was crooked, his eyes occasionally crossed, and a sole eyebrow arched across his forehead. But, for all that, the two brothers were inseparable, and begrudged each other nothing.

The dreamy younger brother, weary of night-fishing, gazed at the figure in the distance.

Ap Jn 2:1 At first, <John saw a young man holding the lantern. But the more he looked, he thought he saw an old man. Then, the young man changed his appearance once more, and became like a child.>

“James,” John said, troubled. “Who do you see calling us from the pier?”

James let up the oars a moment and turned around.

Acts Jn 88 “I see a child. <What would a child want with us?” the elder brother wondered.

But John asked uncertainly, “A child?”

“The one calling us from the shore!”

“We’ve worked long and late tonight – maybe your eyes are deceiving you. Don’t you see a handsome youth smiling at us?”

Flustered, James replied, “You must be dreaming! Let’s get in closer and see *who* this fellow is..!>”

Meanwhile, the sons of Jonah had already reached the pier.
Acts Pt 2:10 From his craft, Simon gazed at the hooded figure and saw <a man in a long white robe, with only his brow, hands and feet exposed. The stranger was holding a styrax-wood staff, and looked like a rather unusual merchant.>

"Ahoy there, brother and friend!" Simon called out. "Are you in need?"

The man in white answered, saying: "<Rightly did you say, Acts Pt 2:34
'brother and friend'.> For my name is Lithargoel and I am a pearl-
seller. I've called you because I'm looking for <labourers and Th Cont 138:34
apprentices.> There's much work to be done <– while we still have Th Cont 138:4
time!>"

Simon cast a befuddled look at Andrew. "Couldn't this fellow wait till morning?" The elder brother with rosy cheeks and a red-beard was still thinking of their empty fishing nets.

But the fair-haired Andrew, who was as youthful and dreamy as John, was staring at the gilded silhouette glowing in the lantern light. The younger son of Jonah seemed entranced by the sound of the stranger's voice.

"We are poor fishermen," Andrew said to the pearl-seller, "and have laboured all night without reward."

"<The man who labours has found his true reward – for he has Gs Thom 43:7
found life!> Now, if you come and work for me, you'll be rewarded a thousand-fold for your efforts! You'll deal exclusively in pearls, and forget all about night-fishing..."

"As apprentices to a pearl-seller?" Andrew wondered.

"First you must acquire your pearls!" Lithargoel laughed.

At that moment, the sons of Zebedee brought their craft
alongside the others. As the hooded stranger turned to them, <John Acts Jn 89
stared in awe at an old man – rather bald, with a thick flowing beard. Meanwhile, James marvelled at a golden youth – with beautiful curls and the fuzz of a first beard on his cheeks.>

"To be my apprentices," Lithargoel continued, "<you must be Gs Thom 40:11
shrewd as serpents and innocent as doves!> Indeed, a true apprentice
of the pearl-seller is no different from a shrewd fisherman. <Such Gs Thom 33:28
a man once cast his net into the sea and drew it up filled with little fish. Among them he found one large fish. The shrewd fisherman released the myriad of little fish, but kept back the one large fish – for therein lay the reward for his labours.>

The four of them sat, unmoving, in their boats.

"<Whoever has ears to hear, let him hear!" the saviour cried.> Gs Thom 33:28

"At least the shrewd fisherman," Simon complained to his mates, "could choose from a net full of fish. We haven't caught a thing all night."

"Cast your nets back into the sea – and the choice will be yours!"

John and James, who were frightened by this tripartite apparition – alternately old man, youth and child – immediately turned their boat and rowed out to sea. The sons of Jonah took up their oars and followed.

Within minutes they had spread their nets and swept the depths of the lake. As the two boats approached, the lanterns on their prows illuminated thousands of silver fins churning the surface of the sea.

"Pull!" James cried, "pull for your lives!"

And Simon, seeing that this was indeed the greatest catch of their lives, leaned over the boat and tugged with all his might.

But the net, burdened by its treasure, tore along the seams. Hundreds of little fish started swimming back into the sea.

"Grab as many as you can!" James cried. And Simon, leaning over the side of his boat, pulled armloads of sardines into the listing vessel.

But Andrew and John gazed calmly at the myriad of shapes in the water. Then, with a lightning movement, Andrew seized a large fish. A moment passed, and John did the same.

Simon peered into the water with tears in his eyes. He had never seen such a shoal of fish – and now it was disappearing from view. Distraught, James watched their loaded nets sink down to the bottom of the sea.

Suddenly, a single *musht* surfaced and James, startled out of his wits, caught it. A broad smile spread over his face.

The two sets of brothers rowed their boats back to the pier. At Simon's feet, a pile of sardines were flipping and jumping.

"Did you make a good catch?" Lithargoel asked. The first light of morning was now spreading across the horizon, illuminating his hooded features.

The sons of Zebedee moored their boat and climbed upon the dock. Each was holding a huge *musht* in his hands, with its gracious dorsal fin sparkling in the morning gleam.

The sons of Jonah, their craft now secured, also mounted the pier. Andrew felt sorry for his brother, who stood there empty-handed. Simon was staring, ashamed, at the scores of little fish jumping and flipping in their boat.

"Three of you would indeed make worthy apprentices!" Lithargoel remarked.

"But where," Andrew asked, "are the pearls that would make us pearl-sellers like you?"

Lithargoel approached Andrew and looked him in the eyes.

"You – you are the son of Jonah, are you not? Where did Jonah find the pearl?"

Understanding, Andrew gazed down at his catch. With two fingers, he extracted a shiny white pearl from the belly of his fish. The sons of Zebedee did likewise, removing their tiny white treasures.

Immediately, the pearls disappeared. Instead, with the *gnosis* in their grasp, the three of them *saw* the pearl-seller for who he truly was: his face radiated calm, his passible features glowed with infinite compassion. Before them stood the Messiah. Andrew, John and James trembled with awe.

Turning to Simon, the saviour asked: "And you, *Cephas*, have you found no reward for your labours?"

Red-faced and tongue-tied, Simon could do no more than mutely shake his head.

<Suddenly, in the span of a heartbeat, he cried aloud: "Do you Acts Pt 9:1
know me? Didn't you just call me *Cephas*?"

The saviour answered, "Tell me, *Cephas* – who gave you that name?"

"Jesus, whom I've known for many years. He... he gave me that name..."

"Then *recognize me*."

Lithargoel dissolved his appearance, letting fall the pearl-seller's guise – and revealed, in truth, *who* he was.>

"Jesus?" Cephas asked incredulously. "Jesus of Nazareth?"

The Bethsaidean's heart filled with joy. With his eyes newly opened, he began laughing and crying at the same time.

"I left you for dead at the Temple," he heaved with sorrow. Then, lowering his head, he babbled, "I ran away in fear, and never returned, afraid they would seize me. Like a coward, I hid myself here. I am so ashamed..!"

Jesus brought his face close to his friend's. "We were *all* misled. And you acted courageously, my brother. When called upon, you followed me – even unto death."

"But I've failed you, even now!" Cephas lamented. "I stand before you – with nothing in my hands. I'm weak, unfaithful – unworthy of your friendship..!"

"No. Earlier you addressed me as 'brother and friend' – then you spoke truly. For you shall establish my brotherhood here on earth, in the companionship of the faithful. You shall gather the little fishes unto yourself."

The saviour looked into the eyes of Cephas with a gaze that calmed and re-assured him. In a flash, the feelings of shame and grief fled from him like invisible shadows.

"You, *Peter*, are solid as a stone. And to remember this, I shall
Ap Pt 71:15 call you, henceforth, by *that* name. <I have chosen it for you because,
+ Ap Pt 70:26 in you, I have found my strength and my faith. Through you, I will
establish the foundation of my community – the church that shall become a sturdy *bedrock* for all those called *by faith* to the Father. In this way you, Peter, shall become perfect in accordance with your name...>"

Peter's eyes opened wide and he saw the glories that awaited him. He saw Jerusalem's temple transformed into a domed and steepled cathedral. And he, the new High Priest, wore a stole and chasuble crowned with a three-tiered tiara. But in a flash, the vision passed, and he found himself once more standing on Gennesaret's shores.

"But – who are you?" Peter asked in wonder. "I left you for dead in Jerusalem, and now you appear to me here – like the man I knew, but also – a bestower of glories."

Dial Sav 126:14 "<It is the one who *sees* who reveals,>" Jesus said mysteriously.
"Andrew, John and James have been given the *gnosis*, which is *knowledge* of the hidden. They see me as I truly am. But you, my friend, have been given the *pistis*. Through *faith*, you and all of
yours must come unto me. And yet, even though you remain blind,
2Ap Jas 57:8 you may still *see* <He-who-is-hidden.>"

Jesus touched his hand to Peter's forehead and caressed his brow.

"The blind are those who have eyes to look, and yet they do not
see. But those *with faith*, even with their eyes closed, may look upon
Ap Pt 72:9 the true saviour and *recognize* him. <Put your hands over your eyes
– that is, over the body that shrouds your perception like a veil – and tell me what you see."

Peter did as he was told, and the corners of his mouth creased to a frown. "I don't see a thing..." he murmured, and removed his hands.

1Ap Jas 27:3 "Do it again!" Jesus urged.> "But this time, <cast away the
bond of flesh that encircles you,> and look upon me *with faith!*"

Again, Peter did as he was told, but this time the corners of his
Ap Pt 72:9 mouth rose. <He experienced an unparalleled awe – a fear mixed
with joy – for he saw a light which glowed greater than the sun at mid-day.

Then, the light slowly descended upon Jesus, and he saw the
saviour as he truly was.> Peter *saw* <He-who-is-hidden.> 2Ap Jas 57:8

"Blessed be the Nazarene!" the Bethsaidean cried. "<For he is L Pt Ph 133:26
truly an Illuminator!> <The Son of Light> <opens the eyes of the 2Tr Seth 51:2
unseeing!>" Gs Tru 30:15

This time, when Peter removed his hands, he continued to see
the luminous Christ that had descended into Jesus. A flame of faith
had kindled in his soul, illuminating the face of <the heavenly, Gs Phil 58:17
perfect man.>

As one, the four fishermen bowed their heads before the Messiah.

With great satisfaction, the Nazarene closed his eyes and stared at his newly-found apprentices. The four men before him, in their dingy fisherman's aprons, blazed with the light of the Upper Aeons.

Jesus smiled to himself. In the shadowy forms of these four Galileans, he had discerned the lineaments of a higher world. Before him stood the Four Lights – *Armozel*, *Oriel*, *Daveithai* and *Eleleth.*

III

It was the fifteenth year in the reign of Tiberius, when the Herodians ruled Israel under the auspices of Rome, and Pontius Pilate was governor of Syria-Palestine. It was the month of *Támmûz*, when the High Priest Caiaphas celebrated the Mid-summer Feast, and wood-gatherers brought timber for the altar's eternal flame. But for generations afterward, when the Galilean farmers and fishermen remembered this blessed hour, they called it 'the summer of the Messiah'.

Each morning, the disciples launched their boats onto the lake, and wherever they landed, Jesus addressed crowds that grew from seventy to seven hundred to seven thousand or more. In parables and riddles he revealed the invisible kingdom, hidden like a pearl in the coils of a world-circling serpent.

When Christ walked from Capernaum to Magdala, flowers sprung up under his feet. When he crossed the Jordan from Chorazin to Bethsaida, the fish leapt in the air to greet him. Wherever he passed, the oxen bowed and the sheep bent their forepaws.

After their day's labours, the disciples returned to the Widow's Tower in Capernaum. And at night, from the top of that tower, they surveyed the new kingdom arising in Israel. Each hour, the kingdom came a little closer to 'now', and its walls circled the 'here' in every peasant's heart.

Jesus awoke with a stifled cry. In the darkness of a dream, halfway between waking and sleep, he had heard a plaintive whisper. His heart was pounding, his ears ringing.

Nazareth was calling to him.

In his vision he had seen a small cottage on the hill. Still wrapped in swaddling bands, he had awoken to find his mother leaning over him, smiling. It was she who was singing to him, an old shepherd's song, with its strophes and cries from a long-forgotten
Gs Egypt 66:21 lullaby. <*U aei eis aei! Ei o ei! Ei os ei!*> And then, he heard the secret words hidden in the syllables. The consonants and vowels
Gs Egypt 66:21 that combined to cry: <*Son! Forever, you are what you are..! You are who you are!*>

Jesus leapt up from his mat. It was so early that the swallows in the trees were still sleeping, and the eastern sky was a pearly grey.

"My twin and my bride!" he cried, "My four lights – rouse yourselves!"

Drowsy and dishevelled, the companions awoke. From her room, Magdalene came running, her long unbraided hair wrapped loosely in a scarf.

What labour was demanded of them now – so urgent that it couldn't wait until daybreak?

Zost 4:19 "<Our time in this world is short!> We must set out for Nazareth – *now!*" he screamed. "The sabbath begins this evening, and the synagogue will meet after sunset. We must address the sons and daughters of Nazareth – before it's too late!"

The Nazarene splashed cold water on his face, then threw handfuls at his disciples. "Get dressed! We're leaving!"

Within minutes they had gathered up their sandals and staffs, closing the door behind them.

The walk to Nazareth, once the sleep had been wiped from their eyes, was pleasant and invigorating. With the sun rising over the hills of Gaulanitus, the lake sparkled like a thousand angels arrayed in golden armour.

The Nazarene marched ahead, his bare feet flying over the Roman pavings. Andrew and John, the youngest and most vigorous, followed close behind. Magdalene dragged the sluggish James. Peter and Thomas fell far behind.

Halfway towards Magdala, Jesus turned right, following the road that led northward unto Tyre. Magdalene, remembering this road all too well, said nothing. But Peter could not hold his tongue.

“We’re crossing out of Israel – without a bite to eat?” the Bethsaidean’s large belly was knotted with hunger.

The saviour didn’t respond, and continued marching at a dizzying pace. He kept looking right and left, as if trying to distinguish strange markings in the landscape. Around them were nothing but olive and fig orchards.

“Here!” he cried at last. The saviour was staring at a lone fig tree at the top of a hill. Satisfied, he sat down on the ground to wait. The disciples, glancing at one another, reluctantly followed their master’s example and sat down.

The morning’s first sparrows began to sing. A hawker passed, pushing a wooden cart loaded with bread. His tanned features and the bleached tips of his flowing auburn hair spoke of long days outdoors in the heat.

“Peace be to you, passerby!” Jesus said, rising again to his feet.

“And to you!” the peddler replied with his hand on his heart. Bowing his head, he continued along his path.

“Where is the one accompanying you?”

The bread-seller’s cart ground to a halt.

“...Do I *know you*, stranger?” The peddler looked at the man by the roadside.

“<I am a passerby, just like you...>” Jesus replied mysteriously. Gs Thom 40:19

Meanwhile, the six disciples had risen and gathered round the bread-seller’s cart. Nervously, the man looked from one face to the other.

“Are you thieves – come to rob me?” he asked in a low frightened voice.

Upon hearing this, the saviour laughed. The bread-seller also let out a high nervous laugh to hide his fear.

“None of the seven robbers shall detain the passerby,” Jesus assured him. His intonation was strange and laden with mystery.

The hawker grew nervous. He didn’t like the looks of these strangers – especially the one with the red beard, hungrily eyeing his bread.

“And the other who was with you?” Jesus asked again. “– Where is he?”

The peddler gazed guardedly at the man in white. He had the frightening feeling that this wayfarer was going to rob him of all of his possessions – and he was going to get down on his knees and thank him for it.

He panicked. *"Nathanael!"* the bread-seller cried.

A slender man emerged from his hiding place. He wore a tanner's apron and was carrying a knife. He didn't have a single hair on his head, and seven earrings pierced the length of his left ear.

Nathanael stalked them slowly. The tanner's knife, in his expert hands, balanced on the edge of his fingertips.

Without fear, the saviour approached the menacing tanner.

"Greetings, passerby!" Jesus cried aloud.

Jn 1:48 "<Do you *know me?*" Nathanael asked.>

Jesus gazed deep into the man's eyes and slowly nodded yes.

Jn 1:48 "<Before Philip called you, I saw you... under that fig tree." Jesus indicated the tree on the hill.

Suddenly, Nathanael dropped his knife. He fell to his knees and cried, "Rabbi! You are the Son of God!>"

Philip's heart skipped a beat. His only friend had surrendered their knife to this unruly band of brigands. Their bread was forfeit, maybe even their lives. And – for reasons he still couldn't understand, this made him feel happy.

Jn 1:47 "<Behold," the saviour said to his disciples, "– a man freed of deception!> This Nathanael, though a stranger, *recognized* me at once – for he knew me, just as I *know* him."

For a long time, Philip eyed the man in white. After a pause, he asked, "Are you the one they call the Messiah?"

Jesus did not reply.

Gs Thom 48:20 "<Tell me, stranger, *who* you are – so that I might believe too."

The saviour said, "You can read the face of the earth and sky, but you haven't recognized the one standing before you, and you still don't know how to read this moment...>"

Slowly, Philip nodded his head.

"If you *are* the Son of God," he bartered, "then couldn't you at least *show* me... so that I can believe it with my own eyes..."

Jn 14:8 "<I am in the Father and the Father is in me," Jesus replied slowly. "Whoever has seen me – has seen the Father.>"

Philip nodded his head again. Somehow, he knew the man in white was going to say this... The peddler believed in him, trusted him completely – and this worried him.

Gs Thom 38:1 "<I have chosen you, as one from one thousand, and two from ten thousand," Jesus said. "In this way, all may stand as a single one.>"

Nathanael kissed the saviour's hands, eternally grateful. Philip smiled weakly.

And the Nazarene, feeling sorry for this peddler who didn't dare separate himself from his worldly goods, said: "So that you, Philip, may *know* the Father, and *see* him as we do, I offer you this gift."

He placed his hands on the other's cheeks.

"<Whoever drinks from my mouth will become like me..." He Gs Thom 50:28
pressed his lips onto Philip's. "And I myself will become as he. So
that all that is hidden will be revealed to him.>"

The peddler began trembling from head to foot. Thunder cracked, and a whirlwind passed through his soul. He smiled as tears welled up in his eyes. Looking at the Messiah, and at all the disciples around him, he saw the same face. He saw his own face in them, and their faces were smiling with warmth and kindness.

Welcoming Philip and Nathanael into their ranks, the disciples broke into laughter.

But Philip turned to Jesus and asked, "What has happened to me? *Where am I?*"

The saviour took one of the loaves of bread from his cart, and held it in his hands.

"You have stepped into the kingdom," Jesus replied. "<The Gs Thom 49:2
kingdom of the Father is like a baker and his bread. He took a little
bit of yeast and concealed it in the dough. From that small bit of
leaven came forth huge loaves of bread – enough to feed the entire
kingdom. Whoever has ears to hear, let him hear!>"

Jesus pressed the freshly-baked bread to his lips and smelled its sweet aroma.

Immediately, Philip took all the loaves from his cart and offered them to the disciples.

"Breakfast..!" Peter cried.

The nine Galileans continued along the same road, munching their bread with a few dates from the roadside.

Jesus walked with his arms round Andrew and John, who leaned their heads against the saviour's breast. Philip and Nathanael smiled at each other, happy as children playing in the sunlight.

Meanwhile, James had wiped the sleep from his eyes, only to realize that his dream, at last, had come true: he was far from Gennesaret's shores – a wayfarer with a staff, walking to destinations unknown.

As they mounted a bridge near the crossroads, a customs depot came into view. Herod's publicans were adjusting their scales, opening their ledgers and sharpening their quills.

"Matthew!" Jesus cried.

A short man, his beard tightly-braided and his hair well-oiled, poked his head out the window.

"Jesus?" Levi cried. "Jesus of Nazareth?"

He flew out the door and embraced the Galilean he'd last seen in Jerusalem.

"Come with us Matthew – now! The old kingdom is crumbling.
Tr Res 48:24 <The rich have become poor, and the kings have been overthrown.>
Leave everything and join us..."

Levi looked at his companion and smiled weakly. He had heard that the Nazarene was crossing the countryside, preaching of the new kingdom arising in Galilee. It was only a matter of time before he passed through Sepphoris.

Tr Res 48:26 "Yes, yes... <Everything's prone to change and the world's an illusion...> I've heard it all before!" the publican replied, rubbing his elbows. His arms and shoulders were still covered with scars from the last time he'd followed this self-proclaimed messiah.

Tr Res 47:14 "<While you dwell in this world, what is it that you lack?>" Jesus asked him, his eyebrows rising.

"Money," Levi stated flatly. "Sovereigns, shekels, drachme – all will do just fine, thank you."

Gs Phil 53:23 "<Names given to worldly things are deceptive, Matthew. They distract our thinking – diverting it from true to untrue.>"

Gs Phil 53:35 "I'll give you that much," he allowed. "<The names which we hear in this world deceive us...> But that's just a question of numismatics. *True money* never deceives."

Gs Phil 54:18 "<The rulers of this world deceive us," Jesus replied sharply, "taking the names of the good and giving them to those that are evil – to confuse us through the very names they use...>"

Levi tapped his chin thoughtfully. Then he moved in close and asked: "Have you found it then – the secret of the Five Seals?"

The saviour stared at him in silence.

"*The power of powers*," Levi whispered, "– have you learned its secret?"

"I have," the Nazarene replied.

His eyebrows rising, the son of Sepphoris leaned in closer: "Would you share it with me?"

"The secret?"

Levi nodded.

The saviour opened his mouth: "<Anyone who has found the Gs Thom 51:4
world and become rich – should renounce it all and follow me.>"

"Un huh..." the publican replied. "Anything else?"

"Yes. <If you have money – don't lend it out at interest. Rather, Gs Thom 48:35
give it to those from whom you'll never get it back.>"

"Ahhh!" Levi responded. "Well, that settles things."

The crafty merchant looked Jesus over from head to foot.

"One more question... Why do you keep calling me *Matthew*?"

"Because that is the name by which you are *called*. It is not I who gave you that name, but the Father."

"Matthew..." Levi said, weighing up the sound of it.

"Tell me, Matthew, <how is one to hear, if his name has never Gs Tru 21:32
been called?> <His name comes to him, and if he recognizes it, then Gs Tru 22:12
he knows where he has come from and where he is going to...> <He Gs Tru 21:25
understands that the Father himself has uttered his name – a name
known from the beginning, and to be called again at the end.>"

"And my name is Matthew?"

"You're the one who answered when I called that name..." Jesus remarked in a calm, even tone.

The tax collector scratched his bearded chin and shifted his weight from foot to foot.

"<If one is called," Jesus continued, "he hears, he answers, and Gs Tru 22:4
he turns to him who is calling. Because he knows *why* he is being
called. With that knowledge, he does the bidding of the one calling
him – the will of the Father.>"

Levi pondered this much. His whole life, thus far, had been spent in the pursuit of money. Not possessions, but *money* and the power that it brought. Now, the Nazarene had articulated the self-same thought that had been nagging him for years: that money's only power... – was to satisfy our greed, wants and desires. Whether he possessed sovereigns or shekels, it was all quite the same. The names had misled him. Coins, once their images had worn off, were nothing more than metal pieces. And money, though valued, was actually quite worthless.

Now the Nazarene had called him by his *true name* – a calling he could not refuse...

The son of Alphaeus withdrew the key-ring from his pocket, with the keys to the customs depot. He threw it behind him and smiled. For the first time in his life, he felt as if he had done something for himself. He felt free. And with this new-found feeling growing inside him, Matthew followed Jesus and the others.

IV

The Galileans retraced their steps, then took the Roman road that cut through the Bet Netofa valley. They could see Sepphoris on their right, perched atop its low hill, and Mount Carmel rising majestically to their left. Between them, nestled in the slopes, lay Nazareth...

The Nazarene's heart rose in his chest and his throat constricted. Despite the painful moments he had passed in this place, it was his home, and his blood flowed with the richness of its soil. The terraced slopes around the town were filled to abundance. Slender fennel stalks brushed their hands; clusters of wild capers shaded their brows.

Jesus and his disciples, now ten in all, raced up the paths between the farming plots. In the golden light of evening, the village on the hill glowed resplendent.

They reached its familiar watchtower, bound on all sides by rubble walls. In the village square they passed the communal wine-press and pottery kiln. All the houses looked empty – their gates closed, their windows shuttered. A lone watchdog barked as they passed.

It was after sunset, and the whole of the village had gathered in the synagogue to celebrate the sabbath. Jesus ran ahead, knowing every narrow lane between the limestone homes. At last he came to the simple house of prayer that served as their synagogue.

The son of Nazareth burst through the door and ran up the main aisle. His face was aglow, his smile radiant. In his heart he felt an overwhelming compassion for these simple tradesmen and farmhands.

Word had long-since reached the villagers of this wayward son of Nazareth who had attracted huge gatherings along Gennesaret's shore. They knew him as a simple carpenter, that unstable son of Mary – and could not believe that he, the village idiot, was hailed by thousands as the Messiah. It went beyond all reckoning.

But now, here he stood, gazing at them with eyes afire and his hair in flames. Any moment, he would start screaming revolution and the end of the world.

"*Yeshua*," the village rabbi said, taking him by the arm, "what brings you here?"

"The sabbath..." the son of Mary replied.

"Have you come to expound the Law?"

Jesus looked over the congregation. There, in the front, was Eleazar, the stiff and grim-faced village elder who had cursed him since birth, claiming that Jesus was a *mamzer* – an illegitimate bastard. For this, the youth had been ostracized as 'unclean' and barred from the synagogue. The rumours of his birth had even banished him, as a child, from their village walls. Now, Eleazar was gazing at him fixedly. Why had the mamzer messiah entered their house of prayer?

Beside this hook-nosed notable stood Heli his grandfather, uncle Theuda and his father Joseph. These elders were flanked by his four fledgling cousins: James, Joses, Jude and Simon. Nervously fingering the tassels of their prayer shawls, they stared at their brother uneasily.

Further back in the women's section stood Mary his aunt and her three daughters, Anna, Athalia and Arsinoe. *But where was his mother?* His nine companions, meanwhile, had discreetly filed inside and were standing in a row along the back wall.

With a nod to the village rabbi, the son of Nazareth stepped up to the lectern and opened the scroll at random. Under his eyes, the words of the prophet Isaiah appeared. He scanned the flame-like
script with his finger. *<For this people's heart has grown dull, and* Isaiah 6:9
their ears are hard of hearing.>

The Nazarene stared at the text and said nothing. Was that the message YHWH wanted to impart to his people?

He wracked his brain until a different passage came to his lips. It was a strophe from the prophet Asaph, whose words were preserved in the Psalms.

"*<I will open my mouth to speak in parables,*" he chanted to Psalms 78:2
the congregation, "*I will proclaim what has been hidden from the foundation of the world until now.>*" He rolled up the scroll.

"I stand before you here as a Nazarene. I know you as my neighbours and as members of my family. For years we trod the grapes together – winnowed the husks and ground the grain. Then, to celebrate the harvest feast, we gathered as one – to break bread and pour out the new year's wine. Yet, for all that, I know that I am also a stranger among you. My years at the monastery and the rumours of my birth exclude me as an outsider."

His glance fell upon Eleazar, who barely concealed a malicious smile.

"But I stand here today, for the first time in this synagogue – 'to open my mouth and proclaim what has been hidden from the foundation of the world until now'. *It is the Kingdom!* The invisible kingdom that lies spread out before you! A kingdom that exists *here and now!"*

The congregation opened their mouths, and stared at the *mamzer*, confounded.

"In this kingdom, all are gathered as one, to break bread and pour out the new year's wine, because they know that *the harvest time has come*. Not the end of the year, but the end of time as we know it on earth!

Gs Thom 51:6 "Yes, <the kingdom is *already* here, within you and among
+Gs Thom 32:25 you.> And it is a time of rejoicing, when debts are forgiven, our
+ Lk 17:21 hampers are opened wide, and each gives without reckoning."

Eleazar frowned. The elders on their benches began to shift and squirm.

Tri Tr 96:35 "<For the kingdom, fellow Nazarenes, is like a village filled with
all that is good – with brotherly love and wide-reaching generosity.>
Gs Phil 77:31 Yes, generosity, because love is the brother of giving! <Love never
calls something its own. It never says, 'this is yours' or 'that is mine'
but 'all of these are yours'.>"

A discomforting silence descended over the synagogue.

"Look around you! Has our community recognized *its hidden unity*, in which each of us stands *no different from the other?* Has our community manifest this love and goodness, this sharing and forgiveness?" He leaned over the lectern and asked, "Have you welcomed the stranger into your midst?"

Many members of the congregation coughed loudly. The stalls creaked and a prayer scroll tumbled to the floor.

"In Nazareth, that Kingdom *has yet to be seen*. It is like a treasure – hidden deep in your hearts. None of you here will see it until he steps into its realm. When you open your hearts, love one another, and give freely without asking – then its gates will open wide to receive you."

Eleazar was shaking his head, hissing loudly in Heli's ear. But the eyes of the younger ones, like Jude and James, were glistening with hope.

"*'I will open my mouth and speak to you in parables'* the prophet Asaph proclaimed. Listen to me then, so you may know the kingdom buried in your breasts – a kingdom no different from the very village wherein we dwell."

A hush fell over the entire congregation. Outside, a lone dog howled. In plaintive cries, it wept for its master.

“<The kingdom,” he began, “may be likened to a peasant who Gs Thom 109
had a treasure buried in his field. His whole life long, he didn’t know the treasure was hidden there. And so, when he died, he left the field to his children. But they, unaware of its buried treasure, took the field and sold it to the first man who came along. The stranger ploughed its furrows – and behold! He found the hidden treasure.> For the rest of his days, he rested upon the bounty that was revealed to him, and *to him alone*, through his labours.”

“So it is with you, peasants of Galilee. <The kingdom already Gs Thom 32:25
exists – *inside* of you, and *outside* of you.> <But first, you must Gs Thom 37:20
make the outside like the inside,” he cried, “ and the inside like the outside..!>” You must take the treasure hidden in your hearts and share it with every man and woman.”

More grumbling was heard, among sighs of discontent.

“It is not a question of following the Torah, with its commandments and its laws – but of acting in accord with our unseen oneness. If one knows the unity hidden in their community, then he loves the other as himself, and does him no evil. You offer yourself to yourself, and thus, to others, and to God.”

The villagers shook their heads, and their mumbling rose to a noisome clatter.

“<To enter the kingdom, you must make the two into one,> just Gs Thom 37:20
as a man and a woman, when in love, come together as one. In that love, in that unity, lies the image of our kingdom!”

Joseph slammed his hand down on the wooden bench. The congregation protested loudly.

“<If you wish to enter into the kingdom, you must first become Gs Thom 41:10
like a little child!>” Jesus stared at Eleazar. “For the new-born child is perfect in every way! He is, as yet, untainted by people’s fear, judgement and prejudice...”

The village elder stood up and cried angrily at the impudent youth. “Who are you to say these things? You’re ill-born, cast out, unclean! How can you – a pariah! – stand there and judge us?”

“<I am the Son of the Father, just as you all are my brothers and Jn 17:21
sisters,” Jesus replied calmly. “I say these things, to remind you that we may all be one.>”

The son of Nazareth looked at his villagers plaintively. He was pouring every drop of love and sweetness into his words, but they fell like oil on the villagers’ anger, igniting their fires of hate.

“You are not my son!” Joseph said, standing up from his place in the congregation. “I’ve disowned you – banished you from our family home! Your place is no longer here, among the Nazarenes!”

Ap Jas 7:1 “Listen to me please!” he cried. “<At first, I spoke to you in
parables, but you didn’t understand. Now I’m speaking to you plainly and openly – and you still cannot see your way to the truth!> Open your minds, lest your hearts be hardened with contempt!”

“Liar!” they cried. “False Messiah! Deceiver!”

For a long slow moment, Christ said nothing. But the gaze in his eyes transformed from a sparkle of light to a burning and searing flame. These Nazarenes – his neighbours and family – had hardened their hearts against him. To them, Jesus remained a *mamzer*, cursed by his birth and ostracized like a leper. The villagers would never reverse their judgement, and accept him once more in their homes.

Th Cont 143:24 “<You neither realize your perdition,” he warned, “nor have
you understood that you dwell in darkness and death!>”

“Illegitimate bastard!” they taunted him. “Untouchable!”

Ap Jas 12:39 “<Woe to you,” he cried, “who have heard and not believed!>
Th Cont 143:9 <Woe to you,” he cried again, “godless ones> of Galilee! <How
Th Cont 143:12 long will you be oblivious?> <Woe to you,” he cried a third time,
Th Cont 144:13 “village in the grip of demons!>”

The elder Eleazar tore at his garments and cried “Blasphemer! Blasphemer!”

But, like a fiery sword, the saviour’s voice cut through them all.
Ap Jas 9:24 “<You wretches! You pretenders! You falsifiers of knowledge! Can
you still bear to listen, when you should have *spoken* these things from the first? Can you still sleep at night, when you should have *awoken* from the first – so the Kingdom might receive you? Verily, I say unto you, had I known you wouldn’t listen, I would *never* have come among you! Now you, who are *outside* the Father’s inheritance – weep! Mourn!> For you, village of Nazareth – are banished from the Kingdom!”

Furious, the congregation leaped up and surrounded him, seizing him by the hair.

“Stone him! Stone him!” they cried.

His disciples fought their way through the mob, but the nine were far-outnumbered. As he was dragged out the door, Jesus could see, in the faces of those around him, the dark countenances he knew all too well: wickedness, depravity, abuse, wrath, ridicule, torment and spite – all of them demons laughing in cruel delight.

“Death! Death!” the villagers chanted as they dragged him

to the edge of a cliff. Then, arming themselves with stones, they backed away. As soon as the elder came to give the sign, they would fire away until the victim fell to his perdition. *That* was the Law; *that* was the command decreed for blasphemers.

As the peasants jostled left and right, a cry came up from their midst: "Clear the path for Eleazar! Let the sentence be passed!"

The mob parted just enough for the old man to squeeze through. The white-haired elder turned around – and they were all shocked to behold a fragile old woman. It was Mary, the heretic's mother.

The blessed Virgin stood between the crowd and her son, looking at all of them with a gaze that froze the blood in their veins. She hadn't left her home or been seen in the village streets for longer than any of them could remember.

Mary wasn't frightened; she wasn't angry. Her eyes beseeched neither pity nor comprehension. Instead, she looked at all of them with wonder – a stupefying wonder that fused insanity with sanctity. On her face was the sage smile of a holy fool.

Then, three of her family came running and huddled by her side. It was young Jude and James, along with their sister Arsinoe. The three were trembling with fear, but would rather stand and die there, by her side, than see any harm come to her.

One by one, the villagers dropped their stones, which fell with a deadening thump to the ground. No one dared speak as, slowly, they turned and retreated. Each returned to their homes, burning with anger and stung by shame.

"*Yesseus...*" the Virgin cried, turning to her son as he knelt in her embrace.

"I'm sorry my mother," he cried, as large tears came rolling down his cheeks. "I turned them all against me – then cursed them – condemned them *all!* How will I ever be forgiven?"

His face burned with shame, seeing his younger sister and brothers there, so innocent, staring at him in fear.

"Don't blame yourself, my son," she said, caressing his hair. "It could not be otherwise."

And then, with the unsettling gaze of a holy fool, she started
singing softly: "*<U aei eis aei! Ei o ei! Ei os ei!>*" Gs Egypt 66:21

But, hidden in that ancient lullaby, he heard the words she
intended for him alone: '*<You are what you are – forever, my son...* Gs Egypt 66:21
You are who you are.>'

V

Abandoning Nazareth, the saviour and his disciples headed north. In Cana they hoped to find a small repast and a place to lay their heads for the night.

Despite the day's sad outcome, the evening was pleasant and peaceful. The trill of nightingales sounded in the trees and a refreshing wind rustled the leaves of the acacias.

The elder Mary marched beside her son, who walked with his head bowed. In sullen silence, he was thinking of the Nazarenes.

But his aging mother had suddenly grown wings. After years of confinement, she was now free to roam the countryside. She looked left and right, stumbled then scurried on in tiny steps.

The three young ones had elected to accompany their forsaken brother. James was sixteen and Jude was barely twelve, but they were firmly resolved to follow him along this thorny path. Every so often they turned and watched while Nazareth receded from view.

Magdalene cast a glance at the two youths, so slender and graceful in their movements. In a strange way, Jude reminded her of Jesus at that age: pensive and withdrawn, but with a hidden fierceness and determination.

1Ap Jas 40:22 Their sister Mary-<Arsinoe> had just reached eighteen, and her face radiated a mysterious allure. Her long dark hair hid her fine-cut features and she watched the world attentively through large eyes glistening with brilliance. But, the enchanting sister never spoke, and her uncanny silence had long-since exasperated her brothers.

Their heads buried in their cloaks, John and Andrew were whispering to each other. It was just as Magdalene suspected. These two angelic apostles, one dark-haired and the other fair, were staring at Arsinoe with dreamy eyes. Which of them, Magdalene mused, would be the first to approach Jesus' sister? And what would the master have to say?

The younger Mary caught up with Jesus and his mother, who were still marching in silence.

"There will always be three," the Virgin announced in a voice laden with mystery.

They turned and looked at the old lady. Her mind was elsewhere, as always, but her words still intimated some hidden truth.

"Three ages of the world," she continued, "three ages of Man. And so, there are three types of men."

The saviour's brow rose a notch.

"And what type are the Nazarenes?"

"The last," she replied, "quick to anger; slow to understand. In that regard, you are very much like them..." She smiled at him a wicked smile, full of wise and gentle humour. "But look at Peter there, and that Thomas marching beside him. The other types of men are more like them. One is full of soul, the other filled with spirit. One burns with faith, the other with the quest for knowledge. It has been so from the beginning."

"That is what the Baptist said," Magdalene remarked, looking down the dark path before them.

Jesus glanced at Miri curiously.

She fingered a long stand of her hair, lost in remembrance. "When John spoke in Jerusalem, Salome was there, and recounted to me every word that had fallen from his lips. The prophet said
<three phoenixes will fly into the coming fire. The first is immortal, Orig Wld 122:7
the second will die but rise again, and the third will be consumed forever.>"

She looked up at the passing cypresses. Their dark silhouettes reminded her of condemned men with their heads bowed.

"He called these three types: <'the pneumatic', 'the psychic', Tri Tr 118:14
and 'the hylic'.> <One is spirit-endowed, the other soul-endowed, Orig Wld 122:7
and the last nothing more than earthly substance.> <Each type will Tri Tr 118:14
be known by its fruit. Their numbers are mixed for now and their differences pass unnoticed. But, with the coming of the Messiah, the nature of each will be revealed...>"

Jesus thought of the Nazarenes. Had they just declared their true nature?

"<The spiritual race is like light from light and spirit from Tri Tr 119:16
spirit," the elder Mary said, her confused gaze growing clear. "When + Tri Tr 118:29
knowledge is revealed to them, they recognize it immediately. They will receive salvation in every way. The soulful race is like light from a flickering fire. They hesitate, and so their fate is left undecided. But the material race," she bowed her head, "lives in utter darkness. It shuns the shining of the light, and has no knowledge of unity. They will receive destruction in every way.>"

The saviour's face grew dark.

"But the psychic race still has hope?" Miri asked.

"<It was in the middle when begotten and created," the Virgin Tri Tr 119:16
said, "and remains double according to its capacity to do good or evil.> Though wavering in unknowing it may still be saved," she

glanced at Peter marching ahead of them, "by faith..."

As they rounded a hill, the distant town of Cana came into view, sparkling with torches and lanterns. In unison, the companions cried with joy. The city of light was indeed a wonder to behold.

Then, from the surrounding hills they heard the gentle tinkling of a hundred tiny bells.

"Shelama!" came a voice from the rocks above, offering the traditional greeting of peace.

"Shelama!" the companions cried in response.

In a moment they saw him – a broad-shouldered shepherd with a lantern hooked to the crook of his staff. He was descending with a herd of sheep, their tin and copper bells echoing in the evening air.

"Have you come for the celebration?" he asked. "Tonight, all of Galilee is Cana's guest!"

As he came closer, the companions could see a huge man with unkempt hair and beard. But a broad smile brightened his pock-marked face.

Then Peter cried, "Simon? Simon the Cananaean? I never thought I'd see your ugly face again, you crazy Zealot!"

The shepherd peered at the faces in the darkness. And a sudden cry of joy leapt from his lips. "The Galileans! My brothers-in-arms! The freedom-fighters of Jerusalem!" He howled in delight, and half his flock scattered with fright. "I see you've re-united! And recruited a whole pack of rebels to join us in the fight against Rome! Women, children, an old lady – you've come well-prepared this time!"

First Peter and Thomas, then Matthew and Jesus gathered round the fierce-looking but gentle-hearted shepherd. Each gave him a great hug, Matthew embracing him longest of all.

The Zealot's eyes filled with tears. "Come with me tonight to my home. I'll put a roof over your heads and tomorrow we'll eat and drink to celebrate our re-union. My little cousin's getting engaged to a delightful girl from Saab and they're celebrating the betrothal – the whole countryside's invited for the three-day feast."

With a festive cry, the companions let fly their rapture and delight. But the saviour cast a forlorn glance back at Nazareth, remembering its dark inhabitants.

Wiping the sand from his feet, he looked ahead at Cana in the distance – lit up for the feast like a thousand-candled *menorah*.

"Brothers and sisters!" he cried. "We've left Nazareth behind, where the dead may bury the dead. But in Cana, preparations are being made for the Wedding Feast! Let us rest. And tomorrow, we'll greet the future groom and toast his bride-to-be!"

Then he turned to Simon.

"<And thrice-blessed are you> who, on a dark night, invites a Ap Jas 14:41
stranger and passerby to the future wedding feast. You are one from one thousand!"

Stepping lightly and laughing, they set out for the sparkling city in the distance.

IX. Cana

I

Simon Zealot lived alone in a large old farmhouse, its many lofts and chambers built like steps descending the valley of Cana. Its central courtyard housed a large den, with benches of wood and lamb's wool arced around the hearthstone. Above their heads, the moon shone through vine leaves and grape clusters hanging from the arbour.

Having washed their hands and feet, the disciples reclined in a circle while the shepherd fetched olives, bread and freshly-skimmed goat's cheese. This simple repast with refreshing wine soon filled the fifteen brothers and sisters to contentment.

Jesus laid back and admired the joyful sight of his apostles revelling and conversing. Thomas to his left was deep in debate with Peter and Matthew. Magdalene to his right was teasing John and Simon. Across from him, Andrew was glancing furtively at Arsinoe while whispering to young Jude and James. Meanwhile, the elder James was laughing foolishly with Philip and Nathanael. Twelve apostles in all, plus the two relaxing in the alcove above him. For Mary-Arsinoe, his mysterious sister, was resting her head in the lap of Mary his mother.

Twelve. The number acquired a curious sense of completeness. After wandering far and wide, he had laboured hard, chosen well, finding the twelve finest companions to accompany him. His sister and brothers were the earthly fulfilment of his upper world visions.
They were the Fullness <– the true brothers and sisters, upon whom Gs Tru 43:5
the Father had poured out his love. And in their midst, that love

would never be lacking...>

The more the saviour stared at his twelve companions – was it the wine? was it the day's events? – he saw them with eyes awakened by ardour, rapture and ecstasy. Each of them, like a luminous and multi-layered silhouette, was emanating waves of love and goodwill, which he felt like a warm glow burning upon his cheeks. If one tear were to roll off his lids, it would immediately be consumed by that heat, so powerful was its radiance.

In wonder he watched as they started glowing, transforming, growing into winged and luminous beings. Each one bore the Nazarene's features, as if he were gazing into a twelve-fold reflection of himself. It was not his mortal face that Jesus saw, but
Unt MS the countenance of <Christ the Verifier, who stood as the sonship in their midst. This Christ bore twelve aspects> which were manifest in
Unt MS the twelve apostles. Meanwhile <the twelve beneficent ones gazed upon him and saw themselves in him,> unified as one.

Unt MS In this unexpected vision, <each of the twelve powers surrounding him had a crown upon his head, and was blessing him as the only-begotten king.> They stood with their hands clasped before them, their arms interlinked, forming one continuous chain of interlocking circles.

Unt MS And they raised their voices, crying: "<Through your image we have seen you, we have fled to you, and we have stood with you. We received the unfading crown, which has became known to us through you. O glory to you forever, only-begotten one.>" And together, they pronounced the closing strophe, Amen.

Then the Christ in their midst responded with the words:
Pistis ch 7 "<Behold, I have chosen you from the beginning. Rejoice now and be glad, because when I entered the world I brought with me twelve powers, who I took from the Treasury of Light. These were cast into the wombs of your mothers, and into the bodies you now wear, in preparation for my coming into the world.>"

The vision of the Twelve Chosen expanded, until each of them lost their bodily aspect, and became a pure and holy light in Light.
Ap Jn 7:30 Peter, Andrew, James and John shone the brightest, as *Armozel*, *Oriel*, *Daveithai* and *Eleleth*... And each of these four Light-givers shone between two lesser lights, making twelve lights in all.

He saw the twelve as they first stood in the Upper Aeons, the twelve faculties of his own mind which expanded into the twelve aeons of the divine Mind. He 'stood at rest' in their midst, as the only-begotten Son, and each of them manifest an aspect of God's seeing, thinking, and *knowing*.

Peter stood between Thomas and Matthew, but he knew these Ap Jn 7:30
three as truth, grace and form. Andrew stood between young Jude and James, but they became memory, afterthought and perception. The elder James stood between Philip and Nathanael, but now as love, understanding and idea. And last of all, John stood between Simon and Magdalene, but they were peace, perfection and wisdom. Yes, Wisdom was last of all... Wisdom – called 'Sophia' in the Upper Aeons, but named 'Magdalene' here below.

Through these twelve mindful aspects, he was able to know himself and, transcending this, know his Self – the inner source of knowledge that was the Father of all. The living Light shone on him from above, pouring its watery luminescence upon him. And he was entirely immersed in its all-pervading awareness.

From this new perspective of absolute mindfulness, at one with the totality, he could survey the heights and depths of the Upper Aeons. Above him his mother stood by the Father, as the eternal Virgin *Barbelo*. She was the Mind's first Thought, the *Ennoia* of *Nous*, joined to the Father as 'Mother of all'. Together, the Mind's thinking and its thought formed the self-reflective Parent, who was the Mother-Father, the androgynous source of all.

Then, slowly lowering his gaze, he looked down into the light's furthermost depths. In contrast to his mother above him, he saw his bride Magdalene below, she who was *Sophia*, the last of the twelve Upper Aeons. The younger Mary stood like a lower reflection of the elder Mary.

It had been so from the beginning. Magdalene was the lower Wisdom and his mother the upper. The Upper and Lower Wisdoms were named with different names, hidden holy names: the upper
was called *Barbelo*, and the lower, *Achamoth*. The upper was 'the Gs Phil 60:10
Virgin', but the lower was *'the Prunikos'*. The meaning of that epithet could not be denied. She was Sophia *the fallen*, Sophia *the whore*.

But why this epithet? What had she done to deserve such a title? The deeper he looked into the darkness, the less he could discern. The nature of her deed was hidden – obscured by the darkness, lacking
in light, and so utterly unknown. <Covered by clouds and unseen by Ap Jn 10:11
immortals,> her impulsive act remained shrouded in mystery.

Jesus awoke from this vision, only to find Arsinoe staring at him. Still with her head in the Virgin's lap, Arsinoe smiled at him curiously. Then, she closed her eyes and plunged back into the depths of rest.

The twelve apostles were still laughing and conversing. Simon and John were listening to Magdalene, enthralled by her charms and entranced by her conversation.

Miri lay down her cup and glanced at her beloved. She sensed at once that something was amiss. He was staring at her strangely.

"What is it?" she asked, caressing the back of his head.

He grabbed at her wrist and pushed away her hand.

That abrupt gesture, performed with such malice, shocked himself as much as her. He felt anger, jealousy – even frustrated desire. Yes, he had to admit to himself – he felt desire for the Magdalene. Despite his spirit's higher calling, his limbs were aching that moment for Miri: the fullness of her lips, the warmth of her touch...

"I'm tired," he said at last. "The day has been long, and our labours demanding. We each deserve a little rest." A weak smile crossed his lips.

"A quiet room has been prepared for you," Simon said in low, gentle tones. And he added with a deep bow of his head, "...my master."

Soph JC 91:21 "<You give me peace. My peace I give to you.>" He leaned over and kissed Simon.

"And may peace be unto all of this house," Jesus added, gazing at his apostles, exhausted but satisfied.

Then the two of them rose, and Simon led Jesus to a quiet chamber on the roof.

II

Above the vine arbour, the heavens sparkled and the Milky Way spread its pale mist of light.

Beyond the courtyard walls came distant sounds in the darkness: shepherds piping, crickets chirping, and a passing caravan of Batanean camels with their copper bells.

As the earthen lamps flickered out one by one, the shepherd of Cana led his guests to their designated chambers. Philip and Nathanael supported one another as they stumbled down the hall. Matthew, Peter and Thomas continued arguing loudly over Hebrew and Hellenic polemics. Sprawled out on the floor, lanky James was deep in sleep, dreaming of night-fishing.

In a quiet corner of the house, Magdalene lay next to Arsinoe and the Virgin. But Miri could find neither rest nor peace. She kept thinking about her beloved's strange response, playing it over in her mind. Why did he refuse her touch? Did he think she was teasing him? Trying to arouse him?

And what if she were... – after all that had passed between them! They had played like children in their nakedness, kissed and caressed. When he fought for her she had refused him. When he called her his bride, she had blushed like a virgin. They were two-as-one, engaged as body and soul. His mother, yes, even Mary sleeping beside her – wished for no joy greater than their marriage...

But how? Where was the mysterious Bridal Chamber and its 'marriage made perfect by the Father'? Did even *he* know – he, her beloved bridegroom?

And as Magdalene dropped off to sleep, she recalled the Baptist prostrated at her feet, beseeching her – 'Know yourself, before it's too late!'

The dream began as it had a thousand times before. *She had given birth*, but could not *see* the mysterious child she pressed to the cleft of her neck. Then, as the dream progressed, she remembered
how the child had come into the world. She had whispered, <*Child,* Orig Wld 100:10
pass through to here.> But somehow those words came out of her
mouth as, <*Yalda baoth.*> Orig Wld 100:10

With the utterance of that name came a terrible feeling of anxiety. It spread through her limbs like a sickening fever. Her hands grew cold, her brow burned hot. Somehow, she was the sole cause of this impending evil – immense, overwhelming – but she didn't know how or why. Thousands upon thousands would suffer through her act. Yet, its nature was so heinous that she had hidden it – hidden it from everyone, even from herself.

'Know yourself!' came the prophet's voice, interrupting her dream. And for the first time, the sequence of events took on a different colour. She watched them unfold as they always did – but this time she was conscious and lucid – awake within her own dream.

She felt her child nuzzle its dark face into her neck, licking and purring. She felt as its serpentine tail wrapped itself seven times round her body. And this time, she knew the words it would whisper – the words that always shocked her out of her sleep.

"My mother," Yaltabaoth hissed, *"Sophia... Achamoth... Prunikos..."*

But this time, she did not awaken with fear. Because she was aware that her waking was nothing more than prolonged sleep, and the insertion into another level of dreaming. All she lived was a lie and deception, an illusion and forgetting. But this dream, if she could remember and unravel it, was the truth. Through its images shone a higher hidden knowledge.

Her serpentine child recoiled slightly, and stared at her with a frightening smile. *"Sophia Prunikos,"* he repeated, *"Sophia the Fallen! Sophia the Whore!"*

Then, as she gazed in horror upon its leonine face, the monster grew to immense proportions. Its face became bright as the sun and its coils wrapped themselves seven times round the horizon. She wanted to scream, but her voice was caught in her throat. She wanted to flee, but she knew there was no place to turn.

'Know yourself!' the prophet called to her again. She was about to flee from the dream – rouse herself from the nightmare by surrendering to fear. But the prophet's voice gave her strength, even as the nightmare deepened.

Ap Jn 11:4 She watched in agony as <the Great Archon, joining with his arrogance, begot twelve Archons more. As he uttered aloud their names, from *Athoth* onto *Belias*, his fiery breath transformed into frightening demons with the faces of beasts. One was like a hyena; another, like a dragon. In all, seven celestial monsters appeared in the skies, and five more over the surface of the earth.>

Then the seven malevolent spirits joined with her in the heavens, and she was powerless to resist them. They controlled her very soul – her thoughts and moods, the movements of her limbs. It felt as if her arms were weighted down with stones; her legs forced open and pinned apart. Fearing that she was descending into total delirium,
Ap Jn 28:11 <one by one, they lay upon her.> The seven demons entered her
Iren 23:2 flesh <and she suffered every abuse at their hands.> Cursing
and maligning her, each of them cried: *"Magdalene the Fallen! Magdalene the Whore!"*

Raped in this manner, again and again, she felt herself tumbling into utter madness. The atmosphere around her grew denser, colder, darker as she dropped through the seven heavens and into the five sublunary realms. A body and soul enveloped her spirit like so many dark and heavy garments hiding her luminous core. They grew over her – like flesh, sinew and bones, like marrow, blood, skin and hair – all of them rank and putrid, with the smell of rotting corpses.

'Know yourself!' the prophet cried a third time. But Magdalene feared she was descending so far into insanity that would never

re-emerge. Still, the nightmare continued and still, she refused to awaken, clinging onto the last and fading flicker of her lucidity.

She watched as her body was born, then aged and died. But her spirit, once expired from that rotting shell, was seized by the demons and thrust anew into another body. In each life she'd sinned; in each life, she'd consorted with demons, powers and Archons. Having abused her body and raped her soul, they had gained mastery over
her sorrowful fate. <Thus, she was cast once more into another Iren 23:2
mortal form.>

She watched in horror as her vital spark <survived over a Iren 23:2
thousand years, passing through body after body. In one life, she was honoured as the Trojan Helena; in another, she was scorned as a prostitute from Tyre. She wandered through life after life, like a lost sheep> searching and beseeching its master – until finally, her spirit entered the body she now possessed. The features she so loved, the hair she so cared for; the oils she rubbed between her breasts and the henna she traced over hands and feet – all of this was temporary, an illusory garment and entrapment.

And already – it was too late! The spark inside her, which had witnessed all this with the faintest glow of awareness, was smothered over and extinguished by a thousand screaming demons. The shadows rose up from every crevice of her body, they cried from every corner of her brain.

In every conceivable manner of madness, her mind was tormented. Trapped in her nightmare and unable to awaken, she suffered a thousand tortures as she lay, unmoving, in her bed.

III

The valley of Cana, covered with dew and morning mist, shimmered golden green in the new day's sun.

Magdalene awoke feeling irritable and miserable. She had some vague notion that the same nightmare, which she had dreamt so many times before, had returned to her this night. But, like a faded tapestry, its images were dark and ill-defined.

The apostles rose from their mats, joyous and refreshed after a long pleasant rest. They greeted this dawn with great expectations, for today they would celebrate the engagement feast. Working in wood and stone, they prepared their gifts, then bathed and perfumed themselves.

Magdalene kept herself apart, wondering if her strange moods and nascent folly had not returned. Curiously, Mary-Arsinoe accompanied her wherever she went, nodding warmly with the gentlest of smiles. Wordlessly, the sister of Jesus bathed her and braided her hair; she anointed her with aloes and traced fresh designs on her hands and feet.

The companions set out in the early evening, when the air was cool and the twilight lasted for hours. In the surrounding fields, the ox-carts stood empty, the plough-shares abandoned – all had gathered in Cana to greet the bride and groom-to-be.

Now into its second day, the feast at Cana had reached its height. Under a garlanded awning, the newly-engaged couple received their guests one by one. The betrothed greeted each with a heart-felt kiss, while his future bride flashed emerald eyes from behind her embroidered veils.

The Messiah was welcomed as a special guest. After presenting their gifts, Jesus and his companions mixed with Cana's town folk. They feasted, drank and danced. They sang traditional psalms and, like competing minstrels, improvised bawdy songs, which were hailed with whistles or laughter. The moon glowed bright while the sun lingered in the heavens. It felt, on this night, as if the sun and moon were to be wed, witnessed by the earth and sky.

After midnight, the companions regrouped, wishing to find their centre once more in the saviour. Among their ranks, three more had been added. From Bethany, just east of Jerusalem, Martha and Mariam had come to celebrate Cana's feast. But secretly, they had journeyed to distant Galilee in hopes of hearing the Messiah. And now they had found him here – celebrating the promised wedding. At once they had pressed themselves to his sides and not left him since.

The third was Susanna, a solitary wayfarer who gathered herbs, folk-remedies and old wives' tales. Despite her compelling appearance – tall and slender with ginger hair – she rarely smiled. In fact she had been widowed young, and chose this solitary path rather than re-marrying her husband's brother – for such was required by law.

In her usual, respectful but reserved manner, she had asked the saviour if she could follow him. When asked why, she replied
Acts Jn 95 without hesitation, "<Because you are the way for the wayfarer...>"
And nodding, the saviour had taken her into his embrace.

The Nazarene sat in a corner of the courtyard, surrounded by his disciples. The three new ones sat closest, while the others lay casually across one another, cradling cups of wine in their hands. Only Magdalene and Mary-Arsinoe kept their distance, huddled in a dark corner across from Jesus. From time to time he glanced at Miri, and was met with a cold stare he could hardly decipher.

The son of Nazareth began: "I had a vision last night. As we sat in a circle, I saw you all glowing with light, and each was crowned with the Father's glory. You stood at rest in the upper heavens, as the Twelve Aeons of the Father."

Andrew raised his eyes. "<Tell us of the aeons, so we might Soph JC 112:19
understand...>"

Jesus looked at the fair-haired son of Jonah and smiled.

"The Upper Aeons are so many emanations or extensions of the
Father's unity. Like <light from his Light and life from his Life, they Ap Jn 4:2
are knowledge of his Knowledge.> And like names echoing in the silence or images in the watery light, each of you reflects the Father to himself. Thus are you, the Twelve, like twelve aspects of his Mind or twelve manners of his thinking. When He remembers himself, Jude *is* his memory; when He sees himself, James *is* his perception; when He is at peace with himself, Simon *is* that peace."

Jesus looked at his disciples one by one, remembering and marvelling at their unique qualities.

"The Upper Aeons are 'the Fullness', or *Pleroma* as we say in Greek, because they are *filled* with the Father's thoughts. Indeed, each person with the *gnosis* becomes one of the Father's thoughts. As that person regains awareness of divine unity, knowing God within himself, the Father's thought returns and, through it, He reflects upon himself. Like a circle, God's self-knowing is made complete.

"That is why we call the Upper aeons the *Pleroma*, because the
Fullness is *made complete*; it becomes <the Entirety,> the Totalities, Hyp Arch 97:13
and the All. It is <the Storage-house of the seeds, the Treasure-house Auth T 28:22
of the light,> <and the ultimate Dwelling-place> of the All." Auth T 33:4

The Nazarene looked up. Above his head, a thousand invisible stars were shimmering in the night-sky.

"What can I tell you about the All? <The All exist within Unt MS
him and nothing exists without him. He is a boundary to the All, enclosing them all, since they are all within him and there is no
place outside him.> <The All are the small ones who join the big;> Dial Sav 140:6
<they are the little ones who are made great.> <Since the Father of Dial Sav 136:23
the aeons existed *before* the All, He remains an incomprehensible Unt MS
and solitary One. Yet, He is the One who comprehends the All.>"

"Then what of the Lower Aeons," the Iscariot asked, staring into the darkness. "How do they fit into his greatness?"

Soph JC 114:18 "<The Father created a curtain between the immortals and those
Hyp Arch 94:9 that came afterward.> <This is the veil that hangs between the world
above and the realms below. Nothing more than shadows came into
being beneath the veil> – images lacking in light. The Lower Aeons
Dial Sav 139:13 are <the Deficiency,> lacking in knowledge, love and life – even
existence!"

He gazed at his twin, whose face remained dark and disturbed. The Iscariot was still fascinated by the darkness, and its lure of unknowing. The saviour pressed on.

"Where the Pleroma is timeless and eternal, the Deficiency is bound by space and time. Above, all are immortal and imperishable; below, they are born to perish and die. One is light and spiritual, the other dark and material. And yet, these oppositions in our thinking exist solely in the lower world. Above, all is one – the totality of Existence – and the Deficiency *does not even exist!*"

Thomas shook his head ever so slightly. But Matthew, sitting beside him, asked:

"So how do we live here and now?"

"You live, *knowing* that the Kingdom exists! It is invisibly here and unfolding now. But most of what you see around you, misleads you. Like fog and a dark mirage, it distracts you; like a smoke-filled mirror, it tricks you with temptation, turning you away from the invisible light. We must remain focused on the Kingdom. Only in this way may it expand and flourish..."

"Then how does the Kingdom grow?" Peter asked.

Christ gazed upon the Bethsaidean, and his heart swelled with joy. This man was the bedrock of his community. But still, the elder son of Jonah would encounter many difficulties in comprehending the mystery.

"It increases without any loss of its unity! It increases, just as the One became many in the Upper Aeons. When the One first reflected upon itself, it became two. But it became, not just thinking
and thought, not just the masculine *Nous* and the feminine *Ennoia*,
Ap Jn 20:9 but the Father and Mother. Together they form <the Mother-Father,>
or more simply, the Parent."

He turned to Susanna, Martha and Mariam.

"Many times, when addressing the crowds, I will speak of 'the Father'. But you must know that the divine One is not a Father alone. The unity is the Mother and Father *together*, as *the Parent* of the All.

And the Parent is neither masculine nor feminine as we understand them, but androgynous...

"Indeed, all the angels in the Upper Aeons are androgynous, as extensions of the Parent. Here below, the family expands because the man and woman lay with each other. Indeed, that is the very mystery of marriage – whose betrothal we are celebrating this evening."

He glanced at Magdalene, whose cold stare continued to beguile him. Indeed, it intrigued him, drawing him to her, tugging at his heart with renewed desire.

"<Marriage in the world is a mystery because no one can know Gs Phil 81:34
when the husband and wife will come together in their marriage
bed, except the two of them.> <As the male moves upon the female, Th Cont 139:41
and the female upon the male,> <each contributes to the child's NH Ascl 65:31
begetting.> <When the semen reaches climax, it leaps forth – and in NH Ascl 65:19
that moment, the female receives the strength of the male. But the male, for his part, also receives the strength of the female.> In her womb she forms their offspring, who will then be born either male or female. And so the cycle continues.

"<If there is a hidden quality to marriage in this world, then Gs Phil 82:4
how much more is the marriage above a true mystery!> <Whereas, Gs Phil 76:6
in this world, the union is between husband and wife; in the Upper Aeons, the form of the union is different, although we refer to it by the same name.> We call it a 'marriage and begetting', though in truth it is a 'consent and creating'. It is a *consent* between two *consorts*."

The saviour looked at his brothers and sisters. All were listening intensely. To make himself clear, he began again at the beginning.

"Through the union of the Mother and Father, the Parent produced a third, which is the Son. This is the third part of the mystery. The One by itself is the first aeon. The One as two – the Mother and Father, the thought and its thinking – is the second aeon. But the third aeon is the One as three – the Mother, Father and Son as thought-thinking-itself. Through the Son, the One reflected upon itself, and its self-knowing was made complete.

"That is why the Son came into the world – to find the particles of light scattered in the darkness, enlighten them, and turn them toward the One. As each returns to the One, divine self-knowing expands to the very limits of the Entirety. The One is made All and
the all are made one. How great is this mystery! <For in the One, Soph JC 110:15
the multitude revealed themselves, and that multitude will gather together once more and return to the unity.>"

Suddenly, simple Nathanael raised his eyes to the heavens. In a flash, he had understood.

But Susanna asked, "Tell us of the consorts. How did the Mother and Father create the Son, if they are androgynous?"

The saviour smiled at Susanna. She was more perceptive than most. He opened his mouth and said:

"Each angel in the Upper Aeons is created androgynous, but <is
Soph JC 104:10 given a male and female name> – like the Parent who named itself
Father and Mother. And each one thus named becomes a *consort*.
In Greek, we call each of these a *syzygy*, since it is the complement
of some other. The Upper Aeons expand each time a consort seeks
Soph JC 101:16 out its complement <– the one with whom it was destined for union
Gos Eg 52:3 from the beginning.> <These two join *in consent* and, with the
Parent's final consent, the consorts create a third, to bring about the
completion of the aeons.>"

Jesus cast another glance at Magdalene, who was staring at him from the shadows. How intriguing her beauty seemed to him tonight.

Gs Phil 59:2 "<It is by a *kiss* that the perfect conceive and give birth,>" he
said. "They approach each other, they gaze upon each other, and they
Eugnos 77:4 recognize their own features in one other. <For she, as his feminine
aspect, resembles her brother and consort,> just as he resembles her.
Eugnos 81:7 <In greeting each other, they embrace and from that kiss comes the
mutual recognition and reflection, by which they create the third.>
For, together, they have reflected the One's original unity and,
together, they create an extension of his unity."

Many of the apostles nodded, having now perceived the beauty of the mystery. But others gazed into their cups, at a loss to understand. Seeing this, Christ continued.

Tri Tr 73:19 "<The emanation of the Totalities from the One does not come
about *through separation*, like a child cast off by its parents in
Soph JC 104:10 begetting.> Rather, when <he reflects with she who is his *syzygy*,
they reveal their androgynous offspring with a male name and a
female name.> But it remains one and, in its androgyny, the offspring
reflects the Mother and Father *equally*; it remains a *unique* reflection
of the Parent to itself."

Magdalene gazed at her beloved and wondered – *who* was the *syzygy* of the Son; the consort of Christ?

Tri Tr 73:19 "<In this way," Jesus concluded, "begetting becomes a process
of extension, as the Father extends himself to those whom He loves.
His love expands, so those who have come forth from him may

return to him – by *becoming* him,> joining with him once more in loving unity. They become a part of the One's totality, in joyful union and communion."

It was well after midnight, and those who had not understood, now made weary by the effort, were utterly exhausted. Though his words would never reach these, others had attained new awareness.

The saviour rose and gave all of them a look that made their tired eyes grow wide.

"<From this day onwards, I will speak with you openly about Pistis ch 6
the beginning of the truth unto its completion. And I will speak with
you face to face, without parable. I will not conceal from you, from
this hour onwards, any of the things that reside in the height.>"

"<But *rabbi*," Peter said, "who will be able to climb up to such Dial Sav 135:7
heights or, for that matter, down to the bottom of the abyss?> Our
minds cannot encompass it all!"

The saviour approached Peter and caressed his hair. "Even I
have difficulty in comprehending these things, since the mystery
has not been revealed to me completely. But little by little <I began Test Tr 43:23
to know myself, and speak my mind concerning these things – the
unbegotten aeons, the Virgin who brought forth the light. Now,
when I open my mouth, I speak with the Mind of the Father.> But,
in truth, not even the Word knows whereof it speaks, until its words
are spoken."

He then turned to James and Philip, who were looking at him with wonder but an utter lack of comprehension.

"<Whoever is worthy of knowledge will receive it. And with Soph JC 93:18
that knowledge, he will become an immortal in the midst of mortal
men.>"

Next he turned to John, who was gazing at the master with an intense spiritual ardour.

"<He who has come to know the Son of Man has come to know Test Tr 36:23
himself.> <And he who has known himself has, at the same time, Th Cont 138:17
achieved knowledge of the depths of the All.> Therefore, look upon
me, and <behold me in truth. For I am not the things I have said, but Acts Jn 101
the things that you are able to *know* through me. And in this way,
you too will become like these things.> You too will become a light
in Light, a son of the Son, and one with the All."

Together, they whispered the word, "Amen..." and the evening came to an end.

IV

That night Miri lay awake in her bed as a tumult of strange emotions wracked her heart. At the same time, a chorus of taunting voices raced through her head. Fragments from last night's dream kept resurfacing, but she couldn't remember their meaning or proper order. The unity and clarity she had felt after Christ's first kiss had been replaced by a myriad of passions in conflict.

Unable to withstand the onslaught of voices, she rose from her mat. In the darkness, she could see Arsinoe's crystalline eyes glistening as they gazed at her, wide and awake. But the mysterious sister said nothing.

From the inaudible stillness she heard the Virgin's muted timbres.

Thund 16:31 "Have you forgotten? <Whenever you hide from me, I will appear.> You are hiding Miri... hiding *from yourself*, hiding from us *both...*"

Miri gazed into the darkness. "Because I cannot admit, even to myself, what I've done."

"Or what you've become," the Virgin said.

"You know what I am!" she replied, her voice breaking with sorrow. "Neither wife nor virgin, neither daughter nor bride! All I've become... is..."

She hesitated, unable to say the word they all knew. The ensuing silence was filled with the Virgin's breathing.

"We are more, much more than that..." the elder Mary said at last.

"Then what..?" the younger Mary pleaded.

"You know it yourself."

And from the thousand cries echoing in her soul, Miri heard the one voice she hadn't heard for so long, reminding her. *'The whore and the holy one'*.

"I am ever-virgin," the elder Mary said, "and you are ever-whore. But *Barbelo* and *Achamoth* are one in their wisdom. Together, we become *the holy one* – She who is 'Mother of all'."

The Virgin leaned forward into the moonlight, and her face was shining with such compassion that all tears were erased from Miri's face.

"In the earliest hour of the morning," the mother said, "the darkness meets the light. Go now, it is time..."

Miri waited a few moments until her heart grew calm. Then, without another word, she rose and departed.

Magdalene climbed up to the roof, and drew aside the curtain to Christ's chamber. Her beloved was fast asleep, like an effigy laid out in its tomb.

Naked, she climbed into his bed and began caressing him. Roused to life, he appeared pale and slender as a spectre.

With her fingers enmeshed in his long tresses, with her lips pressed hard to his cold mouth, she arched her body over his.

"Miri..." he whispered, half-awake, "did I call to you in my sleep?"

"Sometimes," she replied softly, "<the soul moves of her own Ex Soul 134:8
accord.>"

He opened his eyes, and gazed at her face in rapture. Was this a dream? Her face had transformed, and become even more beautiful than he remembered it. Her eyes and lips, so familiar, so much like his own – manifest a higher hidden presence.

Miri smiled through her tears, seeing him as he saw her. Their two faces had blended into one. But over and above that, she saw his higher aspect, the mysterious presence that had entered him at the Jordan. She saw the bridegroom.

And he, his eyes growing wide, suddenly awoke to the higher
presence in her – ancient, wise and eternally-knowing. She was
Sophia, his bride from the beginning. Trembling with ardour,
shaking with fear, <he recognized his counter-image...>" Ap Jn 23:9

"<The bridegroom and bride belong in the Bridal Chamber,>" Gs Phil 82:23
she said, her voice resonating with Sophia's.

"But it is not yet time. That mystery is still hidden from us..."

Magdalene nodded. "Because you have not yet embraced me as your bride or consented to our union."

He watched her fine features hovering in the half-light, her words surrounded by a halo of truth.

"<No one shall see the bridegroom with the bride," she revealed, Gs Phil 82:24
"unless he becomes such a one.> <Know me and recognize me, you Thund 14:24
who know me not...> The bride is <she who gives herself joyfully in Tri Tr 93:1
the hope of union.>"

She pressed her lips to his brow, his hands, his chest, whispering
with each kiss: "<After the saviour cleansed his soul, renewing it Ex Soul 132:10
like a virgin, she entered the Bridal Chamber. And filling it with
perfume, she lay herself down, awaiting her true bridegroom.>"

Powerless, speechless, still he resisted.

She brushed her fingers over his sides and caressed the last of
Ex Soul 132:34 his ribs, his Adam's rib. "<Once the saviour and soul unite, they
become a single life. Wherefore the prophet said of the first man and
woman, 'They become a single flesh'.>"

She moved her weightless body over his in a slow rhythmic motion.

"But we cannot, here and now, in the flesh..." he pleaded.

Like a soul floating over his sculpted effigy, she smiled and
Test Tr 30:2 responded, "<The Law commands us to take a husband or wife,
beget and multiply, like the sands of the sea.>"

In his delirium, he declared, "How much I long to join with
Ap Jn 21:30 you! But the first man and woman learned that <to taste such fruit *is
death*.>"

But even as he said this, his longing mounted to insatiable desire.

Ap Jn 21:30 "<The root of that tree is bitter!" he cried, reminding himself.
"In all its branches lie mortality. And nascent desire, housed within
its seed, sprouts only in earthen darkness!>"

Still caressing her consort, his bride replied, "In its fruit lies
knowledge and awakening! I have tasted it – and I know! It's hidden
seed *is life!*" And again, she brushed her long fingers over his ribs.
Gs Phil 68:22 "<Eve was separated from Adam> <because, it was not in the Bridal
Gs Phil 70:20 Chamber that they united.> But I have come to you tonight – to join
them now, and re-unite them in the flesh."

"Would you enter the Bridal Chamber blindly, unknowingly? We remain flesh of their flesh..!"

"In her wisdom, Sophia knows the secret hidden from the first
Gs Phil 70:19 – hidden even from you, Jesus my brother. <Those who have united
in the Bridal Chamber will no longer be separated...>"

His desire for her rose, and she lowered herself over his supine figure. Their limbs entwined; their bodies pressed together. But the moment before their union, he saw the fires dancing in her eyes – seven flames undulating like seven fiery demons: lust, pleasure and dissatisfaction, then desire, frustration, jealousy and rage.

From her eyes to his, the demons leapt. And he, trapped by his desire, was powerless to resist them. They possessed him entirely, spreading to his extremities. Anger rose like a fire through his limbs; fury blazed in his eyes.

His hands rose above her breasts, then locked around her neck – tightening, squeezing, suffocating her every breath.

Gasping for air, Miri clawed at his face, digging her nails deep in his brow. She tore at his flesh.

In one impulsive act, he seized Miri and threw her from him. Then, recoiling in fear, he began thrashing his arms blindly, as if, fighting off invisible armies. He writhed on the ground, slithering like a wounded serpent, crying and convulsing.

Suddenly, his anger turned inward, and Jesus scratched at his own flesh – lacerating his thighs, tearing open a huge gash in his side. He was clawing at his own skin, as if ripping it from his soul like a blinding, suffocating garment.

Seeing this, Miri threw herself on her beloved, seizing his arms, trying to stop him from harming himself. In agony they struggled – pulling, tugging, rolling over one another. All the while she was screaming for him to stop.

They landed with him on top of her: his hands pressing her arms to the floor, her legs pinned apart. Gazing into her eyes, he pleaded: "Out seven demons!"

But he knew it was hopeless.

She had planted her seed of desire in him, and now it had taken root. From one evil seedling, six more had sprouted. His lust was unsatisfied; his anger unsatiated. And from those frustrated cravings came the pleasure, jealously-guarded, for revenge.

Miri could see these seven afflictions swimming in his face and knew her worst fear had come true. Her demons had finally become his own, and neither of them could cast them out. By acting on desire, she had released in him an array of evil passions.

Tears welled up in her eyes. "Forgive me," she pleaded, "for who I am and what I've become! It's my fault, even if I don't know the nature of my sin."

And, raising her hands to her brow, she hid her face in fear and shame. But through her sobs came an unrequited flow of self-recrimination and remorse.

"In spite of it all, <I deserve the things I've suffered..." she Val Exp 34:23
cried in deep lament. "I accept! *I am* what I've become.>"

Though her hands were pressed hard to her face, the tears still squeezed through the crevice in her fingers.

"<I am sinless," she whispered softly to herself, "and the root Thund 19:15
of sin derives from me..!> *I am* Sophia the fallen; *I am* Magdalene – the whore..."

Jesus gazed at the woman under him, curled up in agony. And from a sudden stirring in his heart, the evil in him recoiled. His fury and desire, like frightened demons, fled. Instead, from compassion came a heart-piercing sorrow which he'd never felt before. It came like a light, hidden in his soul, pouring love's healing into his eyes and hands.

Now he wanted nothing more than to share in her suffering, take her to him and hold her in the hopes of soothing her misery.

"So so so..." he said, prying her hands from her face and kissing her steaming forehead. "I love you *for who you are* – Sophia, Magdalene – *you are who you are*, forever..."

And as they stared at one another, the veil of their shared misery was rent in two.

"Miri, my beloved," he whispered, kissing her hot moist cheeks, "We each have our angels and demons – uprising unbidden, hidden within. But you are everything to me – my love, my life! You are my soul, whether fallen or forgiven. You are my bride, in every manner of passion."

Then they gazed at one another, knowing that the fires in their eyes had been extinguished by a flood of healing tears. He looked at her, and through his newly-awakened eyes, he beheld that vision of the Fall which had appeared to him many months before.

He saw Miri the way Adam first saw Eve – their eyes freshly opened to nakedness and desire. Feeling neither fear nor shame, they recognized that in their fleeting embrace lay oneness, and that this was the secret hidden from the beginning; this was the beginning of love.

Still leaning over her, he marvelled at she who was his counter-image, his consort, his bride.

Why, in *The Poimandres*, had the First Man fallen for his reflection in Nature's mirrored pool? Because she, the goddess so long forgotten, embodied in her flesh that *eros* which passed through all of nature. On the surface of her sea, he saw the thousand myriad reflections that formed her web of life: the ram that tumbled the ewe, the stallion that mounted the mare. Even when serpents entwined, these two lowly beasts bode man no evil but bore all the signs of life's healing and renewal.

Those signs lay everywhere: in the spiralling fall of a winged sycamore seed; in the he-goat and the she, engendering their offspring; in the roots of two cypress trees, one female, one male, enmeshed in the cold dark earth; in the repeating design of a creeping vine traced on Miri's skin.

Deep in her womb, the Goddess nurtured life's eternal cycle, and he, the First Man, wanted nothing more than to fall from his austere heights into her image of plenitude.

Gently, Jesus planted his lips into Miri's palms, then touched her hands to his hot forehead. In bowing to the sacred designs traced upon her skin, he wished to recognize, in her, Nature's striving for eternal growth through death and renewal.

Seeing this, a myriad of images uprose in Miri's mind. Her entire journey, long-since buried in her memory, came surging to the surface. She remembered the ancient love-poem sung in honour of Baal and Astarte. She recalled all the goddesses forgotten by her people – *Hochmah*, *Asherah*, *Astarte* and *Zoe*, whose gifts they had long-since forsaken – wisdom, fertility, love and life. All of Sophia's aspects appeared once more: She, who was honoured and scorned; She, the great and disgraced; She, who was life and death. Last of all, Miri called to mind the Virgin who had whispered to her: <*I am* Tri Prot 19:15
the womb that gives shape to the all.>

Impossibly, she saw her own face in all these images. All were one, and manifest the Parent's hidden aspect – the feminine half who was 'the Mother of all'.

Still leaning over Miri, staring at her with intense ardour, Jesus acknowledged this higher presence dwelling in her. Then, as Sophia gazed in wonder, her consort came closer. As if, from a great height, Christ's face lowered slowly toward hers. And in a moment of mutual recognition, they kissed.

In a flash, all became light, <shining without shadow.> All the Soph JC 113:19
dark places of her soul were illuminated, and Miri saw the entirety, from the uppermost heights to the bottom of the abyss.

Just like Jesus before her, she saw the Aeons of Light, with *Barbelo* and *Achamoth*, the Upper and Lower Wisdom. In awe she saw how she and the Virgin were equal aspects of Wisdom – the one younger, the other older, but both timeless reflections of the same eternal deity: the virgin and whore as Holy One. Together, these two became 'the womb that gives shape to the all'.

This vision filled her with an overwhelming joy. And though her eyes were closed, she started laughing with delight, shaking with the ecstasy of *gnosis*.

But from her place in the heights, as the last of the Upper Aeons,
<Sophia looked down.> And there, unlike the other luminous beings, Zost 27:9
she was able to discern all the shadows dwelling in the dark below. Though covered by clouds and obscured by fog, she could see the

light-lacking beings, whose sombre shapes were shifting – the lowly creatures whose life was hidden, whose wisdom was unknown to the light of the uppermost heights.

What Miri saw frightened her so terribly that she started trembling in horror. Writhing from side to side, moving to and fro, she closed her eyes and cried for it to stop.

"Do not be afraid!" her bridegroom cried. His voice came to
Th Cont 138:17 her as if from a great distance. "<To know yourself is to acquire knowledge of the depths of the All!> This vision is yourself! Look at it and do not be afraid."

Magdalene opened and closed her eyes, but it made no difference. The nightmare would not stop, and now it fused dream and wakingness into a single horrific vision of forgotten self-knowledge.

All the images from last night's dream came flooding back into her memory. The entire sequence flashed before her, passing over her eyes with incredible speed, and she felt the full impact of its atrocity in the span of a single heartbeat.

But, as if she were tied to a huge turning wheel, Miri watched with horror as the torturous sequence of her dream cycled round. With a dizzying feeling of falling into insanity, she passed through life after life, consorting with Archons and demons, then dying and rising again. Repeatedly raped, falling past aeon after aeon, the dream recommenced, and she innocently imagined she'd just given birth...

"Know yourself!" the distant voice cried. Was it the prophet calling to her from her dream or the voice of the saviour still clasped in her arms?

She felt his burning lips pressed to her lips, and heard the saviour saying "*You are who you are* – Sophia, Magdalene – do not be afraid!"

From that kiss came renewed illumination. Like flashes of lightning, the dark places in her soul, for a few brief instants, were bathed with luminosity. And in that terrible epiphany she saw the impulsive act which darkness had hidden from her, which time's forgetting had shrouded in ignorance.

In the beginning, Sophia had stood alone. Though her consort
Val Exp 34:25 stood with her, as her *syzygy* and complement, <*she had renounced*
Soph JC 104:14 *him*> – calling herself <'First Begettress' and 'Mother of the Universe'.> Though the Son, as her male reflection, shone with an
Val Exp 34:38 abundance of light, <*she cut herself free from him*,> <calling herself

‘Life’ and pouring forth its plenitude as ‘Mother of the Living’.> Ap Jn 23:20

She knew of her *syzygy* <– the one with whom She was destined Soph JC 101:15
for union from the beginning.> <But Sophia desired to create *alone*, Hyp Arch 94:5
without the aid of her consort.> <Thus, She conceived a thought Ap Jn 9:25
from herself, bringing forth a likeness from herself *without* her
lover’s consent. And though the person of her maleness had not
approved, still *she brought forth*.>

But, because it was not a complete reflection of the Parent,
her offspring appeared, lacking the fullness of unity. Indeed, it was
imperfect, multiform, monstrous and misshapen. <Like a woman Orig Wld 99:17
giving birth, all her superfluities flowed out> and her offspring burst
forth <– an aborted foetus, entirely lacking in spirit.> <That watery Hyp Arch 94:14
substance took shape, like an image> without light, <and its shadow Orig Wld 99:9
became matter.> Hyp Arch 94:12

<When she saw the consequences of her desire,> Sophia Ap Jn 10:7
trembled with fear. For <her offspring assumed a palpable form. Hyp Arch 94:16
Molded out of darkness; it became an arrogant beast – resembling
a lion.> <With eyes of fire flashing like lightning, it acquired the Ap Jn 10:8
shape of a lion-headed serpent.>

In horror and fear, <she cast it away, hoping none of the Ap Jn 10:11
immortals would see it. She surrounded it with clouds, to hide it from
them all.> This was <the Archigenetor of ignorance who reigns over Tri Prot 40:22
chaos and the underworld.> <This was the First Archon> <– the Ap Jn 10:19
Arrogant One> who claimed ‘<It is I who am God; and there is *none* L Pt Ph 135:15,
apart from me.>’ Hyp Arch 94:21

But the fauvean serpent turned towards its begetter, and the
moment she saw his horrendous countenance, she cried aloud in fear.
Her senseless cry acquired form, becoming the being’s unspeakable
name <– *Yalda baoth*.> Thus, in ignorance and fear, she named the Orig Wld 100:10
aborted thing.

Yaltabaoth seized the spirit which had escaped Sophia’s lips,
and acquired it for himself. In this way, <the Arrogant One took a Ap Jn 13:26
power from his mother,> which was the seed of light within her. And
with the *pneuma* now in his breast, he glowed like fire. This flame,
mixing with the darkness, glowed dimly in the Upper Aeons, though
below it blazed with all the fury of the sun.

<When Sophia had seen the wickedness of her deed, she Ap Jn 13:21
repented – weeping, lamenting, moving to and fro.> Indeed, so
terrible was her deed that *she hid it from herself*. Having repressed
all memory of the event, <she was overcome by forgetfulness and Ap Jn 13:24
the darkness of ignorance.>

Thinking that her consort had refused her, Sophia dared not return to the heights. Instead, she entered the intermediary realm, 'the eighth heaven' which lies just above the realm of her wicked
Unt MS son. <This is 'the Middle', the outer limit of the light, which forms a boundary and veil between the aeons below and above.>

But already, it was too late. Yaltabaoth commanded his Archons
Iren 23:2 to lay with her, <so she could not re-ascend to her Father.> And she, having refused Christ as her consort, was renamed the *Prunikos* – Sophia 'the fallen', Sophia 'the whore'. She fell from the eighth realm, passing through each of the Archon's aeons, acquiring the body and soul-garments that hid her vital spark.

Iren 23:2 It was just as Magdalene had seen in her dream: Sophia <was cast into a bodily prison, passing for ages from one vessel to the next,> until finally she entered the daughter of Magdala. Her whole life long, Sophia's life-spark had hidden in her breast – but Miri, blinded by the flesh, had remained ignorant and unknowing.

This entire vision, in all its horror and complexity, came to Magdalene in a flash, and within a moment it was over. But its epiphany was so overwhelming that she cried aloud in agony, shuddering from the shock of self-knowledge.

The Nazarene took her into his arms, caressed her hair and kissed her, mingling his tears with hers.

Trembling, she recounted the entire mystery, denying neither her wilful deed nor her shameful role. *She* was the mother of evil, the cause of this world's ignorance and suffering. *She* was at fault – she, the Sophia hidden in Magdalene's flesh, just as Christ was concealed in her consort, the Nazarene.

Christ gazed upon Sophia and acknowledged her unwitting role in the creation. Though sinless, the root of all sin lay in her. Though willing good, she had done evil. And though repentant, she had never been fully forgiven for her deed. Only he, her consort, could remedy that fault.

"Your kiss," she whispered, wiping away her tears, "has exposed my hidden act; it awakened me from my ignorance." A painful smile
Thund 17:35 broke upon her trembling lips. <You have wounded me, my beloved, and you have shown mercy.>"

Then Sophia lowered her head and murmured, "In your infinite mercy, I beg of you please – forgive me for my fault."

Gs Phil 75:3 The saviour held his consort close and said: "<The world came about through a mistake.> But you will *never* be forgiven for your

trespassing... You have committed a sinless sin and faultless fault.
<Though ignorant, you have been knowing; though senseless, you Thund 14:26
alone have been wise.> You are what you are, Sophia, Magdalene, Thund 15:29
forever...”

She raised her eyes and stared at him, at once comprehending and still lost in unknowing.

“<All you have done has its origin in love,” Jesus said, letting Iren 2:2
the voice of Christ speak through him. “Because you, the Mother
of all, *imitated* the divine Parent – desiring to create *just as* He had
created. You acted alone, multiplying from one to many, just as He
had done. Thus, in ardour and passion, you longed *to know yourself!*
You searched into yourself, and began to expand to the very heights
and depths of the pre-existent Parent.>

Sophia-Magdalene gazed in wonder, as the Word revealed the mystery in full.

“<In your infinite longing, you desired nothing less than to Iren 2:2
comprehend the Parent’s greatness. And when you could not attain
that end, you suffered every agony of mind – stretching yourself
outward ever further, until you finally met with *horos*, the Limit that
is his knowability. With great difficulty, you were brought back to
yourself, knowing that the Parent is incomprehensible.>

“And yet, like the Parent before you, <your resultant thought Ap Jn 10:2
did not remain idle.> For the product of your desire was *ignorance*.
And from that ignorant thought grew <the shadowy darkness and Orig Wld 99:10
watery depth that ultimately became the Archon of the all.>”

For a long time, Magdalene and the Nazarene remained silent, reflecting upon all the Word had revealed. Each of them remembered the desert prophet, engaging Jesus with his darkly-ringed eyes and demanding: ‘Who created Yaltabaoth? *Whence comes evil?’*

Now, at the price of terrible pain, they knew. And Miri, through the painful ordeals of this night, had come to *know herself.*

“By suffering her own passion,” the Word revealed once more,
“<Sophia created the veil between the immortal beings and those Orig Wld 98:20
who came afterward. She established ‘the Limit’ of the eternal aeon,
whose light is everywhere, and whose exterior is now shadowy
darkness.>”

He brushed the back of his fingers over his cheek, wiping away the last of her tears.

“Do not think that you suffered without purpose. For Sophia
acted out of love. Her ardour and passion <belong, not to desire, Gs Phil 82:8
but to the will.> <Nothing happens without the will of the Father, Gs Tru 37:20

though his will be ever-inscrutable. He alone knows the beginning, middle and end.>"

"Then what?" Magdalene cried. "Why so much suffering from love, if the only result is ignorance? Why would the Father *will* for darkness to enter the world through her?"

But the moment she said this, she heard a voice uttering the answer. She heard the Virgin – who *was* Wisdom, but *Barbelo* – that
part of Wisdom which Sophia did not know. Speaking for them both,
Tri Prot 45:6 the Virgin said: *<I am the Womb that gives shape to all. And I give*
birth to the Light that shines in splendour.>

In that moment, it all became clear to her. The Father – through Sophia – had willed darkness into being. But the Mother – through Christ – had willed the coming of the light. She had given birth to the Light that shines in splendour, and he would come, to remedy Sophia's fault, and chase away the darkness. He would restore everything to how it formerly was.

The bride gazed upon her bridegroom and marvelled. He
Tri Tr 79:1 would make <the end like the beginning.> Through his own terrible
Gs Thom 36:11 entrance into the world, <the end would be where the beginning is.>

X. Gennesaret

I

The summer of the Messiah lasted late into the winter months. *Tíshrî* passed with its Feast of Tabernacles. The Pilgrims carried their freshly harvested dates through Jerusalem's torch-lit streets, then drank in abundance the new year's wine. They built *Sukkoth* huts from branches of palm and willow, then recalled in psalms their forefathers' forty years of wandering through the deserts of Sin and Shur.

The months of *Márhéshwan* and *Kíslew* saw the Feast of Lights, when eight lamps were lit, night after night, to celebrate the rekindling of the Golden Candlestick. But the *gueshem* – the winter rain – still did not fall, and their summer's joy was prolonged.

Jesus and his companions raced around Gennesaret, mooring their boats and amassing the crowds, which wilfully surrendered their scythes to bask in the coolness of the Messiah's shadow.

His words fell upon their burning brows like a soothing rain. They laid fresh loaves and olives at his feet, repaying him gladly for the few moments of peace which he had brought to their toil. The poor were comforted and the hungry were fed. All the while, the Roman soldiers looked upon these gatherings with stern bewilderment. Herod's soldiers reported back to him; the Levites kept the High Priest abreast of these deeds. But Galilee had thrown up invisible walls. It was the new Kingdom, brilliant, glowing, unseen – its gates as clear as glass, its towers transparent as shimmering crystal.

Everywhere one turned, the Messiah was there. "<I am the light Gs Thom 46:23
that presides over the all,>" he cried, and he shone forth on all of

them, like the rays of some higher, unseen sun.

Gs Thom 46:23 “<I am the all,” he said, “for all come forth from me, and to me the all will go.>” They came to him, like water-carriers basking in his stream.

Gs Thom 46:26 “<Split a piece of wood,” he told them, “and I am there. Lift a stone; and you will find me.>” In every face, in every rock and tree, the Messiah’s face was reflected, smiling with inner calm.

On the hillside just outside Ginnesar, a crowd of thousands gathered. The Nazarene walked among them, sometimes addressing hundreds, other times speaking to a select few. All listened with wonder on their faces; all heard and were satisfied. For a long time afterward, they recounted his words, remembering that late afternoon as ‘the Messiah’s last sermon’.

“Speak to us of Love!” a gentle shepherd cried.

Gs Phil 77:35 To the crowd, the saviour replied: “<Love is like an aromatic oil – all those, who anoint themselves with it, will enjoy its benefit. While those who are anointed enjoy its fragrance; others nearby will also take pleasure in its scent.> So must you anoint yourselves with love, and spread its sweet distillation to all around you.”

Gs Tru 33:39 Then he gazed at the peasants at his feet and added: “<The children of the Father are his fragrance, for they come from the grace of his countenance. Indeed, the Father loves his fragrance, and manifests it in every place.> Like the crown of thousand-petalled flower, he exudes the honeyed-nectar and draws it back to himself. He exhales it like sweet-smelling breath; and you, in spirit, are that breath from him. When he draws it back into himself, you are subsumed once more in the richness of his aromatic splendour.”

In the shadow of a carob tree, publicans and merchants shook their heads, whispering among themselves.

Gs Tru 34:18 “<But when fragrance grows cold,” he said in a stern voice, “it loses its scent. From hatred, spite and division, the holy aroma turns acrid. But once the breath draws it back in, it again becomes warm and sweet. For this reason, the sonship of the Father has come, to dissolve hatred and division, and unite us once more in the fullness
Tri Tr 138:22 of his love.> <For the One is filled with Love.> In the brotherhood of faith, we *all* become true sons of the Father.

Gs Phil 61:36 “Trust in faith!” he cried. “<Faith receives, love gives! No one will be able to receive without faith. No one will be able to give without love. Because of this, in order that we may indeed receive, we believe, and in order that we may love, we give.>”

He stopped and gazed at the Galileans sitting round him.

"Look upon your brother, and see him as you would see
yourself! <Love your brother like your own soul, and protect him as Gs Thom 38:10
you would the pupil of your eye.> For, just as your small reflection
lives in his eye, so his soul lives in you."

Then the Nazarene continued among the tradesmen and day-
labourers, touching their heads and saying: "<Blessed are you who Gs Thom 43:8
have laboured, for you have found life!>"

Coming upon an old anchorite from desert, he cried: "<Blessed Th Cont 140:41
is the wise-man who sought after truth! When he found it, he rested
upon it forever, and trembled not before those who dared to disturb
him!>"

A young man turned to him and said, "Lord, am I coming closer
to the Kingdom?"

The saviour turned to him and said: "<The person who is far Gs Thom 47:17
from me is far from the Kingdom. But the person who is near to me is
near the fire.> For know this: <it is through fire that the whole place Gs Phil 57:22
will be purified.> And so, you must become <like the salamander, Test Tr 71:27
who goes into the flaming fire which burns exceedingly,> but is
neither burned nor consumed."

"But how?" the man cried, in fear for his soul.

"Have you not heard me? <Love and goodness are the beginning Dial Sav 142:4
of the path...>"

A woman asked him, "Then how will we come to *know* the
Father?"

The saviour replied: "By seeking him. <If you seek with a Allog 56:15
perfect seeking, then you will know the good that is in you. What is
more, you will know yourself, as one who has come from God> and
one who will return to him."

Then he raised his face to the multitude and cried: "<Blessed Gs Thom 41:27
are the solitary ones, the chosen few, the Elect. For you will find the
Kingdom! You come from it and you will return to it.>

"<Blessed is he who *was*, before he came into being!> For he is Gs Thom 36:17
pre-existent, and he shall exist afterward.

"<Blessed is he who *is*, before he came into being! For he is, Gs Phil 64:10
and was, and *will be!*>

"<Thrice-blessed is the man who, from the beginning, has Gs Thom 36:14
'stood at rest'. For he will know the end, and death will not overcome
him!>"

A young Pharisee called out, "Blessed are you, O Lord!" This
youthful rabbi had come all the way from Jerusalem, wanting only
one thing: not to believe, but to know absolutely. "<No one can Soph JC 93:24

find the truth except through you, master. Teach us, therefore, the truth!>"

Ap Adam 83:11 The saviour smiled and answered: "<Blessed is the soul of
that one who has known God, and received the knowledge of truth!
For he shall live forever! He has not been corrupted by desire, nor
accomplished the works of darker powers, but has knowingly stood
in God's presence – like light come forth from fire and like life come
Soph JC 117:8 forth from flesh and blood!> <Whoever, then, knows the Father in
pure knowledge will depart to the Father and repose> in his eternal
rest."

Then for a long time he was silent. A cold wind blew over them from the lake, and many began shivering. Jesus sighed, shook his head and cried out.

"You walk the earth, not knowing what lies in the skies spiralling over your heads. Above you lie the planetary rulers, unseen, like robbers lying in wait. They command legions of demons to tempt your soul and consort with it – leading you astray. But when your hour finally comes, and you must leave this place of sojourn, then you will truly know their mastery. For having submitted to them here, you will belong to them there. As you rise, they will demand payment, like toll-collectors blocking your route. And you who have obeyed them will be cast down, not just once, but again and again, until your soul finally repents, and finds the perfect passage through their seven gates."

"Then how will we rise, deathless, from the flesh?" a woman cried. Her name was Annabel, a well-known courtesan from Tiberias. And though she had sung at many weddings, secretly she longed to become, herself, the bride one day. The saviour knew this longing hidden in her heart.

Ex Soul 127:19 "<Wise men of old gave the soul a feminine name," the Nazarene
replied, "because she is feminine by nature> – loving truly but also
foolishly."

The courtesan lowered her head, ashamed that he had read her heart. Gazing at the crowds he cried:

"Each of you must become acquainted with the soul hidden in your own flesh – she who is your sister, silent and unheard."

He sat upon a rock where Magdalene, a few paces away, was reclining with Mary his mother. He acknowledged them and said:

"Bear with me a few moments, and I will tell you her story – how she wandered far from her home, and became fallen in the world. I wish to tell you 'the Parable of the Bride' – she who dwells invisibly in each of you."

Many in the crowd gazed at their own shadows: the inseparable double that the day revealed but the night concealed.

"Your soul, <when she was still with the Father, had remained Ex Soul 127:22
virgin and pure. But when she came into this life, she acquired that
bodily garment> <which made her a sister to lust, hatred and envy.> Auth T 23:12
<The rulers of this world prepared their temptations quite artfully, Auth T 30:26
spreading them before her like a banquet. They wished to make the
soul incline herself to them – drawing her by force of ignorance,
deceiving her, until she succumbed to the fruits of desire, envy and
fleshly pleasure.>

"<In this way, she fell into the hands of evil men – some of Ex Soul 127:25
whom were merchants, who seduced her with many gifts; others of
whom were robbers, who took her by force.> <She had turned to Ex Soul 128:7
these men, thinking that one would become her respectful husband.
And indeed, they deceived her much, pretending to be true, when
they were no more than unfaithful adulterers.> <For they were Auth T 23:29
well-versed in all the pleasures of life – in proud passions, hateful
envies, and vainglorious things.> <In body, she prostituted herself Ex Soul 128:1
to them, and they defiled her one and all. Then one day they left and
abandoned her.>

"<She fell into drinking much wine, for wine brings debauchery. Auth T 24:14
And, having left knowledge behind, she fell into all forms of
bestiality.> <She raged at herself like a woman in labour, who writhes Ex Soul 132:2
in agony at the hour of her delivery.> <Finally she became a poor Ex Soul 128:17
and desolate soul, like a young widow without means.> <Dwelling Auth T 27:26
in a house of poverty, she became feeble, ill and alone.>"

The saviour paused, and nothing could be heard except the cool breeze blowing from the lake.

"<Perceiving the empty deception she was in, weeping over Ex Soul 128:26
the darkness that had entrapped her, she mourned her pitiful state.
Sighing, repenting, she prayed to the Father, calling upon him with
all her soul. She repented of her prostitution, calling her Father
by name and saying in her heart, 'Save me, Father, for behold: I
render account of myself. I abandoned my house and fled from your
shelter.> <I tasted sweet passions, only to realize they are transitory. Auth T 31:24
I revelled in evil, and now I have left its deceitful food behind.>
I beg you, Father, <restore me to you again.>' <She prayed, not Ex Soul 129:2,
externally, with the lips, but from the spirit within, which rises up Ex Soul 135:4
from the innermost depths.>

"<When the Father looked down and heard her cry, He was Ex Soul 128:26

overcome with mercy, and counted her as worthy – for many are
Ex Soul 132:7 the afflictions she suffered after abandoning his house.> <From
heaven, her Father promised to send her her man, who is her brother
in heaven, the one called the bridegroom. So as to become his bride,
she renewed herself, giving up her former prostitution. She prepared
the Bridal Chamber, filling it with her perfume, and entered it. Then
she lay herself down, waiting for her true bridegroom to enter.>"

Christ stood up and walked among them; an inexpressible delight lit up his face.

Ex Soul 132:23 "<With the will of the Father, the bridegroom came down to
her, and entered the Bridal Chamber. She gazed upon his face,
Ex Soul 132:33 and when she recognized him, she rejoiced with tears.> <For she
remembered that, originally, they had been joined, one to the other,
when they were still with the Father – in that time before Eve led
Ex Soul 132:33 Adam astray – Adam, who was her brother.> <Now, this marriage
had brought them back together again. The soul was joined to her
Ex Soul 133:31, true love;> <she enjoyed her beloved and he also loved her.> <This
Ex Soul 134:5 is the marriage made perfect by the will of the Father.>

Ex Soul 134:9 "<She received her divine nature from the Father, so that, like a
virgin, she could be restored to the place from whence she had first
Auth T 35:8, come.> <She found her rising.> <This is the ransom from captivity.
Ex Soul 134:13 This is the upward journey through the heavens. This is the way of
Auth T 32:16 ascent to the Father.> <She gave the body back to those who had
Auth T 32:2 given it to her.> <She stripped off this world, and discovered the
Auth T 35:10 true garment which clothes from within – the bridal raiment.> <She
reclined in the Bridal Chamber, receiving rest from her labours. She
ate of that banquet which provides immortal food. She found what
she had been seeking all this time. For, within the light that shines
in the glory of revelation, she came to repose in Him who is at rest
– for ever and ever, Amen. >"

There was a long silence. Then, from various places in the crowd, there came the scattered response: Amen.

But the courtesan of Tiberias, who was overcome by tears, cried, "Speak the words that will make each of us a bride!"

Soph JC 107:11 And Christ said: "<By the will of the great Light, I have come
down from the places above, to cut off the work of the robbers and
awaken the drop of light in you. I descended in secret, evading their
bonds of fate, so that, through me, you may become perfected, and
bear much fruit.>

Ap Jn 31:5 "<Let he who hears," the saviour cried in a loud voice, "*get up
from his deep sleep!* When the soul asks 'who has called my name?'

And ‘where has this hope come to me, while I’m still bound by the
chains of this prison?’ I will respond, ‘I am the knowledge of the
light!> <I am the remembrance of life! I am the one who is, and was, 2Ap Jas 58:6
and will be with you forever!> <*Arise and remember!* For you are Ap Jn 31:14
being called! Follow your root, and ascend to the greatest heights!
But beware the deep sleep and your enclosure in the walls of Hades.
Guard yourself against the angels of poverty. Renounce the demons
of the abyss, and all those who will ensnare you!>’”

He pointed to the heavens, where clouds were rolling and forming into darkly threatening shapes.

“<But if the robbers ask you, ‘where have you come from?’ Gs Thom 41:31
Then say to them, ‘I have come from the light – from that place
where the light first came into being, and where I first appeared – as
an image in the light.’> And the gate-keepers will not detain you.
<You will be spared from their bond, and freely enter that place Tri Prot 41:18
where you were from the first.>

“For you are the chosen ones,” the saviour cried, his exhilaration
enlivening every word. “You are <the assembly of the Elect, who Soph JC 113:21
exist in the Light that shines without shadow! And your anticipated
joy cannot be described, for it is an *unutterable* jubilation. In the
radiant Silence, the lights will delight themselves, forever without
end, in unchanging glory and immeasurable rest!>”

Ecstatically, a beggar cried, “<O you, our light, enlighten us O Th Cont 139:20
Lord!> Reveal to us the Light!”

“<The Light exists inside a son of light – and with that light, he Gs Thom 38:7
illuminates the entire world. But if he does not shine, then there is
darkness, nothing more.> <Therefore I say to you: to become like Gs Thom 43:31
God, you must become full of light. But if you will be one separated
from God, then your heart will remain in darkness.>”

By now the sky had become heavy as led. A downpour threatened to break any moment.

“Do not be afraid! <For I have come into the world, like a light, Jn 12:46
so that whoever believes in me may no longer dwell in darkness.>
Do not tremble before <the revelation of the light, which comes like Tri Tr 131:9
a blast of lightning! Rather, bear witness to it, for it is the sign of
your salvation.>”

The moment he said this, lightning streaked across the sky, illuminating the lake and its lower depths.

“<For in me is life – the life that enlightens every man.> <That Jn 1:9 + Jn 1:4
luminescence will shine amid the darkness, and the darkness will Jn 1:5
not overcome it!>”

The people grew frightened. It was, as if, the world itself obeyed the Word's command.

Jn 8:23 "<You are from below; I am from above. You are of this world;
2Tr Seth 52:9 I am not of this world.> For <I am a stranger to the regions below.>
Jn 12:36 Thus I say to you <– walk while you still have the light, lest the darkness overtake you. He who walks in darkness knows not where he goes. But the light will be with you a little longer yet. While you still have the light, therefore, believe in the Light – that you may all become sons of light.> For only the sons and daughters of light will enter the illustrious Kingdom."

"Teach us of the Kingdom," an old man cried, his body shaking, his lips trembling.

Unt MS "The Kingdom <is like a crystalline ship, laden with all things good. It is like a city of light, filled with every race of man.>

Tri Tr 124:18 "<It is entrance into the great Silence, where there is no need for voice, nor for knowing, nor for understanding – but where all things glow with light, without need of external illumination.>"

As he said this, the clouds over their heads began, mysteriously, to disperse. A strange glow spread across the heavens.

Hyp Arch 97:13 "<All the children of the light will know their root, which is the Father of the entirety. Unto ages and ages, they will sing with a single voice, 'Holy! Holy! Holy!'> And though their voices may be many, they will sing their praise, in an eternal round, harmoniously
Tri Tr 132:20 as one. They will sing, from themselves to themselves. <For in the end, they will receive a unitary existence, just as their beginning was unitary. They will go to that place where there is no male nor female, nor slave and free, but the all in all.>"

Gs Tru 32:31 Christ held up his hands and bade them, "<Say to me from the heart that you are the perfect day, and that in you dwells the light that does not fail..!>"

Like bees drenched in sweet pollen, they cried to him, "Before you leave us this evening, speak to us – if it is permitted – speak to us of the Father!"

The crowds, he could see, had become saturated with the sweetness of God's breath. They wanted nothing more than to inhale his eternal fragrance, again and again, without end.

Mars 4:20, Tri Tr 53:40, Tri Tr 53:7, Ap Pt 76:14, Tri Tr 52:6, Gs Tru 22:25 "He is <the silent One> <– good, faultless,> <complete, perfect, one...> He is <the eternal One> <– without beginning, without end;> <the one who encircles all space, while there is none that encircles him.>

Allog 64:31, "He is <the eye of revelation that is at rest;> <a being without

evil – imperturbable, sweet.> Yes, <joyous, sustaining, delightful and Gs Tru 40:29,
true,> you will recognize him by his majesty and beauty. Standing Tri Tr 55:15
at rest, in the fullness of the Father, you will *know* him, in <the first Allog 65:18
emergence of the stillness... and tranquility ... and silence.>"

The saviour bowed his head and surrendered himself to speechlessness. Above him the skies shone with the radiant splendour of day's end, when the light lingers in the heavens as if, in fear of departing. The lake of Gennesaret never looked more glorious.

Slowly, the crowds dispersed, wondering if this were not the first day on earth.

II

As the companions retreated to their sailing crafts, a gentle mist rose above the olives groves. The sky grew dark and starless over their heads, casting the myrrh and lilac bushes in shadowy relief. The evening air was filled with their intoxicating aromas.

As usual, Thomas and Peter tarried behind the others. Peter recognized at once that the Iscariot was in one of his moods – brooding, silent, secretive. But Peter's own heart was seething with resentment. He decided to speak to the Iscariot, unburden his heart, and try to draw him out.

"Did you see it – the way he glanced at Magdalene, just before the Parable of the Bride?"

Thomas gazed at the tangled branches of a passing tree, and the black birds perched on its boughs. In spite of himself, his voice rasped low with resentment.

"I saw it – the secret glance, the tacit pact of complicity, just between the two of them..."

A wicked smirk creased beneath the Bethsaidean's beard. "Yes, but did you catch what he said? He told her, in so many words, that she has a *womanly* soul – she tries to love him truly," he smiled with spite, "but all she does is foolish..."

The Iscariot's eyes flashed grey with irony. "His whole theology, it seems, is founded on her – the soul who prostituted herself, then repented, hoping to gain the bridegroom's love."

"You think it's love she's after?" The Bethsaidean shook his long red locks. "She wants to conquer him, nothing more – tempt
him with forbidden fruit. If it were up to me, <I'd banish Mary from Gs Thom 51:18
our movement. Women aren't worthy of the life.>"

The Iscariot cast a curious glance at Peter. Did the Nazarene know that Peter – his rock, his foundation to the faithful church – wanted to exclude women?

The Bethsaidean looked at the disciples marching ahead of them, and Jesus at their front. A flash of fury passed over his face, seeing that Magdalene, of course, was close by his side. The saviour was confiding his thoughts to her in whispers.

Gs Magd 17:7 “<Does he prefer her to us?” Peter asked, his anger rising. “Would he rather entrust his secrets *to a woman* – than speak openly with all of us?>”

Gs Magd 18:6 Thomas shrugged. “<You’ve always been hot tempered, Peter my brother. Now you’re contending against women as you would with our adversaries. But if he’s made her worthy, who are we to reject her? He knows her well enough – even... loves her *more* than us.>”

“That’s what worries me...” Peter mumbled.

They walked on, their heads bowed in silence. The Iscariot returned to his abject state.

“Women are corrupt by nature,” the son of Kerioth remarked,
his voice dry in his throat. “It is the man who must restrain himself.
Th Cont 144:8 <Any man who loves intimacy with womankind is woeful indeed,
Th Cont 140:25 and pollutes himself by contact with them.> But it is <his own
insatiable lust that blinds him.> The Nazarene spoke truly when he
Auth T 31:24 said <all passions are transitory> and <the pleasures of life, sheer
Auth T 23:29 vanity.>”

As Thomas spoke, he could feel his darker twin emerging. It was Judas who had said these things – Judas, who hated Magdalene and all she stood for: love, desire and all the pleasures of the flesh. Monasticism was the true path – desert asceticism and rejection of the flesh.

“Then we’re agreed,” the Bethsaidean said, concluding their conversation. “Magdalene is a bad influence. We must keep her away from the Messiah.”

As they skirted the shores of the lake, the saviour walked with
Gs Phil 59:6 three women <– Mary his mother, Mary-Arsinoe his sister, and
his companion Mary Magdalene. Indeed, his mother, sister and companion were each named Mary, and these three always walked beside him.>

“I fear for you Jesus,” Magdalene began. “I can feel it – we’re losing you.”

The Nazarene looked at his beloved, a confused expression

overcoming his features.

"Miri's right," his mother affirmed. "He's taking possession of you..."

"Who?"

"Christ!" Magdalene exclaimed, her voice shaking. "The Son of God with his league of angels! He's overpowering you – *possessing* you as much as the Archon did with his army of demons! When you open your mouth, he speaks through you at every turn."

"He is... and I am... the Messiah. <The Word must become Jn 1:14
flesh> in order to be heard by men."

"But what will happen *to you?*" Miri asked, her heart breaking with remorse. "I've felt it – I know! Sophia acted through me, making me suffer her passion. What will happen to you – in the end? Will you suffer because of him?"

"What choice do we have, you and I? Christ and Sophia must speak through us – not just *be*, but *become* themselves through us..."

"Refuse him!" Magdalene cried. "Recover yourself, before it's too late..."

In the shadowy path before them, the Nazarene caught sight of a dark figure awaiting their approach. They came upon a blind man, his gaunt figure draped with an anchorite's robes. The desert prophet bowed low before the Messiah.

"I have waited for you for many years," the blind man began. "If it be your will, free me from my affliction. You are the saviour – save me!"

The companions came upon Jesus and the blind man, surrounding them on all sides. They stood in a desolate place, the farmers and field-hands having long-since retreated to their homes.

Hesitatingly, the Nazarene cupped his hands round the elder's face, whose cheeks were scarred and whose eyes were glazed over with a thick blinding mist. The corners of his mouth twitched and rose slightly.

In a moment, Jesus saw them there – the multitude of demons glaring from behind the clouded eyes. For a long time, the man of Nazareth gazed into their darkened depths, sensing the infinite abyss beyond the blinding veil.

He saw, beyond the myriad of demons, greater and darker forces at work – the powers and Archons, and greater still, the Archigenetor himself. Then, with a cold icy chill running down his spine, he realized he was staring into the face of Yaltabaoth made flesh. Before him stood the Archigenetor's Son.

His fiery serpentine eyes hypnotized the saviour, whispering, "Come to me, if you will. My name is Barabbas. Meet me now!"

Jesus released his grip, recoiling in agony.

"Leave me!" he cried. "Leave me in peace! I'll have nothing to do with you..!"

The apostles, bracing the fallen Nazarene, gaped open-mouthed and amazed. Meanwhile, the blind man remained where he was, unmoving, with a satisfied smile upon his face.

The Nazarene turned away and walked on, his head bowed in pain and humiliation.

Where was the saviour now? He felt powerless and confused – unable to accept or deny his divine counterpart, the Christ within.

"I have no choice," he said to Miri in a strangulated voice. "If I must sacrifice myself, I will – for the Messiah to reach the end."

They came upon their crafts, moored in the shallows of the lake. Gennesaret was dark, silent and deathly still.

The sons of Zebedee released their boat from its mooring; the sons of Jonah following suit. The companions piled into these two sturdy crafts, then set sail for Capernaum. After a long hard day, they wanted nothing more than to build a fire, dine and then rest in the warmth of Magdalene's home.

From the far-off villages came the inviting smell of cypress wood burning in the hearths.

At once, Jesus lay himself down – utterly exhausted from his day's labours. The sails unfurled, the rudder slipped softly into the lake, and the son of Nazareth soon fell into a deep, dreamless sleep.

Andrew lit the lanterns fore and aft while Peter guided their vessel. In the boat beside them, John did the same while James steered their craft.

The younger son of Zebedee whispered to his brother, "I don't like the look of the moon tonight."

In the starless sky above their heads, the silver moon turned to rust and sanguine hues.

As the boats sliced the water, John noticed that the blind man was skirting the lake, following their every movement.

As soon as they reached the centre of the lake, the moon disappeared, plunging them all into darkness. A strange wind started ripping against their faces, whipping up the waves. This was not a storm, but some great disturbance churning the skies and seas.

It circled round them, like a beast beneath the waves, moving at incredible speed. Was this Leviathan, the legendary sea monster that sailors always feared? And was that the great beast Behemoth in the skies, stirring up the storm clouds? They felt an encroaching evil, restless and malevolent.

Suddenly they were caught in a violent commotion. Like a maelstrom, the currents whirled under their vessel; like a cyclone, the clouds spiralled over their heads. Their boats were pulled into the mighty vortex – rocking, swaying, threatening to overturn.

Still, the Messiah slept.

In desperation, Peter tried to wake him, but the saviour couldn't be roused. He lay still and rigid as a corpse.

Then, leaning over their crafts and looking deep into the swirling abyss, they saw the beast. Like an electric eel, the Archigenetor slithered under their vessel, illuminating the turbulent depths with an eerie phosphorescent glow.

Jude and James, in fear for their young lives, started crying. Nathanael prayed. Arsinoe stood up in the boat, as if hypnotized. She was drawn by the beauty of that horror, wanting to plunge herself into its paralyzing depths.

At last, Magdalene understood their predicament, and why this horror had broke upon them. Wisdom whispered to her the truth she'd refused to hear – that *she* was the cause of this suffering, and only Christ could resolve it.

The waves lashing her face, the tears blinding her eyes, Magdalene leaned over Jesus. From within, the voice of Sophia erupted onto her lips: "<*Yesseus... Mazareus... Yessedekeus* – Save us!>" Gs Egypt 64:9

Then Magdalene, her lips trembling with remorse, kissed the saviour's mouth.

The boat rocked violently, throwing her back. She would have tumbled over the side had not Thomas grasped her and pulled her to him.

The twin and the bride watched as a glowing spectre rose from the Nazarene's recumbent figure. The son of glory straddled the side of the boat and stepped onto the waves.

All of them gazed in wonder as the Messiah walked upon the water.

Then, balancing on the edge of the maelstrom, he wilfully plunged into its fearful depths. An apocalyptic battle broke beneath the waves. Flashing blue and white, electric charges of light illuminated the dark abyss, while the black serpentine body churned the surrounding waters.

And suddenly, from the centre of the vortex, a rippling calm spread in all directions. The waves expanded, growing in circles, until the waters achieved an absolute stillness and serenity.

It was frightening, the perfect silence that came afterward. They sat in their listing vessels, listening to the last of the waves breaking on distant shores. The sky was cloudless and still, the sea as smooth as glass.

But Magdalene – crouching close to her beloved, caressing his brow as his eyes slowly opened – cried aloud in pain, knowing she had sacrificed him. Now, the Messiah would move through him always – just as Sophia moved through her – to remedy her ancient fault. But Jesus, her beloved, would be no more.

XI. The Upper Jordan

I

For three days and nights, the Messiah did not move from his refuge in Magdalene's tower.

Each morning, he woke with his disciples, broke bread with them, and shared in all their menial tasks – repairing torn cloaks, washing muddied tunics and preparing their winter clothes. They spoke of earlier times, drank wine by the hearth-side, and not once did the Nazarene speak with authority. It felt as if Christ had departed, leaving the man Jesus behind.

Then, on the evening of the third day, the Nazarene announced their imminent departure. His suddenly stern demeanour warned them of impending hardship. They gathered up their sandals and staffs, donned their heavy cloaks and departed.

Cool rain was falling, and the wind on their backs sent chills through their cloaks.

Walking north along the lakeshore, they reached the Upper Jordan, where 'the Descender' flowed into the Gennesaret delta. The Messiah sought a secluded spot where they could comfortably camp for the night. He found a place on the banks of the fast-flowing river, next to a small, calmly rippling inlet.

They built primitive shelters from willow and palm; they scooped fresh water from the Jordan's pool and prepared a fire to warm them. Then, gathering his disciples round him, the saviour spoke with terrible gravity.

"It begins now," he said, his dark eyes flashing, "– the battle between the sons of shadow and the sons of light. We've been granted a short reprieve, to prepare ourselves. But know this: in three days' time I will send you forth in pairs, so the battle may commence in earnest."

The brothers and sisters glanced at one another, fearful of their impending task.

"The Baptist has been seized; his mission will soon be over. But
Jn 3:30 <as *he* decreases, *we* will increase!> He prepared the path; we will
walk it together. Why did he say 'the Messiah will come – bearing Five Seals'? Because those seals will be given *to you* – to mark you and protect you. You are the chosen ones; you are the Elect."

He pressed his palms together, staring into his hands as he spoke.

Gs Egypt 59:1 "<The Father brought forth the Five Seals from the fullness
of his bosom.> And gradually, He reveals them to the Son for the
Unt MS benefit of all. <I am the Son who stands in your midst as Christ the
Verifier. For I have come to verify each of you, and seal you with the
Ap Jn 31:22 seal of the Father.> In this way, <I will raise you up, and seal you in
the watery light, so that death will no longer have power over you – from this time onward.>"

Andrew turned to John. What had happened to the Nazarene? His joyful countenance had turned to brooding and foreboding.

"You should have died three days ago – perished in the abyss stirred up by Yaltabaoth. I cannot bear the thought that the
Archigenetor would have claimed you for himself. You are precious
Pistis ch 7 to me, precious as pearls from <the Treasury of the Light.> Therefore,
for your protection and salvation, I will initiate you this night into the preliminary mysteries. We shall not sleep, but spend the whole of the night in preparation."

His voice was low, barely above a whisper.

"Then, with the coming of the light, you will be initiated into the *gnosis* of the Third Seal."

From afar came the cries of desert predators: hawks and foxes, jackals and hyenas.

"And the last of the Five Seals..?" his mother asked flatly. "What of the fourth and fifth?" She was staring into the fire, which was hissing and crackling from the damp wood.

"Here below, where knowing unfolds gradually, the Father's wisdom comes to me a little at a time. The final two seals have not yet been revealed..."

These words did not sit well with his companions. Peter cast a side-glance at Thomas, whose brow was creased with doubt.

The Nazarenre raised his voice:

"In the Jordan, John revealed the First Seal, which is the *baptism* in three forms. Through his grace, the Second Seal was confirmed: the anointing with oil which we call the *chrism*. These two will prepare you for the Third Seal – the visionary ascent we call the *resurrection*."

Christ gazed at his companions, turning slowly from Simon to Susanna to Matthew.

"Tonight, you will be baptized three times and anointed, so that you may be resurrected. In this way, the power of the first Three Seals will pass into your hands."

Rising, he walked among them, placing a hand on Philip's shoulder, then on Nathanael's.

"You have already received instruction concerning the first and second seal. But you must penetrate deeper into their mysteries before acquiring the third. We have built this fire by the Jordan to ready ourselves for that task."

He poured some water into a cup – water from the free-flowing Jordan – and handed it to Philip. Taking an ember from the fire, he handed it to Nathanael.

"<It is from water and fire that you are made sons of the light.> Gs Phil 67:2
<And through water and fire, you will be purified. For there is water Gs Phil 57:22
in the baptism; and there is fire in the chrism.>"

Cradling the sacramental cup and baton, Philip and Nathanael trembled. Something invisible and strange was stirring in the water and the fire.

"<The mysteries," Jesus said, "are revealed through images and Gs Phil 84:20
their archetypes.> <Everything above is concealed> <– hidden, as Gs Phil 59:14, Gs Phil 84:23,
if, by a veil.> <Only the things below are revealed.> <But when the Gs Phil 59:14, Gs Phil 84:23
veil is rent, all that is hidden will be shown forth.>"

He held out his hands. In the flickering light of the fire, his figure appeared like a transparent spectre.

"<I have come to make the things below like the things above, Gs Phil 67:30
and unite them – through images.> Once you <*enter through* the Gs Phil 67:17
image> you will see the mysteries hidden above."

"Then what lies hidden in the water?" Philip asked. He was gazing into the cup, as if, into the infinite depths of the sky.

"When you go down into the Jordan <you are baptized in the Ap Adam 85:24
living water,> <the water that flows from above.> The baptismal Melch 8:1
waters, together with the oil of the chrism, reflect the watery light of the Upper Aeons."

"And the fire?" Nathanael asked. He was mesmerized by the glow of his burning ember.

Gs Phil 67:5 "<In the chrism is the fire, and in the fire, the light> – that light which shimmers throughout the aeons' waters."

Jesus held up a clay lamp – flat and round, with a small handle on one end and a spout on the other. "The fire in the chrism's oil is hidden. Still, it may be made visible." He poured some oil into the lamp and touched an ember to it – the oil burst into flames.

"Of course, the light we see in this fire is not the true light.
Zost 48:3, The fires above give light but <do not burn;> <they are beautiful
Gs Phil 67:5 and bright, whiter> than the fire of the stars. Here below, fire and water do not mix because they are opposites. But above, opposites exist harmoniously: the fire mixes with the water and makes it luminous."

"Then why a watery light?" Matthew asked, scratching at his beard. "Why are the Upper Aeons composed of fire *and* water?"

"Because these best reflect the Father's unity. Fire, when divided, suffers no loss; it may pass from lamp to lamp, growing in number – while remaining one from the source. And water, like a mighty ocean, may become many droplets – yet how willingly those drops plunge back into the ocean! Like sparks and dew drops, the Father disperses himself into the multitude. But they, returning to him, may unite as one at their source."

He smiled at them and added: "Both fire and water are *vehicles* of his light. Fire concentrates it and, like a lamp, diffuses it for the benefit of all. Water retains light and, like a mirror, reflects it back to our eyes. The Upper Aeons have this quality, since they receive the Father's light – like a seal or impression – and manifest it as his luminous images."

Concentrating his gaze on Susanna, Mariam and Martha, he said: "In order to impress your image in the Upper Aeons, both the
Gs Phil 69:8 baptism and chrism are necessary. <No one can see himself in a mirror without light. Nor can he see himself in the light without a mirror. The baptism provides the watery mirror; the chrism, the fiery light. For this reason, it is fitting to perform *both* rites.>"

Philip and Nathanael nodded, having understood this aspect of the mystery completely.

"Through the mystery of these two seals, you *come to exist* in the Upper Aeons, both in image and in name. I have already explained how the Father sees himself in your image, and names himself through your name. But for you, that luminous reflection becomes the key to the mysteries – it becomes your garment of light."

The sons of Zebedee glanced at the sons of Jonah, remembering when Christ had first made them his disciples. They had seen it then – the glowing raiment...

"Many times you have heard me speak of the body as a garment.
That garment is nothing more than a <perishable rag,> <a cloak of Gs Tru 20:28
darkness,> which clothes your soul in death and corruption. It is Ap Jn 13:32
<the robe of ignorance, the dark enclosure, the living death. You CH VII.2
carry it like a portable tomb, and you are its perceptible corpse.>
But once your image is impressed in the watery light, it will become
your <true garment> <– the garment of life> which <clothes you in Auth T 32:2 Dial Sav 138:20
the perfect light!>" Gs Phil 70:5

"<How will the garment be brought to us?" Jude asked. Dial Sav 138:20

The Lord said, "As you enter the watery light, there are those
who will receive you, and others who will provide you> with your
raiment – the angels <who immerse, enrobe, enthrone and glorify.> Tri Prot 45:12
<*Micheus*, *Michar* and *Mnesinous* – they will immerse you in the Tri Prot 48:15
spring of life; *Yammon*, *Elasso* and *Amenai* – they will invest you with your robe of light; *Bariel*, *Nouthan* and *Sabenai* – they will crown you and enthrone you; and *Ariom*, *Elien* and *Phariel* – they will glorify you with the glory of the Father.>

"<Thus you will strip off the garment of ignorance, and put on Tri Prot 49:28
the shining light. All darkness will dissolve; all ignorance will die.>
<You will shed the chaos of the uttermost abyss, and put on the Tri Prot 48:7
shining light that is true knowledge of the Father.>"

A blissful smile overcame his features.

"Once you are washed three times and anointed, you will enter
<the light-place of the Fatherhood,> where angels will <inscribe Tri Prot 48:29
your name in glory> <and seal your image in the great radiance.>" Zost 6:7

The saviour's smile glowed even brighter; his face was bathed Zost 6:7
with light.

"Yes, in the Fullness of the Father, your name <will be written Zost 5:11
in glory and your image will be sealed in the light. You will receive
your true image> and <put it on> like a robe of light. Tri Tr 128:19

"<Whoever has a name and an image," he pursued, "will be Melch 15:4
raised up – from unknowing to understanding, and from death *to*
life!> <You will receive the luminous seal, partake in the mystery Tri Prot 49:30
of knowledge, and become *a light in Light!*> For <you have been Zost 5:11
baptized in the watery light, you have received its image – that power in you which is set over the darkness, since it contains the

light, *the whole* of the light...>"

The saviour paused, overcome by the glory and beauty of that vision. Some, like Peter and James, felt trepidation, confronted by the awesome nature of the initiation. Others, like Andrew and John, felt prepared for the experience – no matter how overwhelming it might be.

"All of this is necessary so that you may live. The garment of light will *protect* you – for now and for always. Once you are
Gs Egypt 67:2 <armed with the armour of light,> no Archon can harm you. <As
Gs Phil 86:7 long as you dwell in this world, none of them can torment you.>"

Christ looked up and gave them all a pregnant stare.

Gs Phil 86:11 "<And when you leave this world,> you needn't fear death.
Gs Phil 70:5 For the garment will protect your soul *in its ascent*. <The Archons cannot see those clothed in the perfect light, nor can they detain
Gs Phil 75:21 them.> <Having gone down into the living water, you have shed
Gs Tru 20:28 the bodily corpse and put on the living man> <– you have donned imperishability, so that life eternal clothes you.>"

"Will we see it then," Peter asked "– the robe of light? Will we see it with our own eyes?"

Jesus looked down at the ground and slowly shook his head. Staring hard at the elder son of Jonah, he rebuked him.

"Peter, Peter... have you already forgotten what I told you?
1Ap Jas 27:3 Once you <cast away the bond of flesh that encircles you,> then you
Ap Pt 72:21 will see <the light that shines greater than the light of day.> But you, my brother and friend, must embrace these things *through faith*. You will never grasp my teachings without *pistis*."

Act Pt 12A 11:1 <Peter was afraid to reply a second time. He whispered to the one beside him, who was Thomas, "You speak to him this time..."

Thomas answered and said, "Lord, before you we are afraid to say too many words...> But tell us of the resurrection, so that we may know and be prepared."

Now he smiled and said, "Blessed are you, Thomas, for you will be given the *gnosis*."

Peter, blushing to the roots of his red beard, cast a bitter glance at the Iscariot.

"The Third Seal contains a mystery equalling the other two. For it is *knowledge of the soul's ascent*. It is an initiation into the hidden names of all who will greet you – from the Archons below to the angels above."

Then, staring at them with eyes that made them tremble, he
Melch 14:13 added: "Therefore, <do not reveal to anyone that which is hidden,

unless it is revealed to you to do so.>"

The disciples greeted these words with an uncomfortable silence.

"I pray that <you, in your minds, will understand all I will reveal 1Bk Jeu to you during this discourse – so that you, my disciples, will be saved from the Archons' persecutions. Hasten to receive my word, and *know* it with certainty, so that no Archon will triumph against you.>"

The saviour looked up. Slowly the moon was inching itself to the highest point in the heavens. He had only a few hours more to reveal the mystery of the Third Seal.

"Open your minds! Remain attentive, but at rest. Do not fight against the drowsiness, but seek the mid-point between sleep and waking – which is mindful contemplation. Then you will absorb my words, in that state which we call 'standing at rest'."

The Nazarene drew himself up, inhaled deeply, and said in a calming voice, "Let us pause now and concentrate on mindfulness, so that when you are prepared, we may continue."

One by one, the disciples turned their thoughts inward, seeking the place in the Silence where the Word spoke clearly and truly.

II

For many days, Salome hadn't stirred from her quarters. Though the palace in Tiberias was buzzing with preparations for Herod's jubilee, she remained locked in her apartment – planning, scheming, plotting the darkest of intrigues.

She had set her heart on this one conquest, and would countenance no failure. Tonight, when the celebrations reached their height, she would flee with John to a refuge in Batanea. She had planned it down to the slightest detail. The only uncertainty that stood in her way was John himself – and for that she was prepared to sacrifice everything.

But like a little girl, she'd fussed for hours over one final detail: what to wear during this, the most important hour of her life. At last, she'd settled on a suitable attire: the sheerest of seven veils to swathe her slender limbs; the finest of emeralds to complement her olive-green eyes; the most enchanting of ointments to perfume her seduction – but all covered over with a coarse leather cloak.

At the appointed hour, she descended into the palace dungeons. The guards had been well-bribed – then drugged and securely bound.

Whatever transpired between her and John would not pass beyond these walls.

In the cold limestone dungeon, Salome's lamp burned dimly, the only source of light in the darkness. She found the Baptist in chains – emaciated, foul-smelling and unattired except for his thin loin-cloth. Her guards had reeled in his chains, which passed through iron rings on the walls, then threaded a loop in the ceiling. He hung with his arms outstretched, his feet barely touching the hay-strewn flagstones.

His head bowed, his long matted hair hiding his fine features, John seemed to be lost in delirium. The bearded prophet was whispering to himself – not prayers, but prophecies of his own dark future.

Wordlessly she approached, and pressed her burning brow to his cool forehead. That touch, after the numerous tortures he'd suffered, stung him into cruel awakening.

He gazed at the diaphanous figure before him, the blinding lamp held high in her hand. For a moment, he mistook her for an angel, one of the heavenly consorts who greeted the newly-risen soul. But then, those adoring, child-like features reminded him that he was still on earth, still breathing, still awaiting his final trial.

"John..." Salome murmured, delighting at the sight of her small image in his eyes, "your sufferings are over now. Trust in me – place your fate in my hands, and we'll flee from here."

The Nazarite wanted to fall back, recoil from her advance, but the walls and iron chains held him fast.

She caressed his cheek, drawing in each breath that fell from his chapped white lips.

"I have the keys to free you from these chains, and unlock you from your prison. We can even flee Herod's realm, and find freedom for ourselves... this night!"

John's dark eyes sparkled mysteriously.

"You *will*, Salome... You'll lift the chains of my fate and free me from my prison. You'll do it *all* – tonight."

She felt the keen double-edge to his words, but refused to be cut by them.

"I have never loved *any* man in my life – *never*, until I embraced you in Jerusalem. At that moment, I knew, I would make you my bridegroom."

She hooked the lantern to the wall. With her face half in shadow, half in light, Salome's beguiling features had the ambiguity of a sphinx.

"Like this?" John asked, the tendons on his neck tightening. "You would make me your bridegroom – here below, in the darkness?"

"No," Salome replied, "<Brides and bridegrooms belong in the Gs Phil 82:23
Bridal Chamber.> I wish to stand with you in the light."

The prophet's eyes opened wide. He had heard it in her words – light as a whisper, but unmistakeable – *the Voice.*

"Oh yes... I've dedicated myself to the teachings, and learned their language... I'm not from the Archons and rulers, John. I'm just a child – a virgin who wishes to become a bride."

The anchorite gazed hard at this bewitching apparition – uncertain if she was filled with truth or deception.

"Then why have you come to me tonight?"

"You – who know *all* futures – you haven't seen your own fate?"

"No – only the fate *of others*. Yours is like a path in the forest, twisting then forking left or right. Now tell me: what do you want with me?"

She moved her lips close to his... close enough to kiss – then immediately withdrew them.

"– Your *consent*."

The word hung in the air for a long time.

"You know it yourself, John beloved – each of us has been seeking the other – as their consort. When two halves of the heavenly *syzygy* recognize each other, they offer their consent – in the form of a kiss."

She caressed the lips she so desired.

"Recognize me," she commanded, "as I recognize you. In the aeons above, we were one – only to become separated in this dark place. 'John' is the male name; 'Salome', the female name. Give me the kiss that would re-unite us." With tears glistening in her eyes,
she whispered, "<For you and I were destined for union from the Soph JC 101:16
beginning...>"

The Nazarite gazed at Salome for a long time. Was she the one destined for him? Like a virgin soul, this daughter of the Herodians stood before him – so unknowing, laying herself open – an innocent child offering herself to him willingly and without fear.

But then, he smelled the sweet fragrance on her neck, and saw the emeralds encircling her throat.

"My bride – my *true* bride – would stand naked before God, <as Dial Sav 143:18
a child of truth. Look at the jewels and finery you're wearing, the

transitory garments you've put on! Strip yourself of these,> and then you may enter the Bridal Chamber."

Salome lowered her eyes.

"I put these on for you. Your soul is beautifully arrayed, flawless as a precious gem. And *I am your soul*, John – perfect, young, virgin... But command me to lose these things, and I would in an instant."

Gs Thom 46:28 "<Why do you think the people searched me out in the wilderness? To see someone dressed in *soft clothing* like a king? Or – to see a reed shaken by the wind! I've lived by the Nazarite vow, forsaking bread, wine and all worldly goods. Because no one
Gs Thom 39:27 dressed in soft clothing will ever recognize the truth!> <But if you strip away these garments, with neither fear nor shame, and trample them under your feet like a little child> – then you will learn to stand naked before God."

She nodded her head willingly. "Come with me now and we'll flee to Batanea. It's barren and wild, beyond the reach of this kingdom. We'll have no home, but a tent! No soft robes, but stitched pelts against the wind! And our only possessions, we'll carry with us on camels through the desert!"

She pleaded with him, pressing her clenched fists against his chest.

Test Tr 41:4 In a low voice he intoned, "<No one knows the truth except the one who has forsaken *all* the things of this world – having grasped their garment's fringe and renounced *the whole place*.>"

"Your bride, your true counter-image, surrenders those things willingly!" she cried, wanting nothing more than to flee this ostentatious palace and live out her dreams with him.

"The path is not easy," he warned. "It twists and turns, testing you with many ordeals. But in the end, the reward is great. For
Act Pt 12 A 10:22 <wisdom surpasses all gold, all silver, and the most precious of jewels.>"

She tore the emeralds from her throat, trampling them into the straw and mud. "These things mean nothing to me!"

Act Pt12A 5:21 "<To walk that road, you must forsake it all! For many will stalk you along the way: *robbers* and *beasts*... If you wear an expensive garment, the robbers will murder you for it. If you carry a loaf of bread, the dogs will stalk you for it. Instead, you must learn to fast daily, from stage to stage. Even if you walk that road, eating meat or vegetables, the lions will devour you for the meat, and the bulls will gore you for the vegetables.>"

"Believe me when I say to you that *I am your soul!*" she cried.
"<I'll renounce it all – the world and everything in it!> I give you Act Pt 12A 10:13
my word – my vow! Now pronounce the vow that I wish to hear – our *marriage* vow! Recognize me as your consort – and we'll seal that consent with a kiss!"

Salome was shaking from head to toe, trembling with desire for that one kiss which would make him hers.

But slowly, determinedly, the Nazarite shook his head from side to side.

In a choked voice, he said, "Would you renounce even that one kiss?"

Large tears began to roll down Salome's cheeks. She shook her head. "Would you ask me to renounce life itself?"

"I would ask no less of my soul – to renounce this life, in favour of eternal life."

Salome's dream – of a life in the desert, dwelling peacefully with her beloved prophet – began to vanish and disperse like so much sand in the wind.

"Do not refuse me John – not *now*, not *in this place*... You don't know how terrible the consequences will be."

John looked at her with a look that made her shiver. He looked sad – infinitely sad, full of longing and regret.

"I *know* the consequences – I have heard the Voice that whispers through you..." His throat tightened so hard he could barely breathe.

Salome gazed hard into his sallow eyes. "I came here, prepared – willing to give up everything. The garments, the jewels – they were nothing: gambits to be risked without loss. Even food and wine, I would do without! But I knew, even before coming here, that I would not leave without you..."

She swept the tears from her cheeks and inhaled deeply. "No woman can take a man by force. Even you, chained to this wall, stripped bear, almost naked – I still couldn't command. Yes, I could caress you, attempt to arouse you... but I wouldn't have what I want! I wouldn't have the kiss that is given freely and willingly – in consent!"

"As long as we wear these fleshly garments – it will not be
given. As long as the soul wears seven soul-garments – inconstancy, CH I:24
greed, lust and pride; wrath, injustice and deception – the perfect marriage cannot be celebrated."

"But *how* then..?" Salome pleaded. "By what rite of passion can we two be made one?"

Auth T 31:24 "<The passions of the soul are transitory;> the desires of the
Gs Phil 66:16 flesh, fleeting. But you – if you <strip off the flesh> and shed your
seven soul-garments – you will enter the Bridal Chamber, you will experience eternal union."

Salome shook her head. In the lamplight, her face took on a terrible, hysterical expression.

"Before I entered here, I had prepared myself for our sacred marriage – the one, the *only* rite that would bring us together. Because it contains a mystery greater than you or I..."

Her look was dark, almost deranged.

"*...The sacrifice*. I learned its ancient meaning on a journey far from here." She gave him a look full of pity. "Man cannot live without consuming life, my beloved. You may try to renounce it – eating no meat or vegetables, even scourging your flesh. But that is the way for you, a *man* steeped in the *spirit*, to sacrifice to his God.

"A woman is different: she feels all the good things of the earth like life growing in her womb. She makes her sacrifice to the Goddess – offering all these things on the altar, *killing* them, *consuming* them, in the full knowledge that their life will be replenished. In the womb of the Great Goddess, they will come to life once more."

"Idolater! That is *not* the perfect sacrifice! The ancient ways were
flawed." Then, knowing that his words would turn her against him
Eugnos 85:7 forever, he said: "They are marred by <the defect of femaleness.>"

Salome stared at him as if the knives in his eyes had pierced her breast.

With the voice of the ancient prophets, John thundered: "All life in this world comes from the female – from the goddess Sophia and her unforgiven fault! *She* gave birth to the darkness, to desire, to the Great Demon who rules us all through passion."

"The Goddess gave us life!"

"Perishable life! The corruptible life of the flesh!"

"No! Eternal life, which cycles round in her womb – forever and without cease! That is why we sacrifice to her – in *knowing recognition* of that mystery!"

1Ap Jas 35:10 "<Sophia is female from female,> without the redeeming
quality of the male. *Achamoth* was begotten by *Barbelo* – the
Gs Phil 75:3 Lower Wisdom came from the Upper. And <she brought forth the
Ap Jn 9:31 world by mistake> <because she acted *without* the consent of her
consort. Without the approval of her maleness, her desire acquired a bastardized form, becoming the Archigenetor of the abyss!>"

The veins on his neck were bulging.

"That is why the Son of glory has come into the world. He is
male <– *three times* male!> <He will divide the light from darkness; Allog 58:12
the corruptible from incorruptible – and the male from female!> Test Tr 40:21
Through the three *parousias*, he will bring about the end, and restore us to the beginning. Through *his* sacrifice, he will correct Sophia's fault, raise her up from her falleness, and redeem her in the Bridal Chamber."

The prophet's voice gave out. In a hoarse whisper, he admonished Herod's daughter.

"Renounce this world with its <feminine desire> <– flee from the Zost 1:10
bondage of femaleness, and choose the salvation of maleness!> For, Zost 131:5
only <the male race will inherit the eternal realm!> <Every woman Gs Egypt 44:19
who makes herself male will enter the kingdom of heaven...>" Gs Thom 51:24

Gazing at John in disbelief, Salome scratched her nails deep into his flesh. She screamed at him a primitive, guttural cry.

"Tonight, each of us will make their sacrifice – John... beloved! It will be a total consummation, transcending even the flesh! For I will willingly *take your life*, even as you *renounce mine!* If we must, we will sacrifice ourselves to each other..!"

III

Christ stared at the moon, which had now reached its apex in the heavens. Half the night remained – and then, at dawn, he would initiate his disciples into three of the Five Seals.

He threw fresh logs on the fire and stoked its flame. The fire blazed back into awakening. In a similar manner, the disciples woke from their restful contemplation and looked expectantly at the Messiah.

They could hear the deep urgency in his voice as he continued their instruction.

"There are mysteries within mysteries; there are names within names. The first seal is the baptism in three forms; the second is the chrism. But the Third Seal is like a prelude and conclusion to those
rites. In order to prepare you for your three baptisms, <secret names Gs Egypt 63:4
and signs will be entrusted to you – first of all, for the *renunciation* of the lords of the Lower Aeons, and secondly, for the *invocation* of the angels who dwell in the Upper Light.>

"But the names which I give you shall be spoken by you *once only*. The renunciation and invocation are *rites* of naming – and

the hidden names, once spoken, *grant existence* to what is named.
Tri Tr 61:12 Indeed, <all that exists, exists through its name.>"

Philip and Nathanael gazed inward. Each was trying to comprehend the mysteries *within* the mysteries, like so many layers of knowing.

The saviour, meanwhile, was staring into the invisible heavens, remembering the mystery that had manifest itself *before* the foundation of the world.

Gs Egypt 41:4 "<The unproclaimable Parent> exists in the great Silence. <He
Gs Egypt 40:16 is the Parent *whose name cannot be uttered*.> But when He named
himself with the names of the Mother and the Father, these two *came to exist* – as extensions of the One, as aeons expanding outward in circles, but remaining one in their centre. Each name in the Upper Aeons, spoken with the *pneuma*'s breath, reflects the One back to itself – in name.

"All the aeons possess these hidden names. Even you, through the baptism and chrism, come to possess such a name: it is your
Gs Tru 21:27 hidden spiritual name, <a name that the Father himself pronounces>
Gs Tru 21:25 when you are sealed in the watery light and <inscribed in the Book
of the living.> Thus you are made one of the Elect, one of the living *who truly exists*."

Looking into the blazing fire, Jesus said: "Even the twelve
Ap Jn 12:26 Archons have their names <– names given to them by their Originator,
+ Mars 7:24 to extend his darkening power. But the Archons also have a hidden
name, devised by the one above the heavens – by the One who *exists alone*, in the Silence. This name signifies their powerlessness and
Gs Phil 56:3 destruction. Thus, the Archons have two names> <– a hidden name,
Norea 28:30 and a worldly name.> But these two, <when spoken together, create
a single name.>"

He gave a meaningful glance to Arsinoe, who nodded her tacit understanding.

"Tonight, you will be baptized three times. The first time you enter the watery light, you will pronounce the Archons' names in such a way as to *renounce* them. For these names grant you *command* over the forces of evil. But you must be careful, for you can also *conjure* them forth – *by speaking them into existence*. If you abuse that power, and seek mastery over the demons for your own ends, they will soon make you their slaves."

In the stillness of the night, they heard the wind whispering in the trees – an eerie, ominous wind. The stars above their heads glared down at them with cold anger and discontent.

"In that same spirit, the names of the angels in the Upper Aeons are spoken as an *invocation* – to give them glory and praise. When
you enter the watery light in the second baptism, <you will *confess* Tri Tr 127:25
faith in those names, and bear witness to them, giving voice to your belief... *that they exist!* Through this confession, you gain your salvation.>

"The renunciation and invocation, intoned before the first
and second baptisms, become a prelude to the third, which is <the Tri Tr 128:5
baptism in the fullest sense. For it is a complete immersion into God. You will rise up through the aeons with the firm hope of attaining angelic glory. If, in your confession, you have truly *believed* in the angels' existence, then you will return to them, and receive their perfection. The Father who gives union-in-knowledge will be with you, and you with him, in *one knowing*.>"

Suddenly, the saviour grew silent. He looked to his right, where the three Mary's were reclining – Arsinoe in the lap of Magdalene, with the Virgin embracing them both.

For a long time he looked at them, while the night grew evermore silent.

"Is it possible to utter a mystery?" he said, barely above a whisper.

Without a word, Arsinoe rose from her place and embraced her brother, giving him a ritual kiss.

She assumed her place beside the saviour – looking at all of them with infinitely mysterious eyes. And then, to their great wonderment – she spoke.

"<Among those born of women," she said, "from Adam all the Gs Thom 41:6
way down to John the Baptist, none has been greater than John.>
That is why, on this night, <the head of prophecy will be cut off with Ap Jas 6:28
John.>"

She gave them all a forlorn look that froze the blood in their veins.

"John spoke with the eternal Voice. And each evening, he
instructed his disciples concerning <the Voice – hidden, dwelling Tri Prot 35:32
within, coming from the immeasurable Silence.> <That voice, Tri Prot 45:27
he said, carries the breath> – which *is* knowledge of <the Silence Tri Prot 35:34
surrounding us all.>"

As Arsinoe spoke, the Voice behind her words mesmerized them all with its sweet and resonant timbres. In every phrase, with the rise and fall of her words, it seemed to whisper hidden hymns of praise.

Tri Prot 41:26 "John prophesied to us, saying <the Voice would dip below the Archons' language, and speak its mystery to the chosen few.> Now, we know – you *are* those few..."

The disciples shifted uneasily in their places.

Gs Phil 71:3 Arsinoe looked at Jesus and nodded. "<One must indeed utter a mystery,> my brother, so John's prophecy may be fulfilled..."

From her slender and delicate throat, the Voice resounded with infinite depth.

"Know this. Each of you possesses a secret treasure – the pearl, the particle of divine light planted in you. But your unseen spirit is also *unheard*. It is the *pneuma* – the divine *breath* in you that speaks with the Voice of the Silence. Not even the Archons possess it. Through the *pneuma*, you may speak the hidden, unutterable names which the Archons themselves cannot pronounce."

She paused a moment, listening to the silence around her. The forest was deathly still. Only the calm rippling of the river could be heard.

Unt MS Then she said, "<Every name which came into existence through the Father is an unutterable name, since it comes to exist
1Bk Jeu within his Silence.> These hidden names, we say, <are spoken 'in the tongue of the Father'.> But the worldly names, which came into
Unt MS being through Yaltabaoth, <are spoken 'with a tongue of flesh'.> The body utters them and the body hears them.

"That is why there are names within names. The Archons possess both a hidden and a worldly name, making a single name once these two are spoken together. Your *pneuma* gives you the power to pronounce their *hidden* name and *render them powerless...*"

Susanna felt a cold chill run down her spine.

"How mysterious are the workings of the almighty Father! For
Orig Wld 125:14 <He sent the Word into the world with this purpose: to reveal the hidden names, and condemn the twelve Archons to their deaths.>"

Arsinoe looked at her brother.

Tri Tr 127:8 "He is <the revelation and the path,> <for he enlightens each
Gs Tru 18:19 one of us, and shows us the way> from the world below to the world above – by teaching us the names of all the aeons."

The owls in the trees grew uneasy. From the distance came more cries of jackals and hyenas.

"And herein lies the greatest part of the mystery..."

Arsinoe paused, collecting her thoughts and listening to the Voice inside of her.

"In each of these names, vowels and consonants are combined.

The consonants are pronounced with the tongue of flesh, but *the vowels... are sounded... with the tongue of the Father*. In time, you will learn how to do this. Tonight, I will speak them for you."

Mariam, Martha and Susanna nodded slowly, fully understanding the gravity of the task that lay before them.

"The consonants you may form quite easily, since you do so everyday; the consonants give voice to the Archons' worldly names. But hidden in each vowel sequence is the secret name, which you must learn to say with the silent Voice. *Only that Voice will command them...*"

All of the disciples were now listening intently, hanging on the edge of every word.

"You must learn to release the *pneuma* – the sacred breath – *through* the vowels. Listen as I pronounce the simple vowels, which are the most expressive in power..."

Arsinoe concentrated herself in all of her being – inhaling deeply and then slowly releasing a melodic succession of tones which reverberated deeply.

"<aaa, eee, eeeh, iii, ooo, uuu, OOOh!>" Mars 28:21

The effect on the listeners was breath-taking. They felt themselves drawn up, leaving the earth behind them and, for those few short moments, enclosed in a sphere resonating with absolute fullness. Within a second, it was over.

"<From these simple vowels are made the diphthongs,> Mars 28:28
which possess lesser or greater power, depending on how they are combined. The most common ones sound like this..."

Again, she pitched the voice in her throat and emitted a series of vowel combinations – each growing deeper, richer and more complex in its resonance.

"<ai, au, ei, eu... auei, eueu, oiou... aueieu!>" Mars 28:5

For a few seconds, these sounds transported them into a series of different spheres, each resonating with its own distinct harmony. The effect was disorienting, but spell-binding.

"Finally come the consonants. When a hidden name is woven
into a worldly name, <the consonants fall under the vowels' Mars 29:20
command, and must submit to them. Thus, in the nomenclature of the angels and Archons,> there is always a space for the silent Voice to exercise its power.

"All the names will be revealed to you by my brother. Over time, I will teach you how to sound them. And once you have learned these things, you will also teach them to others – but *secretly*, and

only to those who have been properly initiated into the baptism and
1Ap Jas 36:13 chrism. Otherwise, <guard them in silence, and keep them hidden
within.>"

The hardness in her voice left no doubt as to the gravity of this injunction.

The Nazarene nodded to Arsinoe with deep respect.

Then he said: "After death, each of us must undergo the soul's
NH Ascl 76:21 ascent. <Many will not complete that passage, and be thrown down.>
But there are those few, whether by faith or by fore-knowledge, who will survive, and enter into the Pleroma of the Father."

He looked at Peter and Thomas, giving them each a stare replete with mystery.

"The seals are given to you – as power. For knowledge *is* power. The first and second seals contain the powers of washing and anointing. The Third Seal contains the power of *naming*, which will become manifest in the preliminary and concluding rites.

"During the preliminary rites, you will renounce the demons and invoke the angels. But there is also a concluding rite – which is *the vision of the resurrection*."

Upon hearing these words, Peter grew unaccountably frightened. His hair tingled on the back of his neck, and he shivered uncontrollably.

"The Third Seal is called the resurrection because, in the concluding rite, you will speak the names and see the images in such a way as to *experience the resurrection*. Indeed, the Third Seal is an immersion into *vision* – where you will *see* the soul's ascent, and receive *the image* of your soul's resurrection.

He gazed at the flickering faces of his apostles through the heat and smoke of the fire.

Gs Phil 67:9 "<There is the awaited resurrection, and *an image* of that
resurrection. To be fully initiated, you must rise up and *enter through* the image of the resurrection.> It is a prolonged glance into the after-death experience – not at all easy to bear, and fearful to the extreme."

Matthew and James grew nervous. They had felt a certain trepidation before, but now they were overcome with panic and despair. Still, the two of them held their shivering limbs and listened intently.

Gs Phil 73:1 "<If you do not receive the resurrection while you live, then
Gs Phil 66:16 when you die, you will receive nothing.> <Therefore, while we are
still *in* this world, it is necessary for us to acquire the resurrection. In

that way, when death strips us of our flesh, we will still *know the way* to our rest.> Without eyes to see or mouths to speak, your soul will still know how to thread its way through the Archons' labyrinth."

Susanna gazed at the saviour, frightened but confident that he was, indeed, 'the way for the wayfarer'.

"And you must undergo this visionary ordeal *without fear*. But the promise of reward is great, since the vision passes from resurrection to *redemption*."

As he gazed into the fire, his face glowed with its flickering light.

"In the end, <the vision of resurrection becomes a revelation Tr Res 48:34
and transformation – a transition into newness called 'the final redemption'. For imperishability descends upon the perishable; the light flows down upon the darkness, swallowing it up; and the Pleroma fills up the deficiency. All these images and symbols become *present and actual* in the resurrection.> Though frightful to the extreme, in the end it becomes a vision of bliss."

"So the first two seals prepare us for the third?" Philip asked. "The washing and anointing prepare us for the resurrection and redemption?"

"Yes. From the Jordan we get the living water of the baptism;
and from the baptism, our redemption. In that same spirit, <from Gs Phil 73:17
the olive tree we get the oil of the chrism; and from the chrism, our resurrection.>

"It is good and proper that you learn these things. <For the Gs Phil 74:16
Father anointed the Son, and the Son will anoint his apostles, so
that they may anoint others.> <He who has been redeemed may, in Gs Phil 71:2
turn, redeem others.> <He who has been anointed, has received the Gs Phil 74:16
resurrection,> and he may, in turn, resurrect others."

Philip and Nathanael slowly nodded. But John said, "Before you, I have become confused. In what order will all this occur?"

The saviour smiled at his beloved disciple and replied: "Indeed,
it is not easy to impart the mysteries through words alone. But
listen and try to understand. The Three Seals are so composed as
to become mysteries within mysteries. Together, they make up <the 1Bk Jeu
Fire Baptism,> which is <the baptism *in the fullest sense*.> Tri Tr 127:25

"Why is the Third Seal included with the baptism and chrism?
Because it is like an *immersion* into vision and an *anointing* with
images. Thus, <'the baptism in the fullest sense' includes the Gs Phil 69:25
resurrection and redemption> that are particular to the Third Seal."

The saviour smiled at his beloved apostle and said:

"In general, the sequence of the rites is quite simple: renunciation and the first baptism, then invocation and the second baptism, followed by the chrism's anointing and the third baptism. Last comes the resurrection and redemption."

John nodded his comprehension and Jesus continued:

"Understanding the sequence of the Three Seals is more complicated. During the first part of the rite, all of us together will renounce the Archons and you will be washed with water – that is the first baptism. Then together, we will invoke the angels, and you will be washed a second time – that is the second baptism. All of this is to prepare you for the third and final baptism – which is a total immersion in the Jordan.

"First, you will be anointed with oil, in the rite of the chrism, and then you will be plunged into the river's inlet. The sensation is sudden and overwhelming. From the Lower to the Upper Aeons, your soul will be transported immediately, and you will enter the Father's watery light. Your baptismal name will be spoken, and you will be granted your garment of light. That vision will break upon you like a flashing illumination.

"Thus, through the washing and anointing – you will have acquired the powers of the first Two Seals.

"The Third Seal's power lies in its naming. It was present in the preparatory renunciation and invocation. It will also be present in the concluding rite, where we will speak and conjure forth a vision of the soul's resurrection and redemption. It is, as I said, a terrifying vision. And after your third baptism, we will lead you through your soul's celestial journey.

"This vision will become a gradual, aeon-by-aeon ascent from the lower to the upper, from the darkness of the Deficiency to the Fullness of the light. It will break upon you slowly, unfolding like a nightmare that ends in a final revelation."

The saviour eyed each his apostles. Though his face was filled with bliss, they trembled at his final words.

"But through that experience, you will finally have lost your fear of the Archons, *even your fear of death* – for you will *know* what lies beyond the sufferings of this world."

IV

Herod Antipas, the archon of Perea and Galilee, sat upon his mighty throne as emissaries brought gifts and laid them at his feet.

From Egypt came gold, emeralds and rubies. From Assyria came the rarest of incenses – nard, frankincense and myrrh. From Africa came animal pelts of softest fur – leopard, panther, minx. All were piled before the *basileus* in honour of his jubilee.

To his right sat Herodias and, to his left, Salome. The vizier Chuza and his wife Joanna announced each gift as the courtiers applauded. Then, as minstrels sounded their drums, flutes and lyres, the courtesans danced and acrobats leapt in the air.

The bilious king, made wild with drink, turned lustily to Salome.

"How beautifully you've arrayed yourself this evening! Your ointments are intoxicating and your silken veils stir up the blood! But, my precious creature, what gift have *you* brought me tonight?"

"You are difficult to please, my king. Already you have more riches than King Solomon himself! Still, I have arranged two very special presents. The first sits just outside the hall. The second – you have hinted it to me well enough! The second sits beside you, beautifully arrayed."

She gave him a conspiratorial glance.

"Forget the first! Tell me about the second! Is it true – the hierodules of Tyre taught you the dance of seven veils?"

"It is true indeed. But the ways of their people are mysterious to us – at once, seductive and demanding! No woman bestows her gifts without first demanding some small token, some small offering from the one who will receive it."

Feeling the full, dizzying effects of the Cypriot wine, he cried out, "Demand it from me and I will grant it without reserve! Only do as you promised! Dance for me Salome!"

Salome gazed at him like a cat, awaiting the exact moment to pounce.

"The wine makes you bold and reckless, my liege. What token will you offer me first?"

"Take my ring, with its signet of a palm branch. On any document, you may impress it *once*, taking whatever you desire – up to half my kingdom!"

"It is not your kingdom I desire, great tetrarch, nor your power. But grant me absolute mastery over one of your subjects, and you will have what you want..."

"One of my subjects?" he queried, gazing at her blankly. "Over Chuza? Is that it? You want his stewardship, to command my armies? *Ha hah!* Or is it..." He leaned in close. "Is it Herodias you want? To replace her – your own mother?"

Salome smirked and shook her head.

"Neither Herodias nor Chuza. This subject of yours is neither courtier nor freeman. He is lower than a slave."

Herod thought hard, unable to imagine the feint that was concealed in her request.

She leaned in close and caressed his arm. "Do not fear my selfish whim. It's for me alone – a playful fancy. No harm will come to you, I promise. But offer me this one small token of your affection."

Baffled, Herod nodded. "Mastery over one subject – neither courtier nor freeman?"

"I swear it on your throne! Now swear it to me! And I will dance before you – down to the last veil. I will stand before you, fully exposed, and hand you that veil – as one token in exchange for the other!"

At last, Herod laughed. "Your request is granted. I swear it – swear it on my throne!"

Salome stood up, and the long robe covering her slender figure fell to the floor. She was swathed in seven diaphanous veils.

At once, the minstrels stopped playing and the acrobats dispersed.

With anklets tinkling, her bare feet padded down the seven steps of the dais. The palace floor, a massive mosaic, was framed by meanders with a labyrinth laid in the middle. Standing at its centre, Salome cried out:

"I promised two gifts to our great king. *Both* will bring you entertainment and amusement! The first is rarer than all the gold, incense and furs that lie at his feet. I present you with a most special guest. The king's jubilee would not be complete without the Prophet of the Five Seals!"

A great hush fell over the court as John the Baptist was brought out – still bound in chains, but freshly washed and perfumed. The desert ascetic wore his legendary robe of rough camel-hide. But he was wreathed and garlanded like a bridegroom. His combed hair and trimmed beard could still not hide the fiery eyes that glared at them all with uncompromising spite. The most poisonous of his stares he directed at Salome.

"Insolent vipers!" John cried. "Ignorant beasts! Your rich perfume and soft clothing reek worse than all the whores of Jerusalem!"

Herod stood up, unsure if Salome was trying to mock or amuse him. But, when all the courtiers began clapping and cheering, he smiled uneasily.

The guests jostled among themselves, trying to catch a glimpse of the prophet. They had heard so many legends and rumours. Now, here he was – presented for their amusement.

Again, John thundered:

"You are blinded by lust, fettered hand and foot by your own flesh! Laugh – hyenas! – while you wallow in ignorance and death!"

Salome gracefully waved her arm, and the entire hall erupted with applause.

Like one of the many gifts laid at Herod's feet, the Baptist was chained to a ring at the foot of the dais.

Then, assuming her place once more in the middle of the floor, Salome bowed her head and waited for the music to begin.

V

It was now the middle of the night, and the dome of heaven had reached its darkest hue. This vigil was taxing to the extreme, but their task demanded wakefulness. It was a test of attention, and they each struggled to remain restfully aware.

"The time has come..." Jesus announced, "to enter the mysteries of the Three Seals."

The disciples stared at him. On their faces was joyful anticipation mixed with fear and foreboding.

The saviour stood up and held his hands out at his sides. Immediately, Arsinoe and the Virgin joined him before the fire.

Making a circle round them, the disciples all bowed their heads. Each of them stood silently and at rest. Only the trickling of the Jordan's inlet could be heard.

<Jesus turned to face the four corners of the world, and his 1Bk Jeu
disciples did likewise.> Then, forming a ring around the flaming light, he joined his hands over the fire with Arsinoe and the Virgin. In the greater ring around them, the disciples linked their arms and enlaced their fingers.

Bowing his head, Christ heartfully intoned the opening oratory for the first baptism.

"<Hear me, my Father – the father of all Fatherhoods, infinite 1Bk Jeu
Light! Make my disciples worthy to receive the Baptism of Fire. Release them from their sins and purify them of their transgressions.

Yea, hear us, Father, *as we renounce the Archons* through their two-fold names, inscribed in the aeons, and pronounced once only.>"

For a long time, they remained silent.

Gs Egypt 67:6 Then Arsinoe <stretched out her arms and folded her fingers together, making a circle before her body.> Holding her hands in prayer thus, she opened wide her mouth.

The sister of the saviour pronounced the name of the first Archon. Each vowel, sung in a minor key, rose and fell with a strangely dissonant tone.

"B*eeee*l*iiia*s!" she canted.

The saviour cried out:

"*We renounce thee, Belias,* Archon of the first aeon! Your name is anathema. Your darkness has no power!"

The disciples intoned the curse exactly as Christ had instructed.

"M*eee*lc*eiiiii*r-A*aaa*don*eeeiiii*n!" Arsinoe sang, her voice falling into a frightening basso.

Again, the saviour intoned the renunciation, and the disciples responded with the exact same words.

From *Armoupieel* and *Yobel* to *Abrisene*, they abjured the Archons' names, execrating each of them.

Having repudiated the five Archons of the abyss, Christ gazed into the heavens.

"A*aaaa*b*ee*l!" Arsinoe trilled, and her voice grew more sonorous and restrained.

They renounced the lowest of the seven heavenly Archons, the fire-faced authority who guards the gateway of the moon.

Ap Jn 10:23 And so it continued through <*Cain*, *Adonaiou* and *Yabel*, then *Kalila-Oumbri*, *Harmas* and *Athoth*.> When Arsinoe intoned the final name, she was tottering and delirious, on the verge of collapse from exhaustion. But the Virgin and Nazarene united with her, giving her strength.

At last they all cried "Amen!"

While the Virgin took Arsinoe in her arms, Jesus raised the cup containing the Jordan's cleansing water. One by one, he poured a drop of the living water on the heads of his disciples. And each who received that drop felt its absolution. Their vision grew clear, their ears were opened, and they heard the Jordan's flow like a thunderous wave of renewal.

From that moment onward, their gaze was cleansed of want and their ears could hear no envy. No hidden voice could whisper its evil intimations or temptations. Awakened from drunken slumber, they felt themselves freed of the Archons' insidious bonds. Like Adam before the Fall, they stood: immaculate, untainted, flawless.

A second time, Jesus joined hands with Arsinoe and the Virgin. Standing perfectly at rest, the apostles joyfully linked arms in the circle.

The saviour re-opened his mouth:

"Hear us, Father of unity, for we are your community, <the Gs Egypt 55:2
incorruptible, spiritual church which gives you praise, singing and giving glory *with one voice*, with one accord, with a mouth *which does not rest!*> <Yea, hear us, Father, *as we invoke your imperishable* 1Bk Jeu
names which reside in the Treasury of Light.>"

"Miiicheeeuuus!" Arsinoe sang with all the strength and spirit her voice could muster.

"<Holy are you, Holy are you, Holy are you, immersing angel, Melch 16:16
Micheus, *who exists* for ever and ever, Amen!>" Jesus intoned.

As the disciples repeated this prayer, each of them spoke from the spirit within – concentrating their faith and confessing the angel's existence with steadfast, unwavering conviction.

Rising ever higher, their voices of praise ascended the aeons, from the three immersing angels to those who enrobed, enthroned Tri Prot 48:15
and glorified. And just before the second baptism, they gave praise to the Four Lights, *Eleleth*, *Daveithai*, *Oriel* and *Armozel.* Ap Jn 7:30

Again, the Nazarene poured the Jordan's lustration over their inclined brows. And with that water came a momentary vision of *all* the aeons. They saw the angels whom they had named. In the watery light, *Micheus*, *Michar* and *Mnesinous* stood ready to receive them Tri Prot 48:15
and immerse them in the spring of life; *Yammon*, *Elasso* and *Amenai* were holding their robes of glory, ready to invest them with undying radiance.

"The third and final baptism," Jesus pronounced, "is preceded by the chrism."

He looked into the distance, as if remembering.

"The Last Prophet indicated the way, when he baptized us in the Jordan. But he immersed us in the water, knowing full well that one would come after him <who would baptize with the holy spirit and Mt 3:11
with fire...>"

"John," he said to the son of Zebedee, "<bring me the grape 1Bk Jeu
vines for the Baptism of Fire.>"

Flustered, young John found a sprig of grape vines near the fire, and ceremoniously handed them over.

Carefully, the Nazarene dipped these in a cup containing blessed
1Bk Jeu incense. Then, tossing the drenched branch into the fire, he <offered
up the strangely aromatic balm consisting of juniper berries, myrrh,
frankincense, mastic, nard, cassia flowers and turpentine, all mixed
in oil of myrrh.>

The smoke wafted up, a perfumed but pungent odour that entranced them all with its sweetness.

He took up another cup, containing the holy oil of the chrism.
Exod 30:22 It contained the ancient recipe of <cinnamon and myrrh, ground in
cassia and aromatic cane, then pressed in olive oil.> As one final
1Bk Jeu ingredient, he added a distillation of <the dog's head,> a rare herb
with healing properties.

Standing before his beloved disciple, Jesus dipped his fingers
and applied the ointment onto John's forehead, then over his ears,
1Bk Jeu under his nose, and finally <onto his tongue.> All of this was
performed in reverent silence.

Fifteen times he stood before his disciples and anointed each of them.

Then Arsinoe and the Virgin led them individually to the banks of the small pool in the Jordan. The saviour stood in the middle of the inlet on a rock, half-submerged in the cool flowing current. The water was dark but inviting.

John was the first to descend. The son of Zebedee stood before his beloved master, trembling with fear and ardour.

"John, son of Zebedee – so you have been called, for it is your
Melch 16:11 worldly name," Jesus said with a smile. "But I have been sent <to
+ Gr Pow 36:15 baptize you in the Living Water, and pronounce your hidden name.
It will become a name among the living names inscribed in the water
and the light.>"

He placed his hands over his disciple's brow.

Ap Adam 85:22 "<This is the holy baptism of those who know the eternal
knowledge – born of the word written in the Living Water.> Come,
Tri Prot 45:12 *Bonarges*, son of the Thunder <– I am inviting you into the exalted,
perfect Light!>"

He plunged the trembling youth into the Jordan's living water. With a mighty rustling, the trees over their heads shook. A low thunder rumbled through the heavens and, in a flash, the initiate emerged from the Jordan, simultaneously laughing and crying.

In ecstasy, he saw the three enrobing angels, descending with his garment of light. It bore his shape and reflected his countenance, while shimmering in gold, silver and white. And on its hem was woven through his hidden name, glowing in gems and pearls – *Bonarges.*

<Jesus crowned him with a woven sprig of pigeon's grass,> but 1 Bk Jeu
the beloved disciple saw *Bariel*, *Nouthan* and *Sabenai* holding the Tri Prot 48:15
lustrous crown, which burned delightfully as it was pressed upon his head. And as he stood in the light, the angels *Ariom*, *Elien* and *Phariel* glorified him with the glory of the Father.

In a daze, John was led away from the water. The surrounding disciples gazed at him in silent amazement. He looked utterly transformed. Light in step, graceful in his moments, he smiled at them radiantly, and his face emanated love, compassion and enlightenment.

"Peter!" Jesus cried. "It is your turn. Come into the water and kindle the light!"

VI

With her palms pressed over her head, Salome swayed to the music, letting the rhythm flow through her, animating each of her movements. Her dance was entrancing, mesmerizing every eye in the hall. As one, the percussionists wove complex patterns while the lyre and flute improvised melodies over top.

Even the Baptist, burning with anger and humiliation, could not keep his eyes off this wavering apparition.

Though Salome was deeply immersed in her oceanic motion, she opened her eyes just wide enough to glance at John.

"Like a reed shaken by the wind..." she cried for his ears only.

And indeed, he *saw* it. She was moving like a willow, blown by invisible winds. The music carried distant desert sands, and she was alternately buffeted and caressed by their sweet and stinging nettles.

He gazed, his stare unbroken, at this undulating spectre while a voice from within – Salome's voice – whispered to him, 'Behold: this is your soul!'

The waifish figure turned slowly on one foot, her hands rising and falling like waves. Then one of the veils was pinched between thumb and forefinger. As her figure turned faster, the hand rose and the unravelling veil was lifted away.

With a thousand tiny steps she circled the hall, the gossamer kerchief fluttering behind her. Then she leaned over and, with a broad arc of one arm, laid it on the pile of treasures.

Salome turned to John and whispered: “One kiss, and you will save us both...”

A cold sweat broke out on John’s brow.

Salome waited. Though the music played on, Salome waited for the sign that would grant her his consent.

John bowed his head in refusal.

Indignantly, Salome turned – but whispered before she left him, “Your love is fickle, my beloved – inconstant as the moon..!”

Immediately, she leaped and then landed, drawing a large circle in the air with her hair.

That cyclic motion, so poetically inscribed, seemed to speak to John with all the vagaries of a prophecy.

It showed, like a mysterious sign, the monthly cycle of the moon – alternating between light and darkness, mutable but regular in its ever-changing aspects.

In a flash, the prophet recognized the message implicit in her graceful gesture. This was the dance of his soul, stripping away garment after garment as it rose through the aeons. She had stripped away inconstancy, like a soul-garment. Indeed, like a raiment given by the moon, swathing his soul – now it had been mercifully lifted away.

The daughter of the Herodians danced, and Herod Antipas clutched his throne, unable to control his mounting desire. He would see Salome this night, see her bare as Bathsheba bathing on the roof. No king, not even David, could withstand that temptation.

VII

Huddled in their heavy woollen cloaks, the disciples gazed into the fire. Except for Arsinoe and the Virgin, each of them had gone down into the Jordan. And each had emerged with his view onto the world irreparably altered.

The Upper Aeons, the angels, the Fullness of the Father – all of this had been experienced as unquestionably real. In a flash, they *had seen* it, and *knew* its existence was truer than any earthen shadow.

And though each of them had seen the same thing, they sat in silence because no words could convey the epiphany they’d shared – the transformation and awakening into all-knowing bliss.

The Nazarene stared at the moon, whose scarlet hues deepened and coagulated like blood. The night was almost over, and he still had to initiate his companions into the mysteries of the Third Seal.

"It has been written from the beginning that those <who are Gs Egypt 65:25
worthy of the seals, granted in the spring baptism, will receive the resurrection. Through the renunciation and invocation, they are instructed about their receivers, and will know them, just as they will be made known to them.>

"Therefore, do not fear the vision of the soul's ascent. Stare into the fire and see their terrible faces – fanged, venomous, poised to devour you. Though the Archons will stalk you, *do not be afraid!*
<For your fear gives them power! And if you fear the bestial gate- Dial Sav 122:1
keeper, he will surely engulf you! Indeed, there is not one among them who will spare you or show you mercy...>"

Jude and James began trembling uncontrollably. But an inner voice told them to stifle their anxiety.

"<But *you* needn't fear them, since you have mastered every Dial Sav 122:1
name and sign while still on earth.> <Through the anointing, you Anoint 40:11
may trample the snakes underfoot, and tread on the heads of the Melch 10:28
scorpions!> You have <renounced the Archons,> so <all the powers Anoint 40:11
of the Devil will fall before you.> <Your enemies can in no way Melch 13:11
convict you.> <Though the crossing place is fearful – you, with a Dial Sav 123:23
single mind, will pass it by!>"

The flame of their campfire seemed to slow in its flickering. The interval between each movement lengthened, until the glowing tongues undulated like fiery serpents. Strange shapes moved in and out of the furnace.

The saviour raised his voice, pitching it with confidence and encouragement.

"Remember! Your garment of light will protect you! <Not one Gr Pow 46:6
of the Archons can seize you or drag you down, because you wear the holy garment, which neither darkness can touch nor fire burn. You needn't shut your eyes nor avert your gaze...>"

A loud hissing escaped from the fire, and a log exploded in a shower of sparks. In a flash, they saw Yaltabaoth's face, surrounded by twelve auras of flames. It was horrendous, this unocculted view unto the source of all evil.

Slowly, the face dissolved, but its flaming halo expanded, like twelve silhouettes in a spectrum of colours – growing stronger, more intense, blinding them momentarily.

"Do not turn away! See in that hellish glow the Archons' many aeons – seven in the heavens and five over the abyss!"

In the deepening spectral glow they saw a black serpent biting its tail. Suddenly, the viper released its tail and lashed out at them, its five mouths spitting poison and hissing noxious fumes. This was no illusion. The scaly serpent had five heads, which turned and twisted round each other.

One was black, earthen and misshapen, like volcanic rock. Its eyes were fearfully hollow; its mouth a gaping emptiness. Another was white, airy and transparent, like a crystalline skull. The third was aqueous and azure blue, vomiting a torrent of ill-smelling gall. The fourth blazed like a fiery dragon, spitting blinding flames into their eyes. And the last, the fifth, kept moving in and out of their vision, ethereal, fleeting, invisible.

"Behold the Archons of the abyss!" the Nazarene cried. "Dwelling lower than the lunar sphere, they control the four elements and the ether."

In awe the apostles saw the hidden forces animating earth, water, air and fire.

"Do not avert your gaze! Only the lowest form of man need fear them – he who is wholly flesh, with neither soul nor spirit – the man of the *hylic* race. For these five Archons have mastery over the material body, which itself is an admixture of the four elements in the ether. They strip away the flesh, burn it and consume it. For these
Test Tr 36:29 gate-keepers know: *none* will rise *bodily* in the resurrection. <Nor should you, therefore, wish for a carnal resurrection...>"

The five-headed serpent plunged back into the depths of the fire and disappeared. The flames continued their strange, slow wavering in expanded time.

In a low voice, the saviour warned them of the next impending vision.

"Once the body has been burnt away, the soul rises toward the seven heavenly spheres. All those who possess a soul – those of the *psychic* race – will fear the next seven gate-keepers. Even the third race of men, who possess a spirit as well as soul, yes, even the *pneumatic* race must confront them. Though their garment of light protects them, their soul must still tremble before the Archons' wrath.

"Seven times your soul will stand before the seven evil Archons. And they will examine your seven soul-garments, which were fitted over you when you first descended into this world. For each garment bears the mark of its creator.

CH I.24 "The gate-keeper who stands before the gate of the moon seeks out *inconstancy*. He who stands before Mercury's gate looks for *greed*. At the gate of Venus, *lust*; at the gate of the sun, *pride*;

and at the gate of Mars, *wrath*. Finally, at Jupiter's gate he seeks out *injustice*; while at Saturn's gate, *deception*. These are the seven passions of the soul – enveloping you as seven soul-garments, each inscribed with an Archon's hidden sign."

Again, the fire blazed up, and a fearful appearance materialized in the flames.

VIII

Salome spun and twirled, like a thin clay figurine spinning on the potter's wheel. Her skin was glistening with sweat, and her garments clung to her flesh, revealing the slender lines of her sinuous figure.

The second sheath was lifted away, and tossed upon the treasures at the foot of Herod's throne.

Her small chest heaving, fighting for air, Salome stood before John a second time – and waited.

He gazed, spell-bound, at this miraculous image of his soul. Knowing her desire, his body pulled at the restraining chains like an animal awaiting slaughter. One kiss would release them both. But, with a supreme effort, he tumbled forward. Pressing his head to the floor, he manifest his stubborn refusal.

"Give yourself to me – in love!" she cried. "If two lovers possess each other, that isn't greed – it's love freely given!"

She turned and walked away. John watched as his soul turned and walked away. How much it had cost him – that surrender. But the soul-garment of 'greed' had been cast off, and his soul's slender image was passing through its gateway into the next aeon.

The third dance commenced, a sudden explosion of unrequited desire. She caressed her swelling breasts, gyrated her hips and thrust her hands repeatedly between her glistening thighs. She simulated every sexual act, performed every rite of passion. It was, in its lewd and obscene gestures, a wild and orgiastic celebration of lust.

She ripped the third garment from her body as if she were stripping away her own flesh. The pain and ecstasy on her face was manifest for all to see.

Herod slid off his throne and fell to his knees, his mouth open, his eyes in a daze.

But John, crouching like a wounded animal, barely managed to lift his head.

Salome fell to the floor. Thrusting the third garment away from her, she moved her head close to John's.

Breathless, she begged him, "Now! Plant your lips on my lips and I'll be yours forever!"

But John, burying his head in his cloak, murmured, "Not now, not ever..."

Stiffening, Salome growled through clenched teeth, "Love *is* lust! It's two bodies thrust against each other – flesh against flesh – clawing to be united! It is a moment of passion that is never repeated and never perishes!"

Thrusting herself to her feet, she marched away, her head held high. Relieved, John felt his soul pass under the archway of lust, and enter the fourth aeon.

The next dance began with a serpentine motion, her head moving from side to side and arms undulating like an ancient goddess of the snakes. Everywhere she turned, she opened wide her eyes and hypnotized anyone who dared to meet her commanding stare. Mesmerized by the Gorgon's gaze, they all turned to stone.

Haughtily, she drew off the fourth veil, exposing the small pert breasts that rose, sharp and erect, from her chest. Her glistening skin reflected the flickering torches of the hall, which danced in flames all along her body.

When this time, she dropped the kerchief on the pile, she barely stooped to recognize the anchorite curled up at her feet.

"Love is pride," she said, "and knows no mercy."

Barely hesitating, without a moment's waiting, she walked away.

But John watched, defeated, as his soul departed. Without pride, without ambition, forsaking all worldly glory, it passed out of this aeon and into the next.

The sharp and jagged movements of the next dance manifest a violence almost incongruent with Salome's girlish figure. But she seethed and raged, releasing a stream of scorn, a storm of vengeance and anger. Her hair whipping and flying, her hands clutched to her head, she flung herself across the floor. The frightened courtiers stepped back, fearing they would become the victims of her unchecked fury.

But the object of her scorn lay heaped upon the floor, trembling at the demon that had gained possession of his soul.

She tore another veil from her body and shredded it into pieces. Wrapping up the fragments round her fist, she threw them hard at the quivering figure before the dais.

Falling to her knees, she grasped John's head by the hair and pulled his face towards hers.

"Love is anger – beloved! It is the seething fury of desire denied – lashing out in blind vengeance, punishing the one who scorned you, who bled you... who refused you even the slightest kiss..!"

Heaving a sigh of relief, John watched as his soul, divested of its wrath, turned away.

As the flutes and lyres improvised new melodies over the complex rhythms, Salome's body responded immediately to those strange conjurings. She conveyed, through her variegated movements, the unusual sensation of balance suddenly tumbling into disorienting confusion.

At times, whirling like a dervish, she would manifest a perfect centripetal motion, spinning no less than seven times on a single arched sole. But, as if blown by invisible winds, that centre would be upset by a debilitating force. It was the most artfully executed of her dances, its choreography spontaneous and alive.

When she emerged from the last of seven spirals, a slender shift had wound itself round her upheld wrist.

Slowly, she surrendered this with the others. Moving closer to John, she bowed her head and whispered, "Love is unjust, my beloved! But love also forgives. Will you cling to injustice? Will you refuse, even now, to forgive Woman for her fault? Or with a kiss, will you make it right? It is not too late... Be merciful, just and fair. Embrace me."

She gazed at him with beseeching eyes, seeking the minutest sign of compassion.

Tears welled up in John's eyes. His heart was torn in two. But he knew that such a kiss, even now, could not be surrendered. His soul had still to suffer its final passion.

Reading all of this in her lover's face, Salome bowed her head.

And as she withdrew, John watched his soul escape one of the most difficult of the Archons' bonds.

Salome gazed down at her trembling limbs – naked, except for the one shift that swathed her slender hips. What had John said? *My bride* – my true bride – *would stand before God* – naked *as a child,* naked *as the truth...* Was that his final demand? Was this the only way he would grant his consent?

Then she looked at Herod Antipas. His eyes were fixed on that last sheathing. Writhing on his throne, he couldn't wait for the final moment when she, standing naked before him, would hand him her final veil as a token. In exchange for what?

Would John *renounce her* to the end – *sacrifice her* and *her love* – to obtain *his* vision of worldly transcendence? Was his God so demanding? And so utterly deceiving?

What the Goddess taught was manifest for all to see. Every one of her creatures could feel her flow of life in their limbs, could see the suffering of life-blood spilled, even as they consumed it once more as a sacred offering. Her sacrifice was the true sacrifice: the manifestation of life, taken and given, even as it was eternally renewed in the Goddess' womb.

Resignedly, Salome began her final dance.

IX

A terrible apparition rose up from the fire. Its face was like a blazing furnace; its eyes were like blackened coals, which glowed hellish red in the deep fiery pit. The air smelled of seared flesh and burning hair.

Suddenly, the beast lunged, scorching the apostles' faces with an infernal blast.

"A*aaaa*b*ee*l!" Arsinoe cried, and her screeching decree warded off its vicious attack. For the command contained the Archon's hidden name.

From the midst of the fire, it glared at them furiously, barely restrained by the incantation.

The saviour's voice grew low and ominous.

"This is the first Archon that awaits your soul in the heavenly ascent. This is Abel with the devouring fire-face. But you, with your knowledge of its hidden name, may pass it by!

"Listen – and listen well – as Arsinoe utters the protective spell."

Breathing in deeply, Arsinoe intoned:

Fr Bruce *"<When they take my soul to the place of Abel,*
the great and powerful Archon with the face of fire,
who waits upon the way, and carries off souls by theft;
when they take my soul to that place,>
2Bk Jeu *<I will seal myself with the protective seal,*
pronouncing its name once only:
'Fall back Archon of the first aeon,
For I challenge you
A*aaaa*beel!>"

The pronunciation of that name had an utterly eerie effect. The beast grew in size to monstrous proportions. Then, cursing aloud, uttering an unearthly, ear-rending scream, it opened wide its mouth.

And, as the maddening vision expanded, they were sucked through its open maw. All of them felt the first of their seven soul-garments rent and stripped away. It was like a sudden liberation from one of the invisible bonds imprisoning their blind and captive souls. Momentarily plunged into utter darkness, they made the harrowing passage into the next Archon's realm.

Like a burnt holocaust, the fiery beast had been consumed by its own flames. But no sooner had the furnace died down when a new face rose up from the fire. Saliva dripped from its bared fangs. The beast drew back, ready to strike.

Immediately, Arsinoe cried: "C*aaaaii*n!"

Before the beast could pounce, its wrath was restrained by her command.

The disciples trembled at this frightful apparition. But, remembering their armour of light, they stifled their fear and gazed directly into its glaring eyes.

Arsinoe repeated the protective spell, and the second soul-garment was rescinded. It was torn away like an invisible skin enveloping their flesh. All greed and want were blissfully lifted away.

And so the maddening vision deepened, through *Adonaiou*, *Yabel* Ap Jn 10:23
and *Kalila-Oumbri*, then *Harmas* and *Athoth*. The combinations of
vowels in the Archon's names grew more complex; the faces of the
beasts ever-more frightening – hyenas, hydras and dragons... Ap Jn 11:22

At last they stood before the gate of the Archigenetor of the Abyss.

X

Salome began her final dance. Her legs felt heavy as lead, and her arms felt like stone. The entire court began spinning around her. Nothing... none of it seemed real. The more she moved her limbs and displaced herself through space, the more she felt utterly removed from the festive hall. Time slowed, and space became a liquid light, swimming with appearances.

Weightlessly, she floated through the myriad of shapes. This world was nothing more than a mirage, an endless series of images that flowed in and out of manifestation. She herself was a mere semblance, a fleeting apparition in time's endless flow.

The entire hall became entranced by this beguiling spectre. John gazed, spell-bound, at her transporting illusion. At times she appeared ethereal and transparent. At times her flesh, in the throes of desire, seemed like the most palpable and compelling of forms. Which one hid the naked truth – the flesh or the veil?

When Salome finally stood, in utter nakedness, with the veil in her hand – these two choices appeared insoluble.

Crying uncontrollably, Salome wrapped the veil round her hand and knelt before John.

"Love is no illusion, beloved bridegroom. All of this is real. I am yours to possess, in body and soul. Behold the naked truth. If you renounce me now, then you will have sacrificed us both!"

With one hand naked, the other bearing the veil, she cupped her palms round his face. "Kiss me now, beloved consort, or renounce me completely."

The tears in John's eyes, mixing with the torch-light, bathed Salome's face in a radiant aura. The voices and visions had led him this far – to this moment of decision. And then, the path had divided, and he had seen two futures, equally clear. In one he embraced Salome; in the other, he renounced her. Only one led to their union.

Where did the sacred marriage take place – here, on earth, or in heaven? Did one reflect the other? How did God unite with the Goddess? How would the Son, the Bridegroom, unite with his Bride? The mystery was beyond him.

The only way he knew, the only path that had opened before him – was renunciation.

"Salome beloved, you are my true bride. But our marriage is the surrender of one to the other, in sacrifice..."

Salome gazed at him in horror and wonder.

"No, my husband," she whispered. "Ours is the sacrifice... of a man and woman to each other – in love."

Seven times her bare feet kissed the seven steps of the dais, until she stood naked before the king. Surrendering the last veil to him, she spoke loudly for all to hear.

"This garment, I give to you, my earthly king, in exchange for my heart's greatest hope."

Herod stared fixedly at Salome. Her nudity enthralled him, but the expression in her eyes inspired fear.

"Then speak that wish, and by all the powers of my throne, it will be granted."

Salome turned and looked at John. He looked pathetic, bound and chained, made ready for slaughter. But in his eyes glowed a holy fire which gave her strength. She pronounced the binding words which, once spoken, could never be withdrawn. She spoke them as her wedding vow.

"Make John mine – as I will be his, forever. Slaughter him like the offerings of old... slice his throat and sever his head – so my heart's last wish will be granted."

XI

In the aura of early morning, a swallow circled over their heads three times, screaming with joy and ecstasy. Then, like a terrible portent, it hurled itself into the fire – and was consumed.

Arsinoe cast a forlorn glance at the saviour, who trembled in recognition of the augury.

A single tear formed upon her lid, but she refused to let it fall upon her cheek. How, he wondered, could she receive the sign with such knowing resignation?

But the most painful and illuminating part of the initiation still awaited them, demanding their full attention.

Mustering all his powers of concentration, the Nazarene joined his hands and spoke.

"The last gate leads to Yaltabaoth's realm. Not only does he rule the Archons – he is their complete manifestation, indeed, the summation of all evil. The Archon's twelve shapes constitute differing aspects of his one terrifying form. Therefore, do not tremble before this singular image of all-encompassing malevolence..."

The fire before their eyes began to hiss and twist, as if a huge abominable monster were struggling in the blasting furnace of its womb.

A terrible wind made the mighty cedars and oaks above them bow their heavy heads. A strange light glowed in the heavens as insects buzzed madly through the air. The night birds screeched in terror.

And suddenly, from the fire, the huge serpent rose up. Opening wide its leonine mouth, it cried like a bastardized child newly-born – screaming, howling, blaspheming with a thousand inscrutable curses. Its fiery eyes radiated with evil. Entwined in its flaming mane, twelve lesser serpents opened wide their bestial mouths and spewed forth streams of profanities.

Above the deafening malediction, Arsinoe screamed a single high-pitched note. This expanded harmonically as she aspirated the sacred vowels over the earthly consonants. Making him her instrument, sounding the blessed *pneuma* through Yaltabaoth's name, Arsinoe commanded him.

The coiling hydra expanded its hood, disclosing an array of arcane symbols on its scales. Venom dripped from its open mouth, and it gazed hypnotically at Arsinoe. The serpent was poised to strike.

Fearlessly, Arsinoe stood up and approached the fiery apparition. Its noxious fumes assaulted her nostrils and the terrible heat, like a blazing furnace, singed the tips of her hair.

But, concentrating all her emotions on the final incantation, she cried:

"Fall back – Archon of the Final Aeon!
For I challenge you:
Y - *AAA* - LT - *AAA* - B - *AAAOOO* - TH..*!"*

Like a huge ball of fire, the apparition exploded, blinding them with a light brighter than the sun.

All the disciples had the distinct impression of passing through
the sun, as if, through a doorway in the heavens. At the twelfth aeon,
CH 1:24 the seven passions of their souls were burnt away, just as surely as
the body had been consumed after the fifth aeon. They were freed of
inconstancy, greed and lust; pride, wrath and injustice. And strangest
of all, they were freed of deception.

With eyes newly opened, they saw with undying clarity how a thousand demons had kept them in constant blindness, beguiling them with a myriad of appearances – hungering for fresh meat and intoxicating brews, greedy for rich possessions and all the pleasures of the flesh – whose denial had angered them, and whose attainment had made them proud.

Unseeing and in darkness, they had fought with their fellow man – competed with him in envy, enslaved him through labour or imprisoned him through injustice. All the while, unknown to them, they were joined in unity – a brother to that enemy which, in truth, was their own dark reflection. This multiplicity was an illusion, for all were one.

With this knowledge, they passed beyond the last of the Lower Aeons and into the place called 'the Middle'. It glowed with an unusual light, for this realm comprised the curtain between light and shadow. Halfway between the Upper and Lower Aeons, they stood in the eighth heaven, the interstitial realm of Wisdom's repentance.

"As the mother of Yaltabaoth," Christ intoned, "Sophia created this realm when she repented for her fault. And after death, you too will come to exist here, awaiting the final Restitution, when your spirits will finally divest themselves of their repentant souls – and enter the Pleroma."

The saviour stood up, spread his arms, and cried: "Behold, the aeons of the upper light!"

Surrendering their souls, the disciples rose ever higher in their minds. In their collective vision, they beheld a fountain of clear flowing light. It surged upward and outward in a crystalline spray of incandescent light, then cascaded through the aeons in a spectral array of translucent colours.

They did not stand apart from the vision, but *became* it, like droplets of light in a crystalline ocean. As the aeons' fire and liquid fused, its luminous waters bathed them in a multitude of phosphorescent hues. The heavenly stream poured over them and *through* them – aglow with knowing and pulsing with life. They existed here, in image and in name, as part of the manifold angels surrounding the Godhead.

Each apostle, in his own unique manner, became one of the twelve aeons of the uppermost heavens. Though they swam through the light on the wings of awareness, each transported itself in a singular way: Peter was the Grace-filled *Armozel*, and Andrew, the After-thought *Armoze*l. James was *Daveithai*, the Understanding angel, and John, the Perfect *Eleleth*. Together, they shimmered as Four Lights in the heights, each accompanied by two lesser lights, making twelve in all.

Like a mosaic comprised of flawless crystals, their glittering gems combined into God's glowing image. Each of them shone in rainbow shades, like fragments of Phoenician glass in a sun-stained *rosace* – and all of them transparent to the same luminous source.

This vision expanded, and they were struck with holy wonder. They saw the source of life like a visionary tree: the translucent fruits on its golden boughs dripping with God's life-giving sap.

Again, the vision transformed, and the source of life became a celestial flower – a lotus, lily or rose, with syllables stained on its pollen-filled petals. On the uppermost lid, three sacred signs were inscribed: truth, grace and form. On the lid to the left: memory, afterthought, and perception. On the lid to the right: idea, understanding and love. And on the last of the petals: peace, perfection and wisdom. Though separate, each scented lid spiralled to the same aromatic centre, overflowing with perfume and sweet-smelling nectar. All were forms of knowing, and all found their knowing in the one Mind that was God.

Time passed without measure and space grew limitless. Beyond birth, beyond death, they stood at rest in a realm where movement and stillness combined into a timeless dance of eternal joy.

Linked arm in arm, they spun like unseen planets round an invisible sun. Turning in circles, this cosmos expanded into a celestial city glistening with light: its four glass walls and twelve-gated towers the outward sign of God's hidden kingdom. Here was the heavenly Jerusalem, the true archetype shaped in the divine architect's mind.

Passing from image to abstraction, the light exploded into a network of jewels where each luminous nexus reflected the node that glowed at the centre. Like ruby, emerald and amethyst gems, their angelic bodies glowed with rich inner radiance. And yet, like gold, silver and polished stones, their crystalline forms also reflected each other's light.

In interlacing patterns of incredible complexity, they manifest the geometric perfection of God's infinite matrix. A myriad of shapes – pentagons, triangles and squares – combined into shining polyhedra, increasingly complex, one within the next, until all were inscribed in a vibrant, twelve-sided spheroid. It was the One's divine latticework, endlessly expanding yet flawlessly unified.

Enchanted by this beatific vision, entranced by its diamantine perfection, still they heard the distant timbre of Arsinoe's angelic voice.

Unt MS Though she spoke <with a tongue of flesh,> they heard her
1Bk Jeu speaking <with the tongue of the Father> as, in ecstasy, she cried:

"We call upon you, we invoke you:
Norea 27:11 <Father of all, upright *Nous*,
the Mind dwelling silent in the heights!
And *Ennoia* of the light, ineffable voice,
The Thought speaking the mind of the Father!
And you, the living, untouchable *Logos*,
the Word speaking two names that are one.>"

Then, in an upper-worldly voice that resonated with the sound of each sacred vowel, Arsinoe pronounced three names, three hidden holy names, wherein the mystery of the beginning became manifest:

Noesis!
Noesis Noeseos!
Noesis Noeseos Noesis!

Enraptured in a state of absolute mindfulness, ecstatic, elated, the disciples rose up to the uttermost heights. When Arsinoe intoned *Noesis*, the first sacred name, they saw the greater Mind or Thinking which was *Nous*, the Father. And after Arsinoe had pronounced the two holy names, *Noesis Noeseos*, they saw, with joy rising in their hearts, how He stood together with Thought, the Mother *Ennoia*. Then, as one, the Thought and its Thinking, the Mother and Father, engendered the Son: *Noesis Noeseos Noesis!* And in that moment, the Parent became complete in itself as the tripartite unity of *Thought-Thinking-Itself.*

In a timeless and eternal moment, all become one, and they finally 'stood at rest' within the Parent. Their endless striving was at peace, for their spirits had found their true and restful silence. In the stilled state of absolute mindfulness, they entered into knowing union with the omniscient One.

"<The name of the Father *is* the Son," Arsinoe cried aloud. "It is Gs Tru 38:7
the mystery of the unspeakable, coming to our ears and filling them completely. Thus, the Father's name, though never pronounced, is still heard through the Son.>"

With her voice rising ever higher, Arsinoe canted:

"<Yesseus... Mazareus... Yessedekeus!>" Gs Egypt 64:9

"<This is the Word that originated in the Voice.> This is <the Tri Prot 37:3
Son of the silent Silence. His name contains the Voice's *seven* Gs Egypt 42:21
vowels. And in him, *the Logos*, they find their completion.>"

Again, Arsinoe chanted. But, forgoing all consonants, she sang seven vowels – unhidden, holy and pure:

"<iiii... eeeh... ooo... uuu... eee... aaa... oooh!>" Gs Egypt 66:17

"This," she cried, "<is the ineffable mystery! The invisible, Gs Egypt 53:24
unnameable, uninvoked name!> This is *Ieou*, the *Fifth* Light who comprises the *Alpha* and *Omega*: *I-Eh-O-U-E-A-Oh!*"

Upon hearing this ineffable name, the disciples' eyes were opened anew. They saw the blinding face of God, whose countenance bore the lineaments of the Son. The smile on the saviour's face was full of compassion; his eyes were half-closed in contemplative bliss. But the Son, they now recognized, bore their own features. They stared at themselves while staring, inexplicably, into the face of God.

Their spirits dancing, their minds alight, the apostles were overcome with beatific bliss.

Ode Sol 21 Arsinoe <lifted her arms on high, as if they had been loosed from
CH I. 31 their chains.> Inhaling deeply, she made the final <speech offering>
which transported them all into the last and highest sphere:

Gs Egypt 66:12

"<O Being which beholds the Aeons
AIOhN O OhN!
Thou art the Alpha and Omega
EI AAAA OOOOh!
In veritable truth,
Thou art
O Eternal Being

A
EE
EEEh
IIII
OOOOO
UUUUUU
OOOOOOOh!>"

For a fleeting moment of epiphany, they achieved, in silence and stillness, the supreme *gnosis*. Then slowly, this vision dissolved, and the companions found themselves sitting round the fire.

Though they had returned to the world of shadows, the joy and ecstasy of their awakening remained. They felt an unquenchable desire to spread this hidden yet joyful serenity – to embody it here below, in the world of appearances. Through giving, loving and sharing, they could begin to manifest the invisible kingdom in those mindful acts and heart-felt deeds that momentarily evoked the eternal, unforgotten *gnosis*.

PART III

XII. Batanea

I

After a long and peaceful slumber, the disciples awoke. Through the canopy of trees, the afternoon sun shimmered like swords of light. The earth felt warm beneath their cloaks and the sound of the sparrows came to their ears like earthly music.

From their satchels they withdrew bread, honey and dates, distributing them among themselves. Each of them ate in silence, replenishing the flesh so the flame in their souls could burn that much brighter. Only the faint sparkle in their eyes betrayed the hidden joy still swimming in their hearts.

The saviour, they learned, had watched over them as they slept, then departed. After a long walk along the Jordan's banks, he had returned with his face long and cheeks hollow. Most distressing of all was the gaze that blazed from his darkly-ringed eyes.

Some of the disciples recalled that strange look, and it froze the blood in their veins. The Nazarene had the same dark stare as the Prophet John. It was, as if, the spirit of the Baptist had taken up residence in the Nazarene's flesh.

"The battle begins tomorrow," Jesus said slowly, his voice low and grave. "We haven't much time. For this is the beginning of the end..."

Leaving aside their brief repast, they assumed the same places where they had sat the night before. For a prolonged moment, the saviour stared at Susanna, gazing deep into her soul. A shiver passed through her flesh.

"The Archons are twelve in number," Jesus said, "but those

twelve command invisible armies: authorities, powers, and legions of demons. Each of the heavenly Archons has seven powers under him, and each of these powers commands six demons more, making three hundred and sixty malevolent angels in all. In each living body, they exercise their power – by *ensouling* it – animating it with movement and enslaving it with emotion."

The saviour's stare left no doubt concerning their existence, and the potential danger that lay in their influence.

"The five Archons of the abyss mix hot and cold with dry and wet. Keeping these opposites in balanced tension, their mother *Onorthochrasaei* molds the material body. From the four elements in the ether, her myriad imps give shape to each and every limb.

"Thus, the legions of demons rule us – *body and soul.* With cruel tenacity, they master any man who surrenders himself to their influence. Not only are we subject to the needs of the flesh – hunger, thirst and desire – but more pernicious still, we suffer all the passions of the soul. Jealousy, anger and shame – these are the most insidious of emotions; anxiety, fear and mourning – they possess us like so many evil spirits."

The moment the Nazarene pronounced the word 'mourning', Susanna felt a wound re-open in her heart. She had lost her husband seven years before, but still suffered the pain of his passing – guarding his memory jealously, afraid to let it go.

Ap Jn 18:14 "<*Nenentophni* rules over grief, just as surely as *Blaomen* rules over fear.> They are always at work: distracting peace of mind, agitating the calm heart. You must learn to recognize each of these demons – burning unseen in your soul – and master it by name."

The saviour stood up and spread his arms, as if he were crucified upon the world.

Ap Jn 15:32 "You hold *Krys* in your right hand, and *Beluai* in your left. *Treneu* moves the fingers of your right hand; *Balbel* those of your left. Each finger, joint, and nail – *each* bodily organ and extremity bears a demon's mark. You must come to *know* them all, *command* them all – so the battle between the sons of light and the sons of darkness may begin in earnest."

The disciples bowed their heads. None dared question the master, but each was thinking the same thing: how would they ever survive this initiation? The task seemed daunting, unbearable...

Upon the saviour's instructions, each of them lay on the ground with arms outspread and eyes half-closed. After centering themselves in mindful contemplation, they followed his commands.

Arsinoe intoned the demons' hidden names, and they repeated them inexorably, briefly seeing, in a dark and terrible epiphany, which evil imp was animating their limbs, and what elusive passion was occupying their hearts.

When *Nenentophni*'s name rolled off Arsinoe's tongue, Susanna felt a terrible gust of wind rushing through her body. Finally surrendering the memory of her husband, she let his spirit go.

The ordeal lasted late into the night, as they concentrated on each bodily part and passion, while all three hundred and sixty demons were named and commanded.

"<*Asterechme* created the right eye," Arsinoe intoned, Ap Jn 15:32
"*Thaspomocha*, the left. *Yeronumos* created the right ear," she droned
on inexorably, "*Bissoum*, the left. The nose belongs to *Adioreim*; the
lips to *Manen-Ephroum...*>"

The moon arced across the skies and disappeared with the dawn. When, finally, they were allowed a few hours' sleep, the disciples experienced the most tormenting of nightmares – made even more threatening by the certain knowledge that these horrible *incubi* lay hidden in their skins.

On the morning of the third day, the saviour addressed them with unconcealed joy.

"<I have given you, as sons of the light, authority over all the Soph JC 119:4
evil things of this world, so you might *tread upon* their powers.>
<Now that you have stripped away all that is evil and corrupted, you L Pt Ph 137:6
will become illuminators in the midst of mortal men.>"

He bowed his head.

"<In our hearts, we are united. We have made a covenant with Act Pt 12A 1:9
each other, to fulfil the mission appointed us.> In the ensuing battle,
we will defeat the darkness, by turning it into light! <Let us come L Pt Ph 137:23
together, therefore, and teach the world salvation!>"

As they whispered 'Amen', they raised their glowing faces. The saviour's gaze was confident and triumphant. They had no doubt now that the Messiah had come as a warrior, armed with radiance, to quell all earthly shadows.

Gathering up their things, they departed at once. The Messiah marched ahead, the soles of his feet burning. An eagle in the sky circled then dived, as if indicating the direction they must take.

By mid-day, they had reached Bethsaida on the borders of Gaulanitis and Galilee. The ancient walled town, fortified in basaltic stone, was an important marketplace for nomadic traders. From Phoenicia in the west to Philip's kingdom in the east, camels came laden with sacks of rare spices, rich weavings, and amphoras filled with wine. The sardines, mushts and barbels, fished from Gennesaret's depths, were traded here in abundance. Sealed in clay jars, conserved in a rich sauce, they travelled from here to the four corners of the known world.

With his companions close behind, Christ entered the marketplace. To Matthew's great delight, the Messiah overturned tables and sent their goods flying. Simon Zealot quickly followed suit, smashing cruses of perfumed oil and spilling sacks of precious spice. The disciples went wild. Birds were freed from their cages; animals released from their tethers.

In a thousand different tongues, the merchants and traders starting cursing, spitting in the air and shaking their fists.

Christ stood on the steps of a raised platform where slaves had been auctioned that morning.

Gs Phil 62:26 "<Jews and Romans!" he cried in one breath. "Greeks and
Gs Phil 63:11 Barbarians! Freemen and slaves!> <Turning and turning, like asses
tied to the millstone, you've walked a thousand miles – and still kept
to the same spot! Like blind desert tribes, you've walked a thousand
Gs Phil 66:20 journeys – but still made no progress to the end!> <How many times
will you go astray along the way?> How long will you wander the
earth, lost and forgotten, a race far from home?"

The merchants and traders, like desert jackals, crowded round the Messiah, stalking his every movement.

"Who will be the first?" the Messiah cried. "You have heard my
Test Tr 44:30 <testimony of truth> – who dares contest me?"

A hefty slave-trader, his whip held high, was the first to mount the steps. But Simon and Peter, standing at the saviour's sides, held the man fast.

Suddenly, the Messiah seized him by the head and stared into his wide, furious eyes. Screaming the demons' names, Christ cast them out one by one. The body convulsed and a series of shadows rose in the air – darkening broad daylight, spreading noxious fumes.

The crowd pulled back. But another merchant, made furious by the loss of his goods, threw himself against the saviour. Again, the demons were seized and cast out. He joined the slave-trader, who was sitting in a daze, staring at the crowd in utter bewilderment.

But from the midst of the mob came a terrifying, strangulated cry. The buyers and sellers struggled against each other, trying to escape the horrific presence in their midst. A huge man stood, covered with rags – his leprous flesh a mass of stinking contusions.

The crowd drew back in fear.

Even the Nazarene was overcome by disgust and revulsion. The leper approached, extending the gnarled stumps of his ravaged, bandaged hands. A tremendous pity overwhelmed Jesus, quelling his fear. The saviour grasped the man and gazed deeply into his cruelly distorted features.

In horror, the son of Mary gazed into the leper's eyes, seeing his own face covered with rotting folds of flesh. Then the pain and, even worse, the man's shame and self-loathing, overwhelmed his soul. He had never felt such hatred directed infinitely inward.

In the eyes of others, this pathetic man had never experienced acceptance, only fearful reproach. And so he had lived his entire life in self-revulsion, despising pity and revelling in his own fleshly mortification.

For a few moments, it seemed like the Nazarene would lose himself in this vertiginous, maddening vision. He felt, in a cruel and twisted way, an extraordinary vanity for his ugliness. He clung to his deformity, finding a final, perverse pleasure in his monstrous existence.

If it were not for Arsinoe and the Virgin, Jesus would have become trapped in this strangely distorted mirror, frozen for all time in its evilly narcissistic gaze. But the two women tore his face away from the leper's, even as he was stretching to embrace him.

Both the saviour and the saved were thrown back. The ragged man let out a scream as painful as an animal's dying cry. The sky was suddenly darkened by a thousand shadows convulsing in the air.

Amazed, the Nazarene saw the man before him stand erect. His limbs straightened out; his skin grew smooth and clear. But more amazing still, his soul was freed of its darkly-distorted reflection. His heart beat calmly, his mind became sober and at rest.

Seeing this, the crowd grew agitated. Some tried to flee; others stood in blind amazement. But the beggars of the marketplace, the blind, lame and infirm, came hobbling forward. Some had tears in their eyes, others cowered in self-effacing shame.

The disciples led them one by one before the Messiah, who gazed into each tragic, fearful face. For a few moments, the blind made him blind, the mute shrivelled his tongue and the lame paralyzed his limbs. But he recognized each hidden affliction, recalled its name, and commanded it to flee.

"Peter!" the master called. "Believe in me when I tell you that you too possess this power. But *look upon them with faith* – and you will free the blind of their affliction!"

Shaking from head to toe, Peter nodded. Accepting a blind man into his embrace, he stared deeply into his unseeing eyes. A momentary darkness descended. But, remembering that darkness – the same blindness which had overcome him when he had put his
Ap Pt 72:21 own hands over his eyes – as then, so now, <he suddenly saw a light greater than the light of day.> The scales fell from his eyes, and he
Acts Pt 138:7 saw the blind man just as the blind man *saw* him. <With eyes of the flesh and eyes of the soul,> they stared at each other, as if, into a strangely luminous mirror. And then both of them started laughing and crying in wonder of the miracle they had wrought.

Susanna stepped forward and took a woman into her arms. This pitiful creature – withdrawn, cataleptic, her eyes glazed over with madness – barely met Susanna's tearful gaze. But when their eyes locked, the two of them tumbled into a labyrinth of confusing memories. Staring, as if, into a cracked looking-glass, Susanna saw a thousand fractured images of suffering and abuse, their pain compounded by a deep desire to be loved. Finally a veil of numbness had descended – clouding the mirror, obscuring its reflection – until her soul could no longer see its own dark image.

But the woman, equally entranced by Susanna's tearful gaze, began to identify herself with this loving disciple. She saw beauty, compassion, wholeness. She saw herself as Susanna – healed, renewed, her heart at rest. And as her own eyes filled with tears, the woman's self-image grew clearer, her face became radiant and bright.

Finally, the mirror was shattered, and they gazed at one another with ecstasy in their hearts. All darkness had been eclipsed. Like shadowy silhouettes, the demons departed, cursing Susanna as they fled. The two women tearfully embraced.

One by one, the disciples began to perform healings. Each manifest a different power, but all succeeded in freeing tormented
Test Tr 33:5 souls from the Archons' bonds. <The lame, dumb and blind; the paralytic and demon-possessed – all were granted release> through the disciples' healing gaze.

II

That evening they returned to Capernaum in a jubilant, indeed, a triumphant mood. Outside the Widow's Tower, a cloaked figure waited in the shadows. As Magdalene grew closer, she suddenly exclaimed, "Joanna?"

The veiled woman pulled back her hood, revealing that it was indeed Salome's former tutor. The wife of Chuza desperately looked left and right, her face deeply lined with sorrow and fatigue.

The companions entered Magdalene's home. Some lit lanterns and kindled the hearth-fire while others drew the shutters and fetched water from the cistern. Then, sitting in a circle before the warming fire, they quenched their thirst and massaged their tired limbs.

But Joanna couldn't keep still. She paced back and forth, not knowing how to release the flood of anguish in her heart. Finally, the Nazarene grasped her by the shoulders and, with deep concern in his eyes, calmed her of her dark despair.

"We've had many omens concerning John," he said. "We knew his fate lay in Salome's hands..."

"She cut him down!" Joanna cried, "like wheat at the harvest! Those were her exact words – that he be bound and beheaded like a beast led to sacrifice!"

The noble woman shook her head, unable to believe that her own charge could act so callously.

"And Salome – what happened to her?" Magdalene asked, fearful of the response.

Joanna stared at Magdalene, her tongue cleaving to her palate. At last, she said:

"Whatever soul she once possessed has perished with the Baptist. Salome shows *no feelings at all* – neither bitterness nor remorse. Instead, she fled Herod's court and installed herself with Philip in Batanea. We are told that she indulges in every form of excess – bathes and perfumes her body for hours, feasts in the Roman fashion, sleeps with slaves and concubines, then drugs herself to sleep each night. She confides in no one. But her servants say she wanders for hours in the desert. When the wind rises, she exposes herself to the burning sands and stinging nettles, laughing and singing hysterically like a child."

Magdalene lowered her head, remembering the delicate girl who had confided so ardently her hidden desire for the Baptist. A cold chill ran down Miri's spine. Would her love for the Nazarene fall under a similar curse?

When Miri looked at Jesus, he was looking back at her, his eyes darker than ever.

Joanna turned to the saviour, an urgent message burning on

her lips. "While in prison, John often cried out in delirium, uttering strange prophecies. Herod had each of his words transcribed, hoping to find some sign. He and Chuza are obsessed with the Five Seals – they think the seals' power will bring down the kingdom..."

"They aren't entirely mistaken," Jesus replied.

"I hope it will be so!" the noble-woman announced, disgusted. "I've renounced the whole place – my king, my husband and all my titles. I've thrown it all aside and come over to your kingdom – if you'll have me..."

Joanna was a proud, uncompromising woman. But, she lowered her head and gazed at the earthen floor. "I have been so blind..."

"Why do you wish to follow me?"

Acts Jn 95 "Because <you are the lamp for those who wish to see,>" she replied, her eyes gilded with tears.

Jesus nodded. "Then you are welcome among us."

Magdalene breathed a sigh of relief.

"I hope I may prove myself worthy," the new disciple announced. "You should know that Herod's spies follow you at all times. Even Pilate and the priesthood are tracking your movements. You must be careful! They could seize you any moment. And we know what happened to John..."

The ensuing silence spoke for her. Worried, the disciples turned to one another. But the Nazarene seemed unconcerned.

Joanna's voice then grew deep and troubled. "There are strange events unfolding in Jerusalem. Another prophet has been seized, a blind anchorite from the desert named Barabbas."

Jesus turned to her, deeply disturbed.

"They say he has been stirring up the Zealots. But at every turn, he's spoken against you, claiming Jerusalem will fall if the Messiah of the Five Seals enters Zion's Gate."

"Then why have they seized him?" Magdalene wondered.

"It is all part of the High Priest's scheming. He wants to make a martyr of him – as if, by condemning him, his prophecies will be proven true. From his prison cell in Jerusalem, Barabbas is gaining notoriety, and the faithful now tremble at the sound of his voice. He's turning the mob against you."

The disciples wondered at this strange turn of events.

"Barabbas also spoke against John, calling him the False Prophet. And you, it seems, are now regarded by the Jerusalemites as the False Messiah."

Jesus nodded, marvelling at the genius behind this evil scheming.

Was this really the work of Annas and the High Priest? Or was the Archigenetor shaping his fate?

"In prison, John called out to you directly. Maybe he knew someone would bring you his message..." Suddenly, Joanna broke out in a cold sweat. What her coming here pre-ordained?

"He spoke of Barabbas, saying: '<A demon will come forth P Shem 44:31
from the belly of the serpent! He will conceal himself in an empty place, but many will be awed by his works.>'"

Upon hearing this, Jesus realized just how serious a threat Barabbas was. Yaltabaoth's Son was leading a multitude astray.

"Then he spoke to you directly," Joanna paused. "His words were strange and cryptic. He said: '*Yesseus* – bring the bride and twin to Delphi! *Mazareus* – stand before the sphinx! *Yessedekeus* – inscribe the omega over the alpha!' And his last message was: 'When the swallow is consumed, your hour will grow short!'"

The saviour stiffened. One glance at Arsinoe confirmed his worst fears. When the morning swallow had consumed itself in the flames, the Baptist had given his sign. The Messiah's appointed hour was approaching fast.

And still – two of the Five Seals exceeded his grasp.

"Do you know what he wished to tell you?" Peter asked in quiet desperation.

The Nazarene made no comment. Instead, he raised his voice confidently. "The fore-runner prepared the path. We, who have walked it, have found the way to be straight and well-guided. Today was another good sign: you have gained the seals' protection and manifest their power. Tomorrow you'll join in pairs and set upon your own ways."

Whatever foreboding they may have felt was soon erased when they saw the smile on the saviour's face. Some hidden joy was swelling in his breast.

"But," he said, glancing at each of them warmly, "we'll meet again in three weeks' time. We have already attended the betrothal. Now, the bride and groom have invited us to their wedding feast. Once our labours are finished, we'll enter the bridal hall and join in the celebration. The wedding feast of Cana awaits!"

The disciples lay their heads that night with a strange anticipation. A dark garment had fallen over Galilee, but the morning would come, clothing the land with light. Undoubtedly, hardship awaited, but so did unexpected miracles.

III

Dawn came, unveiling a blanket of snow over the black and barren fields. The crowns of the sycamores were gilded with frost, and crows picked berries in the snow. Standing by the hearth-fire, the Nazarene paired his disciples in twos.

Andrew, bashful and smiling, was paired with Arsinoe; the hefty shepherd Simon would accompany Susanna. Philip and Nathanael were kept together; John would care for the Nazarene's mother. Mariam went with Matthew, and Martha with tall and lanky James. Young Jude and James, the saviour's younger siblings, were sent forth as brothers. Peter was paired with Joanna to teach her along the way. That left Thomas and Magdalene – whom Jesus kept behind.

He stood back and admired his eighteen companions – eleven
1Ap Jas 38:15 men and <seven women.> They were his fellow labourers, his true
Ap Adam 83:1 brothers and sisters <– the light-givers whose illuminating works
Pistis ch 7 would shine> <from the Treasury of Light.>

2Tr Seth 67:31 "<I am standing among men and women," he began, "who are forever united in the friendship of friends, knowing neither enmity nor evil, but united in word and peace - through the *gnosis*. You have come to know fully and completely *who* the One is, and indeed that *all are one*. Thus, *you are* the community in unity. Through the spirit of mutual friendship, you shall come forth into the light. You have taken on my likeness, and now will appear to all as the Word.>"

Ap Jn 2:16 With tears rising to his eyes, he said: "<I have come to teach
Gs Tru 33:30 what is, what was, and what will be.> <Yet you too, my beloved companions – shall *manifest* the will of the Father, for you also come from him...>

Ap Jas 9:9 "<Trust in me, and understand what the Light is!> <In you
Gs Truth 32:31 dwells the Light that does not fail. Say then, from the heart, that *you are* the perfect day! Speak of knowledge with those who err. Speak of truth with those who search for it...>"

He walked among them, grasping them by the shoulders and engaging them with his mysterious eyes, black and sparkling like obsidian jewels.

"It is said that the lame and blind, the paralytics and demoniacs have suffered because of their sins. But I say to you, they have suffered
Jn 9:1 <so the works of God might finally be made manifest to Man.> All of us have experienced suffering, and been illuminated thereby.

Gs Tru 33:1 "<Thus – make firm the foot of those who have stumbled! Feed

those who are hungry, and give repose to those who are weary! Stretch out your hands to heal those who are ill!>"

He stood before Susanna, and a complicit stare passed between them.

"<The physicians of this world heal the body, which belongs Act Pt 12A 11:14
to the lower world. But the physicians of the soul – *they heal the*
heart! Thus, heal the body first. But, through that healing, reveal
your greater power, and heal the greater illnesses of the heart.> Gs Truth 33:5
<Awaken those who sleep! And to those who wish to rise – lift them
upward!>"

He turned to Arsinoe and Andrew.

"Each of you is blessed with their own particular gift, their own
unique power. <And it is fitting, in this way, that each of you enjoys Int Kn 15:23
the gift given to you by God. Therefore, *do not be jealous of one*
another, lest it become an obstacle on your path. Does one possess
the gift of prophecy? Does another seek to write the divine word?
Share it without hesitation. Rejoice in your brother's gift and give
thanks to your sister's grace! In this way, you too may share the
divine grace that dwells in each of you.>

"In the evening, as you rest from your labours, <sit down and Ap Jas 2:8
recall what I've said to you, whether secretly or in the open.> <Write Gr Pow 42:31
down my words, according to your desire, and put it in a book.>
None of you has authority over the other, or may say 'I understood
the master's teachings, but you did not! *Each of you bears your own*
proper witness! <If one makes progress with the Word, do not let Int Kn 16:31
the other say: 'Why does she speak while I remain silent?' For what
she reveals is yours also. The one who delivers, and the one who
discerns, are *both* moved by the same illuminating power.>

"<Become earnest about the word! Hearken to it, know Ap Jas 9:18
knowledge, and love life!> <For the first part of the word is *faith*; Ap Jas 8:10
the second part, *love*; and the third part, *works*.

"Like a grain of wheat, let the word be sown *in faith*. Like a grain that sprouts into many seeds, let it grow *through love*. And like the bounty of its harvest, let it nourish and save, *through your works*. The grace of knowledge is given to you, so you may plant the kingdom's seed, spread it to all, and make it grow.>

"<Now is the time and the hour,>" he cried. "<Now is the eternal 2Ap Jas 63:24
day.> <In union and communion with the spiritual fellowship> – go 2Ap Jas 53:29
forth, and spread the Kingdom over all the earth!" Ap Pt 79:1

Hearing this, they were filled with joy. <They parted in four L Pt Ph 140:10
directions, to preach the word and perform many healings.>

IV

The Nazarene cast a forlorn look around the room. The Widow's Tower felt so empty without the joyful faces of his apostles. There, hanging from a nail, was Susanna's veil of black tulle. And here, alone in the corner, was Matthew's broken sandal. On the window sill were frosted figs gathered by Arsinoe that morning. And Simon, whether by accident or design, had left his knife behind.

Magdalene and Thomas felt the same sad emptiness. They hadn't realized, until now, how attached they had grown to their sixteen brothers and sisters. If only the seed which had sprouted so lovingly in their midst could blossom throughout Israel...

In a whisper that was barely audible, Jesus said: "I've reserved the hardest task for us."

He turned and looked at his bride and twin. His chin was low on his chest, and he sighed deeply.

"We can't afford to wait any longer. You heard John's prophecies. We must leave – *now*..." His face was rigid, betraying not the slightest emotion. "We must go to the place where John's questions find their answers."

The Iscariot cast an unsettling glance at his double, and said, "...The desert."

"The only way I know, is to go as far as you can... into the borderland between life and death... where the silence whispers with your innermost fear. For the answers to appear, we must confront the unknown in ourselves."

Slowly, he nodded his head. "I'm going into Batanea's eastern steppes. Will you accompany me?"

There was a prolonged moment, during which Magdalene and the Iscariot searched each other's eyes.

Thomas tried hard to remain calm, hoping his gaze would not betray his innermost schism. Would Judas, long since banished into the shadows of himself, appear once more in the wilderness? In the desert wasteland – would the hanged man return to life?

Magdalene stood rigid, listening to her heartbeat, and the fearful pause before each pulse. In the darkened silence, would Sophia raise her voice?

Suddenly, the expressions on their faces were adamant and clear. Swallowing their fear, they would accompany him.

Without taking the slightest provision, the three of them turned, and walked out the door.

Perched on the town's eastern slope was a Roman fort, with SPQR engraved over its gate. Pilate's soldiers and Herod's spies were stationed here – S*enatus* P*opulus* Q*ue* R*omanus* – 'in the name of the Senate and the people of Rome'. The spies watched, stern-faced and silent, as the three Israelites skirted the lake and passed out of Capernaum.

Though the snow of last night had melted, hearth-fires continued to burn in the nearby homes. The Gennesaret fishermen were sitting with their nets stretched between their toes, repairing the holes with needle and twine.

Near Bethsaida, the three companions crossed the Jordan, leaving the basaltic soil of Galilee behind. Entering Philip's territory, they felt that here, at least, they were beyond Herod's reach. As they passed Gaulanitis and penetrated deeper into Batanea, the earth grew rocky, arid and dry.

Magdalene, whose henna-stained brow had become lined with anxiety, finally broke their prolonged silence. "The Baptist's prophecies," she asked Jesus, "did you understand them?"

The Nazarene looked at her and a slight smile creased his lips.

"Miri, no oracle is without ambiguity..."

Jesus drew in a deep breath. "I know this much: 'the swallow consumed by fire' tells us we haven't much time..."

"Before..?" Miri asked, a terrible chill rising up her spine. She shivered uncontrollably.

"...Before we inscribe the omega over the alpha," he replied, his voice as prophetic as John's. "We will bring about the end, by making all things as they once were – at the beginning." And he added, his eyes flashing mysteriously, "– as they were, *before* the Fall of Man."

The Iscariot stared at Jesus, his temples throbbing, his heart beating wildly. "Then, have you seen it? – The Fall... the *true* Fall of Man..?"

"...What *really* happened in Eden?" Jesus frowned and shook his head. "No. But the answer became clearer with John's second oracle. 'Stand before the sphinx' he said..."

Dark and brooding, the Hellenist nodded. "The riddle of the sphinx. What walks on four legs in the morning, on two in the afternoon, and on three in the evening. Like a child, a youth and an elder with a staff, the answer is – Man."

Jesus stared at a scarecrow in the middle of an abandoned

field.

"Yes. That was the question which John put to us in Perea: *What is Man?* Who was Adam? And Eve? Solve the mystery, he said, and the path to your own end will be made straight."

Miri asked, "Then how do you hope to solve it?"

"What do you think John meant when he cried 'Bring the bride and twin to Delphi! Why do you think he fell at your feet?"

The Iscariot stopped suddenly, his eyes opening wide. "*Know Thyself!* The Baptist spoke the same words inscribed on the Oracle of Delphi..."

Silently, Thomas and Magdalene recalled that strange moment when John hugged their knees and tearfully kissed their feet, pleading *'Know yourselves – before it's too late..!'*

The sun behind their backs cast long shadows ahead of them.

"So that is why you've taken us with you into the desert..."
Dial Sav 139:12 Magdalene said. <She spoke as one who had understood completely.>

"Only you two can solve the mystery."

Miri thought about this for some time. Hadn't she already looked into herself? Didn't the saviour kiss her repeatedly, screaming *'know yourself!'* as she fell deeper into a terrifying trance. Hadn't she seen Sophia's terrible fault, the mistaken act of creation? At the price of terrible suffering, she had answered the question *whence comes evil.*

Was there more?

Their path mounted the dry, barren steppes. At the foot of a cliff, a black goat had fallen, and carrion were tearing off bits of its flesh.

Thomas watched them with morbid curiosity, and the dark birds nodded their heads as he passed. At once, his brooding melancholy intensified.

"But why me?" Thomas wondered aloud. "Out of all the apostles, why single me out?"

Jesus smiled knowingly at his twin. "It wasn't I who imposed this task upon you. John recognized something in you that makes you unique."

The Iscariot walked on in silence, his mind besieged by dark thoughts. Was it *Judas* that the Baptist sought – the shadow side which Thomas had tried to quell in himself?

Thomas felt the dead man stirring inside of him.

"Your task is to know yourself," Jesus confided to his twin. "But you've always guarded another truth, close to your heart, and never let it go – the truth for which even Socrates sacrificed himself."

Slowly, Thomas gave voice to the Hellenic truth he always revered. "I *know* I *do not* know..."

"Exactly. Why do you think John phrased his oracles in the Greek manner? Because he was speaking to you. And he gave you this task. You must reconcile the two Hellenic truths: 'know thyself' and 'I know I do not know'."

The Iscariot's brow darkened. If all he knew was that 'he didn't know' – then he'd never 'know himself'. But if he did try to 'know himself', then he would have to know... what he did not know...

Thomas broke out in a cold sweat. There, in the desert, he would have to confront Judas – the unknown in himself. What moved the 'hanged man'? Asceticism and life's denial? Hatred for Jesus and Magdalene? Jealousy? Resentment? Or a deeper longing, hidden and forbidden, to sacrifice *all* that was dear to him?

The Iscariot looked at his two companions. His ears were buzzing with the sound of a thousand locusts.

"Don't you know what's at stake here?" Thomas cried aloud. "Why did you ever ask me to accompany you?"

"You were the perfect choice," Magdalene said, caressing his shoulder. "We must answer the question 'What is Man?'"

"And Man," Jesus explained, "does not *'know himself'*. Even on the day of his death, he'll doubt himself, hanging on to the terrible truth, 'I *know* I *do not* know... I do not know *myself'*. That is what makes you – and what makes Man – so unique..."

The Iscariot's throat constricted; his breath grew short. He was afraid he would faint any moment.

"And that," Magdalene said, "is why you are so important to us. We couldn't answer the question without you. In your own way, you are... our Man."

For seven days they walked east, taking shelter at night in the tall dry grass. The desert steppes rose gradually, and nomadic herders became increasingly scarce as they approached ancient Ashtaroth. The hawks and falcons, circling in cloudless skies, soon gave over to vultures and crows. At night, packs of desert dogs roamed the wilderness.

At last, the three collapsed in a secluded place where large outcroppings of rock shielded them from the wind. They built a fire from dried brush and twigs. The melted snow, from tepid pools embedded in the stone, tasted bitter. They hadn't eaten since setting out.

Jesus traced a circle in the earth and, for three days and nights, they didn't move from that place. Their flesh took on the same depleted hue as the surrounding desert brush. If they opened their mouths to pray, their cracked lips bled. Their thoughts grew unclear, skirting the borderland between wakingness and sleep.

On the third night, the Iscariot awoke to stoke the fire. The stars above his head looked like pointed spears of light. He paused, delirious, and stared at his two companions. Shivering in her sleep, Magdalene had curled up close to the Messiah.

He regarded these two for some time, wondering what their fate might be. What mysterious force kept them apart, just as their love drew them together? He had seen it from the beginning – she was the one destined for the Nazarene. They were two halves of the *syzygy*, but in the flesh they could never meet.

As long as they bore their bodily garments, they were like Adam and Eve – separated by gender, no matter how much they desired to join as one.

Magdalene stirred, and their bodies drew closer. The fire cast a warm glow over her trembling limbs. Its flames seemed to course up and down their enmeshed figures. But the more he watched, the more he felt himself falling into a trance.

Was this a dream? A strange glow covered the recumbent pair. It grew, until he could clearly see a silhouette of light, gleaming with pearly opalescence. Then the colours deepened into ruby red, amethyst blue and malachite green. The scintillating hues overlapped and fused, forming a spectral white radiance.

The light seemed to refresh and awaken him, even as it rose up and transfigured into a single shimmering spectre. In a breath-taking vision, he beheld an angel, standing erect, its face holy and peaceful. It hovered slowly over the dormant figures below.

At first, Thomas wanted to avert his gaze. But the glowing aspect was so intriguing that his eyes were drawn to it inexorably. In the angel's enigmatic smile, he beheld the familiar features of Magdalene and the Nazarene – fused as one. His heart thundered in his chest at the moment of recognition.

Then, a strange transformation occurred, as his vision doubled. From one, the angel became two, and he clearly saw a transparent spectre like the Nazarene to the right, and another like Magdalene to the left – each resembling the other like brother and sister.

They stood with a glowing sphere held between them, the

Nazarene's hand atop and the Magdalene's hand below. It glowed with life, and <within its transparent glass he could see a diamantine jewel, where two more spheres revolved around each other. Their phosphorescent hues of yellow and blue seemed to radiate with knowledge and insight, with fore-knowledge and wisdom. Around the glowing sphere, a blackened serpent circled with its tail in its mouth.> The entire vision overwhelmed him with mysterious awe.

Ophite diagram

"We have waited for you since the beginning," the female angel said. "For your task is to re-unite us. Only you can make the left like the right, <and the man like the woman, and the two into a single one.>"

Gs Thom 37:24

Then her male counterpart spoke:

"For we come from a single one. I am the Christ who has stood from the beginning. <And she, Sophia, is my consort who, from the first, was destined to be in union with me.>"

Sophia JC 101:16

Thomas bowed his head, knowing that a terrible mystery had been revealed to him. But why – to him?

"Only you," Sophia said, "can <make the above like the below, and what is within, without.> <What you see within you, you must see outside of you – by making it visible.> You must bring the unity from above, and manifest it here below."

Gs Thom 37:24
Thund 20:22

Shivering, Thomas admitted, "I haven't understood. How does that task fall to me?"

Christ replied:

"At the end of this seance we will call upon you to act in accord with our desire. For the present, Jesus the Nazarene and Magdalene his bride must remain ignorant of these things. The secret has been entrusted to you alone."

The apostle looked down at the couple fast asleep. With his blood pounding in his ears, he realized that Jesus and Miri were oblivious to the heavenly angels floating above them.

"But first," Sophia cautioned, "you must *know yourself*. You must know the mystery that Yaltabaoth has hidden from the beginning – hidden from *Man – until now*."

The glowing sphere which they held between them started to expand, and Thomas felt it encompassing him completely. It seemed as if he were rising through seven heavenly spheres, until he came to a place radiating with a most unusual light.

"The place you call Paradise," Christ revealed, "lies in the eighth and ninth heavens – an intermediary realm between the Upper and Lower Aeons. It is 'the Middle', where Sophia and her ill-begotten son Yaltabaoth have contested with each other since the beginning."

"In my repentance," she said, "I created this place. Then my spark fell through seven heavens, and was trapped in a bodily prison. At the end of each life, I aspired to rise above this place, but failed with bitter tears. Each time I've tried – and Yaltabaoth has thrown
Ap Jn 14:9 me down. Nor will I rise beyond this realm, <until my fault has finally been rectified.>"

She lowered her head. "My spark, this time, is trapped in Magdalene's flesh – awaiting forgiveness and its final resurrection."

Christ made a broad arc with his arm, showing forth 'the Middle'.

"This is a place of appearances – the veil between light and shadow. Here, the light of the Upper Aeons takes form in shadowy images. Here, the events of the past are made present, so you may behold the truth."

In response to these words, a blinding succession of images passed before the apostle's eyes. He saw the terrible serpent Yaltabaoth rising from the earth. The Archon shed seven skins like seven colours of the rainbow, becoming saturated with white radiance. As the fiery serpent emerged into the eighth heaven, it opened wide its leonine mouth. From the belly of the beast, an ancient bearded prophet emerged. This venerable old man in a flowing white raiment had all the appearances of the divine creator. Spreading wide his arms, He proclaimed:

Orig Wld 112:28 *"<It is I who am God.>"*

As Thomas gazed directly into the fiery face of the creator, its aureole of flames expanded in all directions. The Lord stood upon a
Orig Wld 102:15 heavenly chariot, surrounded by <armies of angels and archangels, unto countless myriads.> But the heavenly hosts seemed hollow and
2Tr Seth 53:27 dim, <lacking true glory.>

"I am the creator of heaven and earth!" He proclaimed.

Darkness separated from light. Then day from night, earth from heaven, and the waters below from the waters above. At the meeting place of four rivers, a garden sprouted, overteeming with life – lions and oxen, wolves and lambs, birds of every colour.

"This," Christ explained, "is Paradise and its creator."

Thomas began trembling before the strange revelation.

"The one whom generations have called YHWH, Lord and Creator, is no more than a blind god, inflated with pride. It is

Yaltabaoth made mad with vainglory."

Spontaneously, a terrible question came tumbling from the apostle's lips.

"And *He* created Man?"

"Not from the first. By reflecting upon himself, the One in the Upper Aeons created the Son of Man, and in his image, Man himself. It was the divine Parent who made the luminous image, and *spoke it* into existence."

Thomas heard the resplendent Voice resounding from above:
"<Behold the Son of Man, and he who exists in his image – Behold Ap Jn 14:13
the Man!>"

Through the shadowy veil, he saw a luminous image assume form in the Upper Aeons – human in shape, but neither male nor female. It resembled the image Thomas had seen earlier: the angelic *syzygy* of Christ and Sophia.

"This is <the heavenly *Anthropos*,>" Sophia said, "the divine Gs Phil 58:17
image of Man. His form reflects the Son of Man, who is the true
image of the Father. This is <the perfect Man,> spiritual in substance, Gs Phil 58:17
<the Adam of the light!>" Orig Wld 108:19

As Thomas gazed upon this figure, it felt like his own flesh had been transfigured. He was staring into his own true image, no longer burdened by flesh or blinded by passion. The Adam of the light stood absolutely erect, his body in perfect balance.

Sophia spoke once more:

"When Yaltabaoth saw the heavenly image glowing with perfect
light, he said to his Archons: '*<Come, let us create a man according* Ap Jn 15:1
to the image of the true God and according to our likeness, that his image may become a light for us.>'"

As Thomas gazed on in horror, the Archons created a human form, each of them contributing an equal part: bones, sinews, flesh and marrow; blood, skin and hair. And their hosts of angels, three hundred and sixty in number, shaped each of the lesser organs and limbs. These were not fleshly, but the soulful forms that animated the body.

And the Archons said: '*<Let us call him Adam, that his name* Ap Jn 15:5
may become a power of light for us.>'"

Before Thomas' unbelieving eyes, the soul of Adam took on a dimly translucent form. But the human figure lay supine on the horizon – unmoving, lifeless. It resembled the Adam of the light, but lacked its glowing radiance.

"This," Christ said, "was <the second Adam, invested with Orig Wld 117:28

soul, but lacking the spirit of the first Adam.> For the *pneuma* belongs to the light. None of the Archons possess the *pneuma*, with the exception of Yaltabaoth, who had acquired it from his mother. But even he remained ignorant of the *breath* within him."

"Thus I petitioned the Parent," Sophia said, "with fervent prayer, asking that the particle of light, which glowed in Yaltabaoth, might be mercifully retrieved. The Parent heard my prayer of repentance and sent down Christ with his Four Lights. With one voice, they
Ap Jn 19:22 whispered into Yaltabaoth's ear: *'<Blow into Adam's face, and he will rise.>'*"

Thomas gazed in wonder as the Lord hovered over Adam's recumbent figure. The Almighty leaned over and breathed his spirit into Adam's face. At once, God's face grew dark, while Man's face
Ap Jn 19:32 grew luminous and bright. <Gaining strength, Adam stirred, stood up, and shone with great glory.>

Suddenly, the angels and archangels were thrown into terrible pandemonium. For Man, though he was the Lord's creation, shone brighter than the Lord himself.

"Because Adam outshone him," Christ revealed, "Yaltabaoth tried to *hide the light* by burying it in a corporeal body."

With thunderous wrath, the Lord called his angels to order and
Hyp Arch 87:24 commanded them: *'<Come, let us create a man that will be soil from the earth!>'*

Ap Jn 20:33 "<With the four winds," Sophia said, "they mixed earth, fire
Hyp Arch 87:24 and water> <to model their earthen creature.> From mud, matter and
Ap Jn 20:33 dust, they formed his body, a covering of mortal flesh. <Then they threw the glowing Adam into darkness, ignorance and forgetfulness. The Archons brought Adam into the shadow of death, and he became a mortal man.>"

Thomas watched, with unbearable sadness, as this luminous and perfect image of himself was caked in clay and bemired with muddy earth. Once more, Adam lay recumbent on the ground – naked, unmoving, immersed in a deep, deceptive sleep.

Orig Wld 117:28 "<This is the third Adam," Christ said sadly, "the Adam of the flesh.> His soul slumbers, and his spirit is trapped in layer upon layer of the Archons' creation."

"But Yaltabaoth was still unsatisfied," Sophia lamented. "He wanted to retrieve the *pneuma* buried in Man's flesh. He could see it like my luminous image – hidden within, beautiful and feminine.
Ap Jn 22:28 <He desired to bring it out of Adam's rib. So He resolved to make another creature, after my likeness, in the form of a woman...>"

"Even the third Adam," Christ said, "<resembled the angels of Ap Adam 64:6
the Upper Aeons.> He was an androgynous *syzygy*, like the divine
image of the *Anthropos* before him. <But the Great Archon, in his Ap Adam 64:6
wrath, decided to divide Adam – so he would become two, a man
and woman.>"

"<When Eve was still in Adam," Sophia recalled aloud, "death Gs Phil 68:22
did not exist. When she was separated from him, their separation
became death. If the two can again be made one, then death will be
no more.>"

Thomas stared in disbelief as the mystery became clear to him at last. Like Adam and Eve, these two – yes even Christ and Sophia – longed for nothing more than to be re-united. But they, like Magdalene and the Nazarene, *were fallen* – divided by gender, and could not re-unite until Sophia's fault had been rectified. If Adam and Eve could somehow be brought back together, then Christ and Sophia would return to their state of unity. *Was that the task reserved for Magdalene and the Nazarene?*

Before Thomas could give the question further thought, the frightening vision extended. As if, in the concluding act of a terrible tragedy, the *true* Fall of Man unfolded before his eyes.

The Lord said: *'<Come, let us cause a deep sleep to fall upon* Hyp Arch 89:3
Adam.>'

"<And as Adam slept," Sophia cried, "God made an opening in Hyp Arch 89:3
his side like a woman's.> Then He drew forth from Adam's flesh a
female companion."

At once, a line from the scriptures echoed in the apostle's ears:
'<Thus male and female created He them...>' So it was *Yaltabaoth*, Gen 5:5
Thomas accepted with great sorrow, who had *separated* man from
woman.

Again, Sophia spoke: "But the moment the woman took form, even though she was molded as flesh from his flesh – she became luminous and bright. Due to the *pneuma* in her, she stood erect, shining with a light brighter than the light of God."

In a moment that stilled the apostle's beating heart, the luminous
woman stood before her recumbent partner and cried: *'<Arise,* Hyp Arch 89:13
Adam!>'

"Immediately, Adam rose up from his deep sleep. <He became Ap Jn 23:4
sober from his drunken slumber, and recognized his counter-image
– for she had lifted the veil which hung over his mind.>"

Newly awakened, Adam rejoiced and exclaimed: *'<Since you* Hyp Arch 89:14
have given me new life, you will be called Eve, the mother of the

Ap Jn 23:9 *living.> <Because of you, a man will cleave to his wife. His consort
will be sent to him, and they will both become one flesh.>'*

Hyp Arch 89:17 "But the Archons," Christ said, "<when they saw Adam
speaking with his female counterpart, became greatly agitated.>
Perceiving that Adam was again luminous, and shone as bright as
Eve, they flew into a great tumult."

"Thinking that these two had deceived him," Sophia added
softly, "Yaltabaoth decided to deceive them. He drew a veil over
their perception, and placed them between two trees in Eden."

She sighed, saying: "Disguised in God's glowing raiment,
Hyp Arch 88:26 Yaltabaoth addressed Adam and Eve with the words: '*<From any
tree in the garden you may eat, except these two. For the day you eat
from them will be the day of your death.>'* He indicated to them the
Tree of Knowledge and the Tree of Life."

"He did this to trick them," Christ explained, "hoping they
Ap Jn 21:24 would be tempted by the second tree, which is <the Tree of *their*
Life. It sprouts in darkness, and desire is its seed. The root of this
tree is bitter, and hate lies in its shadow. Its branches are death;
its leaves, deception; and its blossoms have the ointment of evil.
Indeed, if one tastes its fruit, one has truly tasted *death.*>"

Ap Jn 23:20 "So I," Sophia said, "<came down and entered the Tree of
Knowledge, in order that I might rectify my fault. Secretly, I
placed the *gnosis* in its fruit, the knowledge of the light, to awaken
them from the depths of their sleep. For Adam and Eve no longer
recognized their nakedness.>"

"Their nakedness?" Thomas wondered aloud.

"The first Adam," Christ said, "the *Anthropos* of the Upper
Ap Jn 20:5 Aeons, was <*naked* of all imperfection.> But as he descended
Ap Jn 13:32 into the second and third Adam, the Archons <*clothed him* in
imperfection,> corruptibility and mortal flesh. Thus Adam and Eve
wore the garments of ignorance over their naked innocence and
omniscience."

Ap Jn 22:9 "But how did they eat?" Thomas asked. "<Wasn't it the serpent
who taught them to eat?>"

"That is what you have been taught from the beginning," Christ
responded. "And the serpent has beguiled you with that untruth up
to this very day..."

Ap Jn 22:3 "As the serpent," Sophia revealed, "Yaltabaoth <placed himself
before the Tree of Knowledge, in order that Adam and Eve would
not recognize its hidden knowledge.> But, to save man from
Ap Jn 23:26 wickedness, Christ descended <in the form of an eagle, and perched

on one of the branches of that tree. It was he who brought about that they ate from the Tree of Knowledge.>"

Upon hearing this, the apostle's mind started reeling. He could not believe what he had just heard.

Christ smiled and said: "Yes, I bid them eat of the fruit where
Sophia had hidden the *gnosis*, for I sought <to awaken them from Ap Jn 23:26
the depths of their sleep. Through Sophia's sacred fruit, they tasted
perfect Knowledge, and at once their minds were awakened. They
recognized *that they were naked*> – yes, that they were truly naked
of all imperfection, even though the Archons had clothed them in
ignorance."

"Thus, we had secretly planted the seed of knowledge in Man," Sophia said. "But Yaltabaoth became furious once more. For the great Deceiver recognized that, in truth, *it was he* who had been deceived..."

The final moments of the Fall passed before the Apostle's eyes, making him cringe with despair.

"When Adam and Eve recognized their nakedness, they turned their faces away from the Creator, because they were ashamed of all the evil and deception He had wrought.

"His wrath and fury rising," Sophia said, "Yaltabaoth cursed
them. Out of spite, <he made them drink the water of forgetfulness, Ap Jn 25:7
so they would no longer know *from whence* they came.> <Then he Ap Jn 24:7
cast Adam and Eve out of Paradise.>"

Thomas watched in horror as the Lord and his angels <turned Hyp Arch 91:3
to Adam and his wife. They seized them and expelled them from the
garden.> And as they fell, <they were clothed in gloomy darkness.> Ap Jn 24:7
Finally, Mankind was thrown into <a life of toil and terrible Hyp Arch 91:7
distraction, becoming overly-occupied by worldly affairs> and the
cares of the flesh.

"<Because you have eaten of the tree," Yaltabaoth thundered, Gen 3:16
*"cursed is the ground because of you. By toil you shall live the rest
of your days, and in pain you shall bring forth your offspring.>"*

"Sadly," Christ remarked, "they acquired the seven soul-garments of the heavenly rulers, and the five material-garments of the earthly Archons. Thus they fell under the last and most bitter of all the Archons' bonds – the *Heimarmene* that men call Fate."

Suddenly, all grew dark. His vision of the eighth and ninth heavens started dissolving, and Thomas felt himself falling, a terrible feeling of weightlessness as if he were tumbling to his death. The fear was terrible, dizzying and debilitating.

But when he opened his eyes, he found himself back in the circle where Magdalene and the Nazarene were sleeping. The glowing sphere, which had encompassed him with its vision of Paradise, was cradled once more in the hands of Christ and Sophia. It glowed as before, but encircling it – the blackened serpent seemed more menacing than ever.

"All men," Sophia said, "have been denied the vision of the
Ap Jn 28:28 truth that has just been revealed to you. Through Fate, <the whole of
creation has been made blind.> Henceforth and without cease, the
circling of the planets dictates Man's destiny: altering his will and
Ap Jn 28:21 influencing his every action. Men are now trapped <in ignorance
Ap Jn 28:32 and the chain of forgetting.> They are bounded especially <by time.
For Fate, the *Heimarmene*, rules over all.>"

"And the hidden knowledge?" Thomas asked, clinging to hope.

"It has remained hidden in Man up to this very day," Sophia said. "It is knowledge of the *pneuma* – the divine spark, the particle of light. It is the remembrance and the awakening; the pearl and the seed. It is awareness of inner freedom, and the unforgotten *gnosis* that man comes from God, and to God he may return."

Thomas was trembling. He was unsure his mind could encompass the mystery.

"Now you know the true nature of the Fall," Christ said, "and
how Eve was separated from Adam. I have descended through the
Archons' aeons to awaken Man, and remind him of his true origins.
Gs Phil 70:12 <But I have also come to repair the separation which was from the
beginning, and again unite the two.>"

The apostle stared in awe. This was the last piece of knowledge which he had yet to comprehend.

"You have come to re-unite Adam with Eve?" Thomas asked, "– to make them as they *once* were... in the Upper Heavens?"

"Such is the mystery of the Bridal Chamber," Christ revealed.
Gs Phil 70:12 "<For those who have united in the Bridal Chamber will no longer
Gs Phil 70:12 be separated.> <Eve has remained separate from Adam, because it
was not in the Bridal Chamber that they first united. But when the
woman joins with her husband in the Bridal Chamber,> they will
again taste perfect oneness."

Thomas felt faint. It was a truth he had suspected from the beginning, but now he could not doubt its veracity.

"You shall reveal the Fall of Man to Magdalene and the Nazarene," Sophia said, "but the mystery of the Bridal Chamber must be withheld until the proper time."

The Iscariot was too afraid to demand why. But Christ spoke for him.

"The Bridal Chamber is the Fifth and final Seal. You must wait until the Fourth Seal has been revealed. Until then, we charge you with silence."

With deep respect, the apostle nodded his acceptance.

"In the meantime, you must act," Sophia said. "To you has been granted secret knowledge of the mysteries, so that you may answer when called upon – and *act* in accord with our desire."

Sophia stared at the Iscariot with a gaze which rooted him to the spot. Whatever they asked of him he could not refuse.

"I am your servant," he whispered, lowering his head.

"Only when Sophia's fault has been rectified," Christ said resignedly, "will man and woman re-unite in the heavenly Bridal Chamber. And Sophia's fault may only be rectified – by my sacrifice..."

Christ bowed his head in silent surrender.

For a long time there was silence as the apostle tried to grasp the meaning of this pronouncement. Suddenly he stared at Christ in mute awe and bewilderment. But Christ lifted his eyes and directed a piercing gaze at the man before him.

"And you," he said, "have been chosen... to deliver the Messiah to his fate."

The apostle fell to his knees before the glowing angel, whose features had become frozen into a mask – hard and pitiless, brooking no contradiction.

"<You will sacrifice the man who clothes me,>" Christ said, Gs Judas 56
pointing to the recumbent Nazarene. "When a stranger in Jerusalem asks if you are the one named *Judas*, you must answer and – in accord with our desire – you must betray Jesus to his death."

The apostle opened his mouth, but was speechless.

Then Christ, before departing, offered him a final word of consolation:

"Yes you, Thomas, <shall stand in someone's stead, even though Gs Judas 35
it grieves you terribly.> But take heart: only the name of <Judas will Gs Judas 46
be cursed by the coming generations.>"

The angels vanished, and the Iscariot fell forward, burying his face in the sand. For the whole of the night, he watered the earth with his tears, begging that he be freed from the holy oath he had sworn.

For days, Didymos Judas Thomas dared not speak.

When, at sunrise, he left the sacred circle and started walking toward Galilee, Jesus and Miri followed him in mute incomprehension. It was only at Bethsaida, one day's distance from Capernaum, that he opened his mouth.

As they camped on the banks of the Jordan, a torrent of words suddenly came tumbling from his lips. He revealed the bizarre vision in detail – the three Adams, his separation and Fall at the hands of Yaltabaoth – but held back the mystery of the Fifth Seal, and the terrible fate that awaited his twin.

Jesus and Miri were overawed by his words, but could not doubt the veracity of his vision. It had all the markings of a true revelation.

V

When, towards nightfall, Magdalene and the Iscariot lay down to sleep, Jesus shifted uneasily in his earthen bed. A thousand thoughts assailed him, and he could not sleep. In the darkness of the night, he heard the voice of Zostrianos, the venerable hermit from the Cave of Darkness. *'Do you know who the Messiah is?'* the Persian mage had asked him. And without awaiting a reply, Zostrianos had answered: *'He is the one who brings history to its conclusion. He is*
Avesta 46.3 *<the Saosyant, the saviour whose sacrifice will end time.>'*

The words resounded as a terrible portent. What sacrifice? Jesus wondered, his heart thundering in his chest. As if in answer to this unanswerable question came yet another question. It was John's enigmatic oracle: *'Who are you – the Bridegroom? Or the Lamb? Can you make these two into one – and celebrate the Wedding of the Lamb?'* Was that it? Was that his fate – to be offered up like a lamb at the Paschal Feast? Or was it a wedding – like the bridegroom and the bride at the marriage of Cana?

The answers to these oracles exceeded his reach. And what of the Fourth and Fifth Seals? His breath grew short, knowing that these last two eluded his grasp.

Were their mysteries bound up, somehow, in the answers to the oracles? *When* would the last seals finally be revealed to him?

Again, the Baptist's voice rose up in his memory:

'In Jerusalem, at the Passover!'

The next Passover was less than a month away.

After the wedding feast at Cana, he realized, he must celebrate the Paschal Feast in Jerusalem. That is the path the prophecies foretold. The Messiah must enter Zion's Gate.

The Nazarene arose at once and walked along the river's banks. A deadly silence brooded over Israel. Only the sound of the cicadas could be heard, like a strange buzzing in his ears. He wandered for some time in a daze. Then, falling to his knees, he bathed his face in the Jordan's cool waters.

The full moon dipped toward the mountains, reflecting his countenance in the river's calm surface.

For a long time, he gazed at his own face, wondering at his gaunt and haggard appearance. This flesh, it seemed, was only a mask, but it still bore meaningful traces. His eyes, he noted, had the same mysterious stare manifest in his mother's gaze: curious, compassionate, questioning...

And the more he looked, the more he saw his mother's face in his own. But it was not the fleshly resemblance that intrigued him. Rather, the spirit animating the face seemed oddly familiar.

With great wonder, Jesus watched as Anna's face also appeared in the watery reflection. She, as Mary's mother, also seemed to possess the hidden radiance. Then, his grandmother's face also transformed, and he saw an even more ancient visage in the fluid mirror.

The moonlight shimmered, the pool rippled, and he watched as generation upon generation passed before his eyes. The son of Mary marvelled at the myriads of ancestors that had lived and died before him. They paraded before his eyes in unending succession, faces without names, all bearing the hidden spark that illuminated them from within.

Suddenly, the waters were disturbed and a terrible flood engulfed his vision. He recognized at once that this was the Deluge which the Baptist had called the first *parousia*. Though thousands upon thousands had perished in its cleansing waters, *one line* of descendants had survived. Those whom he had seen, all those
familiar ancestral faces, he now understood, were <the descendants Ap Adam 73:13
of Shem, Noah's eldest son.> Not Ham, not Japheth, but Shem... + P Shem 34:31

Again, his vision receded backward through time. Yes, his ancient ancestor Noah had survived the great catastrophe, and had preserved a line of descendants that retraced the genealogy for eight generations more. With fear and wonder the Nazarene watched as a new face took shape in the water, a face that resembled his own to a remarkable degree.

But this venerable forebear, he recognized at last, was none other than *Seth*, the youngest of Adam's sons. The same strange radiance illuminated Seth's visage, meaning that he alone, of all of Adam's sons, preserved the hidden *pneuma* that had been planted in the first couple. Not Abel, not Cain – but Seth...

Suddenly, a woman's face mingled with the man's, a face that betrayed a remarkable beauty. The longer he gazed at this visage, the more its lineaments became clear in his mind. This, he strangely understood, was the face of *Norea*, Seth's hidden sister, who had also become his bride.

Yes, there was a daughter born to Adam and Eve, *but she had*
Hyp Arch 91:34 *been kept hidden from all the generations*. She was <the undefiled
virgin who would aid many generations of mankind.> For, like Seth, she too possessed the *pneuma*, and it was only the descendants of these two who carried traces of the hidden radiance.

Indeed, he realized, his eyes opening wide – it was not only
Mars 26:12 Noah who had passed on <the imperishable seed>, but Noah's bride,
whose name had gone unrecorded through history. With a terrible chill, he called forth her appearance, and recognized that she was *Orea*.

As Norea's direct descendant, Orea had preserved the perfect seed, the hidden light planted in Eve and passed on through the generations. Thus, Norea had united with Seth, and her distant daughter Orea had joined with Noah, to become the true bearers of the sacred seed. They were the hidden mothers of Mankind – forgotten, forsaken, erased from all memory.

But Norea and Orea's seed, after surviving the flood, must have finally come to rest in a woman of his own generation. The Nazarene's heart beat wildly as, in his vision, he suddenly recognized Magdalene's serene visage.

Was it possible? The *pneuma* which Sophia had expired when she named Yaltabaoth, that same *pneuma* which Yaltabaoth had lost when he blew it into Adam's face – that sacred spark was hidden in Eve, then passed through her from one daughter to the next. Past Norea and the Fall, past Orea and the Flood, until Sophia's spark had finally come to rest – in Magdalene.

For an extended moment, the Nazarene marvelled at this newly-revealed piece of the *gnosis*.

Finally, in a vision of crowning glory, he saw the faces of his most ancient forebears. Like brother and sister, Adam and Eve appeared before his eyes. At times, he could see their faces separately, as man and woman. But their faces also seemed to merge, and become a single countenance. How was it that these two could also appear as one?

As quickly as the vision had appeared, it vanished once more, and Jesus was left staring at his own face in the water. But what unsaid message was hidden in these images? And why the watery catastrophe that had intervened in history?

At once, the Nazarene stood up and walked with a slow ponderous gait along the Jordan's banks. The swallows in the trees cried for the day's awakening. In the distance, the donkeys brayed and the cocks announced the early morning.

And it was there, as he stood under an ancient terebinth tree, that the terrible truth came to him.

One race had survived the Flood. For they stood <on a high Ap Adam 85:7
mountain, as upon a rock of truth, and generations had passed
without knowing them.> They were the *true* sons of Adam and Eve,
<the chosen race,> the *'Electi'* – whose name, in ancient Greek, 1Bk Jeu
meant 'the shining ones'. By Norea's grace, <the children of Seth> Melch 5:20 Auth T 25:24
<had been kept apart> like a portion of <imperishable seeds.> Mars 26:12

Generation after generation passed, and they had survived, <an Gs Egypt 68:20
incorruptible, holy race> who knew the secret truth – *that they were*
not fallen. <Innocent, free of evil, born without sin,> they were, 2Tr Seth 62:32
in truth, <the *faultless* ones,> <another race *not* of this age.> They Tri Tr 62:29 Ap Pt 83:15
were <the great generation, which no Archon ruled over.> For the Gs Judas 53
Father <had granted his knowledge to Adam and his kin, so that the Gs Judas 54
underworld lords might not rule over them.>

<Three Adams,> Jesus thought, and <three types of men – one Orig Wld 117:28
fleshly, one soulful, and one purely spiritual.> <Only the solitary Orig Wld 122:7 Dial Sav 120:26
race, the Elect, *knew* their true Parents.> <They were the perfect, Ap Jn 28:3
immoveable and unwavering race> who <had been predestined, +Ap Jn 25:22
from the beginning, *not to fall*.> +Ap Jn 2:20 Tr Res 46:25

<As Norea's offspring, the children of Seth came from the Hyp Arch 96:19
primordial parents. Indeed, they came from above, from the androgynous *Anthropos* in the imperishable light. Neither the Archons nor their demons could defile them. For they were the Pneumatic race, and existed immortally in the midst of dying men.>

<Sealed in the watery light through the Five Seals, death had no Ap Jn 31:22
power over them.> <The immovable race were saved and purified Ap Jn 25:22
from all wickedness. They had no care except for incorruption, to which they directed their attention by living without anger, envy,

jealousy, greed or desire, knowing they were not affected by anything except the state of being in the flesh. Thus they endured, to complete the long struggle and inherit eternal life. They alone were worthy of the calling; they alone would be granted eternal existence.>

Ap Pt 78:22 But <these sons of the light,> Jesus recognized at last, *were*
Gs Egypt 60:9 *limited in number*. From the beginning, <Seth had sown his
Gs Tru 21:25 descendants in the Upper Aeons.> But how many had <had their
names written in the Book of the Living?> It was a mysterious sign,
Pistis ch 26, <the *cipher of Melchizedek*,> which foretold <the number of perfect
Pistis ch 23 souls who would inherit the height.>

1Ap Jas 27:10 When that number finally reached its completion, <and those
who were unnumbered were named at last>, then the second and
third *parousias* would pass – the Conflagration and the Judgement
everlasting. The race of Seth awaited the second and third *parousias*,
Pistis ch 26 confident in the knowledge that, *with <the completion of their*
number, they would finally enter the Treasury of the Light.>

But what of the remainder? In a flash, the Nazarene recalled
the vision of the end which he had read in the monastery's hidden
NH Ascl 72:17 manuscript – when *<Darkness will be preferred to light*> and *<he*
NH Ascl 71:22 *who is dead will not be mourned as much as he who is alive*.>

Suddenly, these words from *The Poimandres* transformed into a timeless vision, and he saw it all as actual, real and frighteningly true.

Gr Pow 43:33 <The earth trembled, the cities were overturned and the
mountains dissolved. The earth became desolate, mourning its
former inhabitants. The carrion ate the dead, and were filled to
Th Cont 141:14 abundance.> <From hollowed tombs, shapeless shades rose up, and
hovered over their corpses. For an eternity, these souls suffered all
the agonies earned by their imperfection.>

Gs Thom 51:6 Would <the heavens and the earth will be rolled up> in this
manner?

Jesus fell to his knees. Looking up, he saw nothing but the pale sky of morning – pitiless, grey, unmoving.

Would he, as the Messiah, sit thus on the throne of judgement? Could he, with one downward movement of his left hand, condemn the greater part of Mankind to perdition?

The Nazarene bowed his head, understanding at last the full meaning of his task: he would make the end like the beginning. But those who could never be saved would return to their true state. Two-thirds of Mankind would perish – and become nothingness forever more.

XIII. The Wedding Feast

I

In the surrounding trees, garlands and lanterns shimmered like a thousand stars. Clad in a long white tunic, his hair dripping with costly spikenard, the groom waited before the entrance of the wedding hall. Suddenly, the young shepherd turned to the distant sound of singing in the streets.

A cortege of lily-crowned virgins appeared, waving palms and chanting psalms as they led the bridal train through Cana's torch-lit lanes. His beloved, carried aloft in her litter, was veiled and embroidered in all her linen finery.

Rams' horns resounded and the good folk of Cana cheered as the bride was presented to her groom and the wedding couple entered the festive hall. The village elder read aloud the *ketuvah* and the groom announced in a clear voice that he consecrated this gentle maid to him as his bride.

At once, he brought his heel down on a fresh pomegranate, and its rich juices flowed – an auspicious sign of the fertile years to come. Musicians broke into ancient folk-melodies and the wineskins were slit to pour out the season's freshly-fermented juices.

Returning in twos from their far-flung journeys, the apostles joyfully embraced, greeting one another with heart-felt kisses. After three weeks of wandering, they began recounting all their strange adventures. Blushing, Peter admitted to many cures and conversions, particularly among the gentiles. Meanwhile, young James had established a massive following for the Messiah right in the heart of Jerusalem.

When the Nazarene finally appeared, his arms happily linked with Magdalene and the Iscariot, the apostles' joy was made complete. Though the three desert-wanderers could not hide their gaunt and haggard appearance, they had stopped at the Widow's Tower to replenish their strength and perfume themselves. Now dressed in clean white linen, they looked forward to the peasants' simple joy and revelries.

The disciples led their master to a private chamber which had been specially prepared for the Messiah. On a low side-table lay brass trays loaded with olives, lentil dips and spiced cheeses. Bread was heaped in abundance and the Galilean wine was in high supply.

As they sat upon woven mats, Matthew drew forth from his satchel a papyrus scroll. The former publican read aloud the inspired
A Gs Mt words he'd dutifully recorded: "*<The first step to knowledge is momentary wonder...>*" he said solemnly. Meanwhile John, who had travelled with the Virgin as far as Antioch, had returned with an account of a most startling vision. In a quiet voice, he read:
Ap Jn 1:30 "*<Behold, the earth shook, the heavens opened, and the whole of creation shone...>*"

But Philip, his eyes sparkling like a mischievous child, fished around in his pockets and drew forth a pack of little cards, each with minutely scribbled phrases. He shuffled these at random and read:
Gs Phil 61:30 "*<You saw Christ, you became Christ...>*" Smiling playfully, Philip shuffled them again.

In hushed tones, Martha and Mariam recounted some of the wondrous healings they had wrought. Meanwhile, all could see that a strange, wordless intimacy had grown between Andrew and Arsinoe. Even Simon and Susanna leaned their heads together and whispered confidentially.

The Nazarene was deeply moved by his companions words and deeds. The Kingdom, he thought, may be likened to a fig: the abundance of orchards lay hidden in its core.

The wedding feast of Cana carried on for three days and nights, growing more festive with each passing hour. They sang their praises to the host, rose to toast the union of two families, and danced in circles round the bride and groom.

When the wine gave out on the third day, the Messiah did not hesitate to work a miracle, turning clear water into a dark distillation more potent than any Cypriot wine. Even stones, when the bread gave out, were converted to freshly-baked loaves.

But these transformations wrought a most delirious effect on all present: the celebrants had the dizzying sensation that their long-awaited Kingdom had come here and now. Time lost its measured pace, and they felt that this present joyful moment would continue for all eternity.

In a daze, Magdalene wandered from room to room, overwhelmed with euphoria. This was the bridal celebration, she thought, which the Nazarene had foretold. This was the final seal, she whispered to herself, the Bridal Chamber. Her heart leapt in exultation, for she was elated that so many had been invited into the mystery...

As she wandered back to the apostles' private chamber, Miri fell under a curious spell. Was it the effect of the wine and bread? Standing in the dark hallway, she could see the apostles to the left, reclining with the rabbi at their centre. But in the room opposite, just to her right, she could see the exact same scene – as if, reflected in a mirror.

Magdalene paused, uncertain. Looking left and right, she determined that, without a doubt, one room was filled with her companions, and the other was too. More disturbing still, there seemed to be a third room further down the hall, and there she could just catch a glimpse of the Messiah.

When she looked more closely into the chamber on the right, Miri noticed that all the apostles were sitting quite formally, their heads held high in an austere manner as they listened intently to the master. Meanwhile, in the room to the left, they were lazily reclining over one another, their heads gently lolling to the mesmerizing sounds of the Messiah's voice. And indeed, the discourse in each room, though similar, bore startling differences.

Momentarily forsaking the left-hand path, the daughter of Magdala entered the room to the right.

II

As she sat at the back of the chamber, Miri noticed that none of the apostles were drinking wine, and their repast was no more than bread dipped in salt.

Susanna was saying, "We have laboured hard and now look forward to our rest. Teach us, Lord, of the Bridal Chamber which you have promised us from the first."

The Nazarene sat with his legs crossed and his posture entirely erect.

Gs Phil 84:20 He smiled and said: "<Many mysteries have been revealed to
you. But the Bridal Chamber is like the Holy of the Holies:> you
will not penetrate beyond its veil until you have distinguished good
from evil, and learned truth from untruth."

He looked down at his hands, with their palms folded and their
Gs Phil 54:18 fingers interlaced. "<From the beginning until now, the Archons
have deceived man, deliberately confusing good with evil. They
took the names of the good things and gave them to those that are
evil – so that all who are free would be bound to them like slaves.>

Gs Phil 66:10 "<Though the good things of this world are not truly good, nor
the evil, evil,> we may put each in its proper place if we refer to
Gs Phil 60:26 them as belonging to <the right and the left.>"

Unt MS Showing forth his right palm and then his left, he said: "<On
the right hand is life; and on the left, death. In my right hand I hold
the light; and in my left, darkness. One offers me a place of rest; the
other, a life of hard toil.>"

Susanna nodded slowly as the Nazarene continued.

Gs Phil 53:14 "<But light and darkness, life and death – the right and the left
– these too have become inextricably mixed, like brothers that are
often mistaken for each other. Life is not the true life, nor is death...
truly death.>"

"Then which path are we to take?" Matthew asked. "How are we to live?"

"Remember who you are and from where you have come! You are the Elect, and your light belongs to the one Light above!"

Seeing that Matthew was still confused, Jesus explained.

Tri Tr 98:12 "<Those who belong to the right are of the psychic race, and
seek to do good so that their souls may be saved. Those who belong
to the left are of the material race, and they do evil instinctually,
like beasts.> Indeed, they follow their animal masters, the Archons,
Tri Tr 119:16 and <at the end of time they will receive bodily destruction in every
Tri Tr 119:16 way.> But you... you belong to the spiritual race, the Elect, <and
your spirits will receive salvation *in every way*.> For you belong
Dial Sav 120:26 neither to the left nor the right. As the <solitary ones,> you stand
beyond good and evil."

At the back of the chamber, Magdalene wondered at the words she had just heard. Some of the other disciples were also shaking their heads. Seeing this, the Nazarene explained by means of images.

Iren 1.6.2 "<The pearl in you, the *pneuma*, will never fall under the power

of corruption, whatever action you might perform. Even gold, when submerged in filth, retains its beauty and worth.> <And a pearl, Gs Phil 62:18
likewise, remains pure. Even if it is cast down into the mud, it will not be despised; nor, if it is anointed with precious oil, will it become more precious. It always maintains its true value, just as you, the Elect, will always keep value in the eyes of the Father.>"

"Then we are free to do as we wish?" Peter asked, amazed.

The Nazarene shot a withering glance at his chief apostle.

"Peter, I said you are <from the immovable race, whose lot Ap Jn 25:22
is absolute perfection and salvation. But for the present time, you still wear the flesh, awaiting the day when it will be lifted away. To become worthy of your calling, you must direct your attention upon the body. Like one who stands at rest in the world, abiding and enduring all things, you must meditate on your present state, feeling neither anger nor envy, neither greed nor desire.>"

"Then you command us to restrain ourselves?" Peter asked, trying to comprehend his master.

"<I command you in no way whatsoever! Nor do I, like the law- Gs Magd 8:22
giver, deliver unto you 'the Law' – so that you might be constrained by it!> When Moses returned from Sinai, bearing in his hands the tablets of the Law, he sowed Yaltabaoth's deceit among the unwary, claiming – do this, it is good; but thou shalt not do that, for it is evil! And yet you, <the *faultless* ones,> are born without sin. You needn't Tri Tr 62:29
heed any of the Archon's commands."

"If we steal," Nathanael asked, "bear false witness or eat forbidden foods – nothing will affect us?"

"No. <You have achieved knowledge of the truth, and the truth Gs Phil 77:15
has set you free. But the free do not sin.> Why should you lie, when you know it is untruth? Why should you steal, when you know your brother is your other self? When I baptized you on the banks of the Jordan, your eyes were newly opened, and you saw how hunger and want had blinded you – beguiling you with a thousand fleeting apparitions. Would you willingly brand yourself once more with the Archon's mark, so he may claim your soul in its ascent? In the flesh, you hunger for food and wine, for ease and bodily pleasure. But the moment you put on the garment of light, you became a*ware* of these things, and willingly put off the fleshly garment."

"Then we must renounce the world, not by any command, but by knowledge of the truth," Nathanael offered.

"<If you do not fast from the world, and abstain from it *in every* Gs Thom 38:17
way, you will *never* find the Kingdom.>"

Thomas cast a glance at the saviour. Deep in his heart, Judas was exulting: ‘The Nazarene has renounced the world, and prefers death over life!’

Act Pt 12A 10:14 At last, <Peter said: “Lord, you tell us to forsake the world and
everything in it. Fine, we will renounce it for your sake. But what
are we to do about food for a single day?>”

Silv 105:28 “<Do not become a dwelling-place for lions, or a den for
Act Pt 12A 6:4 snakes!> <Whoever becomes anxious about meat or vegetables, the
Act Pt 12A 5:21 lions and snakes will devour.> <Rather, you must learn to fast a little
Iren 1.24.2 more each day,> <abstaining from animated things> <and eating
Pr Thks 65:3 nothing that has blood in it.> Above all, do not let them <find the
Act Pt 12A 7:26 desire for meat in you, nor the thirst for water.> <*Guard against
Silv 104:24 every desire*, lest you be cast down into a pit of mire and the bottom
of the abyss.>”

The disciples nodded their heads in reverent silence. But Simon dared to ask: “Are we to refrain even from wine?”

Auth T 24:14 “<Wine is the debaucher!>” he cried. “<Cast out the animal
Silv 87:27, 87:16 nature in you,> <and seek the austerity of good discipline!> <You
Silv 107:26 must drink, rather, from the vine of truth, in which there is no
drunkeness or error. The true wine marks the end of all drinking.>”

“But sleep?” James asked. “Are we even to forgo sleep?”

Silv 113:31 “<Do not allow sleep to enter your eyes; nor drowsiness to
touch your lids – lest you fall into the hands of the robbers.>”

Now Andrew, who was sitting next to Arsinoe, became greatly agitated.

After a forlorn gaze at her, he dared to ask the saviour: “But even a man and woman who love each other – are they to restrain themselves from desire?”

The Nazarene looked at the fair apostle with a sad and troubled
Silv 84:19 gaze. In a low voice, he said: “<You must struggle against every
folly, even the passions of love.>”

Hearing this, Magdalene was taken aback. She never believed she would hear her beloved speak those words.

But deep in the Iscariot’s heart, Judas gloated in triumph. At last, the Nazarene had vanquished his love for women – and for Magdalene most of all.

“Have you forgotten the Baptist so soon?” Jesus asked, his eyes
burning like the Prophet’s. “He was the forerunner of all abstinence!
Test Tr 41:4 ‘<No one will know the truth’ he said, ‘except the one who has
forsaken *all* the things of this world – having grasped his garment’s
fringe and *renounced the whole place!*>’”

The Nazarene shook his head and reminded them.
"In the desert, John <fasted daily, from stage to stage, forgoing Act Pt 12A 5:21
all meat and vegetables.> That is how he overcame <feminine Zost 1:10
desire> and freed himself from <the bondage of femaleness!> He Zost 131:5
subdued Salome's lust because <he had already conquered his own Test Tr 30:24
desire.> And thus <John became the ruler of her womb.>" Test Tr 31:3

Magdalene felt faint, as if she would collapse any moment. The earth was sliding out from under her. But somehow, she found the strength to cry out:

"Then you would forbid the passions of love, even between husband and wife?"

"<Would you love fornication?> <Would you covet the flesh Silv 104:30
and its unclean rubbing?> <Just to think upon it is death! It were Soph JC 108:9
better you had never lived than lived such an animal life.> <Do Silv 104:30
not burn yourself, men, with the fires of lust! Nor pierce yourself, Silv 108:3
women, with the sword of sin!> Rather, <strip off the garment of Silv105:13
lust, and remember the shining garment which you have already put
on.> For through it, <you have been released from the flesh...>" Test Tr 65:31

Thomas lowered his head. But the Judas-in-him raised his face and laughed hysterically.

Meanwhile Susanna, who had initiated this entire discussion, asked determinedly:

"Then *what is* the mystery of the Bridal Chamber?"

"It is the Fifth and final Seal, the last of the sacraments which I
will initiate here on earth. Why do you think I baptized and anointed
you? Because it was there, on the banks of the Jordan, that you
acquired your garment of light. <That garment is your wedding 2Tr Seth 57:10
robe, in which you will be wed in the heavenly Bridal Chamber.>
And you received that garment to protect you from the Archons'
desire. <It was bestowed in the hopes that you would never strip Tri Tr 128:19
yourselves of it. Only those who have put it on, and *continue* to wear
it, will receive redemption.>

"<But if you insist on living in the body, then you persist in Silv 94:19
ignorance and deception. Become sober I say, and shake off your
drunkenness! Your Baptism was the first step into the Bridal
Chamber. In the final rite of sacramental union, you will renew your
existence and, from that time onward,> <shine in the depths of the P Shem 41:20
world.>"

Magdalene cried out: "But *what union?* What 'sacramental union' will finally take place in the Bridal Chamber?"

"It is not, as many of you might think, <the fleshly union of Gs Phil 81:34

husband and wife, when they have intercourse with one another.
That is the marriage of defilement! But the undefiled marriage is
the true mystery! It is not fleshly, but pure. It does not belong to
desire, but to the will. It does not take place at night and in darkness,
but during the day and in the light!> The sacramental union is a
2Tr Seth 65:33 <spiritual marriage.>”

Shaking his head sadly, Jesus asked:

Gs Phil 82:10 “<Would you celebrate your union in public, so that the bride
plays the harlot and marriage becomes prostitution? No, the true
bride and groom belong to the Bridal Chamber. Like the hidden rites
celebrated in the Holy of Holies, their union becomes a mystery.
No one shall see the bride with the groom unless they themselves
become one.>”

“And this mystery – this union – when will it be revealed?”
Miri pressed.

“To those who are willing, I will initiate them into the rite of the
Gs Phil 85:32 Bridal Chamber this very night! <As you enter the Bridal Chamber,
you will kindle the light, and the mystery of the perfect marriage
Soph JC 122:5 will be revealed.> <I have come among you, to join you in spirit>
Soph JC 122:5 and unveil the Bridal Chamber, <so that the two might again become
one.>”

“Which two?” Peter now asked. “And what one?”

“Though you were one with the Parent in the beginning, you
Gs Thom 34:21 became two the moment you separated from his wholeness. <And
now that you have become two, you ask> What one? And which
Gs Thom 37:25 two? But I say to you, <when you make the two into one, then you
will enter his Kingdom once more.>”

The Nazarene looked at Peter and remained silent for some
time. Then in a low voice, he revealed:

Gs Thom 46:11 “<Only *the solitary ones* will enter the Bridal Chamber.> During
the Baptism and Chrism, your hidden name was pronounced and
your image appeared in the watery light. At that moment, *your image
was sealed in the Upper Aeons as one of the heavenly angels*.”

Gazing at them intently, he divulged a great secret:

“In the rite of the Bridal Chamber, *you will be joined in
sacramental union with your angelic image*. In the spiritual marriage,
you become wed to your own higher self. The two are made one,
Ex Soul 132:34 <and become a single life.>”

Silence followed, as the apostles wondered greatly at these
words. Suspended from the ceiling, the clay lanterns swayed and
their flames flickered.

The saviour spoke to them firmly, with deep conviction.

"From that day forward, you will live *a solitary existence*, freed from desire, and all the temptations of fleshly marriage. For you have experienced the True Wedding, the marriage of unity. Though a man and woman may live together in the same house, and even share the same bed, they know that their true bride and groom await them *above*. <Like brother and sister,> they refrain from all bodily Iren 1.6.3 intercourse, content in the knowledge that a higher union awaits."

Simon looked at Susanna, wondering if such an arrangement were possible.

"But – are desire and temptation to be conquered so easily?" he asked.

"Remember your garment of light – the bridal robe which girds and protects you! And your angelic image is wed to you, to strengthen you against the Archons' influence – though their demons are legion. Like *incubi* and *succubi*, <the evil spirits take the form of Gs Phil 65:1 handsome men and voluptuous women. And in this guise, the male demons try to mingle with a woman's soul, just as the female ones seek out the soul of a man.>"

A curious shudder passed through his flesh as he spoke.

"<Seeing a man by himself, the wanton *succubus* lies upon him, Gs Phil 65:12 to tempt and torment him. So also the lecherous *incubus*, seeing a beautiful woman alone, flatters her with sweet seduction, trying to defile her. But when they see a husband and wife sitting tranquilly beside each other, in the full knowledge that *their images and angels have united*, then the *incubus* cannot lie upon the man, nor the *succubus* enter the woman.> <The husband and wife have remained Gs Phil 65:8 faithful to their true bride and groom, who were joined to them in the mirrored Bridal Chamber.>"

"Then the Bridal Chamber," Andrew asked, the sweat pouring from his brow, "is a vow of sexual abstinence?"

The saviour nodded, elated.

"When one experiences the joys and ecstasies of that union, the spiritual marriage is entered into willingly, and you promise yourself gladly! <For the Bridal Chamber is the unity of those who Tri Tr 128:33 know the Parent and have become known by him. At that moment, the betrothed does not see His light, but *becomes* it.>

"<This is not the way with men and women in the world. Here, Gs Phil 61:20 you behold your beloved, but you certainly do not *become* one with him or her. Indeed, you see everything here, but fail to *see yourself*. But above, you *see yourself* truly – and what you see, you *become*.>

You become one with yourself in God."
Gs Phil 72:21 "<The children of the Bridal Chamber," he said with a smile,
"have just one name: rest. They needn't seek some other form of
existence, because they have contemplation> – the stillness of
repose where, of all in this world, they alone stand at rest."
Gs Judas 47 Jesus opened his eyes wide. "<Listen, so that I may reveal to
you those secrets that no one else has known.> The mystery of the
2Tr Seth 65:33 Bridal Chamber <is made manifest to you, so that you, through your
own appearance in the world, will henceforth symbolize the spiritual
2Tr Seth 67:5 union granted through knowledge.> <It is the Wedding of Truth,
+ 2Tr Seth 67:19 where the aeons below are reconciled with the aeons above! It is the
Love Feast, where those who exist below, rather than manifesting
division and disruption, reveal the unity and community of love.>"
Gs Judas 34 And having said this, <Jesus laughed.

But Peter, deep in indignation, asked: "Master, why would you laugh at us?"

"I am not laughing at you,>" he said, "I am laughing with joy and despising your ignorance."

Gs Judas 34 <Upon hearing this, some of the disciples grew angry, and
began turning their hearts against him.

Seeing their lack of understanding, the saviour pressed on.> He imparted, with an intense spiritual ardour, his austere truths.

2Tr Seth 65:33 "<Before the foundation of this world, the many were united
with the One in a spiritual marriage.> And at the end of time, they
2Tr Seth 67:19 will again consummate that spiritual union. <Those who were
separated will be re-united, in love, *with the One*.>"

A strange ecstasy possessed him as he pronounced his final teaching.

Fl Sophe "<When you enter the Bridal Chamber, you will deathlessly
ascend into the bosom of the One. Anointed in its bath with
everlasting holy oil, you will reach the highest heavens, gaze upon
the divine features, and behold the angel who awaits you.> In nuptial
bliss, your heavenly consort will pronounce its consent, and you two
will become one."

The saviour gazed at them with other-worldly bliss.

Then, he stood up and said: "Your heavenly consort awaits you.
Gs Phil 85:32 Come, let us <kindle the light and enter the Bridal Chamber!>"

In horror and fear, Miri retreated from the room.

III

Forsaking the right-hand path, Magdalene turned and entered the chamber on the left. Here, the apostles were raising full cups of wine to their lips, and their plates were filled to overflowing. Arsinoe was caressing Andrew's blond locks, and Simon had his arms around Susanna.

Jesus reclined in the Roman fashion, plucking roasted meats from his tray. As before, the Nazarene spoke of the right and the left as ways for psychics and hylics, while the pneumatics were beyond good and evil.

To Miri's great surprise, Peter again asked the question: "Then we are free to do as we wish?"

This time, Jesus replied: "<All the things forbidden by scripture Iren 1.6.3
– you may practise freely.> <For your deeds are neither good nor Iren 1.23.3
evil, though the Archons have tried to enslave men through those
names.> <But you are saved *absolutely* – not by works, but because Iren 1.6.3-4
of the spiritual seed in you,> which will transport you unhindered + Iren 1.6.2
into the Pleroma."

Hearing this, Peter was greatly surprised. Uncertainly he asked: "Should we not, rather, *renounce* the world and everything in it..?"

"<A curse upon anyone who would seek such abstinence! For Epiph 26.5.8
abstinence belongs to the Rulers who made this realm,> to sow their
seed of desire, and enslave men through unfulfilled yearning. <Those Gs Judas 40
who abstain, those who say, 'we are like angels' are filled with
error,> lies and untruth. <But you, you have achieved knowledge Gs Phil 77:15
of the truth – and the truth has set you free.> <You are free to do Iren 1.23.3
whatever you wish.>"

Again Peter asked: "Then what are we to do about the food for a single day?"

"<Have no scruples about eating meat, for it cannot defile you.> Iren 1.6.3
Rather, eat whatever appeals to you – whether meat or vegetables.
<You do so as a kindness to created things, since you gather their Epiph 26.9.4
souls into yourself, and transport them thus into the heights.>"

The disciples gazed at one another uncertainly. Looking into his goblet, Simon asked: "And wine?"

"<Drink lavish quantities of wine,> if that is what satiates your Epiph 26.4.3
thirst."

"And sleep?" James asked incredulously.

"<You hold power over the dream-sending spirits – over *succubi* Iren 1.25.3

and *incubi* and all the familiars.> You needn't fear them, and may enjoy your rest."

Finally Andrew, who was leaning close to Arsinoe, gazed at her longingly and asked: "And the desire between a man and a woman?"

Epiph 26.4.3 "<You may give yourselves over to every passion,>" the saviour
replied.

Once more, Miri was taken aback – never believing she would hear her beloved speak those words.

All the while, the Iscariot was shifting uneasily in his place. Deep within, Judas demanded – wasn't Adam deceived by Eve? Didn't the First Man, beguiled by vanity and longing, plunge himself blindly into Nature's pool? Has Christ finally surrendered himself to the *prunikos*, to Sophia the whore?

Iren Adv. 1.6.3 "<When you surrender to the desires of the flesh," Jesus pursued,
"you are only repaying what belongs to it. Render the flesh to the
Iren 1.25.4 flesh, I say, and the spirit to the spirit!> <For you shall not leave this
place until you have paid the last penny.>"

Seeing that the apostles were confused, the Messiah explained by means of images.

Ap Paul 20:16 "<When you rise up past the Archons, you must pay a toll to
Iren 1.25.4 each toll-keeper.> <Indeed, *your soul must do every deed and taste*
every sin, so that when you depart from this life, you will not be
Epiph 26.10.7 found *wanting* in anything.> <Become *full* with the knowledge of
every forbidden thing! Gather yourself out of the world, and you
will no longer be restrained...>"

"Restrained – in what way?" Andrew asked.

Ap Jn 24:26 "Restrained *by desire*, which <the Archons have planted in Man
Gs Phil 66:4 from the beginning!> Rather, <fear not the flesh, nor love it! For if
you fear it, it will gain mastery over you. And, if you love it, it will
1Ap Jas 32:19 paralyze you> with its endless variety of passions. <The flesh is
weak, but you needn't feel timid or afraid.>"

Gazing at them knowingly, he added in a low voice:

Gs Phil 83:8 "<For the root of desire will remain strong as long as it is hidden>
Dial Sav 134:16 <– and it is hidden to anyone who does not come to *know* it.> <But
Gs Phil 83:8 once it is recognized, it will be dissolved. Do not remain ignorant,
lest desire masters you and makes of you its slave.> Rather, taste
every whim, so that you may *knowingly* be freed of the Archons'
shackles."

As if, caught in a recurring dream, Magdalene again cried out: "Then what of the passions of love between husband and wife?"

"<Whoever finds himself in this world should love a woman Iren 1.6.4
fully, and join with her in union. If he does not, he will not be *in*
truth, nor will he ascend *to* the truth.>"

But Susanna, who had initiated this entire discussion, asked determinedly: "Then *what is* the mystery of the Bridal Chamber?"

"<It is indeed a mystery – the mystery of union – and you may Iren 1.6.4
practise that mystery *repeatedly* and in *every* fashion.> For we
know, through the *gnosis*, that *we*, in truth, *are one*. Thus to join
here sexually *as one*, is to reflect the unity and community of the
One above. We do this in the celebration of 'the Love Feast'."

"The Love Feast?" Peter asked, trembling.

"As a signal that we belong together in this secret community,
<we greet one another by extending our hand, and discretely tickle Epiph 26.4.2
the palm that is offered.> <Having recognized one another, we Epiph 26.5.8
bathe and perfume ourselves, preparing for a great banquet.> We eat
and drink to the full, satisfying every hunger and thirst. Then, the
midnight rite begins with the words: '<Rise up, brothers and sisters, Epiph 26.4.4
and celebrate the Love Feast!>'"

"<If a husband is with wife, he withdraws from her, since all Epiph 26.4.1
women are to be shared *in common*.> Or, if he so desires, <a man Epiph 26.11.8
may fulfil his desire with another man.> Without restraint, <all shall Epiph 26.4.3
celebrate their passion in a wild frenzy.>"

Andrew glanced at Arsinoe, and Philip at Nathanael. But the saviour gazed at them mysteriously and said:

"<And when you have become aroused to the point of climax, Epiph 26.5.7
you will anoint your hands with your emissions – both the man's
and woman's – to hold them up in prayer.>"

To the amazement of all, he stood up and placed his hands on
his side. In a moment that made their hearts stand still, <the saviour Epiph 26.8.2
brought forth a woman from his side> – a woman that strangely
resembled himself <– and began to unite with her. Then, taking up Epiph 26.8.2
his emission in his hands,> he said:

"<First, hold up the seed of man, and say: 'This is the body Epiph 26.4.5
of Christ. Because of this, our bodies undergo the passion.' Then,
hold up the blood of woman, and say: 'This is the blood of Christ,
which is offered up for you.' You raise these up as sacraments to the
Parent,> saying: '<We do this, so that we may live!>'" Epiph 26.8.2

Magdalene stood up, and began backing out of the chamber. Her head was spinning, and she felt that she would fall into the delirious clasp of madness.

At the same moment, the Nazarene cried to his disciples: "The

Epiph 26.4.4 Bridal Chamber awaits. <Rise up, brothers and sisters, and celebrate the Love Feast!>"

In horror and fear, Magdalene retreated from the room.

IV

Finding herself once more in the hallway, the daughter of Magdala gazed neither to the left nor the right. She couldn't bear to tread either path.

But before her, at the end of the hall, she could still see that a middle path awaited. The Messiah stood, half in darkness, half in light, and his image seemed to beckon her forward.

Uncertainly, she stepped down the long narrow hall.

At last, when she entered the dimly lit chamber, she perceived that Jesus and all his disciples were sitting in a circle. Some reclined while others sat rigid and erect. Though Simon had his arms around Susanna, Andrew and Arsinoe sat tranquilly beside each other.

This time, the Messiah commended them neither to ascetic nor libertine acts. Instead, he held up his left hand and right, then said:

"Welcome Miri... We have been waiting for you."

He rose as she slowly approached. Then, placing both hands on the sides of her cheeks, Jesus kissed her fully on the mouth.

"Behold – *the lost sheep!*" he said, turning to his companions. "– the one who makes the Pleroma complete!"

And he sat her down beside him, clasping her henna-stained hands in his own.

Gs Phil 63:32 Seeing this, Peter grew indignant. "<Why do you kiss her thus
Gs Phil 63:32 on the mouth?>" His red face burned with jealousy and anger. "<Do you love her *more* than us?>"

Gs Thom 50:22 "<The Kingdom," the saviour replied calmly, "may be likened to a shepherd who kept watch over a hundred sheep. When one of them went astray, the shepherd left behind the other ninety-nine, and went searching for his one beloved sheep – until he found her. And so great was his joy that he said: *'I love you more than the other ninety-nine.>*'"

The son of Nazareth turned to Magdalene and gazed deeply into her golden green eyes. Miri blushed crimson.

Then he said to his companions:

Gs Tru 31:35 "<The shepherd rejoiced when he found the Lost Sheep, because ninety-nine is the number on the left hand. But once the Lost Sheep is found, then all ninety-nine will pass over to the right> and be saved. With that perfect number, the Pleroma is made complete."

"But why Magdalene?" Peter pressed. "When she was lost, she sinned greatly, consorting with seven demons. How *could* you love a lowly harlot more than us?"

<The saviour answered and said to them: "You ask why do I Gs Phil 63:32
love her more than you? When two stand together in the darkness – even a blind man and one who sees – they will see no differently from each other. But when the light comes, then the blind man will remain in darkness, while the one who sees – will finally see the light.>"

Peter lowered his head, his brow burning red with the shame of defeat. But Jesus clasped Magdalene's hand tightly and continued.

"Miri has been with us all this time, and yet none of you have recognized *who* she is, or heard the Voice that speaks through her. Like deaf and blind men, you have failed to recognize that *in Magdalene lies Wisdom...*"

Slowly, he shook his head.

"She is indeed the *Prunikos*, Wisdom the whore – the fallen Sophia whose fault, from the first, was to act without her consort's consent. And that mistake has indeed caused the suffering of many. For she alone engendered Yaltabaoth, her bastard son. One by one, his Archons consorted with her, cursing her and calling her a whore.
<But when she recognized she'd acted without her consort's consent, Ap Jn 13:34
she fell to much weeping, and repented of her deed.> Through Magdalene's tears, Sophia's fault has finally *been recognized*."

Remembering all that she had experienced – her terrible nightmare, her trying ordeal when she and Jesus plunged into her hidden depths – Magdalene's face again filled with tears. But Jesus caressed her hand and continued:

"<I am the Christ who has come down to Sophia, as the Ex Soul 132:7
bridegroom to his bride> – to unite us all once more in the heavenly Bridal Chamber."

Unable to restrain herself, Susanna asked: "Then *what is* the mystery of the Bridal Chamber?"

"<The Bridal Chamber is the entire Pleroma!> And Magdalene Iren1.7.1
is the image of every repentant soul! <I have descended to awaken Soph JC 107:11
the drop of light that Sophia mistakenly sent into the world. I have come to correct its deficiency, and make it perfect once more. I have come to join *you all* in unity – so that Sophia's fault will finally be rectified.>

The saviour's face lit up.

Iren 1.7.1 "<And once the whole seed has been perfected, Sophia will escape her fallen state, to finally enter the Pleroma. There, she will receive the Son as her bridegroom, so that together, Christ and Sophia may *unite* once more. As the bridegroom and the bride,> as the new Adam and Eve, they will join in their androgynous *syzygy* – so the two may again be made one."

2Tr Seth 70:4 He turned to Miri and said: "<I am the true companion of Sophia.> I have kissed Magdalene to recognize that, *in her*, lies my
Soph JC 101:16 true consort <– the one with whom I was destined for union from the beginning.> And I offer, through this kiss, *the consent* which was withheld from beginning – *before* the world was created."

The Iscariot trembled upon hearing these words. Though the Judas within him cringed, Thomas silently rejoiced. This was the true mystery revealed to him in the desert.

Val Exp 39:29 "<When Sophia receives her consort, and the seeds receive their angels, then all will come to unity through the reconciliation.> That is the final mystery! That is the Bridal Chamber – when the Pleroma
Val Exp 39:13 attains its final oneness. <For Sophia and I, and the seeds and angels, are so many images of the Pleroma, while the *syzygy* is the image of the Pleroma made one and complete.>"

Joy came over the Nazarene's face, then spread to all those gathered in the chamber.

Dial Sav 125:13 "<Those who have known their consorts will neither die nor be
Iren 1.7.1 destroyed.> <Undetained by the Archons, they will rise up and enter the Pleroma. And there, like brides and grooms, they will re-unite in their angelic *syzygies*. In the heavenly Bridal Chamber, the spiritual and the saved undress themselves, body and soul, to enter nakedly into the truth.> As each finds their true consort, the two are made one. Like the *syzygy* of Christ and Sophia, they become androgynous angels. Thus, all who enter into oneness, enter the heavenly Bridal Chamber."

"But what of a man and woman here, in this life?" Andrew asked. He gazed longingly at Arsinoe beside him.

Gs Phil 84:20 "<The mysteries of truth are revealed even now, but through images and their archetypes. The Bridal Chamber is the heavenly image, the true archetype, but its mystery remains hidden.>"

Gs Phil 84:20 With his eyes flashing, he said: "<It remains hidden, just as the
+ 2Tr Seth 58:26 veil conceals the Holy of Holies." Then, in a deep voice, he added: "I have come to rent that veil from top to bottom, so the things that are above may be revealed in the things that are below, and you may *enter through the image* into truth. Although the images are lowly

when compared with the perfect glory of their archetypes, *still* I will
rip the temple's veil with my own hands, so you may enter in secret
to the Holy of Holies.>"

The saviour looked at Andrew with Arsinoe, then at Simon with
Susanna. His face was filled with kindness. Knowingly he said:

"<The Bridal Chamber invites you in.> And you shall enter it, Gs Phil 85:19
here and now, by *entering through* its image. Each of you, here below,
seeks their counter-image in some other, to make you complete in
the heavens, as two halves of one angelic *syzygy*. In the secret rite of
the Bridal Chamber, the husband joins with wife, recognizing that
each has found their true counterpart. And their union here below
becomes an image of their higher union in the angelic *syzygy* above.
<Though you came forth *singly*, you shall re-enter the Pleroma Val Exp 30:23
jointly.>"

Andrew turned to Arsinoe, seeking his own face reflected in her
flesh. And the moment he smiled, her lips rose with joy.

"Like Adam and Eve," the Nazarene pursued, "you are two
in the flesh, born as man and woman. But in heaven, you are one:
the two consorts who seek each other, gaze upon each other, and
recognize their own reflection in each other. Through the kiss freely
given in <the mirrored Bridal Chamber,> the two may re-unite as Gs Phil 65:8
one.

"Thus, your wedding is celebrated in the rite of the Bridal
Chamber. Once <the wedding bed is lovingly prepared, the two Iren 1.21.3
affirm that their marriage reflects, in image and in rite, the joining
of their counterparts in the *syzygy*.> You offer a kiss and utter your
consent, as an image and reflection of your true union above, when
your consorts consent to a kiss in the heavenly union. That is <the Ex Soul 134:5
marriage made perfect by the will of the Father.> That is <the image Gs Phil 85:18
of the Bridal Chamber, which you will *enter through*, into the
truth.>"

In a clear voice, Susanna asked the saviour: "What words are
we to speak, to offer each other our consent?"

With warm concern glowing in his eyes, the saviour said:
"Recognizing the mystery of <the mirrored Bridal Chamber,> you Gs Phil 65:8
say: <*Henceforth, I shall not divide Christ and Sophia, neither in* Iren 1.21.3
the spirit above nor here in the heart.> And from that time forward,
<those who have united in the Bridal Chamber will no longer be Gs Phil 70:9
separated.> For they have experienced the hidden mystery of
union."

Gazing at the Nazarene, Magdalene's heart overflowed with

joy. This, at last, was the mystery she awaited. Neither ascetic nor libertine, it sought the middle path. Through its secret image and rite, it led to the higher unity that awaited each of them above.

The saviour stood up and cried: "Come, each of you who will
Gs Phil 85:32 <– let us kindle the light, and enter the Bridal Chamber!>"

V

Under a vine arbour on the roof, the Virgin found a quiet place of refuge. While songs of jubilation echoed through the festive hall, the distant hills resounded with hyenas' plaintive cries. But here, at last, she had found a sheltered corner for sober meditation.

Above her head, the stars moved in their established circuits, and the moon shone like a sickle – what the vintners called 'the reaper's moon'.

With a cold shudder, her heart suddenly cried out – what will become of the Nazarene?

The stars, she could see, were slowly manoeuvring in the night-
sky – seeking a most fatal alignment. With a stab of sorrow in her
P Shem 38:29 breast, she realized that the Messiah's <appointed time was nearing
its completion.>

But where did Jesus begin, her heart wondered, and the Messiah end? She could no longer distinguish her son from the saviour that had taken up residence in his flesh. Would Christ accompany him to the end – or abandon him at the last moment?

From the distance came a heart-rending cry, as a pack of wild dogs circled and pounced upon their fallen prey. Its pitiful wailing pierced her to the very marrow of her bones.

2Tr Seth 58:23 And what of the Christ who had descended from above? <Was
he restrained by seven chains?> Had he surrendered himself to the
Silv 110:19 *Heimarmene*, the moment he entered the Archons' aeons? <Or did
he, in descending, undo the underworld's shackles and bend its
Gr Pow 42:8 iron bars?> Could *he* save Jesus? <Or would the Archons exercise
their rule over him? But how? How could he gain victory over their
command?> With a cold shudder passing through her flesh, she
wondered – how would he sacrifice himself?

Shaking her head, the Virgin fell into a deep, unceasing sorrow.
1Ap Jas29:9 *In what way will Christ <complete his destiny> on earth?* she
wondered.

Gs Judas 40 Fearfully she looked up at heavens, and the thousands of <stars
that bring all things to conclusion.>

The Virgin sighed. Her mind, with all its wisdom, could not encompass the mystery. But in her heart she felt the sharp and pitiless stab wound, like a sword-thrust long-since foretold and awaited.

In the coiled expanse of the night-sky, the planets moved like so many signs etched onto Yaltabaoth's skin. And the mighty serpent gloated over the astral alignment taking form in his flesh. At last the stars, in constellations unseen, were falling into Fate's awaited configuration.

Yaltabaoth's thoughts, like sleek-winged demons, gathered in the darkness to exult and rejoice.

When the moon grew full in the month of *Nîsan*, his Archons would seize the man called Jesus – and crucify him.

But what of his heavenly parasite – the Christ?

Without the flesh, where could he turn? He would have to quit his earthen host as it slowly suffered onto death...

And flee to the heavens?

How, when each gatekeeper was awaiting his approach? And with only three of the Five Seals, he was powerless to defeat them. The heavenly descender was trapped in a prison with impenetrable walls, and would never re-ascend.

In his mind, the Archigenetor saw a statue frozen for all time. With arms upraised, the saviour stood upon the world, while a leonine face blazed over his head, and a serpent coiled seven times round his crucified body.

Satisfied, the Chief Archon directed his thoughts to the dim mortal sparks trapped in the darkness below. He saw the rooftop of the Temple where the Head Priest was puzzling over his star maps. In dire futility, Caiaphas was trying to convince Annas of the terrible omens attending this Paschal Feast. Annas remained impassive, worrying only about the profits to be gained from the sacrifices.

Meanwhile, in his palace in Tiberias, Herod Antipas was tossing in his bed, his drunken sleep besieged by visions of the Baptist.

Each of these, the Archon knew, would play out their appointed roles. Their hunger for power and their need of the Five Seals bound them to him as slaves. Even his own son, hidden in Barabbas' flesh and preaching now to the crowds from his prison cell in Jerusalem – even he would fulfil his earthly role when the time of judgement came.

No, his true concern lay elsewhere. The serpent of the depths directed his thoughts to a tower in Jerusalem.

There, in the Antonia Palace overlooking the Temple, Pontius Pilate was awake in his bed. In his hands were the writings of the Stoics, and he was pouring over Seneca's words. *Fata volemtem ducunt, nolentem trahunt*, he read. *Fate leads the willing. The unwilling, it drags...* Pilate nodded his head resignedly, and Yaltabaoth smiled.

In the room adjacent, under the curtained canopy of her bed, Pilate's wife Claudia was fast asleep. It was here that the mighty serpent finally directed his attention. In the guise of *succubi*, his thoughts flew through the night and entered her dreams.

She saw her husband upon his throne, dressed in the vestments of procurator. To Pilate's right stood Jesus the Nazarene, and to his left, the blind prophet Barabbas. In the courtyard of the praetorium, the crowds and the elders screamed with bloodlust, *'crucify him!'*

His voice rising in fury, Pilate condemned Barabbas to death while Jesus was granted reprieve.

And then, to Claudia's great horror, the Messiah started laughing – a cruel malicious laugh that froze the blood in her veins. Jesus, the False Messiah, had been pardoned while the true Messiah, Barabbas, had been wrongly condemned to a slow and painful death...

With a start, Claudia awoke, and sought out her husband.

XIV. Bethany

I

Under the scorching sun of mid-day, Paschal pilgrims crowded round the merchants' stalls. The faithful had come, from Mount Hermon down to the Dead Sea, to celebrate the Passover Feast. Over the course of eight days, the High Priest would offer up lambs, bullocks and rams, together with the first fruits of barley – all to expiate his people's sins.

Meanwhile, it was high season for the Jerusalemites. The dove-catchers and lamb-sellers, sheltered by Solomon's Porch, proffered their bound and tethered beasts while the money-changers raked in the shekels. The simple country-folk from distant Idumea, Galilee, and even as far as Elephantine-on-the-Nile gathered to gawk at the city spectacle.

Before their eyes passed Phoenician prostitutes, Abyssinian snake-charmers and Babylonian astrologers. From the Street of the Weavers came bolts of wool, linen and cotton with their richly-woven patterns of pomegranates and grape-leaves. They stared in awe at an Egyptian sorcerer, crouched and silent as a sphinx, who proffered protective gems and tiny scrolls inscribed with foreign curses.

Then, from the direction of the Huldah Gate came a sudden commotion: crowds of pilgrims were waving palm branches and singing *Hosanna*. Word spread fast through the heated crowd: the Prophet of Nazareth had entered the Temple, mounted on a colt.

This was the man whom the prophet John had proclaimed their earthly king and saviour – the Messiah of the Five Seals. But this same man was declared by the prophet Barabbas to be a False Messiah – the basilisk and anti-Christ.

Now, some said, Aaron's true heir was entering Jerusalem to seize the High Priesthood. Others claimed David's true descendant was announcing his rule over Herod's kingdom. A cry went up from the crowd: the long-awaited Messiah had entered Zion's Gate!

Suddenly, in the midst of the marketplace, the Nazarene stood, surrounded by his disciples. He was dressed in a seamless white robe and in his hand he held, not a sceptre, but a winnowing fork.

Jesus gazed into the faces of the merchants and pilgrims, remembering his vision on the banks of the Jordan. Panic seized him. Did he see in these faces the Number of Melchizedek? Would they accompany him into the new Kingdom? Or were these the multitude of Sodom? Would he have the courage, this day, to condemn their greater part to perdition?

Making a sign to his companions, the saviour started swinging his threshing fork. Immediately, tables were overturned and their shekels went flying. The bullocks, released from their tethers, stampeded through the crowd. Cries of panic were raised, and the temple guard sounded their trumpets.

But the Messiah mounted the steps before the Temple.

1Ap Jas 36:16 "<Weep Jerusalem!" he cried, "For a war has been declared on
2Ap Jas 60:20 this land!> <This house," he thundered, sweeping his staff over the
Gs Thom 45:34 Temple, "I have doomed to utter destruction!> <And once I destroy
it, *no one* shall be able to rebuild it!>"

The saviour cast a burning glance at the faithful, his eyes afire.

Gs Thom 35:31 "<You think the Messiah has come to cast peace upon the earth?
He has come, rather, to cast dissension – through war, and swords, and fire! If there be five in one house: then there will be three against two and two against three!>"

He gazed at the faces in the crowd: Zealots, Essenes, Sadducees, Levites and Pharisees. The veins on his neck swelled, and his eyes shone like flaming swords.

Gs Thom 34:14 "I tell you truly – the Messiah <has come to cast a fire upon the
world! And see – *I am guarding it till it blazes!*>"

Upon the highest step, Annas emerged into the sunlight, glaring down at the saviour. The crowd grew restless.

But the Messiah again raised his voice:

"Before he was cut down, the Prophet John stood upon these
Mt 3:7 steps and warned you of <the coming wrath.>"

He drew a deep breath and let cry:

“Now, to mark the Feast of Unleavened Bread, <I have come Mt 3:12
with a winnowing fork in my hand – to clear the threshing floor!>
The wheat <with imperishable seeds> I am <keeping apart and Mars 26:12
gathering into the granary.> But the chaff, which bears neither good Auth T 25:24
seed nor grain <– I am casting into the fire!>” Mt 3:10

Turning, Jesus cast a terrifying glance at Annas. His mouth tasted bitter, like gall and dried blood. Shaking his head at the Sadducee Elder, he cried:

“I have come to declare war on *all those who rule* – the proud,
the vain, the greedy and powerful. Like John before me, I <regard Th Cont 141:26
them *as beasts!* For just as beasts devour one another, so do these
men!> <They seek mastery over their foes, to command them Tri Tr 79:20
– through greed and vain ambition! Possessed by their lust, they imagine themselves superior to their fellows. All are made proud by ambition; all have become *lovers of power*.>

“But I say to you, <let he who possesses power – *renounce* it Dial Sav 129:12
now, and *repent!*>”

Suddenly, a throng of voices rose up to support the Messiah – Nazarites and Essenes, the poor and dispossessed – who had long-since denounced the corruptions of the priesthood.

“<For the glory they so love is *temporary*, and their rule has Tri Tr 120:15
been granted for a limited time. Their end will come swiftly, and they will receive due judgement for their ignorance...>”

His pale face embittered, his eyes blazing with dark ferocity, the Messiah demanded of the crowd:

“But what of you? *They* are slaves of the Archons and powers
– but *you* risk becoming the slave of slaves. <For, whoever sells Gs Phil 79:13
himself into slavery does only his master’s bidding.> <In truth, he 2Tr Seth 65:14
becomes a slave *to his own fear*, and to *the Law*..!>”

He swept his eyes over the Paschal pilgrims, transfixing them with his piercing gaze.

“<But redemption means release! it is the recognition of Tri Tr 117:23
freedom! Before ignorance gained rulership, Truth held sway! And you – who possess knowledge of the truth, yours is the path to freedom!>”

Many cried with joy. But the Zealots, made drunk by the
prophecies of Barabbas, upheld their unsheathed knives and chanted
‘<God is our only ruler!> Death to the False Messiah!’ Jos 18.1.6.23

The Nazarene’s face darkened. Soldiers from the temple guard came to stand beside Annas – awaiting the order to seize the rebel.

His anger and fury rising, the saviour rent the air with his

words:
Auth T 33:4 “<The ignorant do not seek after God, nor do they inquire about
their true dwelling-place. Rather, they go about blindly, in ignorance
and bestiality.>

Th Cont 144:2 “<Woe to you who dwell in error!>” he thundered, his chapped
lips lined with froth.

Th Cont 143:9 “<Woe to you, *Godless ones...* whose hope is set upon *this*
world, and whose only God is *this* life!>”

The Messiah held up his hands, which were shaking with fury.

Th Cont 138:4 “<While you still have time in the world – Listen to me!> <For
Zost 4:19 our stay on this world is short> <and will soon be completed at the
P Shem 21:10 appointed time.> Listen and <I shall tell you of the coming end – the
Tri Prot 42:18 end of *this* Aeon, and the beginning of *the one to come* – the one in
which you shall all be purified> *by fire!*”

Though many bowed their heads, the merchants and elders raised their voices, crying, *‘Seize him!’*

He shouted at the top of his voice:

Tr Res 47:5 “<You received flesh when you entered this world,> like a
cloak of darkness, to blind you with pride, envy, greed and the lust
Th Cont 139:6 for power. <But the body, you now know, is bestial,> <a temporary
Int Kn 6:30 dwelling where the animal rulers keep their abode.> When your soul
Auth T 32:16 ascends to the place from whence it came, <it will give back the
Th Cont 141:6 body to those who fashioned it.> <Indeed, the vessel of the flesh *will
dissolve*,> and its occupant, the soul, will be seized and devoured! It
Th Cont 142:15 will <be punished and slain in the mouths of those very beasts> who
made it, and whom you served as slaves!”

Annas shook his head with slow and measured irony. But the Messiah decried:

Gs Thom 51:10 “<Woe to the flesh that depends on the soul, and to the soul that
depends on the flesh!>

Ap Pt 75:28 “<As long as the hour has not yet come, immortal souls will
Gs Judas 43 resemble mortal ones.> But <when the Kingdom’s hour has finally
come, all spirits will depart and their bodies be left to die. But the
Th Cont 142:30 souls, still alive, will be taken up> <and handed over to their rulers
– who will turn them around, and cast them from the heavens. They
will be cast down into chaos, and the darkness of the abyss!>”

A terrible shudder passed through his flesh.

Th Cont 142:30 “<Imprisoned in that narrow place,> they will be <afflicted by
Th Cont 141:32 all the torments of their own evil nature.> They will be cleansed by
Th Cont 142:1 fire, and <it is *their own fire that will burn them!*>”

Like lightning, the prophecies flashed through his brain, and the world started spinning round him. Breathless, Jesus proclaimed:

"<If the soul flees westward, it will find *fire*. If it turns southward, Th Cont 143:1
it will again *find fire*. Turning northward, it will meet with more fiery
scourges, casting showers of sparks into its face. Not even the east
can save him. For that man did not seek repentance on the day he
was in the body, nor will he find it on the day of his judgement!>"

The elders of the Sanhedrin tore at their garments, screaming, *'Blasphemy!'*

"<Those who have turned away, those who are ignorant, shall Ap Jn 27:21
finally go to that place *where there is no repentance*. Punished with
eternal punishment,> they will fall to <the place of weeping and the Dial Sav 127:13
gnashing of teeth, where they will lament the end of all things.>"

The saviour drew a long breath and fell silent. A terrible hush fell over the crowd.

Then, in a low voice which reached to the ear of every man, he whispered:

"<Only a little while longer, and that which is visible will Th Cont 141:14
dissolve...> <But the time of dissolution will come,> <not only to Dial Sav 122:2
those who seek rulership here below, but to all the powers that rule Dial Sav 127:13
from above!>

"<O unseeing ones," he lamented, "why can you not see the 2Tr Seth 68:25 +2Tr Seth 65:2
great mystery?> <As a sign of the consummation, the phoenix will Orig Wld 122:29
appear *alive* before you, then die and rise again.> <Once that sign Gr Pow 42:20
is given, the present aeon will end, and the new one arise!> <Then Tri Prot 43:4
the great Authorities will recognize the hour of their destruction
– for the elements will tremble, and the foundations shake, and a
conflagration erupt within their midst!>"

Jesus stared into the heavens, and his face filled with frightening awe. Raising his voice, the prophet narrated all that he saw, the terrible unfolding of the final days:

"<Truly I say to you... when the blind god completes the time Gs Judas 54
alloted him, his constellations shall signal their imminent end.> <The Orig Wld 126:10
stars will cancel their circuits," his voice reverberated, "the light of
the moon cease, and the sun become dark.> <The day will wane Tri Prot 44:14
quickly, and time be cut short – for the slackening of the Archons'
bonds has begun...>"

For a long terrible moment, he stared without speaking. Then, seeking out Magdalene in the crowd, who stood beside Mary his mother, he nodded to them gravely and said:

"<And in the final days,> <a great thunderclap will announce P Shem 39:19
the coming of Wisdom. For Sophia, having unwillingly created Orig Wld 126:13

the Archons, will clothe herself with terrible wrath and pursue them. Even he whom she foolishly engendered, the prime parent Yaltabaoth, even he, she will cast down into the abyss!>

Orig Wld 126:13 "<Because of their wickedness, all the Archons will be obliterated! Like volcanoes, they will erupt and cast fire at one another, only to perish at the hands of Yaltabaoth, their own father. And when he has destroyed even them, he will turn against himself, and *destroy himself.*>"

Wiping cold sweat from his brow, the Messiah lamented:

Orig Wld 126:28 "What a terrible day that will be, <when the heavens fall one upon
2Tr Seth 58:14 the next,> <and the flames of the seven Archons are extinguished!
The sun of Yaltabaoth will set, and darkness will overcome the
P Shem 44:13 earth.> <Many places will be flooded; others inundated with blood.>
P Shem 45:15 From nothing, they will return to nothing, <and become just as they
were at the beginning.>"

A threatening quiet fell over the Court. The Temple guards forgot their spears and stood there dumbfounded. The crowd shuffled in uneasy silence. Even the disciples trembled.

Orig Wld 126:35 "Then," he said, his lips still burning with prophecy, "<a great light will shine amid the darkness. The deficiency will be plucked out by its root, and cast down into eternal darkness, while the light will withdraw up to its crown, and fill the eternal realm with endless glory.>"

Suddenly, the Messiah's face was bathed with joyful anticipation. He was like a candle, spreading the light of hope through the cold chill of doom.

3St Seth 127:20 "From that day forward," he cried, "<the way of descent will
Unt MS become the way of ascent,> <and from its going forth, the world
will witness *its coming in!*>"

His face glowed. From the innermost sanctuary of his heart, a multitude of windows blazed with rays of gladness.

Unt MS "<After the dispersal of Israel, we will witness the day of gathering in, when all its members will be united. *All will become one*, as it is written: 'They shall all became one in the One – and *one* only.'> What a joyous moment that will be!"

He walked among the crowd, smiling at Zealot and Essene alike, at Gentile and Jew, freeman and slave.

Tri Tr 123:3 "<When the redemption is proclaimed, I and all those who know me will return in haste to the place from whence we first came forth. We will return in joy to our unitary state and, like images in the sacred mirror, all will stand in a single place, as the restoration

of the Fullness!>"

His joy could no longer be contained; it overflowed:

"<Neither sun nor moon will rule in that place; neither day nor Gs Judas 45
night! For, in that timeless realm, angels dwell in eternal accord with
the holy will.> <We will stand together in the Aeon of beauty, giving Gr Pow 47:9
glory to the unfathomable Unity. And *all* will see Him, because *all* will become reflections of His light. We will shine, having found our light in His light, and our rest in His rest.>"

The Nazarene bowed his head. He felt utterly spent and exhausted. If he were the Word, then nothing more could be spoken, and all that remained was the Silence.

But the crowd, in the aftermath of his prophecies, grew restless and agitated. Some, like the Essenes and the poor, whispered among themselves that the time had come to proclaim him king. Others, like the Zealots and Sadducees, wanted to condemn him to stoning for his blasphemies.

They shuffled uneasily, like wolves and sheep, awaiting some sign. If Annas lifted a hand to seize him, the people would revolt. But if the Elder showed clemency, the Zealots would take action and execute him at once.

From his place atop the steps, Annas stared hard at the Messiah of the Five Seals.

Then Jesus, in a gesture laden with mystery, spread out his arms and bowed his head. Some saw his act as an augury of the crucifixion. Others saw the phoenix unfurling its wings. Whatever its significance, the Messiah departed from Solomon's Porch, and no one moved to stop him.

II

The moment Jesus and his companions stepped outside Jerusalem's walls, they were besieged by a mob. From the Vale of Hinnom came Zion's poor. Draped in rags, famished and crazed, they beseeched his blessings upon their bowed heads. From the Kidron Valley came outcasts and lepers. Their ravaged hands bandaged, their scarred faces concealed, they begged to be touched and healed.

As one, the disciples formed a ring around the Messiah. Peter and Susanna reached out and comforted as many as they could; Joanna dispersed coins among the poor – but they were vastly outnumbered.

The Nazarene, exhausted from his preaching, stumbled along the pavings, nearing collapse. Martha and Mariam supported him, whispering in his ear that their home was not far off.

Pushing their way through the crowd, the disciples set out for Bethany. Near the Mount of Olives, the way narrowed and the crush became unbearable.

At Gethsemane's gate, a stranger came upon Thomas and grasped him by the shoulder.

"Judas!"

The disciple turned, his heart beating wildly.

Gs Judas 58 "Judas," the man cried again, "<What are you doing here?>"

With horror and denial written across his face, Thomas dared not answer.

Gs Judas 58 "<You *are* Jesus' disciple.> The High Priest has sent for you. Come with me at once."

Shaking his head, the Iscariot pleaded: "My name is Thomas..."

"When I called you Judas, you turned to acknowledge it. You've betrayed yourself by that name."

The Iscariot watched in horror as Jesus and his disciples edged further up the slope, and were swallowed by the crowds.

Clouds of black flies rose up in the evening air. The setting sun, reflecting off the mountains of Moab, stained the horizon a crimson red.

Resignedly, the apostle turned, and followed the stranger back into Jerusalem.

Passing under Gethsemane's gate, Peter, John and James escaped the crush. The sons of Zebedee were covered with bruises. And Peter, exhausted by his efforts, couldn't take another step. They watched as the remaining disciples led Jesus past the Mount of Olives.

"Forget the main road," James shouted. "If we cut through the garden, we can follow the ridge."

Peter and John looked across Gethsemane, where the spice gardens of the Jerusalemites were encased by four thick walls. The calm of this oasis seemed inviting, compared with the chaos of the crowds.

At once, they began weaving their way through climbing aloes and bushes of myrrh. Tall cypress trees shaded their passage.

After straddling the outermost wall, they began climbing the

Mount of Olives. At last, the burning sun of mid-day had been extinguished, and a glowing red disc hovered over the western horizon. A pleasant breeze blew over Moab, and the earth grew cool.

Peter, John and James reached the summit, where an ancient altar stood, its huge monoliths weathered by time. For a few moments, they paused, seating themselves on the fallen stones.

Across the Kidron Valley, the walled city of Jerusalem rose majestically, its gates and towers gilded by the setting sun. With the onset of evening, the sacrificing had begun, and a column of smoke rose heavenward.

"Have you noticed," John asked, his blue eyes shining, "that Jesus is not always as he appears to be?"

James cast a curious glance at his younger brother. Suddenly,
he remembered the first time they had met the Messiah. They were
fishing late at night – and he had seen him then, on the shores of
Gennesaret, <in the guise of a little child...> Gs Judas 33

But Peter, recalling that same strange night, remembered the pearl-seller Lithargoel, whom he saw as an old man with a beard...

"Why do you ask it now?" James pressed. He was anxious to reach Bethany.

John began fidgeting with the fringes of his tunic. Stealing an uncomfortable glance at Peter and James, he recounted:

"<Many times, I've glanced at him on the sly, and I've never Acts Jn 89
seen him blink. His eyes are always open!>"

His heart was pounding in his chest. "<And once, when we were Acts Jn 92
all sleeping in the tower at Gennesaret, I peered at Jesus through the folds of my cloak. Without turning, he said, 'John, go to sleep.' I half-closed my eyes, and pretended to be sleeping. Suddenly, I noticed that someone else stood in the room – someone who resembled him completely. The other said, 'Jesus, your chosen ones don't believe in you.' And Jesus said to the other, 'because they are men.>'"

John stared at his companions.

"What are you trying to tell us – that you saw Jesus and..." Peter stopped, unable to mouth the word.

"Jesus... *and* the Christ!" John pursued. "Haven't you noticed
it? <One moment, he appears to us as a simple man, insignificant Acts Jn 89
and small. But the next moment, he looks huge, even reaching to the highest heavens.>"

James shook his head. It seemed to him that his younger brother had given himself over completely to his visions.

Acts Jn 93 "<Sometimes I'd touch him," John went on, "and feel a solid body at my fingertips. But other times, he'd feel immaterial – as if he weren't there at all.>"

A cold chill ran down Peter's spine.

"Then... the saviour we saw on Gennesaret's shores," Peter realized, "changed his appearance..."

"Because we saw the Christ," John said decidedly, "– the one who descended into Jesus at the Jordan. But Jesus himself is just a man..."

The three of them grew silent. The mystery seemed unfathomable.

Suddenly, the earth beneath their feet started shaking, and the summit of the Mount of Olives was bathed in an ethereal light. A
Ap Jn 2:1 figure rose up before them, <whose aspect had three forms shining through each other: an old man, a youth, and a child.> All bore a startling resemblance to the rabbi. But, this glowing Nazarene was transfigured; they were staring into the luminous face of the Christ.

Peter and James began trembling uncontrollably.

The Illuminator beckoned them with a slow motioning of his
Acts Jn 90 hand, commanding: "<Come with me.>"

Peter and James remained rooted to the spot. But John jumped up and followed him willingly.

In fear and wonder, they watched as the beloved disciple vanished behind the huge stones of the ancient altar.

III

By the time Jesus and his disciples reached Bethany, the crowd had dwindled down to a few lost souls. Near the village gate stood a well, its wooden bucket balancing on the stone rim. The Nazarene turned to the poor and blessed them, saying:

Th Cont 145:5 "<Blessed are you, the mournful and down-trodden, for you will be released from every bondage.>"

He made the sign of peace over them. And, feeling that a heavy weight had been lifted from their shoulders, the peasants dispersed.

The village of Bethany was pleasant and restful. Though its inhabitants lived in the shadow of Jerusalem, they prospered by the sweat of their brows, pursuing an honest and simple toil. Wainwrights hammered at anvils and farmhands tilled the terraced fields with song.

Now, in the early evening, the smell of freshly-baked loaves rose up from every hearth. Jesus walked with three women – Mary his mother, his sister Mary-Arsinoe, and Mary of Magdala.

Gazing at a scarecrow in a desolate field, the Virgin shuddered.

"You've been granted a short reprieve," she said. "It's still not too late."

Jesus looked at his mother. Even now, as his final hour approached, she was speaking in riddles.

The elder Mary stopped and stared at him, her virgin face ravaged with anxiety.

"You must obtain the last two seals, before the moon grows full. Have you forgotten them?"

Jesus bowed his head.

"Their mystery pursues me day and night. I have signs and intimations, but nothing more."

"What are you waiting for?" his mother demanded. "<The stars' Gs Judas 54
alignment is nearing completion!>"

Jesus stared up into the night-sky. The constellations made him shudder. And the Paschal moon was almost full...

"Forgive me for my ignorance," he whispered. "I still haven't divined my fate. I see passion and suffering, but that is all..."

"...Passion?" Magdalene wondered aloud.

Arsinoe, in her silent way, cast a forlorn glance at her brother. They could clearly read the expression on her face: all of them would lament the coming days.

"...Suffering?" Miri cried.

"You should ask him," the Virgin said to Magdalene, "*whose* suffering..." She gave her son a look filled with pity. "Will *you* suffer, my son – or the Messiah? What if he abandons you at the last moment?"

"What if I abandon him?" Jesus asked, his heart beating wildly. "Will I have the courage? My only hope is that the Messiah and I suffer the same fate."

"No," Magdalene pleaded, her eyes filling with tears. "*Neither* need suffer..."

Arsinoe turned to look at Magdalene. And to the amazement of all, a smile crept over her features, a smile resplendent with joy.

IV

<It was the fifteenth day of the month, when the moon was Pistis ch 2
almost full, and its light shone brightly on the Mount of Olives. >

Acts Jn 90 <As John, the beloved disciple, drew nearer to the saviour, he beheld him in prayer. The apostle approached in silence, and hid himself so as to gaze unseen upon the Lord.

But when he looked upon him from behind, he saw that the Lord was naked. And appearing thus, unclothed, the Lord did not in any way resemble a man. Rather, the earth seemed to be illuminated at his feet, and his head seemed to reach to the highest heavens.

Terrified, John cried aloud in fear. But the saviour turned, and assumed the appearance of a man.>

The First-born of the Father shook his head, demanding,
Ap Jn 2:9 "<John... John... why are you so afraid? Don't recognize me? I am
2Tr Seth 51:2 the one who is with you always> – I am the Christ, <the Son of
Light,> and the Phoenix of truth."

John stared in awe at the figure before him, who bore the lineaments of his beloved rabbi, but was clearly something more.

"I tremble, Lord, because my mind cannot encompass your greatness. How is it that you appear before me now as a man, when I have beheld you in your great glory, as a colossus reaching to the highest heavens?"

Gs Thom 38:21 "<Because I have taken my stand in the middle of the world, and appeared to you all in the flesh.>"

"But that is the mystery which makes me fear for my reason: are you flesh, or mere appearance?"

Tri Tr 114:31 "<I am your saviour in willing compassion," Christ revealed. "And for your sake, I will manifest myself in unwilled suffering.>"

John bowed his head in fear and anguish. *Who* would suffer thus – unwillingly? And *who* willed to suffer in compassion?

Christ acknowledged the apostle's bewilderment.

Orig Wld 122:29 "<You have already been given *the sign*," he said. "The Phoenix will first appear alive, then die, only to rise again.>

Upon hearing this, John's mind started reeling.

"I have addressed you as John, but your true name is *Bonarges*.
That name has been spoken in the Aeons, and written into the Book
Gs Tru 21:25 of the Living. <Indeed, all those who have received the teaching are
inscribed in the Book of the Living.>"

John bowed his head, acknowledging all that he had seen and received. But a look of terrible suffering came over the Messiah's face.

Gs Tru 18:19 "<Jesus has appeared for this reason: to put on that Book. He will be nailed to a tree, so that he may become a fruit of knowledge for you – a fruit that will bring discovery rather than destruction.>

<On the cross, he will publish the edict of the Father, and establish Gs Tru 19:34
the Book of the Living. Though eternal life clothes him, he will draw himself down to death. And having stripped himself of the perishable rags, he will put on imperishability. For this reason, Jesus will take up that Book willingly, and accept his sufferings with patience, since he knows that his death will become life for many.>"

John fell to his knees, surrendering himself to awe. He was utterly humbled by the immensity of the mystery.

"But who are you," he begged, "Jesus the man, or Christ, the immortal saviour?"

"<Who I am, you shall know when I depart. What I appear to be Acts Jn 96
now – that I am not. But when you next come to me, then you will see me truly.>"

John watched with fear and trembling as <a blinding light Pistis ch 3
descended upon Jesus and surrounded him completely. The disciple gazed after him in mute wonder as Jesus rose to the heights in a spendorous display.>"

Then, <he heard Peter and James calling him, beckoning him Acts Jn 91
from afar. They were angry because he had been speaking secretly to the Lord.

When John returned, they asked him: "Who was *the other one* speaking, the one beside the Lord? Because, from the top of the mount, we heard *two* voices.>"

John stared at them incredulously. <Then, he called to mind the Acts Jn 91
mysterious ways of the saviour – whose unity has many faces, and whose Wisdom gazes at all unceasingly. John said, "You will find out, if you go now and ask him yourself.>"

Peter and James turned to one another, fearful and uncertain.

Then, gathering up their courage, they set out for 'the high place' on the Mount of Olives.

V

At the end of a quiet lane stood Martha and Mariam's home, where they lived together with their elder brother. Pots of dried basil lined the walls, and wild capers grew among crevices in the rock.

Martha turned the key that was kept in the latch, and they entered the quiet courtyard. At the centre of the garden stood an acacia tree, with a nest of black birds in its crown.

Martha went in and looked for her brother, but the house stood silent and empty. He must have left, she realized, for the Feast in Jerusalem.

The companions entered and immediately set about their appointed tasks. Nathanael drew water from the cistern and Philip kindled a fire into life. Susanna refilled the lamps with oil and Simon shook out the mats.

Suddenly, the door opened and the Iscariot entered. His face was dark and his head hung heavily from his shoulders.

They all turned to stare at him, but he didn't utter a word. Instead, he turned to his twin, a terrible anguish distorting his features. A silent stare passed between them.

The Nazarene glanced away, and fixed his gaze on the fire. He stared at it for some time, as if, looking for an answer in the flames.

Jesus sighed and gathered his disciples before him.

"I stand before you," he said, "a simple man, with his worries and his fears."

The disciples raised their voices in protest. "No Lord," Philip said, "you are more... much more than that..."

Gs Thom 34:30 His eyebrows rose, and he turned to Philip, asking: "<Then tell me – how do I appear to you? Compare me to something."

Philip said to him, "You are like an angel, just and fair."

Matthew said, "You are like a philosopher, reasoning and wise."

Finally, he turned to the Iscariot.

Hesitantly, Thomas said, "I... I cannot say *who* you are like – my mouth cannot form the words...>"

The Nazarene wondered at this for some time. Then he turned to his apostles and said:

Gs Judas 34 "<Truly, none of you *knows* me."

When they heard this, the apostles grew confused.

But the Nazarene pursued: "None of you, it seems, can stand before my face – and reveal to me the perfect man."

The apostles trembled and turned away. None dared stand before him – except the Iscariot. But he, unwilling to meet the other's gaze, averted his glance.

"I know who you are..." the Iscariot said, "but I am not willing to speak and reveal it."

Seeing that a higher light reflected in the Iscariot's eyes, Jesus
Gs Thom 34:30 said: "Step away from the others.> <Then Jesus took him and withdrew from the room>

They all waited, watching the door which the twins had shut

behind them.

<When Thomas finally came out, he was solemn and taciturn. Gs Thom 34:30
His companions asked, “What did Jesus say to you?>”

A vision flashed before his face. The Iscariot <saw the disciples Gs Judas 44
crowding round him – with rocks in their hands, and terrible, accusatory glances in their eyes.>

Slowly shaking his head, Thomas replied: “<If I told you even Gs Thom 34:30
one of the words that passed between us – you would take up rocks in your hands ...and stone me.>”

VI

As the moon rose gibbous and bright atop the Mount of Olives, the trees cast menacing shadows over the ground. Peter and James waited, silent and anxious.

Then, a comforting breeze passed over them, and a warm glow rose up from the horizon. For a few moments, their vision grew hazy and clouded. But when they again opened their eyes, the saviour was standing before them.

Immediately, they put off their sandals and fell to their knees. But the Messiah bid them rise.

“<I am Christ,” he said, “the one who is *from you*, and who 2Tr Seth 65:18
stands here *among* you – the Son of Man> and the Son of God.”

Peter turned to James and whispered, “Did you hear it? When he spoke, two voices came from his mouth.”

“The voice of Jesus,” James said softly, “and the Christ...”

A brief smile passed over the Messiah’s lips:

“<As long as the cloud of flesh casts its shadow over your 2Tr Seth 70:1
minds, you will not know me,> <and I will remain an unspeakable 2Tr Seth 65:31
mystery.>”

The apostles bowed their heads.

“Lord,” Peter said, “I have <cast away the bond of flesh that 1Ap Jas 27:3
encircles me> and sought to look upon you *with faith!* Thus I ask, not in knowledge but in faith – why have you come before us?”

With arms outstretched and his head bowed, Christ said: “<I Gs Phil 63:24
have come to crucify the world.>”

Upon hearing these words, the disciples trembled. James felt on the verge of collapse.

But Peter, his faith newly roused, replied, “<Then blessed be 1Bk Jeu
the one who is coming to crucify the world!>”

Christ answered, “<And blessed are you, who have no world to 1Bk Jeu

crucify you. For he who has crucified the world has found my Word – and fulfilled it.>”

At a loss to understand, James turned pale with fright. “If we are your disciples, then how are we to fulfil your word?”

Acts Jn 101 “Soon you will witness <the nailing of the Word, the suffering
of the Word, and the death of the Word.> You too must suffer in the
Jn 8:31 world, and transmute flesh into the Word. <For whoever continues
in my word will truly be my disciple.>”

L Pt Ph 138:13 With tears in his eyes, Peter said, “<If you suffer on our behalf,
then we, too, will suffer with you.>”

The saviour nodded to acknowledge Peter’s faith and compassion.

Ap Jas 5:23 “<When you consider how long the world existed before you,
and how long it will exist after you, then you will realize that your life is but a single day, and your sufferings are but a single hour. Remember my death on the cross, and you will live.>”

Ap Jas 5:35 But James pleaded with him, “<Lord, do not mention death and
the cross – they are far from you.>”

Jn 1:14 Slowly Christ shook his head. “<The Word became flesh to
Ap Adam 77:12 dwell among men.> <Now, the Archons seek to punish the flesh of
2 Tr Seth 65:21 the man upon whom it came.> <For your sake, he will be despised>
L Pt Ph 139:15 and humiliated. <He will bear a crown of thorns, put on a purple
robe, be crucified on a tree then buried in a tomb, only to rise again from the dead. But my brothers – hear me! – Jesus will be a stranger to this suffering.>’”

James and Peter stared, opening and closing their mouths, unable to speak.

2Tr Seth 52:8 “For the Word <is a stranger to the regions below,> <and the
Gr Pow 42:1 nature of his flesh cannot be seized.> <Never will the Messiah suffer
1Ap Jas 31:17 in any way, nor be distressed. For the Archons and their people can
do him no harm.>”

Slowly, a smile crept over Peter’s lips, as he grasped the terrible mystery behind those words. But James’ throat constricted, and his heart weighed heavy in his chest.

Then the air around them grew hazy, as it became saturated with a luminous glow. The Messiah began to rise up into the heavens.

Jn 5:24 “<Truly, truly, I say to you – he who hears my word and believes,
has passed from death unto life, and from this life to eternal life!>”

In the span of a heartbeat, the radiance faded, and they were left standing alone in the darkness.

From the distance, John called them, and Peter and James

returned to the place where they had first taken shelter.

The younger son of Zebedee sat under the ancient arch, his eyes wide with fear and wonder.

"Did you hear it?" James asked his brother. "When the saviour spoke, two voices flowed from his mouth."

"One earthly, one spiritual," John whispered with awe.

"Like the Messiah himself," James now acknowledged, "the Son of God and the Son of Man."

His voice breaking, John cried, "It will be terrible, the coming days. The Messiah must suffer unto death."

The three of them stood in uneasy silence. Among the olive branches, the Paschal moon shimmered.

With eyes full of affliction, James murmured, "Jesus will suffer greatly..."

John nodded. "Jesus... and the Christ."

Peter stared at the sons of Zebedee. He could not comprehend their great sorrow. Fired by his faith, he smiled and said encouragingly, "My brothers, be strong and take hope – neither Jesus nor the Christ will suffer!"

He grasped them by the shoulders and shook them. His face was beaming.

John and James stared at him uncertainly. Then John lowered
his head. "Though he spoke in riddles, this much was clear to me:
<Jesus will accept his suffering with patience.> And Christ, who has Gs Tru 20:11
<appeared to us in the flesh> will suffer with him *<as a sign,>* <as Gs Thom 38:21 Orig Wld 122:29
an *image* of our own resurrection.>" Gs Phil 67:9

James gazed at his younger brother. "What suffering is *that*,
if it is only in image and appearance? No, <the Archons and rulers Ap Adam 77:12
will punish the flesh,> but Christ himself <will neither surrender 2Tr Seth 55:14
himself nor suffer,> <since he is spiritual and remains untouched. Iren1.26.1
Before he is led to his death, Christ will depart, and only Jesus will
be crucified.>"

Realizing the terrible fate that awaited his friend, James hung his head in sadness.

Peter stared at James in amazement. "<Jesus will suffer but Iren1.26.1
Christ depart?> You just heard him say a few moments ago that
<Jesus will be a stranger to his suffering.> Christ <put on Jesus at L Pt Ph 139:15
the Jordan and, when the time comes, he will bear him away from Tri Prot 50:12
the cursed wood.> We should rejoice this night because we know
that neither of them will suffer."

Suddenly, the three of them grew silent. From the distance, they could hear the cries of the lambs being slaughtered in the Temple. Their agony echoed deep into the night.

John shivered. "A terrible mystery has been revealed to us this night. And it seems to me, my brothers, that none of us can fathom it..."

VII

Magdalene gazed at the moon, and its near-fullness made her heart shudder.

Beside her, Jesus lay rigid and still, listening to the sounds of the night. Would this be the last time he ever heard those sounds – the leaves rustling in the acacia tree? The night-birds warbling? And the soft footsteps of John, Peter and James as they found their way home?

The house in Bethany was not large, but it accommodated all the apostles. And here, in a small room on the rooftop, Jesus and Miri had found their final refuge. They had come here seeking shelter and assurance in one another. The Nazarene did not want to be left alone this night, and Magdalene did not want to leave him.

In a broken voice he suddenly cried out: "I'm thirsty..."

Miri poured out a cup of cool water and handed it to him.

He turned and stared at her, his eyes sparkling in the darkness. There was so much beauty and grace in that simple gesture – the giving of the cup.

He breathed in the water's freshness, surrendered the clay to his lips and slaked his thirst. Then, laying back his head, a thousand thoughts assailed him.

How desperately he wanted to close his eyes and sleep. But he didn't dare surrender himself so easily. And it seemed only now, in these rare midnight hours, that he could hear his own voice, and follow his heart.

Over the last few months, the Messiah had spoken through him every time he opened his mouth. And yet, after Jesus had preached in Jerusalem, he felt strangely liberated – as if Christ had finally said his fill, and momentarily departed from his flesh. Even now, he felt free, and was hard pressed to remember what he had screamed at the crowds.

Jerusalem was just another step on the Messiah's path.

"The Messiah..." Jesus mused aloud. "Israel's anointed king. They passed through the Red Sea; he was immersed in the Jordan.

They passed through Sinai's burning sands; he endured the eastern desert. And when they finally suffer judgement – so will he..."

"It needn't be like that," Magdalene responded. Her voice was sad and distant. "The Israelites turned their backs on Wisdom when they renounced the ancient ways. It was they who laid her 'High Places' low. If the Messiah has come, it is to show them a path they have long-since forsaken."

Jesus stared at Miri, uncomprehending.

"In Phoenicia I caught a glimpse of the ancient, forgotten ways. At this time of year, in Tyre, they celebrate another feast. The king enters the Holy of Holies, and joins with his *hierodule* in the Sacred Marriage. It is a time of rejoicing. Through the mystery of their union, the land grows strong and plentiful."

Tears formed on Magdalene's lashes. She had to make him understand now, before it was too late.

"Don't you see it? The Messiah is not the lamb – he's the bridegroom! And Sophia is his bride! If now, he has come to the Holy of Holies in Jerusalem, it is to enter the Bridal Chamber..."

She took his head in her hands, caressed his hair and kissed his lips.

But his mouth, on her mouth, felt cold.

"<Why, when I come close to you," she whispered, "are you Thund 18:35
always so far from me?>"

The Nazarene heard the ancient resonance in Miri's voice, as Sophia echoed her words.

Vainly, he tried to extricate himself from her embrace. "We cannot surrender ourselves, Miri, not even now... How can we embrace, when we still wear the flesh, like seven skins of the great serpent – Yaltabaoth!"

Miri continued to caress him.

"Because we know what lies hidden in our flesh. <I'm the one Thund 16:16
whom you have pursued, and I'm the one you have seized.> <Do Thund 13:8
not banish me from your sight – you who are waiting to take me to yourself!>"

As he looked into her eyes, there was the unmistakeable glance of the ancient goddess in her aspect – powerful, regal, commanding.

Suddenly, a shudder passed through his body, and he withdrew from her in fear.

"Would you be like the others, and join in the ploy to entrap the Messiah? Would you *betray me* this very night? Satiation and desire belong to the Archons."

"And suffering?" Miri asked, her heart thumping wildly in her chest. "If the Messiah suffers – won't the Archons still rejoice? Doesn't't *pain* also belong to them?"

For a few moments, Jesus was speechless. He had become lord over his own mortal vessel, and he did not know which way to turn.

Val Exp 35:30 Sighing, he replied: "No. Although a tumult of <passions
surrounds my immortal seed, I shall separate them, one from the other – elevating the better passions to the spirit, and leaving the worse for the body.>"

Miri shook her head.

"*All* passions belong to the flesh – joy and suffering equally.
Why embrace one and not the other? Come to me, my beloved,
Sirach 6:26 <find rest in me, and I will take the form of joy for you.> Have
Thund 15:29 you forgotten? I am Sophia <– senseless and wise,> <great and
Thund 14:23 disgraced,> <the whore and the holy one.> Come to me this night,
Thund 13:18 and I will reveal *all* my secrets..."

In the cleft of her neck, he could smell Miri's ointment – a fragrance evoking all the mysteries of Nature herself.

"Feel the body's fullness," she pursued. "For a moment, taste
it – the eternal cycle of ecstasy and pain, alternately dying and
Thund 21:20 coming to life again. <For many, my love, are the pleasant forms
and fleeting pleasures which men embrace, until they become sober. And when they finally go up to their resting place, they will find me there once more – I, the ancient Goddess. They will live, and never die again.>"

Thund 16:11 She stared at him in the darkness, and whispered: "<Though
you... continue to call me 'death', I am the one called Life...>"

For a moment, he felt in his flesh all that she had spoken – the mingling of darkness and light, ecstasy and pain...

Slowly, Jesus kissed Miri's hands, following their henna-stained pattern of two serpents entwined on Nature's vine.

And when, this time, they kissed, they acknowledged love's equal share of suffering and joy.

Then, the lovers closed their eyes and lay their heads on the pillow. In the ensuing silence, they heard the evening breeze, and the stalks of wheat in the distant fields as they rocked their heads in hushed lamentation.

That sound came to the Nazarene's ears like a distant calling of his name.

"Have you forgotten *Adonai*?" Jesus asked, turning to Miri.

"Didn't *he* suffer? Even the Phoenicians, in their ancient ways, lament the death of Baal, their lord *Adonai*."

"He was cut down," Magdalene admitted, "like the wheat in early summer – beaten and chaffed, then buried. But when the fertile earth again pushes forth his seed, they greatly rejoice, and proclaim he lives again..."

Jesus nodded his head. "<Alone, a grain of wheat falls into the Jn 12:24
earth and dies. But through its death, it engenders many fruits.>"

"No!" Magdalene cried, lifting her head from the burlap pillow. "That was John's terrible mistake. He was led to the altar like an ancient beast, then bound and beheaded... Salome cut him down, just like the harvested wheat... She offered him up *in the ancient way* – the same way the Israelites did long ago, in the time of Canaan which the Phoenicians have remembered."

Magdalene's aspect grew ferocious, and he trembled to see her so moved.

"Salome offered him up *to the Goddess*, and he became *her* sacrifice. But, believe me, the Goddess no longer demands blood offerings. Israel has forgotten the ancient ways."

"Do you really believe that? What of the lamb – the lambs that are slain, even here in Jerusalem?" Then Isaiah's ancient prophecy
came burning to his lips: "<*He was wounded for our transgressions,* Isaiah 53:5
he was bruised for our iniquities... Yet, like a lamb that is led to slaughter, he opened not his mouth.>"

In the darkness, Miri stared at him, sensing his deep resignation. He still thought the Messiah's path ended in Jerusalem.

"Why do you want to give your life? For what? What do you think it would bring to the people – *forgiveness* for their sins? The High Priest is sacrificing lambs this very night to expiate Israel's transgressions. But you said it yourself – we are born without sin! Would you sacrifice yourself to YHWH, and deliver yourself up to Yaltabaoth?"

"No... But the phoenix must still fly into the fire. That was John's prophecy – do you think he spoke falsely? *I am* the phoenix."

"*Who* is the phoenix?" Magdalene cried, "you, or the Christ? *Who* will suffer – the Son of God or the Son of Man?"

"Both – we share the same fate!"

Miri broke down, repeating to him, "Neither..! Neither need suffer – not you, nor the saviour..."

Jesus shook his head.

"<The Son of God *is* the Son of Man, and unites both natures, Tr Res 44:21

as human *and* divine. As the Son of God, he will defeat death and, as the Son of Man, he will restore the Pleroma> to its former fullness." In a strangulated voice, he murmured, "That is why both must suffer."

"For what fault?" Magdalene asked at last. "It was Sophia who brought death into the world, and divided the Pleroma. Why should Christ suffer on her behalf?"

"Because she created the world without her consort's consent. So she fell, and suffered her own unique passion. Now, her consort must make restitution; *he* must fall like her, and suffer all the passions of this world – freely and willingly – to finally offer that consent which he withheld at the beginning."

Magdalene stared at Jesus, comprehending the mystery at last.

Val Exp 33:24 With dark foreboding, Jesus said, "<Sophia's restoration cannot occur through anyone else but him. At first, he did not *want* to consent to suffering. But, as one half of the *syzygy*, he is bound to. That is why Christ has willingly descended into the flesh> and will knowingly suffer, even unto death."

As he spoke, he could feel himself falling. He remembered the dizzying sensation of tumbling out of control, then plunging into watery darkness.

Jesus lowered his head. Only now did he see how it all fit together: the *Anthropos* fallen into Nature's pool, Adam and Eve, Christ and Sophia.

"But why?" Miri needed to know. "Why this senseless suffering and slaughter?"

"Out of love. He will fall, and sacrifice himself willingly, so that the two may re-unite, and become one."

"The consent..." Magdalene accepted at last. "The two consorts will unite in the moment of consent. But if he consents to suffer *all* the passions of this world, then why surrender to agony alone? Why not unite in the ecstasies of love? Isn't *that* the Bridal Chamber?"

The Nazarene shook his head slowly. "I don't know. I still haven't fathomed the mystery. The Fourth and Fifth Seals... they lie beyond me."

Miri looked at him, her eyes growing wide.

"But – what of the wedding at Cana, when you kissed and embraced me? You spoke clearly of the Bridal Chamber then..."

The Nazarene's blood froze in his veins.

"The Fifth Seal? Miri, no such thing ever happened. What you experienced must have been a dream – or a vision... In Cana, you fell asleep in my mother's arms. She caressed your hair and whispered to you as you slept."

Suddenly, all the bizarre events of that night became clear to her: the room on the right and its distorted reflection on the left, then the third room in the middle. It was all a fantasy and a dream... or a vision – sent by whom? By Wisdom? Or Yaltabaoth...

"You embraced me," Miri began, "and explained that 'all will enter into oneness in the heavenly Bridal Chamber'." She tried to remember more, but it all seemed like a daze. "You said that you had kissed me, as a sign of your consent – that consent which was withheld in the beginning. And so, once Sophia's fault was rectified, then together Christ and Sophia would rise up and enter the heavenly Bridal Chamber."

Jesus stared at Miri, uncertain as to whether this was the truth or a lie.

"But we – yes, it's clear to me now – but we may still join here, in fleshly union, as an image of our higher union in the Pleroma. We do so in the rite of the Bridal Chamber. That is what you said!"

She stared at him, beseeching that he understand.

"That is why Sophia entered my flesh, and Christ entered yours – so that we might manifest, here in this dark place, the mystery of their union. That is the Fifth Seal, the Bridal Chamber..!"

The Nazarene shivered. How much he longed for those words to be true. But a terrible trembling in his heart told him that a darker fate awaited.

"Only one of us knows the mystery of the Fifth Seal," Jesus whispered. "And it is neither you nor me; it has been revealed to someone else."

Suddenly, Miri's heart stopped.

"The Iscariot..." she breathed. "What did Thomas say to you when the two of you withdrew from the room?"

"He lied to me – denying everything. At that moment, I knew
<he was the only one acquainted with the truth. Only he, only Judas, Iren 1.31.1
will accomplish the mystery – the mystery of my betrayal.>" Then
he lowered his head and said, "<...For nine bronze coins.>" Gr Pow 41:30

"No!" Miri cried. "It cannot be! He's misleading you, guiding you down the wrong path – the worst, most terrible path. He's leading you directly to the Archons and their powers – Herod, Pilate, Caiaphas..."

"Yes – where the Messiah's path ends."

She brought his hands to her face, kissed them and anointed

them with her burning tears.

And, in a moment that stilled her beating heart, she saw the
Val Exp 33:19 marks in his palms, invisible but burning with light: <the imprints of the nail wounds.>

"You're wrong!" she lamented. "Wisdom has whispered to me otherwise, and I believe her with all my heart. Your fate lies with me. You must come to me."

"Tomorrow is the Eve of the Passover. Tomorrow will decide."

The Nazarene's face grew rigid with despair.

"*This* is the Bridal Chamber," she cried, kneeling on the bed they shared. "This is where we'll celebrate the final mystery. Tomorrow, when the moon grows full, I'll return here and wait for you. The Fifth Seal will be revealed, the moment we unite in the Bridal Chamber..."

XV. Gethsemane

I

Mariam awoke with a strange presentiment. Still wrapped in cool linen, she tried to go back to sleep – but a disquieting feeling of fear persisted. It was the earliest hour of the dawn, when the air was alive with fresh scents. Tying her long hair with a ribbon, Mariam rose and quit the chamber where her sister Martha lay slumbering in her bed.

Outside in the courtyard, the Bethanite sat herself down in the shade of the large acacia tree. Her heart fluttered between fear and hope as she again tried to remember her dream.

Suddenly, the omen from last night drifted back into her mind. She remembered being immersed in total darkness, and her eyes, though open, were blinded by blackness. Still, it came to her slowly, invisibly – not a figure or image, but a scent. *She had smelled the sweet essence of nard* – a perfume so overpowering that it had pulled her out of her sleep. Even now, she could detect the funereal odour in her nostrils.

At once, Mariam stood up and cried aloud. She called for her brother, who still hadn't returned from Jerusalem.

Hearing this, a kindly neighbour leaned out the window and beckoned her near.

Dressed in black, her face grown long with mourning, the neighbour announced that Lazarus, their beloved brother, had died only three days past. His shrouded remains had been anointed with nard, then walled up on the Mount of Olives.

The moment Martha came out of the house, Mariam took her

sister into her arms and announced the terrible news. The two women embraced, lost in their grief.

Slowly, the disciples emerged from their beds. One by one, they gathered round the sisters and offered their condolences. From the east, the sun broke over the limestone wall, and cast the acacia's long shadow over the courtyard.

When, last of all, Jesus appeared, he found them all dumbstruck
Jn 11:32 with grief. <Mariam came over and fell at his feet, crying: "Lord, if
only you had been here, my brother would never have died.>"

The son of Nazareth stared at her uncomprehendingly. A long
and pitiful gaze passed between them. At last, overcome by the
Jn 11:35 tension and exhaustion of these last days, <Jesus wept.>

Without uttering a word, he turned and entered the sisters' home.

When they came inside, the companions found him sitting by the empty hearth, his head bowed, his mind deep in thought. For more than an hour, the Nazarene brooded by the stone jamb of the fireplace.

In a daze, Martha went about her morning tasks, while Mariam knelt in silence beside the saviour. Her mind was fixed on the memory of her brother. Why were she and Martha absent during the last moment, the most trying hour of his life? How could they have abandoned him?

Finally, Mariam turned to Jesus, her eyes awash with sorrow.

"Surely," she said, "if you wish it, our brother Lazarus could live again."

Jesus turned, and took Mariam's hands into his. A frightening anxiety came over his features.

"How – to live again?"

"Is it too great a miracle – to ask that he be raised from the dead?"

A cold chill passed through his limbs. He thought of this Passover Eve, and what awaited him.

Turning away, his gaze fell upon the Iscariot. Thomas was staring at him, his grey eyes cold with doubt.

The Messiah faced Mariam and, with a slow and measured movement, he shook his head.

"Sister, what you ask cannot be given. The flesh is no more than
Int Kn 7:30 <a temporary dwelling place> – a garment that your brother put on
and has now taken off. Would you ask him to put it on again?"

"Yes, if it would bring him back to us..."

"Do you not see? <The resurrection which you are awaiting Gs Thom 42:10
has already come, but you do not recognize it!> On the banks of
the Jordan, when <you entered through the image> – the image of Gs Phil 67:9
your soul's ascent – then <you acquired the resurrection.> <That Tr Res 49:15
resurrection is the disclosure of those who have risen.>" Tr Res 48:4

Mariam's thoughts flew in all directions, trying to grasp the sense of this mysterious utterance. But her heart and mind remained dark.

She shook her head. Still, she could not bear to think of her brother's body shrouded and entombed on the Mount of Olives. Pressing her forehead into the Nazarene's hands, Mariam wet them with her tears.

"But what of the resurrection of the flesh?" she asked, hope and despair mingling in her aspect.

Jesus stared at her. How desperately he wanted to grant this woman her wish. But when he opened his mouth, Christ said through him:

"I have told you already, <the body is a tomb.> Would you have Ap Jn 21:9
me bring him back – like one buried alive, <like a walking corpse, CH VII.i
one of the living dead?> No, I will not raise the dead, or <proclaim 2Tr Seth 60:21
the doctrine of a dead man..!>"

A terrible shivering possessed him. Then, with wild desperation
in his eyes, Jesus exclaimed: "<Do not await the resurrection of the Test Tr 36:29
flesh!>"

The Bethanite bowed her head in acceptance.

But the Nazarene could not rid his mind of the image that had formed there: Lazarus' gnarled corpse, anointed with nard, devoured by maggots and worms. Would his own flesh take on this dreaded appearance less than three days hence? And his bereaved disciples
– would they <cleave to the name of a dead man?> Ap Pt 74:13

Mariam, meanwhile, came to see her brother's death in a different light. His soul, she thought, would surely rise, even if his body could not.

"But what of those who haven't received the seals, or already
seen their soul's ascent <– where will their souls go?>" she begged Ap Jn 26:23
him.

Jesus stared into her large beseeching eyes as Christ replied:

"<After it has come out of the body, the soul is handed over Ap Jn 26:36
to the Archons, who enclose it again in a prison; they bind it once
more in the chains> of forgetfulness and <cast it down into another Ap Paul 21:18
body.> Thus, the soul will indeed be resurrected in the flesh – it

Ap Jn 27:9 will be reborn, again and again <– until it is finally liberated from forgetfulness and acquires the *gnosis*. If it thus becomes perfect, it will not be cast into another flesh, but is saved.>"

"How – saved?" the Bethanite asked, a glimmer of hope flashing in her aspect.

The moment Mariam asked this, a terrible burden was lifted
Ap Jn 27:14 from the Nazarene's shoulders. He said: "<Truly, you are blessed,
Ap Jn 26:30 for at last you have understood!> <The soul of the saved is taken up
Dial Sav 120:1 to the Aeons, to stand at rest.> <And whoever stands at rest, will rest
Dial Sav 140:11 forever.> <Those born of truth – will not die.>"

All the apostles stopped to wonder at his words. They forgot about their morning tasks, the water-ladling and bread-making. Their souls, it seemed, were flying on out-stretched wings and his voice was the wind that carried them. Only Judas-Thomas remained untouched by his words.

In the ensuing silence, a shaft of sunlight entered the chamber, and fell upon Mariam's face. It's light mingled with her tears, sparkling and glistening in their liquid luminescence.

L Pt Ph 134:15 "<Listen to my words, so that I may speak to you...>" he begged
Gs Thom 32:13 them all. And in a low voice, he imparted: "<For – whoever finds the meaning of these words... will not taste death.>"

II

With a strange foreboding, the companions waited for the Passover Eve. Jesus made no move to enter Jerusalem and address the crowds. No one was told to prepare the lamb and bitter herbs for the Paschal Feast. Peter, John and James glanced at each other uneasily, remembering the Mount of Olives, but none of them dared speak. For the whole of that day, the apostles did not stir from their refuge in Bethany.

But as the sun arced over their heads and sunk towards Moab, the Nazarene suddenly rose from his place beneath the acacia tree and bid them follow.

With a heavy gait they climbed the Kidron Valley and passed under Jerusalem's walls. Jesus led the way through a maze of narrow streets, then indicated a house where the mark of a lamb's paw had been impressed in blood on the door frame. Passing through the quiet courtyard, they mounted the winding stairs to a chamber on the second floor.

2Bk Jeu ch.45 Here, a low table had been laid <with bread, water and wine;

incense, herbs and vegetables.> Though the Passover Meal also
called for a fledgling lamb, <none of the holy food on this table had Pr Thks 65:3
blood in it.>

The low brass table, round and full as the moon, invited them; the eleven men and seven women reclined around it in uneasy silence. None of them knew what to expect this night.

Then the Nazarene knelt before them with a basin of water. One by one, he bathed their feet and anointed their heads with fragrant oil.

When Miri felt the gentle caress of his hands on her feet, a flood of images surged through her memory. How long had it been since they had lain opposite each other, their feet nestled in each other's hair? Tonight, after the Paschal Feast, they would again embrace, but this time face to face. This night, she and he would knowingly unite in the Bridal Chamber.

The Nazarene bid Philip and Nathanael to burn the holy incense; its rich odour soon filled the vaulted chamber.

When Jesus returned to the low table, he sat with Magdalene to his right and the Iscariot to his left. For a long slow moment, he gazed at his apostles, acknowledging each of them with deep, heart-felt stare.

"Though this evening marks the Paschal Feast, we have gathered here to inaugurate, instead, *a new mystery*. This sacrament is the Fourth Seal, the Eucharist, the meal to be shared in remembrance of me. I bid you to gather like this and eat, in ritual evocation of our shared sacrifice."

The moment Peter, John and James heard those words, their hearts froze. A shudder passed through all around the table.

But Jesus smiled and re-assured them. "<All things done in Gs Phil 67:27
the name of the Lord are a mystery – the Baptism, Chrism and
Redemption, the Eucharist and Bridal Chamber.> These are <the Gs Egypt 59:1
Five Seals which the Father brought forth from his bosom,> and
which the Son has brought into the world, to <seal you with the Unt MS
Father's seal, so that you might return as one to exist in him.>"

The moment these words fell from his lips, Arsinoe gazed at the Virgin. Her eyes grew wide with mute wonder. Had he uncovered *all* Five Seals? He had named *each one* clearly and distinctly...

"<Though the Five Seals are ineffable, I have pronounced Tri Prot 50:9
them so that you might abide in me, and I in you.> <The Five Seals Tri Prot 49:26
manifest a glory higher than any glory;> they are <the mysteries 1Bk Jeu
which, though hidden, show the way to the Chosen Race.> For you

Tri Prot 48:30 alone, who <have received the Five Seals, may share in the mystery of the *gnosis*, and become a light in Light.>"

The apostle bowed their heads.

Orig Wld 122:29 "<The phoenix," he whispered, "kills itself and brings itself to life once more.> In this way, it makes an offering *of itself to itself.* That is the mystery which the High Priest proclaims in the
Melch 15:7 sacrament of the Fourth Seal. The most ancient and <true High Priest is designated by the name of 'Melchizedek'. He alone, through that name, bears the name of the Holy One.>"

Peter gazed at his master, and for a moment he saw the mysterious High Priest, venerated for ages by the name of Melchizedek. But John, gazing at that same long face, saw in those blazing eyes the mysterious fire-bird that immolated itself in the flames, then rose again from the smouldering ashes.

In a firm and resolute voice, the saviour addressed them:

"It has previously been revealed to you that the Father is a unity. He is the One who thinks upon himself, who sees himself, and who knows himself. We are the thoughts by which He thinks himself; we bear the names by which He hears himself in the silence. Through our images, He sees himself in his watery light. Whenever we, through the *pneuma* in us, come to know him, his act of reflection is made complete. In one great circle of self-knowing, He knows us and we know him, in the mystery of unity.

"Through the Baptism and Chrism, you acquired the first two seals: your name and your image. With the Third Seal, you were given your robe of light, to witness the vision of your soul's Resurrection. The Eucharist is the Fourth Seal. By eating this bread and drinking this wine, you will be granted one more seal by which you may return in unity to the One.

"And, just as each initiation opened your eyes to the Father, so this sacrament will reveal one more aspect of His mystery – a mystery that transpired *before* the beginning of time, and has not been revealed to the world *until now*."

Breathlessly, the Nazarene gazed at his apostles.

"After the One looked upon itself, named itself, and knew itself – it *acted.* In the beginning, *the One sacrificed itself,* in order to kill itself and die. But, being immortal, the One did not die; it returned to life, recognizing itself *as eternally alive*. It became aware of itself that moment as *Life* – eternal life – dying to itself, rising to itself, forever in the circle. Thus it came to *know* itself, through the mystery of *gnosis*, as life-everlasting.

"The One did this out of love. It willingly and lovingly sacrificed itself to become two: God and Man. For, what is God but life's immortal aspect, while Man displays life's mortal aspect? And yet, these two will be resolved into their original unity. When Man surrenders his mortal self, he returns to God and regains immortality in the divine Self. In this way, the One's act of *self-sacrifice* is made complete."

Matthew stared into Christ's face, and a strange angelic calm came over his features. Somehow, he had understood.

"But, for Man here on earth, this mystery must unfold over time. Though God, in the beginning, surrendered himself to death, Man has not yet reached his end, nor has he transcended death – to join with God in immortal life."

Jesus bowed his head. Suddenly, in his palms, they could see invisible wounds. On his brow, an unseen crown pricked him with its thorns.

"Christ has come into the world to make this mystery manifest. As the Son, he is the Father's furthest extension into the Aeons, from the luminous heights to the darkened depths. He is the particle of light which has descended into darkness, to illuminate it. He is the spirit which has descended into your slumbering flesh, to awaken it. He is everlasting life which has descended into death, to re-animate it. As the phoenix, he will die and rise again, to manifest, on earth, the mystery of the One's self-sacrifice."

Then the saviour held out his hands in a gesture that froze the blood in their veins. Before the crowds in Jerusalem, he had made the same movement: like a phoenix unfurling its wings – or a man fixed upon a cross.

"And, as the High Priest Melchizedek, Christ inaugurates the Eucharist, to mark and remember the mystery of sacrifice – through this shared meal of bread and wine."

The Nazarene held his hands over the offering. On the table lay the wafer of bread, the chalice, and a pinch of salt. <To the right Pistis ch 142
of the bread offering was a cruet filled with water; to the left was another filled with wine.> Taking the two cruets, he poured the water and wine into the chalice, mixing them.

"Thus, by eating this bread and drinking from this cup, you are granted the Fourth Seal, by which you knowingly return to the One. It is not your image or your name which is given to you – *it is your death*, and the recognition of your own death *as a sacrifice*."

"To each man and woman," he said, his voice growing low,

"the mystery of self-sacrifice will become manifest – *through their death*. When your life is willingly offered up, you recognize that you are a particle of divinity which has fallen into matter, darkness and death, and which seeks to return to its source – to spirit, light and life! By dying and rising again, you knowingly participate in the timeless mystery of the One's self-sacrifice."

Mariam bowed her head, remembering her departed brother. Somehow, in her heart, she now felt peace. The terrible breach between life and death, she accepted, would be bridged by eternal life.

He held up the wafer of bread.

"When you take the Eucharist into yourself, you recognize that Christ, through his death, willingly and lovingly offered up his life, to *complete* the mystery of the One's sacrifice. And *you too*, by acknowledging your own death as a sacrifice, will complete that same mystery. By dying and rising again, you reflect the One to itself, not in thought, image or name – but in *deed*."

Gs Phil 59:27 Jesus dipped the bread into the salt, saying: "<May our entire offering obtain salt.>"

Then, he raised the salted bread over the cup, saying:

Melch 15:7 "<I have a name: *Melchizedek*. I am truly the *image* of the true
Melch 16:7 High-Priest, who *is* God Most High.> <I have included myself in the living offering, together with your offspring, and offered them up as an offering to the All.>"

The apostles stared at the saviour. Though they sought to knowingly participate in this rite, his words were utterly mystifying.

Smiling at them, Jesus said:

"When the One sacrificed itself, it offered itself up *to itself* as an offering. This is the great mystery – that his unity became manifest in a *self*-sacrifice. Thus, the One is present, both in *the priest* who makes the offering, and in *the offering* itself. In this rite, *both* are consecrated – the High Priest as the offerer, and the sacred meal as the offering – to momentarily evoke the One's *sacrifice to itself*."

With a solemn gesture, Jesus then broke the wafer in two.

"The priest breaks the bread to make manifest, here and now, the timeless moment in the beginning when the One became two: separating its original unity into God and Man – immortal and mortal life."

James and John gazed at Christ with wonder, seeing how he now held immortality in his right hand, and mortality in his left.

<Would he, nailed upon the cross, divide light from darkness,> life Test Tr 40:23
from death, and the saved from the damned? Would he keep them forever divided? Or would he, like two hands joined in prayer, bring these pairs together once more? Through his death, would he join the two halves of the host once more into a complete circle?

Jesus broke the bread into smaller pieces and distributed them among his disciples.

"The One offered itself to itself, knowing that *all* would join once more in its unifying sacrifice. The priest, and all those who participate in the Eucharist, share the same mystery. They become an image of oneness, divided by death into many; and of the many, rising to life as one."

Raising his hands, Jesus said:

"<I offer myself up to you as an offering, together with those Melch 16:7
who are mine, to you yourself, O Father of All, and to those who have
come forth from you, whom you love,> <forever and ever...>" Euch A 43:38

Together, the disciples recited the response, "Amen."

He passed the divided wafer to his disciples. The moment John took a salted morsel into his mouth, he felt the mystery of unity enter him. He remembered the eternal spark, trapped in his mortal flesh, which only death would release. By dying, he would participate in the sacrifice, offering himself up to the One as the One had offered itself up to him: from the One to the all, and the all back to the One.

All the disciples gazed at one another, sharing in that same realization. For a moment, their experience of life lost its temporal measure, and they felt themselves to be deathless and immortal.

And as they lost their fear of death, they also lost their lesser fears – need, hunger, want and desire. Now they could live *without fear* – giving themselves to others, offering up their works, sacrificing themselves willingly. Through these thousand lesser acts of kindness, they were not really surrendering themselves to others, but sacrificing themselves to the One hidden in the all.

The Nazarene turned to them and said:

"We acknowledge the gift that has been given, by offering up
our voices in prayer. Hence, <when you offer praise, do so like Dial Sav 121:4
this.>"

Touching his fingertips together, he bowed his head:

"<O Father, as we celebrate the Eucharist, we give thanks to Dial Sav 121:4
you, remembering thy Son. Hear us, O Father, as you have heard + Euch A 43:20
your only-begotten Son. Yes, hear us, as you have heard your Chosen

Ones. Through your sacrifice, we have been made complete in every spiritual gift. Through your sacrifice, we enter the Kingdom and are given rest, forever and ever. Amen.>"

The Nazarene then took the chalice in his hands. He held it up, saying:

Melch 7:24 "<We include ourselves in the living offering, by offering ourselves up, as an offering to the All.> We do this, in full recognition of the mystery."

He then drank from the cup, and passed it on to his disciples.

This time, when John swallowed the water mixed with wine, his eyes were newly opened. He gazed at Christ and saw his own features reflected there. But more than that, he saw himself in all the disciples.

He no longer saw difference, but a deep inner likeness. Though he acknowledged that Andrew was a man and Arsinoe was a woman; that Simon came of lowly stock while Joanna was refined – these disparities were deceiving. *All* passed through life and death, which brought them equally into the One. The appearances of this world had misled him.

As long as he remained on the earth, he had to act in the awareness of their hidden likeness. He had to see himself in others, and others in himself. For the other was nothing less than his innermost divinity made visible.

For some time, the companions gazed at one another with this newly found sense of unity and community.

Then the saviour bowed his head and said, "Let us pray." Again he joined his fingers at their tips.

Pr Thanks 63:33 "<We give thanks to you..." for a moment, he paused, leaving a long, profound silence. Then he said: "And every heart and soul is lifted up to you..." Again, he paused. At last, he completed the unspoken utterance: "to you – undisturbed name, honoured with the name 'God' and praised by the name 'Father'.

"We rejoice because You have shown us Yourself. We rejoice, having been illuminated by your knowledge. We rejoice because while we were in the body, You have made us divine – through the *gnosis*.

"To everyone and everything comes your Fatherly kindness. Grant us mind, speech, and knowledge: Mind, so that we may understand you; Speech, so that we may proclaim you; and Knowledge, so that we may know you.

"The thanksgiving of the man who attains to you is one thing only: that we *know* you.

"We have known you, Light of the mind. We have known you, Life of life." For a moment, he glanced at the Virgin and at Magdalene. "We have known You, Womb pregnant with the nature of the Father. We have known you, Womb of every creature."

Then, he concluded the prayer, saying: "There is one petition that we ask: that we be preserved in the *gnosis*. Amen.>"

Having said these words, Jesus turned and embraced the disciples
on either side, kissing Magdalene and the Iscariot. Following his
example, <they embraced each other,> feeling in their kisses the Pr Thanks 65:3
momentary joining of the all in the circle of the One.

III

As night descended over Jerusalem, the Nazarene led his companions back to Bethany. They followed the same road where, only one day hence, they had been besieged by the poor of Kidron. Now the twisting lane was quiet and deserted.

Jesus walked with Magdalene and the Iscariot, keeping these two close by his side. Meanwhile, the apostles' heads were buzzing with the delirious effects of the bread and wine. They walked arm in arm, leaning their heads together and whispering joyfully.

"Why," Magdalene suddenly asked, "did you dip the bread in salt?"

She knew, according to the ancient Law, that <every offering Lev 2:13
was seasoned with salt, as a sign of the covenant between man and
God.> But, had he offered up salt to fulfil YHWH's command?

The Nazarene comprehended her confusion.

"We celebrated the Paschal Feast this night to inaugurate a *new*
mystery. I said, '<May our entire offering obtain salt>' to secretly Gs Phil 59:27
acknowledge Sophia. Only you two may know of this. <Sophia is Gs Phil 59:30
'the salt', and without it, no offering is acceptable.>"

Magdalene gazed at him, at a loss for words.

The Nazarene opened his mouth, and again Christ spoke through
him. "When we call to mind the sacrifice, we must remember that
Sophia also suffered her own *hidden passion*. When she renounced
her consort, Sophia descended into the world <and suffered Val Exp 33:35
greatly.> <She knew what had become of her,> and acknowledged Val Exp 34:32
her suffering as a sacrifice, crying aloud, '<I deserve the passion I Val Exp 34:27
have suffered.>'

"Thus, the bread offering is dipped in salt to recognize that

Sophia is also present in Christ's sacrifice. They are two-in-one, the
Val Exp 34:34 *syzygy*, and <*both* of them suffer> to bring about the final restitution.
She suffered in the beginning; he will suffer at the end. But the end will be where the beginning is. In that moment, their suffering will be made complete, and their passion be as one."

Miri stared at Jesus, slowly comprehending the strange significance of his words.

But when she glanced at Judas-Thomas, the Iscariot lowered his head, hardly able to suffer her gaze.

She saw, that moment, the terrible indecision torturing his heart; his doubt was tearing him in two. He trembled, hardly able to take another step. Still, some hidden, higher duty compelled him to walk with them towards Bethany.

IV

The Nazarene suddenly stopped and turned. He saw, to his left, the terraced enclosure where the Jerusalemites kept their spice gardens. Without another word, he passed under the stone arch that led to Gethsemane.

The gardens were cool and peaceful. The Paschal moon, round and glowing, hung low in the heavens.

Acts Jn 94 "<Before the final offering," he said, "let us sing a hymn to the
Father.>"

The apostles approached, surrounding their saviour in the
Acts Jn 94 moonlight. <He bid them join hands and form a circle, with himself
at their centre.> Though they stood with their hands interlaced, man and woman, each of them saw themselves in his aspect.

Acts Jn 94 "<Answer to me 'Amen'" he cried.
Then, in a low sweet voice, he began to sing:

"Glory to thee, Father!"
And the disciples, circling round him, answered Amen.
"We praise thee, Father; we give thee thanks,
"O Light, wherein no darkness dwells." Amen.

"Grace dances! I play the pipe; everyone dance!" Amen.
"The Twelve Aeons dance above us.
"The Whole on high joins in our dancing.
"I will be united, and I will unite." Amen.

"I am the way to you, the wayfarer.
"I am the lamp to you who see me.
"And I am the mirror to you who recognize me." Amen.

"If you follow my dance,
"See yourself in me when I speak." Amen.
"And you, seeing what I've done,
"Keep silent about my mysteries." Amen.

"In seeing, you have not stood still,
"But have been wholly moved." Amen.
"Through me, you are moved to Wisdom.
"Know the Word of Wisdom!" Amen.

"In suffering, see what I do,
"And be moved to do likewise." Amen.
"For yours is the passion I suffer.
"You who dance, recognize what I do." Amen.>

With each turn, the disciples felt themselves spiralling closer to their master, from circumference to centre. No longer was he the master and they his disciples, but all were immersed wholly in the circle.

When they released their hands, the bonds that drew them to one another were not broken. Compassion joined them in their hearts, and knowledge kept them in common mind. The dance had brought them together in joy, and would unite them still, in suffering.

Suddenly, the saviour paused, and a terrible anguish drew over his face.

"Peter, John and James," he said, his voice breaking, "remain
here, and pray for me. All of you," he said, "<do not go astray or be Act Jn 97
dazed by sleep.> For the time has come when <the rulers will rise Gr Pow 41:14
up in their wrath, and pursue me. Though they cannot recognize me, still they will recognize one of my followers, and kindle their fires in his soul...>"

With fear and denial written on their faces, the apostles turned to one another, wondering – *who* could it be? Only the Iscariot remained silent, bowing his head in acceptance.

"<He will betray me to them – for nine bronze coins. They will Gr Pow 41:14
arrest me, deliver me up to their ruler> and <punish my spirit in the Ap Adam 77:16
flesh.>"

When the Nazarene paused, the apostles erupted with cries of denial; they pleaded and protested, knowing they would be lost without their master.

1Ap Jas 33:4 "Be on your guard! For <a multitude of demons have armed
themselves against you, and now seek to claim you as their own.>
Gr Pow 45:15 For a time, <you will turn from me, and go astray,>" he cautioned
them, "but you will see through their deceptions."

Peter stood forth. Staring hard at Magdalene and the Iscariot, he said: "Others may abandon you, *but I never will!* My faith will sustain me."

Jesus looked hard at his head apostle and said: "Peter, Peter...
Before this night is over, you will deny me three times. And before
Ap Pt 72:2 the next night has passed, *I* will <reprove *you* three times> for your
sore lack of faith."

The Bethsaidean stood absolutely still, mute with fear and horror.

Ap Pt 71:22 "<Be strong!> <Do not let sleep enter your eyes, nor drowsiness
Silv 113:31 touch your lids – lest you fall into the hands of the robbers.>"

Then he turned, taking Magdalene and the Iscariot by the hand, and withdrew.

V

Frankincense hovered at their feet; golden aloes and myrrh filled the evening air. The spice gardens of the Jerusalemites grew fragrant with a rich myriad of scents.

The Iscariot gazed at a redbud tree, and the poisonous henbane growing at its root. Double-minded, torn in two, his mood alternated between a strange elation and dark despair.

But, as Magdalene mutely followed the Nazarene, a different odour assaulted her nostrils – a curious brine, like hyssop and myrrh mixed with sour wine.

They stood in a neglected spot, not far from the hollows where the dead were enclosed on the Mount of Olives.

Magdalene felt faint. The strange odour was still surrounding her, overpowering, suffocating her – a bitter stench of vinegar and gall. She feared she would lose her senses.

At last, seizing the alabaster pendant from round her neck, she broke it and poured out its costly ointment over her hands.

Wordlessly, Magdalene bathed the Messiah's brow with the powerful unguent. Then, falling to her knees, she caressed his hands and even fell to his feet.

But, as she wiped his heels with her hair, she saw there the
marks she had seen the night before: invisible, burning with light
<– the imprints of the nail wounds.> At once, Magdalene cried Val Exp 33:19
aloud, washing his feet with her tears.

All the while, the Iscariot stared at her, a pained expression contorting his features.

"Woman," he said, "your perfume has been wasted. Nard is the ointment of the dead. But Jesus still stands with us, among the living."

Staggering, breathless, Magdalene stood up. She could hardly bare to look upon the Iscariot.

"But you would betray him," she breathed, "to Annas and Caiaphas... to..."

Her breathing stopped.

The Iscariot spoke for her: "...to his death."

Bowing his head, he bore the full brunt of her gaze.

Then he whispered the words, "...For so you have commanded me. It was not I who chose to betray him, *but you*..."

Miri stared at Judas, wondering if the man had lost his reason. But, the more she looked at him, the more she had the terrible, frightening sensation that he was not looking *at* her, but *through* her. He was gazing through her to an aspect of herself which only *he* could see.

The Iscariot bowed his head even lower, and whispered, "*They* charged me – Christ... *and Sophia* – to remain silent, until the Fourth Seal was revealed. Now, I may speak freely."

In this dark corner, where the laurels were overrun by thistles, Judas broke off the branch of a thorn bush and fingered it compulsively, not caring how much it pricked him.

"Sophia herself admitted to me that *she betrayed Christ*." He stared hard at Miri, and his grey eyes would brook no contradiction. "She did so, in the beginning, when she renounced him. She refused him that kiss by which they, together, would have become consorts, and *co-creators* of this world."

Miri turned a wild, frightened eye to Jesus. He nodded
imperceptibly, his brow arched, his eyes half-closed in misery. In
that moment, she realized, Judas was speaking the truth. <He alone Iren 1:30
had known the truth – the mystery of the betrayal.>

As more tears upwelled in her eyes, she recalled all that her beloved had told her last night – how he, as one half of the *syzygy*, was bound to suffer, *just as she did*, by wilfully embracing the cross. Thus he consented to join with her... in the hidden passion.

"*She* betrayed him," Judas repeated, "*before* the foundation of this world. And she chose *me* to manifest the mystery of her betrayal – here and now, in this dark place..."

Magdalene backed away, unwilling to accept the Iscariot's irrefutable logic. *He had known the truth all along*, and hidden it from her. *Who* had hidden it from her?

The epiphany dawned on her like a terrible awakening.

"That is what Christ and Sophia revealed to me in Batanea," the Iscariot declared at last.

"No!" she cried. "The Fifth Seal..." Her eyes opened wide. "It can't be..."

Magdalene stared at the Iscariot, but the Nazarene spoke for him.

"The Fifth Seal is the sacrifice..." Jesus said, whispering the words she dared not utter.

"It is the Bridal Chamber..." she pleaded, a terrible urgency and agony breaking in her voice. "Consent to become my consort this night. Together, we will make the end *as it should have been* in the beginning. Christ and Sophia must unite... to bring the two together: above and below, darkness and light, male and female..."

The two men stared at her, and the expression on their faces was so terrible that she dared not decipher it.

The world started spinning round her, and she feared she would collapse. Breathing in deeply, controlling her emotions, she stared at her lover and said:

"In Bethany, I'll wait for you – wait for the final mystery to unfold. The *true* mystery..." she stopped, unable to say more.

Silently, Magdalene retreated, and ran far from Gethsemane. Once alone, she tore at her garments, hid her face in her hair, and cried aloud. All the while her heart beat alternately between hope and despair.

VI

Judas and Jesus stood face to face in the garden's darkest corner. Their features – barely illuminated by the moon – were like dark and light reflections. Jesus saw his own features in his twin, but could not fathom their faint expression.

"Go to her," Thomas whispered, "before it's too late. The end may *still* reach the beginning," he murmured, "and the two become one."

With terrible urgency in his voice, the apostle spoke of the vision he had seen in Batanea.

"Do you know *who* separated Eve from Adam? It was Yaltabaoth! And he's keeping the two of you separate, even now! What are you afraid of? What are you waiting for? Only you can repair the separation that existed from the beginning, and again unite the two – through Christ and Sophia – as *the new* Adam and Eve."

Slowly, the Nazarene shook his head. And as he opened his mouth, Thomas heard a higher voice echoing his every word. That Voice urged him onward, reminding him of his final duty.

"In the heavenly Bridal Chamber," Christ intoned, "the two will indeed join as one. But first, Sophia's fault must be rectified," he bowed his head, "through the sacrifice."

Judas-Thomas stared at his twin, unwilling to accept the utterance he knew to be true. For a moment he faltered, overcome by doubt and indecision. What if he refused?

"That is the hidden passion," Christ reminded him, "and you, *Judas*, were chosen *above* the others.... To you has been given the hardest of tasks. It is your duty to deliver the Messiah to his fate."

The Iscariot backed away, hardly able to bear the words that had entered his ears. He turned and, like a hunted criminal, fled from Gethsemane, then headed for the holy city of Jerusalem.

The Nazarene stood alone by the gnarled trunk of an olive tree. Above him, the moon had grown full in the month of *Nîsan*, and the constellations had attained their most fatal alignment. He could see the Archons' faces above him: vain, arrogant, triumphant. The Messiah's fate had reached its final hour.

He pressed his forehead to the ancient tree, smelling its sweet resin and embracing the vital sap that flowed through its branches. If only he could stand, unmoving, like this tree, while its boughs were torn, its bark stripped bear, and the crown was severed from its root.

But he was only a man, and when his bones broke, his skin tore and the sinews snapped, his body bled like all men's.

He turned, fearful and confused, wondering which path to take. Wait for Judas till he returned from Jerusalem? Or flee to Bethany for Magdalene's embrace? With a terrible anguish, he realized – *he did not know.*

And the Archons, that moment, where gloating over his ignorance and indecision.

The Nazarene could no longer bear to be alone with his thoughts. In desperation, he ran towards Peter, John and James. He found them
Gs Tru 29:8 all <sunk in deep sleep, dreaming the most disturbing of dreams.>

Gr Pow 39:33 "Wake up!" he cried, "<you who are sleeping and dreaming dreams. Wake up and return> to me. Pray for me – and *for yourselves*."

The three apostles roused themselves from their sleep, none of them knowing how they'd fallen into such a deep slumber.

Ap Jn 23:6 "<Lift the veil that has fallen over your minds.> <Shake off
Silv 94:19 your drunkenness and become sober!>"

He roused them, shaking them awake one by one.

"Pray that the Archons will be kept at bay just a little while longer!"

With his face clouded and his heart deep in distress, he returned to his solitary place by the olive tree. The stars laughed.

He had craved for companionship, and the apostles had abandoned him. But could they, even they, his dearest disciples, *help him now?* He longed for a solace far greater than any human could give. The isolation he now suffered was a spiritual solitude – excruciating, unbearable. Had Christ himself departed from his flesh? *Why did he feel so alone?*

As the first watch sounded, Jesus fell to the ground and prayed.

Gs Thom 38:21 "Christ! <You stood in the midst of the world and, in the flesh, appeared to them. But you found all of them drunk. No, not one did you find thirsty. Yet my soul aches for the children of humanity... who've become blind in their hearts... who've grown drunk and cannot see. They came into this world empty. Will they depart from it – empty?>"

Unsteadily, the Nazarene stood up. He'd hoped to revive his faith through heart-felt prayer. But still, his soul was troubled by darkness and despair.

Cautiously, he approached the place where the remaining apostles had gathered to pray. He found them all fast asleep.

Frowning bitterly, biting his lip, he retreated.

Were they to blame? The spirit was willing but the flesh was weak. All had become victims of the Archons and their powers.
Ap Jn 17:32 *Archendekta* had closed their eyes, and *Deitharbathas* had stopped

up their ears. At that very moment, *Oummaa* was filling their heads with darkly deceptive dreams.

In this, the blackest hour of the night, Yaltabaoth's legions were streaming over the earth, victorious.

He could see, across the Kidron valley, a column of smoke rising in the air. The servitors of the High Priest had begun the night-time sacrifices. But in the swirling smoke, he also saw myriads of demons, like winged predators – hovering, circling, then diving upon their unwary prey.

Gazing at that frightening sight, he recalled the ancient legend
which his mother had told him when he was still but a child. <When Test Tr 70:1
David, Israel's first king, laid the foundations of Jerusalem, and
when Solomon, his son, had built the first Temple, their deeds were
achieved with the aid of demons.

After its completion, Solomon had imprisoned them in seven water pots – hidden deep in the temple's interior. But, when the Romans entered Jerusalem, they found the water pots and released the demons from their prison. Since that day, evil spirits roam over the earth, taking up residence in any man> who lives in Jerusalem's shadow.

The Nazarene looked up at the mist-laden skies of Gethsemane. Here too he could see the demons writhing ecstatically in the evening air – dancing, boasting, rejoicing.

As the second watch sounded, he fell again to the ground in prayer.

"Antipas, Annas and Caiaphas, the Sadducees, <Pharisees Test Tr 29:18
and scribes – they all belong to the Archons now, who've assumed
authority over them.> Soon, <they will seize me,> to mortify my 1Ap Jas 25:5
flesh and torture my soul. Though <they will rain their wrath upon P Shem 36:21
me> I know <it is not really the earthen rulers who will harm me.> 1Ap Jas 31:21
<They've armed themselves against me – in judgement – but they 1Ap Jas 27:21
are armed *with other powers*.> <They've become no more than 1Ap Jas 31:21
images of the Archons> on earth."

He clutched the soil, grasping at thorns, and prayed with cracked bleeding lips.

"<In this place of humanly suffering, I shall bow my head, hold 1Ap Jas 27:27
my tongue, and *not* rebuke them. There shall be silence within me...
and its hidden mystery.>

He pressed his brow into the thorns, inhaling their acrid odour.

"And yet... I tremble <before their wrath, for I've grown weak 1Ap Jas 28:3
and faint-hearted.> <Jerusalem is now the Archons' abode, and 1Ap Jas 25:15

V Allog they've amassed themselves against me in great number.> <O God
above the aeons! Hear my voice, have pity on me and save me from
this evil! Look down upon me, and hear me! Because I am alone in
1Ap Jas 40:19 this empty land.> If it be your will, <cast away from me this cup,
whose only drink is bitterness...>"

Overwhelmed by anguish and fear, the Nazarene stood up, and sought out his companions a third time.

He hadn't taken more than a few steps when he stopped, his heart grown heavy with foreboding.

The night watch sounded a third and final time. He stood, deathly still, knowing that, now, he was powerless. If the Archigenetor's angels had already seized his soul, paralyzing it with fear and anguish – then how could he save his closest companions? The dark forces of Yaltabaoth had reached their zenith.

His only hope was to escape his fate and upset the *Heimarmene*. The Messiah's path ended in Jerusalem. He could see it above him, blazing in the heavens and written on Yaltabaoth's skin...

In the serpent's sky, a new constellation had taken form, which only his eyes could see: the saviour, his arms upheld, was standing on the world, while the lion-headed serpent had coiled seven times round his crucified body. That darkening image foretold his immutable fate.

But now – could he unwrite the prophesies? Could he break open this heavenly omen and alter his destiny? What if he fled from Jerusalem and turned his steps, this very moment – towards Bethany?

Magdalene was waiting for him, and she had seen the truth all along. Even the Iscariot had urged him to it. The Fifth Seal was the Bridal Chamber. *None of them had foreseen it* – neither the angels above nor the Archons below. This was the *unseen* turning in the path...

The moment the male and female became one, the material and ethereal worlds would re-unite. By joining with Magdalene this night, the depths of the abyss could rise up to heaven, and the darkness within would shine with light. Wasn't that the task allotted to Christ and Sophia – to *re-create* the world?

He had to reach Magdalene now, before it was too late. His heart pounded in his chest, beating one syllable only – hope! Abandoning his disciples, stealing himself from Gethsemane, he set out for Bethany.

But there, at the arched entrance to the gardens, Judas was

waiting for him. Seventy-two soldiers stood beyond the gate, their torches blazing like the lights in the darkened heavens. Temple guards, Roman troops, Herodian soldiers – all had gathered in great number, and their alignment here spelled out the same dark fate as the constellations in Yaltabaoth's sky: the Messiah would be seized this night. *All of this was pre-ordained.* Christ must be crucified.

With tears in his eyes, Judas stepped forward. His grief blinded him, and he stumbled time and again. Mustering all his strength, he raised his head and gazed into the eyes of his master.

The Iscariot opened and closed his mouth, hardly able to speak. *Why was Jesus still here? Why hadn't he fled? Magdalene was waiting for him...*

Staring into the face of his master, as if, into a dark mirror – Judas froze. He could not fathom the expression on the face of his twin.

Jesus trembled. The sight of his brother's suffering tore at his heart.

Suddenly, he heard a strange voice, whispering to him from within. It was barely audible, but he had heard this tone before – powerful, regal, commanding. Was it Magdalene? Or his mother? The Voice spoke with the unmistakeable accent of the ancient goddess.

Filled with sorrow and regret, Sophia called to him and said:
'*I* betrayed you when I refused you my kiss. <I deserve the passion Val Exp 34:27
you suffer.> Now I acknowledge it. Will you not acknowledge it, my love, with a kiss..?

Trembling from head to foot, Jesus stepped forward. He could no longer deny the fate which – he now understood – had been ordained by *all* the higher powers.

"<My only true disciple,>" he whispered to Judas, "<do it now. Gs Judas 58
Do what you have come to do...>" Mt 26:49

And Judas, his whole body shaking, fell into the arms of his beloved companion.

Speaking aloud for all to hear, the Iscariot cried, "<My master..! Mt 26:49
Greetings, my master...>"

With quivering lips, he kissed Jesus, and Jesus wilfully embraced him, pressing his lips into the other's with passion, longing and surrender.

The signal was given, as had been pre-arranged from the beginning. At once, the soldiers surrounded them. In the torch light, their faces took on an eerie, inhuman glow.

A soldier stepped forward, his smile a contorted mix of malevolence and glee. With the butt of his sword, he struck the Nazarene on the face.

And as the first drops of blood fell into the earth, the Archons exulted and rejoiced.

XVI. The Praetorium

I

His sight obscured by sackcloth, Jesus stumbled as another blow exploded over his left brow. Smothered in darkness, the world spinning round him, he collapsed to the floor.

"Where are your prophecies now?" a voice called out.

In the ante-chamber of the High Priest's house, seven guards amused themselves with the prisoner by playing blind man's bluff.

"You *are* the Prophet of Nazareth? Well then... prophesy!" Laughing maliciously, they picked him off the floor and stood him up straight.

"Prophesy! Which one of us will strike you next?"

A Roman guard, smiling wickedly, struck the bound and blindfolded saviour. Jesus staggered, till another soldier tripped him, and he tumbled once more to the floor.

His ears erupted with a queer, high-pitched ringing, and the guards roared with laughter. Then Jesus heard, amid the soldiers' cackling, a more evil, unworldly laughter – Yaltabaoth was roaring triumphant.

This night, all of Jerusalem, from the poor below in Kidron to the powerful on the embankment above, were enclosed in their homes for Passover Eve. Zion had shut its gates; its narrow lanes were dark and deserted.

The High Priest's house stood in the Upper City, where the rich of Jerusalem resided in high-walled mansions. Under a large vaulted chamber, Caiaphas paced back and forth, his mind a whirl with plans and preparations for the Paschal Feast.

Each time he turned, tiny bells on the fringe of his robe tinkled. For this special occasion, the High Priest bore the robe of the Ephod, with its bejewelled sceptre, breastplate and mitre. In the flaming torch-light, their gold shimmered and their onyx stones sparkled.

Meanwhile, Annas lazed on the High Priest's throne, dressed in a simple vestment of white and gold. He was confident the Feast would proceed as planned.

"They've brought him here!" Caiaphas screamed, "bound and tethered like a beast for the slaughter!"

"This is the Paschal Feast," Annas mused. "Do your duty – sacrifice him."

The High Priest gazed in horror at his father-in-law, wondering how the Elder could speak those words with such icy candour.

"We have no law to condemn him to death! He's an Israelite! If we stand him before the Sanhedrin, the Pharisees would rally to set him free."

"There are other ways." Annas yawned, stretching out his long, bony limbs. "We can convene a special council, now – in the middle of the night. We'll call up our Sadducee allies, and leave the Pharisees to sleep peacefully in their beds. The council can appeal the case to Pilate, who'll gladly render us Roman justice."

Caiaphas fingered the long braids of his beard as sweat poured over his well-coiffured brow.

"...Crucifixion?" He could hardly bare to pronounce that dreaded word. "You'd defile the Messiah with Roman barbarity? They deny the condemned man a decent burial, leaving him on the cross to rot and putrefy." He shivered at the thought of it. To kill was one thing. To leave the body unburied was the worst possible transgression in Israel.

"No," Caiaphas sighed, "I will not have his blood on our hands, and on those of our children. For generations we'd be rendered unclean."

Annas pushed out a long malicious laugh. "*Unclean*?" He smiled ironically. "Have you forgotten? We usurped the High Priesthood long ago! None of us were born true sons of Zadok. The Essenes say *we defile* the Holy of Holies each time we pass beyond its veil! When you stand before God on the Feast of Atonement and whisper His secret name – does He answer you? Does YHWH appear?"

Caiaphas lowered his large face, swelling with shame and disgrace. He could not bare to answer.

"Then how can *you*, as the High Priest, beg atonement for the sins of our people? *The whole of Israel* has been made *unclean* by your pompous vanity and pride!"

Caiaphas gazed down at his breastplate, where the twelve tribes of Israel were inscribed on it gems. All of this – the *Urim* and *Thummim*, the mitre engraved *'Holy unto YHWH'* – were a mockery and travesty. He was a monkey in priestly robes – and Annas pulled his chain...

"What would you suggest?" he asked, defeated.

A serpentine smile crept over the Elder's lips. "Our only hope is to obtain the Five Seals. If he reveals them, their sacred power will fall to us."

Mute and powerless, Caiaphas nodded in collusion.

Annas clapped his hands, calling for the prisoner to be produced.

When the Sadducee Elder saw the Nazarene – whose brow was beaten, whose ears were pouring blood – he rose from the throne and gazed upon their captive with wonder.

"So this is Jesus Christ..!" he mused aloud. "We meet at last – the Messiah of the Five Seals..."

For a moment, Jesus looked into the eyes of his accuser. Immediately, he averted his gaze. From behind the Elder's eyes, Yaltabaoth glared at him venomously; the serpent's pupils glowed like black flames in yellow opal.

"Our proposition is simple. Reveal the Five Seals, and we will set you free. Otherwise," Annas hissed, "your life is forfeit."

Jesus turned and, for the first time, cast a hard, piercing glance at Caiaphas. The High Priest was cowering in the corner, hoping his garment's bells would not announce his presence.

When Caiaphas *saw* the Nazarene – saw him for the first time with his own eyes – he trembled in fear and recognition. This, he acknowledged without a doubt, was holiness incarnate. He could feel it the moment the Nazarene had entered the room.

"...Not on our hands, or those of our children..." the High Priest prayed in a strangulated voice.

The saviour dismissed Caiaphas from his gaze. Turning once more to Annas, he addressed Yaltabaoth directly.

"*You* would free me from my prison? *You* would lift away my chains?"

The other nodded. "Consider it a simple exchange. We've seized you as expected, taken you prisoner, and now hold your life *in ransom*. You offer the Seals to us – as a pledge – one token in exchange for another."

The smile on Yaltabaoth's face grew wide with satisfaction.

Slowly, the Nazarene lowered his head. "And if I choose to offer up *my life instead* – as a pledge..?"

"For what?" the ancient Elder screamed. "What could you possibly gain in exchange?"

1Ap Jas 28:1 The Nazarene stood, unmoving, his lips drawn tight. '<I shall hold my tongue' he remembered. 'In me there will be silence... and its hidden mystery.>'

Then the rhythmic beating of his heart, for a few moments, altered. In quick staccato bursts, it pounded out its hidden message, which took the form of images behind his eyes.

He saw Magdalene, safely installed in Bethany, waiting for him on the rooftop. And, deep within Magdalene's soul, the fallen Sophia was hidden away – awaiting her redemption. Before this day was over, Christ could save Sophia – ransom her with his life – and return her to the Upper Aeons...

Despite the bruises and contusions on his brow, despite the blood that trickled down his cheeks, for the first time, the saviour smiled.

"Your arrogance has blinded you, so that you no longer see your own ignorance. The Five Seals have led you on with their power, and still – *they elude you*. I would rather lay down my life – silently, willingly – than surrender their power to you."

Annas stepped forward and struck the saviour. In anger and fury, he cursed the saviour, spat on him, and struck him repeatedly.

Then, seizing Caiaphas from the corner, he stood him before the Nazarene and screamed, "Strike him! Tear at your robes and condemn him!"

The High Priest, shaking from head to foot, rose a quivering hand. Then, surrendering himself to weakness, he heartlessly struck the Nazarene. With tears in his eyes, he tore at his priestly robes – the sign that his accusation could not be withdrawn.

Jesus stood motionless, deep in his silence.

Caiaphas turned uncertainly to Annas and whispered, "What is the charge?"

"Blasphemy!" the Elder screamed. "Blasphemy and high treason! You heard it yourself – he claims he's the Messiah, the king who is coming to rule over Israel..!"

Caiaphas turned a trembling eye to Jesus. He hoped, deep in his heart, that the Nazarene's blood would not stain his hands, or those of his children...

"Blasphemy!" he announced. "The prisoner is hereby charged with high treason!"

His voice faltered, and tears bathed his cheeks.

At once, Annas screamed for the Temple guards. The prisoner was ordered to stand before a special council of the Sanhedrin.

II

Pilate awoke in a foul mood.

He had an odd foreboding that this day would auger no good. First, there was the letter from Claudia his wife, full of strange dreams and omens.

Then, while being shaved and perfumed, he received a second missive from Galilee. Herod Antipas wrote, in no uncertain terms, that he was ill-disposed to involve himself in Jerusalem's affairs. True, the Prophet heralded from Galilee, but he renounced any further jurisdiction. The Tetrarch left the matter in Pilate's hands.

His servant cinched the Prefect's belt round a short white tunic, sliding a ceremonial short-sword into its hilt.

What had gotten into the Edomite? Ever since John the Baptist had been beheaded – word of Salome's exploits had spread like wildfire through the empire – Herod Antipas had been acting strangely...

Pilate's spies had kept him posted: the Tetrarch hardly slept or touched his food. In his darker moods, he was want to fall to his knees and pray for hours, beseeching the Baptist's forgiveness. His Vizier Chuza had been dismissed, and this rather capable fellow, the reports said, had converted to the new faith now spreading over Galilee.

Pilate mounted the spiralling stairs to his office in the Antonia Palace.

It was *madness*. Israel was filled with madmen and fanatics – Zealots, Essenes, Pharisees and Sadducees... Now there was this new group – Christianites, or whatever they called themselves. It made him dizzy. How could he govern such an unruly land – and with Roman justice! The Romans, normally a civilized people, had to resort to the worst barbarities – clubbings, burnings, hangings – just to keep these people in order.

His two predecessors, particularly Varus, had made a true mess of things. *Varus* had burnt Judah ben Sariphai and Matthias ben Margaloth like human torches; *Varus* had crucified two thousand of their followers; *Varus* had executed Judas Galilean, the founder of the Zealot brotherhood...

Now, Pilate had to crucify every Zealot that stepped before the Procurator's throne. The next in line for martyrdom was the blind prophet Barabbas, whom the Zealots had proclaimed their new Messiah...

He entered his office and his Praetorian guards stood at attention. Leaning his closely-cropped head in hand, he listened as his adjunct read the day's duty roster. Their contents filled his mind once more with dark foreboding.

"A special council of the Sanhedrin was convened last night, condemning the new Messiah with blasphemy and high treason."

The Prefect gazed down at the papers on his desk. Distractedly, he took up his copy of Seneca and fingered its well-worn pages. Zealots. Christianites. Blind Prophets.

"...Which Messiah?"

"Jesus the Galilean. Last night, he proclaimed himself..." the adjunct glanced down at his scroll, "the Messiah of the Five Seals."

Pilate gazed out the window, unimpressed.

Five Seals. Blasphemy. Treason...

"What does all of that mean?"

"The Messiah is Israel's anointed king, as promised in their scriptures. The Sanhedrin rejected the Messianic claim last night, saying that, according to their laws, it's blasphemy. Now they're appealing the case to you – as high treason."

"Ahhh!" He tapped his Seneca. "Can't they deal with it themselves? What about *stoning* – that's on their books. They can throw him from the walls and stone him."

"Not now, *Dominus*. It's their Paschal Feast."

"Right. The Pasch...."

"They want the prisoner to be judged quickly, before nightfall. They're waiting for you now, just outside the Praetorium."

Pilate gave his adjunct at curious look.

"Outside?"

The adjunct froze. He had hoped his superior would pass over that detail.

"The High Priest refuses to enter a Roman office, saying it would make him unclean for the Feast..."

Pilate burst out laughing.

Unclean!

At a certain point, he rationalized, you have to give up trying to understand these people. In the land of the mad, sometimes you just have to act mad...

He stood up and drew his Procurator's robes over his shoulders.

"Then I'll meet them *outside* the Praetorium."

He looked down at his Seneca. Before leaving the office, Pilate could not resist. Opening the book to any page, he placed his finger on a random passage.

Omnes sub regno, he read, *graviore regnum est.*

Every ruler is subject to a higher ruler.

III

The burning sun broke over Jerusalem's walls. Already, at this early hour, black flies were buzzing in the air, and waves of heat rose from the flagstones.

When Pilate reached the Praetorium, an unruly mass had gathered before its gates: long-robed Essenes, freshly-bathed Pharisees, high-ranking Sadducees and knife-wielding Zealots. The poor of the Kidron were also there, with Paschal pilgrims from distant Samaria and Galilee. It seemed as if all of Israel had gathered before Pilate's door.

Normally, public trials took place in the Praetorium's courtyard, where the Procurator's throne stood high up on a seven-stepped dais. The prisoner was shackled to the *Gabbatha*, a stone bench equipped with iron gyves. Pilate saw he would have to improvise. The Praetorium's balcony, he noted, would suit him nicely. It was shaded by a portico.

"Have the prisoner brought to the upper chamber. I want to see him first."

From the upper chamber, Pilate could hear the cries of the rabble in the square below. He slid into the Procurator's seat, leaning his weary head in his hand. The morning heat was stifling. Holding a perfumed kerchief to his nose, he signalled for his fan-bearers to double their efforts – the stench from the Jewry was overwhelming.

Within minutes, the prisoner was produced: a slender man of regal bearing. The Galilean wore a long white robe – now bespattered with blood – which floated over his bare feet. He held no staff and wore no purse. His long hands, now tethered at the wrists, were finely molded. Black ringlets descended over his shoulders, and his bearded cheeks rose high to darkly sparkling eyes. The prisoner kept his head bowed and stared resolutely at the floor.

Pilate gazed at him for some time. This was not the man he expected. When Israel gave birth to a messiah, he usually resembled the land itself – roughly-hewn, fiery and unyielding, of hot and arid temperament. Somehow, this messiah reminded him of a shady tree or watery spring.

Pilate rose and stood before the accused.

"High treason is a serious charge. Are you what they say you are – the Messiah?"

Hesitantly, Jesus looked into the eyes of his accuser. For a moment, he stared, uncertain of what he saw.

"Are you their king?" the Prefect asked.

This man, Jesus realized at last, was much like himself – stoic in bearing, resigned to his fate, but struggling to free himself.

"Answer me! Where are you from?"

The Nazarene opened his mouth:

2Tr Seth 52:8 "<I am a stranger here.>" His voice had an odd, unworldly tone.
Jn 18:36 "<And my kingdom is *not* of this world.> <I came *into* the world to
Jn 18:37 bear witness to the truth...>"

"Truth?" Pilate's brow rose. "And what *is* your testimony of truth?"

Jn 18:37 "<That, whoever is from truth – hears my voice.>" The Nazarene
cast a long hard glance at Pilate. With frightening irony in his voice,
Test Tr 42:3 he asked: "<Who is the one who speaks? And who is the one who
hears?>"

Then the saviour's voice dropped even lower:

Test Tr 42:3 "<Who is the one who suffers? And who is the one that brings
suffering?>"

Tapping his sword nervously, Pilate took a walk around the room. Somehow those words, in their sibylline strangeness, had stirred his stoic heart.

What power had made him the accuser, and this man the accused? Was not he, Pilate the Procurator, also a prisoner? A prisoner of fate? As Prefect, he was fated to grant suffering, just as this man was fated to suffer...

Pilate stood himself before the prisoner.

"Your people have chosen me, it seems, to decide your destiny..."

The Nazarene rose his head and his lips twitched as he

suppressed an ironic smile.

Seeing this, Pilate grew furious. "<Recognize it! *I* have the Jn 19:10
power to crucify you – or release you..!>"

Sadly, Jesus shook his head.

"<The only power you have, has been given to you... by a higher Jn 19:11
power.>"

Pilate froze. The words from Seneca echoed in his ears. *Every ruler is subject to a higher ruler.*

His anger rising, Pilate drew his sword from its hilt and poised it below the prisoner's throat.

"I'm no fool, Prophet of Nazareth! If you want to die, why don't you do it by your own hand? Why put the blade in *my* hand? *Have you no courage?*"

Jesus stared at Pilate, and it felt as if the sword had plunged deep into his heart. In a timeless vision, he saw Pilate, twelve years' hence, in Rome. The former Prefect was lying in his bath, and with this very sword he had stabbed himself in the chest.

"*Courage*, Jesus of Nazareth! Each of us must stand up to his fate!"

Pilate sheathed his sword and seized the Nazarene by the front of his robe. Dragging him out onto the balcony, he screamed at the crowds below:

"Here is the man! I find no fault in him! In recognition of the Paschal Feast, the prisoner is released!"

Suddenly, a wall of hot air hit Pilate as the crowd screamed, "Release Barabbas! Release the prisoner Barabbas!"

Pilate turned, taken aback by the shouting. Then he smiled at Jesus and said, "It seems your fate is no longer in my hands..."

The Prefect screamed at his adjunct, "Bring me Barabbas!"

Within moments, the Zealot Prophet was hauled out of the Praetorium's dungeons. Pilate stood with Jesus on his right and Barabbas on his left.

"It is the custom to release one prisoner during your Paschal Feast. Two men stand before you, each of them claims to be your king. Which is the True Messiah – Jesus or Barabbas? Which shall I release?"

The crowd erupted with a deafening cry, calling for the blind prophet Barabbas. The shouting of the Zealots and Sadducees drowned out all the other voices.

The prophet of the Zealots raised his hands over his head and shook them in triumph.

"Barabbas! Barabbas!" they cried in adulation.

Then, the blind prophet turned slowly to Jesus and stared at him. Behind his clouded eyes, Yaltabaoth's Son was gloating with victory. A cold shiver ran down the saviour's spine.

"But what of the Messiah of the Five Seals?" Pilate screamed over the rabble.

The thunderous cry from the crowd shook him to the depths of his being.

"Crucify him!"

A thousand voices rose against Christ in their judgement. The deafening malediction left no doubt in Pilate's mind. All of this was ordained by some terrible, higher power.

He wrung his hands, as if, washing them clean.

"So that is your judgement? Then let the Nazarene be flogged..!"

"To the death!" the Israelites cried.

Pilate cast a forlorn look at Jesus. Then, raising his voice to a frightening cry, he completed their sentence.

"...And let him be crucified!"

IV

An ancient olive tree stood in the Praetorium's courtyard. Long ago, its limbs had been lopped off, and iron rings affixed high up on its stump.

The Nazarene's warders drove him into the courtyard, pricking him with the tips of their spears. The morning sun beat down on the *Gabbatha*.

Most of the guards were foreigners – warriors and mercenaries captured in Roman campaigns, some from Germania, others from distant Gaul.

The two lictors assigned to the Nazarene were huge men, heavily tattooed, with strange braids in their long hair. Wordlessly they produced a variety of devices and laid them on the *Gabbatha*: lashes of braided ox-hide, some flared and tipped with iron barbs, others woven with shards of sheep bone.

Seeing this, Jesus was seized with mute anguish. He struggled to stave off the horror, but his eyes kept returning to the whipping block, and its many instruments of torture. Their diabolic construction pierced him through with fear.

For a moment, one of the lictors looked up and stared at the

Nazarene. The man made a strange clucking noise with his tongue, and the sockets of his eyes seemed empty.

Following procedure, the guards stripped the prisoner of his garments and suspended him from the iron rings of the severed olive tree.

Jesus pressed his brow into the bark, hoping to inhale its sweet scent. There was only the acrid odour of dried sweat and blood. *To stand, unmoving, like this tree...*

When the first lash landed on his back, the pain exploded through his brain like a white flash of fire.

"One..." the adjunct droned.

After five lashes, his mind was throbbing with pain and the agony gnawed at his sanity. A myriad of strange faces danced before his eyes: taunting demons, sneering imps, jeering fiends. But above them rose a single horrific face, reminding him...

"Thirteen..!"

The Nazarene's tongue cleaved to his palate; he pounded his brow into the bark. Again the *flagrum* lacerated his skin and its irons barbs tore his flesh. Suddenly, a second frightening face rose up, a face he could recognize.

It was *Blaomen* – the demon of *fear* who worked in concert with agony and dread. And with him was *Nenentophni* – the evil angel whose *grief* inspires pain and bitter passion. He could feel these demons revelling in his flesh, and see them there rejoicing before his eyes.

"Twenty-one!"

The Nazarene turned his attention inward, seeking that centre of calm which neither fear could touch nor grief disturb. And in a moment, he found it: the inner state of rest which existed in his spirit's quietude.

<The Archons ceased to work their command over him, for Gr Pow 42:8
he had triumphed over their rule.> Fear departed from his soul and agony fled his bleeding flesh. For more than a minute, Jesus bore the lictors' lashes – unmoving, at rest.

Then, his own voice returned to him, reminding him: 'I will lay down my own life – *willingly...*' He had spoken those words, less than twelve hours ago, to Yaltabaoth.

At once, the Nazarene renounced his command over Yaltabaoth's legions. And the demons, in a heartbeat, returned to his flesh, tormenting it anew.

"Twenty-nine!"

He clung to the tree, wincing at every lash of the whip. But strangely, he no longer felt alone in his suffering. The Christ, hidden in his flesh, had risen up to endure his agony with him.

Tri Tr 114:31 "<I am your saviour in willing compassion,>" Christ said, and slid his hands into the legated hands of the Nazarene.

As one, the two took upon themselves the burden of the passion.

"Thirty-three!"

They endured the scourging to the end, even as the lash flayed open their skin, and their blood flowed upon the pavings.

When the saviour was freed from the scourging tree, he collapsed in a faint. The Romans justly referred to this punishment as 'the half-death': the stone pavings were covered with blood, and the prisoner had passed out from his ordeal.

Sponging the Nazarene's brow with vinegar and gall, his warders revived him.

And the moment the Messiah rose to his feet, his eyes met with his adversary: the blind prophet Barabbas, now a free man, had come to witness the Nazarene's flogging.

"This man proclaimed himself Israel's king!" Barabbas shouted. "But his words rang falsely in the people's ears. You heard them: *he is the False Messiah!* Treat him like one..."

Amused by the prospect, the guards slung a purple robe over his shoulders, crowned his brow with thorns and threaded a slender reed through his trembling fingers.

"Hail, Messiah of the Five Seals!" the soldiers cried, bowing before the man of sorrows.

Then, laughing heartily, they struck him and spit on him, mocking 'the False Messiah'.

From the guardhouse, two more soldiers lugged out the *patibulum*, the heavy crossbar which the prisoner was condemned to carry through Jerusalem's streets.

The last thing Jesus remembered, as the crossbar was lowered onto his shoulders, was the face of Barabbas. Jesus could see, in the blind man's features the frightening face of Yaltabaoth's Son.

But the blind prophet began to tremble with fright. In that moment, he recognized *the true Son*, the Christ, hidden in the Nazarene's flesh.

Divining his own dark future, Yaltabaoth's Son cursed and swore.

Then, Jesus lost all consciousness.

XVII. Golgotha

I

Magdalene had waited the whole of the night on the rooftop at Bethany. With a terrible anxiety mounting in her heart, she had watched the moon as it arced across the night sky, then slowly dissolved with the dawn.

When the sun's red disc rose up on the horizon, she knew her hopes, like the moon's azure glow, had faded at last. Sad and distressed, she bowed her head, and shed a silent tear of acceptance.

Magdalene gazed at the morning mist, surrendering herself to revery.

She was like this moon, she thought ... mistress of twilight and the night. And he, her lover, resembled the sun... master of dawn and the day. But they were condemned, by Nature, never to meet, and extinguish themselves in each other's light.

The doorway beckoned, with its curtained enclosure. Her head felt heavy, and her feet weighed with each step. Slowly, Magdalene entered their last refuge on the rooftop.

Alone, she laid herself down on the bed where, the night before, they had lain together. Her lids descended and darkness clouded her mind.

A jeering mob had gathered to greet the False Messiah. Screaming and jostling in the city's narrow streets, they cried, "Blasphemer!" and pelted him with stones.

Through Jerusalem's winding streets, the condemned man carried his fateful burden. The crossbeam balanced precariously on his shoulders, and his wrists bled from the bindings.

Two standard bearers led the procession, followed by a soldier with the *titulus*. In three languages it proclaimed the condemned man's crime. Following up the rear was a mounted Centurion, whose onerous task was to execute the criminal before nightfall.

As the mid-day sun beat down on their heads, the air grew thick with hate and blood-lust. He stumbled time and again, and his warders were obliged to whip him to give him strength.

Passing beyond Jerusalem's walls, they were met by a terrifying mob – cripples, lepers, demoniacs – which joined in the procession towards Golgotha.

Bones crunched under their feet and the stench of rotting corpses filled the air. Some of the crucified, still half-alive, called out for water while ravens pecked at their flesh.

On a hilltop scattered with skulls, a single terebinth rose high in the skies, its uppermost limbs forked in the shape of a *tau*. The procession stopped in its shadow, and the condemned man raised his face just long enough to recognize the *tau*'s hidden sign. This cross stood half-way between the *alpha* and *omega*. When the tree of death became the tree of life, the end would reach the beginning.

The whole of the night, the Iscariot had endured his mind's darkest imaginings. From Gethsemane, he had descended like a shadow into the Vale of Hinnom where, within its barren canyon, the lepers and living-dead rotted in their stony hollows.

The son of Kerioth tortured and tormented himself, his heart crying with bitter recrimination. He had performed his duty! But the disciple could not endure his foul deed nor bare to live with himself.

Gs Judas 58 How could it be, that he, <the only true disciple,> had betrayed the man whom he had loved most? He had condemned his twin and, in doing so, had killed *himself* – his better self, his only true self... the one that had saved him.

Jesus had shown the Iscariot his divine self, and had called him by a new name – Thomas – to recognize their hidden affinity. But now, all of that was over. His inner light had turned to darkness, and the shadowy other – Judas – had risen up in his flesh. He was the traitor, the hanged man.

In the distance, the Iscariot espied a redbud tree. And in a darkening flash of glory, he recognized where his steps had led him.

The flowers on its bough, once white and golden, had long-since turned to crimson. The redbud tree was blushing with shame, and the vines entwined in its branches were crying for his blood.

Before the condemned man could utter a cry of terror, his warders turned his crossbeam over and thrust him supine to the ground. Within seconds, two ropes had been thrown over the terebinth's forked branches, and bound to the *patibulum* at either end.

The guards pulled hard on the ropes; and the body, bound to the *patibulum*, rose high in the heavens. For a moment, it hovered, then sunk earthward as the crossbeam fell into the forks. From that ancient tree, the battered body twitched in cruel torment.

Mounting ladders, two soldiers <transfixed the body to the tree, 2 2Tr Seth 58:24
nailing it with four brass nails.> Suddenly, the heavens were rent with a terrifying cry, and the skies turned black.

Though it was still mid-day, the sun was obscured by a terrifying darkness, which lasted from noon till the third hour.

Miri opened her eyes, and was surprised to find that the day had already passed. But the strange darkness obscuring her chamber had an eerie, translucent glow.

Rising, she stepped once more onto the rooftop. All was bathed in a curious half-light. Looking up, she could not believe her eyes: in the darkened skies, the sun and moon had joined as one. She could see the full moon, like a blackened sphere, hovering over the sun.

Was she mistaken, or still dreaming a dream? Had the day not passed, but reached its zenith, only to be eclipsed?

Then – was it still not too late? Even now, at this dark hour, her lover might still be alive... Though condemned to a cruel and pitiless death, he was still suffering, still breathing, still clinging to his last moments of awareness. She had to go to him.

As painful and harrowing as it may be, she had to offer him comfort, kiss his wounds and caress his feet. By this simple gesture, she would acknowledge the sacrifice, and show him that his passion had not been suffered in vain.

At once, Magdalene set out for Golgotha. But, espying by chance the opening to her chamber, a terrible chill ran down her spine. She saw a figure, supine and dishevelled, lying on the bed. It was herself – afloat in phantasms, still deep in darkened dreams.

Could it be, that all this was a dream – even though she felt so awake? She paused, listening to her heart, and experienced that moment another strange epiphany. Why was there no sound in the acacia tree below? Where was the rustling of the wheat in the fields? Everything, in this eerie twilight hour, was bathed in absolute silence.

As she approached the curtained enclosure, she could see the rise and fall of her chest as Miri slept soundly. Not even her breathing made the slightest sound. The stillness was all-encompassing.

Her heart thumping mutely in her chest, Miri resolved not to wake herself. Let the dream continue – whether nightmare or revelation – if it would only lead her to her lover. She retreated from the doorway, and abandoned the house in Bethany.

The darkening heavens frightened her, and Golgotha rose before her like a wasteland. Not a soul was stirring in the hills, and the crows flew silently through the skies. When she rounded the final incline, soundlessly crunching the bones under her feet, she suddenly heard a frightful, deafening cry.

Resounding in the silence, the voice cried out: "I'm thirsty!"

II

James trembled, and the darkness in the heavens fell like a veil over his mind. He could not bare to stand at a distance and watch as his master slowly suffered unto death. The sight of Jesus, nailed to the tree, filled his heart with deep distress.

On a hill overlooking Golgotha, he fell to his knees and prayed that his lord might be spared this suffering. His tears fell onto the dry, barren rocks, and evaporated.

But then, in the darkening sky, he saw a strange light, glowing and ethereal. The light took on a distinctive shape, and acquired the form of a man. James took heart, gazed upward, and at once he knew that his wish had been granted.

1Ap Jas 31:2 <The Lord appeared before him. The apostle ceased praying and embraced him. He kissed him, saying, "Master, I have found you! I witnessed your sufferings, and oh! how I have suffered too!

Now you have acknowledged my compassion...>"

For a long time, the saviour held James in his embrace. Then he released him, saying:

"<Many times have I said to the apostles, and to you alone Ap Jas 8:27
James, 'Be saved!' In this way, I commanded you to follow me.>"

James lowered his face, which was still wet with tears.

"But why must our salvation come about in this way – by suffering?"

Christ nodded gravely.

"<I came down so that I might dwell with you, and you, in turn, Ap Jas 8:37
might dwell with me. I descended, and suffered tribulation, so that
my crown would be granted in saving you.>"

"But Lord," he said, "why did you come down to dwell in the Nazarene? Why did you choose Jesus for this task?"

Christ showed forth his palms, which bore the imprints of the nail wounds. Bowing his head, he said:

"<I am the one who was sent down. And I descended into a L Pt Ph 136:16
mortal frame for those seeds which had fallen away. When I spoke
to him who belongs to me, he hearkened to me, just as you have
hearkened to me today.>"

James thought of the rabbi, and how his master, like a servant, had willingly answered the Messiah's calling.

"But my heart remains troubled. Can't Jesus be spared this suffering?"

Slowly, Christ shook his head.

"The ways of the Messiah are mysterious indeed, <for his unity Acts Jn 91
has many faces.> There are others who will gaze upon the cross
below and perceive it differently. <Therefore, I say to you – be Ap Jas 8:27
sober, and do not be deceived!> The others <will say of him that Melch 5:1
he is not of the flesh – though he is of the flesh. And that he did not
suffer – though he suffered greatly...>"

Tears rose to the disciple's eyes. His compassion for his master moved him to say:

"Then tell me – you who are full with knowledge and great with power – why must the Archons triumph in this way?"

"The Archons have not triumphed... <Pride has been put to Silv 110:29
shame – through humility. The strong and boastful have been
overcome – through weakness. I have refused every exultation, so
that, in God's name, humility will be praised.>"

Christ looked at the sorrowful man before him and said:

"Thus, <I put on humanity.> <For your sakes, I placed myself Silv 111:4

Ap Jas 13:23 under this curse – so that you might be saved.> I submitted myself
1Ap Jas 29:9 to the Archons <to complete my destiny here on earth – and bring
about your redemption.>"

"And what is our redemption? How are we to be saved?"

"By knowingly and willingly embracing your death, as a
Ap Jas 5:33 sacrifice. <Remember my cross and my death, and you too will
live! None will be saved unless they believe in my cross. But those who have believed in my cross, theirs will be the kingdom of God. Therefore, become seekers after death – for the kingdom belongs to those who have put themselves to death.>"

James fell to his knees in deep surrender.

"Then what would you have us do, to become worthy of your sacrifice?"

The saviour gazed at the sad disciple and said:

Ap Jas13:21 "<Be to yourselves as I myself am to you.>"

1Ap Jas 32:23 <When James heard these things, he wiped the tears from his
eyes,> for at last he had understood.

"This is the mystery. From the moment he was condemned, your master held his tongue, and endured his suffering. Only in this way shall the mystery be preserved. Thus, I charge you also to suffer these things, and not open your mouth.

Ap Jas 13:37 "<I have revealed myself to you alone, James; the others have
1Ap Jas 36:13 not known me.> Thus, <guard the secret within you, and remain
silent.>"

As Christ departed, James fell to his knees, and acknowledged the mystery that had been given to him: that in suffering, he would find his final joy, and that, in death, he would return to eternal life.

III

For a prolonged moment, the Iscariot admired the redbud tree, and the vine that hung loosely from its branches. Then, the sky turned dark, and the apostle knew his hour had arrived. He could see it in the heavens – how the sun had hid its face. It could no longer bare to look down on his shameful deed.

Thomas had sacrificed his twin and, in doing so, had murdered himself. He had betrayed all that was good and true within himself. Now, all that was left was to finish off the deed – complete the sacrifice and make himself a true reflection of his dying saviour.

Without a moment's hesitation, he mounted the rocks at the base of the tree and knotted the vine into a noose. Slipping it round his neck, he tightened the notch.

The blackbirds screeched and frightened crows took flight as the Iscariot flung himself from rock, screaming one word only:

"Eleutheros!"

Then he knew... He was free.

Peter opened and closed his eyes, unable to accept the vision on the distant hill. There, in the shadowy twilight, his saviour hung upon the terebinth. The body, impaled by hammer and nail, writhed crucified, while the crowd below cursed him without mercy.

The Bethsaidean's faith was broken, his heart had been torn to shreds. Three times over the course of this night, he'd denied the master. The cock's crow at daybreak had awakened him, as if, from a delirious nightmare.

But *when* had he left Gethsemane? And *how* had he reached Golgotha? He no longer knew where he was or how he'd come here. Had he wandered in a daze, like a man drunk and delirious?

His eyes filled with tears, and he buried his face in his hands.

But a distant voice called to him, reminding him: 'Before this night is over, you will deny me three times. And before the next
night has passed, *I* will <reprove *you* three times> for your sore lack Ap Pt 72:2
of faith...'

When the Bethsaidean opened his eyes, he saw the saviour, hovering above him. Glowing and resplendent, the Christ smiled and said: "Have you forgotten? Your greatest test still awaits you..."

Peter smiled and cried at the same time. Then he shook himself, as if, trying to rouse himself from his profound slumber. Was this really the Messiah? Or was he still asleep in the garden of Gethsemane?

"All this time," the saviour said, "<your heart was drunk and Ap Jas 3:9
delirious. Do you not wish to become sober?>"

Wiping the tears from his eyes, Peter nodded to the heavenly apparition.

"<Henceforth, waking or sleeping, remember that you have Ap Jas 3:11
seen the Son of Man, and spoken with him in person.>"

Trembling, Peter opened his mouth:

"If you are the saviour, then who is the one I see over there, crucified and condemned?"

"Approach him and see for yourself..."

Overcome by fear, the apostle backed away.

"Peter! Must I reprove you already for your lack of faith? Have no fear and do as I say. Approach!"

Terrified, the Bethsaidean stepped forward, then threaded his way through the crowd. Amazingly, none of them turned to acknowledge him. It was as if he were invisible.

"Do you remember, on Gennesaret's shores, I taught you to open your eyes – and *see*?"

Slowly, the apostle nodded his head.

Ap Pt 73:4 "<Now, open your ears, and *hear* what the people are saying!>"

Though the angry mob was hurling insults, Peter listened to the voices hidden in their speech.

Ap Pt 73:4 "<They are praising you...>"

The saviour nodded and said:

Ap Pt 73:14 "<They are telling you this in a mystery. Listen, and guard its secret.>"

Solemnly, Peter accepted. But the effect was eerie: the crowds, even the evil and demon-possessed, were baring their teeth and glaring, but from their mouths came voices of praise.

"Now, turn your eyes once more to the cross, and look upon it *with faith*. Tell me what you see..."

Mustering all his courage, Peter re-focused his eyes and gazed upon the cross. For a moment, his breathing stopped, and his mind throbbed with wonder.

He saw two trees, and two Messiahs nailed upon their branches. One had bowed his head in humiliation. But the other was looking skyward and laughing.

Ap Pt 81:3 "<Lord, what do I see? Is that you yourself whose hands and feet are fixed to the tree – or some other? And who is the other one, glad and laughing, on the second tree?"

The saviour said, "He whom you see, glad and laughing, is the living Jesus. But the other, whose hands and feet are fixed with nails – he is the substitute, who came as an imitator. Now, look at him and look at me."

Suddenly, Peter lost heart. "Lord, let us flee from this place!>"

Ap Pt 80:31 "I have told you – be strong, <and *stand* in their midst. Do not surrender to fear!> This is the second time I've had to rebuke you..."

Trembling, the apostle acknowledged his cowardice. Once more, he turned to gaze at the incredible sight of the laughing saviour and the substitute.

Acts Jn 96 "<I have deceived the others," Christ explained, "so I would

not be deceived by them.> Since the beginning, the Archons have deceived man. And so, to show up their ignorance, *I have deceived*
them, by substituting one Messiah for the other. <The death they 2Tr Seth 55:14
think *I* am suffering, *they* now suffer in their blindness and error. Thus, they've brought their own judgement upon themselves. In their blindness, they have nailed *their own man* to the cross. They thought they were punishing me, but someone else has worn the crown of thorns and borne the cross to Golgotha. He is drinking the bitter gall and vinegar, while I stand apart, laughing at their ignorance.>"

Peter's mind was reeling.

"Then who? ...who is suffering on the cross?"

Christ shook his head.

"Have you no faith? Must I rebuke you a third time? He who is suffering on the cross is the one who came in my likeness – the
False Messiah... Yaltabaoth's Son. This is not the first time <I eluded Tri Prot 40:22
the Archons. When I first descended into the world, I clothed myself +Tri Prot 49:7
as the Archigenetor's Son. And the Archons let me pass, thinking I was their Messiah.> Now, I have deceived them by substituting the
True Messiah with the False. <Thus, they have put to shame, not *my* Ap Pt 82:1
servant, but the son of *their* glory.>"

Peter gazed at the terebinth tree and shook his head, perceiving the strange justice of it all. In Eden, Yaltabaoth had tempted Man
with <the Tree of *his* Life, offering the darkness and deception that Ap Jn 21:30
thrived in its leaves.> Now, Yaltabaoth's Son had made restitution, by hanging on the Tree of Death.

"Then, what of the True Messiah?" Peter wondered.

"The one you see on the second tree is <the living saviour, Ap Pt 82:27
whom they have seized and released. He gazes upon those who did him violence – and laughs at their ignorance and blindness.>"

"Then Jesus..?" The disciple trembled in anticipation.

"<I have borne him far from the cursed wood, and will establish Tri Prot 50:12
him in the dwelling places of the Parent.>"

Peter could hardly believe the joyful mystery that had entered his ears.

"The master has not suffered! And now, he has been released from death!"

Christ nodded.

"<These mysteries have been revealed to you alone.> The Ap Pt 73:14
others, gazing upon the cross, perceive it differently. <Those who Ap Pt 74:10
come after you will cleave to the name of a dead man, and propagate

Ap Pt 73:14 a falsehood.> In due time, the truth will be revealed. But for now, <I charge you to guard this as a mystery, and *not* reveal it to the sons of this age.>"

Peter stood back and marvelled at the mysterious ways of the saviour. As Christ departed, a voice remained, saying:

Tri Prot 41:2 "<This is the ineffable mystery: that I have loosed from you every bond, and broke the chains of the underworld. I have smashed the bars, breached the gates, and thrown down the high walls of darkness. Behold: the Sons of Light shall be released from their chains, and ascend to the place where they were from the beginning!>"

IV

Thomas stood, his eyes wide with wonder, and stared at the redbud tree. A strange wind blew, and the branches creaked, heavy with the weight of the hanged man who hovered above him.

At first the Iscariot could not believe his eyes. But now, he knew for certain. Judas, his shadowy brother, had bowed his head, and surrendered himself to death. Thomas was free.

The darkness that had entered his soul, making him the betrayer, had departed at the last hour.

As the body swung in the wind, Thomas gazed, with fear and fascination, into his own dark and lifeless features. It was over.

In the life he had lived before, Thomas had been torn by doubt, a man divided and double-minded. Now, in the life that was left to him, he would *know* with certainty, with a single mind. The saviour was not mistaken: Thomas *was* the twin, and the time of restitution had come. Now, all would be as it had been before: single, luminous, one.

The Iscariot departed, leaving the vale of Hinnom and the hanged man far behind. Feeling himself full, made one and complete, Thomas smiled, turned, and set his steps to the east.

Acts Jn 97 From Gethsemane <the apostles had fled in all directions, like men gone astray or dazed with sleep. But John, when he saw the saviour suffering, could not bear the sight of it, and had ascended the Mount of Olives,> to the place where he had seen the Lord before in a vision.

Acts Jn 97 <He found shelter in a cave, and collapsed in tears of sorrow. It was now past mid-day, but darkness still reigned over the earth.>

Then, the darkness in John's cavern dispersed, and he saw <the Acts Jn 97
Lord standing in the middle of the hollow, illuminating it.>

The Lord gazed upon his beloved disciple and said:

"John, <I put it into your mind to come here, so you alone could Acts Jn 97
hear these words.>"

The disciple bowed his head in reverence.

"<To the multitude below in Jerusalem, I am being crucified. Acts Jn 97
They have given me gall and vinegar, and have pierced my flesh with their lances. But here I am, speaking to you. Hear then, what I have to tell you,> and open your mind to all which you will see."

Having said this, the Lord transformed in appearance, becoming an effulgence of light which filled the entire cavern. Its radiance dazzled the disciple's eyes, but still he could see, within the watery phosphorescence, a luminous core.

From that centre, a crucifix flared in four directions, creating a blazing cross. Then, the light expanded a second time, and a multitude of sparks danced in circles, like a flickering halo round the cross.

The vision was overwhelming. <Though the multitude moving Acts Jn 98
round the cross varied in size and shape, the cross itself remained singular, still and unified.>

<Above the cross John beheld the Lord, not in appearance, but Acts Jn 98
in voice only – a Voice full of divine kindness.

The Voice said:

"John, I have need of one who hears, for what I say needs to be heard.>"

The disciple nodded and said, "I am listening."

<This cross of light has a name: it is the Word.>" Acts Jn 101

John gazed upon the Word and bore witness to its light.

"<I have cast off my humanity, so you might see me as the Acts Jn 101
Word, and not only as a man who has suffered.>"

John began to understand. <In the beginning, the light had Jn 1:1 + Jn 1:9
come into the world, and the Word had become flesh.> Now, he was + Jn 1:14
seeing the Word as it truly was, fleshless and luminous...

The Voice above the shimmering cross said:

"<This luminous cross is called by many names: sometimes Acts Jn 98
Jesus, sometimes Christ; sometimes resurrection, sometimes life.>

"<Being a unity, this cross stands at the place where the all Acts Jn 99
flowed forth. And through the Word, it will join them all once more,
in unity.> <The multitude that surround the cross, though truly one, Acts Jn 100
are those who have remained below. They have not yet been fully

comprehended, and so they remain in a multitude of forms.>"

The disciple gazed at the flickering halo round the cross, and understood that he himself, and all those who remained apart from the One, were contained in its circle.

Acts Jn 100 "<But those who have risen, are *in* the cross, and have one form
only. All of those who have listened to my voice, and heard me, shall become one with me.>"

John remembered the dance at Golgotha, and how the disciples, though separate in the circle, had also seen themselves in the centre, as one with the Nazarene.

Acts Jn 100 "<If you do truly hear me, then you shall be as I am.> <You will
Acts Jn 100 no longer be as you are now, but above yourself, as I am.>"

"But Lord," John asked, "what of those who have not truly seen you or heard you? Will they remain below?"

Acts Jn 98 "<In truth, this cross is also the limit that separates those above
from those below – raising up the immovable who are at rest, and
Acts Jn 98 leaving behind those distracted and gone astray.> <They belong to
Acts Jn 100 the Archons, with their many powers and demons.> <But do not
Acts Jn 100 concern yourselves with those who are outside the mystery.> <As
long as you do not call yourself mine, I am not that which I am.>"

John thought of the crowds below at Golgotha, who were seeing the Messiah on the cross, but did not *see*, in truth, *who* was crucified.

The disciple continued to gaze upon the cross of light, and the Voice answered his thoughts.

Acts Jn 99 "<This luminous cross is not the cross of wood, which you will
see once you descend from here. And I am not the one who is on the
cross. Those who see me there, do not see me *as I am*. They describe
Acts Jn 101 me in a way that is not worthy of me.> <You will hear that I was
pierced, yet I was not struck; that blood flowed from me, yet it did not flow. You will hear that I suffered – yet I did not suffer.>"

The Voice continued:

Acts Jn 101 "<But, you will hear also that I did *not* suffer – yet I *did*
suffer...>"

John's mind could not encompass the mystery. *Who* hung upon the cross? Who *was* he? And *was he suffering?*

Acts Jn 101 "<Who I am, only I know. I showed my passion unto you and
the others – in the dance – but it remained a mystery.>

Acts Jn 101 "<If one knows how to suffer, then one needn't truly suffer.
Thus, learn to suffer, and you will not suffer. What you do not know,
Acts Jn 103 I have shown you.> <As the Word, I am with you, and suffer with

you always, in compassion.>"

John looked upon the cross. For a moment, he saw himself there, crucified in the light. At last he had understood. It was just as the saviour had said during their dance: 'I am the mirror to you who recognize me'.

As the vision of the luminous cross began to fade into pure undifferentiated light, John heard the Voice say:

"Thus, look upon this cross, hear my Voice, and know that,
<in me is the piercing of the Word, the bleeding of the Word – the Acts Jn 101
nailing, suffering and death of the Word!>"

The light withdrew, and John was left standing in the cavern's darkness.

He descended from the Mount of Olives, knowing that <the Acts Jn 102
Lord had shown himself to accomplish their salvation. He had
shown himself symbolically,> and in the form of an image.

<But all of this, in its great mystery, could neither be heard Acts Jn 93
nor uttered.> It had to be seen, known, and recognized. Thus <John Acts Jn 93
resolved to remain silent.>

V

Shrouded in darkness, suffering in silence, Magdalene slowly descended the hill.

Images passed before her eyes, as if, in a dream. She saw Philip, his head gently bowed, as he comforted Arsinoe, Mariam and the Virgin. The three women were leaning together, rocking back and forth, nodding their heads in awed acknowledgement of the sacrifice.

Wordlessly, Arsinoe turned and stared at Miri. Her face was bathed in horror and wonder. Then, she said something, but the silence left her words unheard.

Arsinoe turned her face to the cross, and Miri mutely followed her gaze.

Jesus hung upon the cross, his chest swelling as he gasped for air through cracked white lips. Again he pushed forth the cry, "I'm thirsty!" and his words echoed in the resounding stillness.

He was staring into the heavens, delirious with pain. But, his eyes had grown wide with wonder. He seemed to be seeking some mysterious revelation or vision. His eyebrows arched into the crown, and their thorns pushed deeper into his flesh.

If only her tears could quench his thirst and their salt give him strength to endure this suffering...

Miri approached the tree, bowed her head, and caressed his feet. She could still smell, amid the vinegar and gall, a slight ambrosial scent – the nard with which she had anointed him last night. But now, bronze nails pierced his feet, and blood dripped into her hands.

Crying aloud, she mingled her tears with his blood, tasting their salt on her lips. She could not bare to endure his suffering in silence.

Stepping back, she rose her head and turned her gaze upon the man of sorrows. *Look at me*, she prayed in the silence, *and see that I have acknowledged your sacrifice. I surrender my will, and share in your suffering. Acknowledge it!*

The Messiah lowered his head to his chest, and in a whisper that only she could hear, he said: *"It is finished..."*

Then, he closed his eyes, as if, in sleep.

Her heart exploded in her chest, and she felt that she had died with him.

Falling to her knees, Miri shuddered and collapsed...

Then, the last light of the mid-day sun was entirely eclipsed by the moon. All was obscured by darkness.

For a prolonged moment, Miri hovered in that darkness, uncertain if she were rising or falling. A thousand memories assailed her.

She became a nine-year old child, immersed in a watery expanse. The dark sea caressed her, a glowing mixture of liquid luminescence. Floating weightless on Gennesaret's surface, she waited, her heart afire. And, a moment later, he was beside her, surfacing from the sea and embracing her. They laughed wildly with childish joy.

More images filed past, and they found themselves on the rooftop of Magdala. Or was it Bethany? *"My sister, my bride..."* he whispered, still a young child. Then, she removed her linen vestment, and the moonlight illumined her nakedness. He in turn, removed his white tunic, and now they embraced – unafraid, unashamed.

In the darkness of their curtained enclosure, she smelled the sweet odour of his skin, an invigorating mixture of tannin, oak and must. And her ears, newly opened, heard a rich variety of sounds: the night birds in the acacia tree, and the rustling of the wheat in the distant fields. The silence had dispersed, and now she knew for certain: they were on the rooftop of Bethany, ensconced in their final refuge: the Bridal Chamber.

His eyes sparkled in the darkness, and a compassionate smile illuminated his face. She smelled the vinegar on his skin, and felt the welts upon his shoulders. But none of that mattered any more.

"My cousin, my consort," he whispered, "the Bridal Chamber awaits." Then, he closed his eyes, and moved his face towards hers. Willingly, she consented to his kiss.

The moment their lips touched, the darkness dispersed. Joining as one, they spun in circles, until she no longer felt herself in her flesh. This, she knew in her heart, is the hidden, holy union, the merging of man and woman. They had confirmed their love with this seal, the Fifth and final Seal.

Singly, they rose up, inseparable, the two-as-one. She had become him, and he was she. They were the unity, the *syzygy*, the unfallen Adam and Eve. In Christ, Sophia now saw her aspect; in Wisdom, the Word had been made complete.

Five dark garments fell from their flesh, seven deceptive passions fell like veils from their souls. The Archons, rendered powerless by their passage, fell mutely at their feet. Rising to the highest heavens, they entered the place of the light.

The Middle dissolved; the boundaries broke, and all the aeons fused. As the depths of the abyss rose up, the darkness was filled with light.

And the material world – once made by mistake – was now made faultless, perfect, and true. The world was created anew.

In nakedness and knowing, Adam gazed upon Eve. Unashamed, their eyes newly opened, they embraced, recognizing that in their union lay love. The end had reached the beginning.

It was like something that had never been.

AFTERWORD

In my presentation of Gnosticism and the life of the Gnostic Christ, I have had to make certain creative decisions which the attentive reader might call into question. Although it was never my intention to impose my own interpretation upon Gnosticism, much of this novel bears, *per force*, the imprint of the author's personality. Thus it is now my intention to lay forth, as clearly as possible, those features of the story which have resulted from my own reading of the Gnostic myth.

As a student of Northrop Frye, I have learned to treat the Bible, with its disparate books, as a single literary whole. In this same spirit, the Nag Hammadi Library and its related documents, in all their diversity, have been treated as a unity. Certainly, alternative views exist among the different authors and their texts, but this should not blind us to their deeper spiritual kinship. And it was remarkable for me to discover, during the elaboration of this novel, the extent to which a passage from one writer could illuminate an obscure passage from another.

This hermeneutic has guided me in my reading of the original texts. I have also had recourse to secondary sources, and have profited much from the writings of Giovanni Filoramo, Kurt Rudolf, John D. Turner, Alastair Logan, Bentley Layton, Gilles Quispel, Jean-Marie Sevrin, Elaine Pagels, Robert McL. Wilson, George MacRae, James M. Robinson and Hans Jonas – to name but a few. (If the reader is searching for an intelligent introduction to Gnosticism, I would recommend Giovanni Filoramo's *A History of Gnosticism* and Kurt Rudolf's *Gnosis*). I would also like to acknowledge Dr. Stephan Hoeller and *The Gnosis Archive* at *www.gnosis.org* for disseminating a broader comprehension of Gnosticism in our own times.

But, I have written a novel, not a doctoral dissertation. And so, the following notes should illuminate some aspects of my own creative rendition of the Gnostic myth.

DIDYMOS JUDAS THOMAS

It was entirely my own decision to combine the apostles Judas and Thomas into one person, and this does not reflect any known Gnostic belief. It was inspired by the prologue from *The Gospel of*
Gs Thom 32:10 *Thomas*, which states: *"These are the secret sayings which the living Jesus spoke and which Didymos Judas Thomas wrote down."*

Of the three names given, only Judas is a proper name, while *didymos* and *tauma* (Thomas) are epithets meaning *the twin* in Greek and Aramaic. Thus, the tripartite name should really be rendered: *the twin* Judas *the twin.*

Although a strong tradition has grown around Thomas 'the doubting apostle', I have chosen to remain true to the Gnostic text and have treated 'Thomas' as Judas' nickname, just as 'Didymos'
Gs Egypt 69:11 later becomes his spiritual name (acquiring a hidden spiritual name during baptism was common practice in Gnostic circles). Thus, in my novel, the character remains *the twin* Judas *the twin.*

The Book of Thomas the Contender also introduces the apostle
Th Cont 138:2 as *"Judas Thomas"* and in their dialogue, the saviour calls him: *"my*
Th Cont 138:8 *twin and true companion."* In Gnosticism, 'twinship' became an important image of salvation, since the Gnostic recognized himself in Christ and Christ in himself. *The Acts of John* made good use of
Acts Jn 95 this 'mirror' motif, so that Christ says: *"I am a mirror to you who see me."* Throughout the novel, I have called upon these motifs of mirroring and twinship.

Due to his doubts concerning Christ's bodily resurrection, the apostle Thomas has become known as 'doubting Thomas'. In many languages (including English and ancient Greek), the word *doubt* is etymologically related to *double* – such as 'to be in two minds' about something. In my novel, Thomas' doubt expands to *double-mindedness*, and so the apostle alternately identifies himself (Thomas) with Jesus or dissociates himself (Judas) from him.

This evolution of the character Judas-Thomas came about naturally over the course of writing. In order to identify this two-sided character in a neutral manner, I chose the epithet 'the Iscariot' or 'the son of Kerioth'. Such epithets, which were common in the early Christian era, became a great aid to me as a writer.

The gospel poses great challenges for the modern author. Of the twelve apostles, two are named Simon, two are named James, and two are named Judas. Of the woman around Jesus, at least four are named Mary, and two are named Salome. To make matters worse, Simon becomes Peter, and Levi becomes Matthew.

I have tried to make some sense of this situation by calling Simon-Peter either Cephas or 'the Bethsaidean' until Jesus finally calls him Peter. Meanwhile, the other Simon is called 'the Zealot'. The two named James, by tradition, are distinguished as 'the greater' and 'the lesser', which I have rendered as 'the elder' and 'the younger'. The two named Judas, also by tradition, are distinguished as Judas and Jude.

Of the numerous women named Mary, I've reserved that name for Jesus' mother by referring to Mary Magdalene as Miri or Magdalene, and to Mary the sister of Martha as Mariam or 'the Bethanite'.

ARSINOE

It is mentioned in the canonical gospels that Jesus had four Mt 13:55, Mk 6:3
brothers and an indeterminate number of sisters. The brothers were named James, Joses, Jude and Simon while the sisters were left unidentified. The existence of Jesus' siblings has caused some difficulties, since it is difficult to reconcile this situation with the dogma of Mary's virginity.

For the Gnostics, virginity was not so much a dogma as an image. Nevertheless, some Gnostic writers struggled with the problem, to
the extent that Jesus' brother James was called his *"step-brother"* 2Ap Jas 50:23
and said to be the son of Theuda and Mary (presumably another
Mary), while another text claims that James was *"not Jesus' brother* 1 Ap Jas 24:15
materially."

Following this tradition, I have assumed that Theuda is the
brother of the Virgin Mary, and that he is married to 'the other Mary' Mt 27:55
mentioned in the canonical gospels. Thus James, Joses, Jude, Simon Mk 15:47 Mk 16:1
and their sisters become 'cousins' of Jesus by blood. But, living Lk 24:10
together under one roof, they were also his 'brothers and sisters' in Jn 19:25
the eyes of the villagers.

In my novel, Jesus has three 'sisters': Anna, Athalia and Arsinoe. Of these, only Arsinoe elects to follow her elder brother, along with her younger brothers James and Jude. I decided on the name Arsinoe from *The First Apocryphon of James*, where the Lord
says to James: *"When you speak these words of this [perception],* 1Ap Jas 40:22
encourage these [four]: Salome and Mariam [and Martha and Arsinoe]." It was entirely my own decision to make Arsinoe silent

until the Gnostic doctrine of 'secret names' was revealed (p. 261).

According to the Gnostic texts, Jesus *had* female disciples. In
1Ap Jas 38:15 *The First Apocalypse of James*, James asks the Lord, *"Who are the [seven] women who have [been] your disciples?"* Unfortunately, the text becomes extremely fragmentary, but the Lord's answer (given above) mentions Salome, Mariam, Martha and Arsinoe. For the novel, I have the Virgin Mary, Mary Magdalene, Arsinoe, Mariam and Martha, Susanna and Joanna as the seven female disciples.

Since Judas and Thomas were combined into one disciple, that left me with a total of eleven male disciples. This number was actually quite convenient. When the Nazarene has a vision (p. 210) of his twelve disciples (the eleven men, plus Mary Magdalene), they correspond to the twelve Upper Aeons. This parallel was suggested
Ap Jn 8:1 to me by the Twelve Aeons in *The Apocryphon of John* and the
Unt MS twelve apostles described in *The Untitled Text* in the Bruce Codex.

Ap Jn 8:20 According to *The Apocryphon of John*, Wisdom (Sophia) is the twelfth aeon. Since Sophia naturally corresponds with Magdalene, this allowed me to see her as the twelfth disciple, while the remaining eleven male disciples correspond to the other eleven aeons. The identification of Peter, Andrew, James and John with the Four Lights is, as far as I know, my own invention.

In certain Gnostic texts, the Upper Aeons expand from twelve to thirty to even three hundred and sixty aeons. As well, in *The Gospel
Gs Egypt 53:1 of the Egyptians*, all the angels and powers in the Upper Aeons have consorts, thus doubling their number. By following *The Apocryphon of John*, where the twelve aeons have no consorts, I have avoided unnecessary complexity and preserved the symmetry between aeons and apostles.

THE ROOTS OF GNOSTICISM

There are various types or 'schools' of Gnosticism, which may be identified with certain places or founding figures. These schools also lead us to questions concerning the roots and sources of Gnosticism. Disentangling these roots, with their different branches and fruits, is a fascinating through extremely difficult process.

Through the three wise men in the Cave of Darkness, I have delved into the difficult question of the roots of Gnosticism. The characters of Marsanes, Enoch and Zostrianos show these roots to be Greek, Hebrew and Persian. For this interpretation, I am indebted to Hans Jonas. I have no doubt that the question is more complex (including Babylonian and Hermetic sources, while questioning the Iranian hypothesis), but I did not want to burden my reader with such a complicated issue.

The different branches or schools of Gnosticism is another thorny question. In my novel, I have tried to give equal emphasis to *all* types: Sethian, Valentinian, Hermetic, etc. But, I have *not* made their differences explicit, since my task has been to present Gnosticism as a many-facetted unity.

I would like to point out here that the myth of Simon Magus and his companion Helena, as described by Irenaeus and Hippolytus, has served me as a model for the relationship between Jesus and Magdalene. As Gnostic saviours, the parallels between Simon Magus and Jesus Christ are too numerous to mention.

Irenaeus Adversus Haereses Bk 1 Ch 23

Hippolytus Refutatio Omnium Haeresium §7-20

But, it is worth noting that Helena and Magdalene also reveal numerous parallels: both are said to be prostitutes, both are called 'the Lost Sheep', both are identified with the fallen Wisdom (or *Ennoia*). And so, in both myths, the saviour descends in order to save this incarnation of the fallen Wisdom.

This explains why, in my novel, Magdalene makes the journey to Tyre (the city where Helena was said to be 'ransomed as a prostitute'). This journey of Salome and Magdalene allowed me to introduce Phoenician beliefs into a Gnostic-Christian narrative. The Phoenicians, it must be remembered, were the descendants of the Canaanites, and preserved many of the Canaanite beliefs which the Hebrews (who settled in 'the Promised Land' of the Canaanites) ultimately rejected.

Such beliefs, involving the Goddess of fertility and her dying/rising consort, would have persisted in Israel, even into the early Christian period – though perhaps as a substratum of archaic customs. For the novel, Salome's and Magdalene's preservation of these archaic customs allows them to serve as foils to the very ascetic, anti-worldly stance of the Gnostic Baptist and Saviour.

Since the Gnostics blamed Sophia for the creation of the material world, their writers used the image of 'the female' in a negative sense. And certainly, in the larger scope of things, they re-evaluated the Goddess of fertility in extremely *negative* terms.

But this should not blind us to several important points. First of all that, through androgyny, the Gnostics preserved a feminine aspect (Barbelo the Mother) *within* the divinity, while also giving the saviour a feminine aspect (Sophia as Christ's consort). Second, that Mary Magdalene, as a female disciple, played an important role in many Gnostic texts. And third, that the example of female discipleship in Jesus' inner circle was followed in practice by many women, some of whom became prominent members in the Gnostic communities.

THE TRINITY

The Gnostics were obsessed by the number three: three Adams, three types of men, three *parousias*, three descents of the saviour. Even their sacred texts were divided in three: *The Tripartite Tractate*, *The Trimorphic Protennoia*, *The Three Steles of Seth*. (*The Hidden Passion* is also presented in three parts). It should not surprise us, therefore, that the Gnostics had a divine trinity.

Ap Jn 9:10 Gs Egypt 41:7 Tri Prot 37:22

Several texts name this trinity as the Father, Mother and Son. It is clear that these three, though separate, are different aspects of the same divine unity. The Gnostic cosmology is founded on the principle that the One expanded into the many with no loss of its unity.

But discrepancies arise between the various texts when this trinity is described in images. For the novel, I refer to the Father as the Silence, the Mother as the Voice, and the Son as the Word. I did this because texts such as *The Gospel of the Egyptians* and *The Untitled Text* in the Bruce Codex refer to the Father as the Silence. And, almost all texts are agreed that the Son is the Word. But the case of the Mother is different.

In *The Trimorphic Protennoia*, the trinity is described in images and, here, the Father is the Voice, the Mother is Speech, and the Son is the Word. Meanwhile, in the Valentinian system, the first female principle (or Mother) is the Silence.

In order to make my presentation of the Gnostic trinity consistent, I decided on the Father as the Silence, the Mother as the Voice, and the Son as the Word. But, I should make it clear here that I have used quotations from *The Trimorphic Protennoia* that are out of context, in the sense that the Voice in this text refers to the Father, but I have used it to refer to the Mother.

Another complication arises when the trinity is described through Aristotle's notion of Thought Thinking Itself. This form of the trinity enters Gnosticism through Simon Magus, as described by Hippolytus. I decided to use it in the novel since it is, in my mind, the clearest example of how the One expanded into the many with no loss of unity.

Hippolytus Refutatio Omnium Haeresium §18

In my novel, the Father is identified with *Nous*, as 'the mind' (or 'thinking' – *noesis*), while the Mother is identified with *Ennoia,* as 'the thought' (or 'of thought' – *noeseos*). Finally, the Son is the reflection, when the mind not only has a thought, but a thought *of itself* (*noesis noeseos noesis* - literally, 'thinking a thought of itself thinking', which is usually rendered more simply as: 'thought thinking itself').

The dyad of *Nous-Ennoia* is mentioned in several Gnostic texts. Soph JC 9[6]:3
But, I wish to point out here that in some Gnostic texts (e.g. Ap Jn Norea 27:11
7:1), the identity of *Nous* is unclear. Although the Mother is clearly Ap Jn 4:2
identified with *Ennoia*, sometimes it is *the Son* rather than the Father who is identified with *Nous*. However, the Son here may be *Nous,* in the sense of an image or reflection of the Father, as the original *Nous*.

THE FIVE SEALS

The Gnostic rite which has been open to the greatest variety of interpretations is the rite of the Five Seals. Some commentators have described this as a five-fold immersion in holy water; others as a baptism in a purely visionary as opposed to ritual sense.

I decided to use a crucial passage from *The Gospel of Philip* as my starting point: *"The Lord [did] everything in a mystery, a* Gs Phil 67:27
baptism and a chrism and a eucharist and a redemption and a bridal chamber."

The Gospel of Philip is the most informative text we have concerning Gnostic sacraments. Nevertheless, the huge number of seams in the text, and the general disorder of its passages, have left scholars with a perplexing puzzle. I allude to this in my novel when Philip appears in Cana with a packet of little cards on which he has written his notes. Like the gospel that bears his name, Philip gleefully shuffles these passages at random... (p. 320).

Still, *The Gospel of Philip* provides us with valuable information concerning the rites of baptism, chrism and the eucharist (which become, for me, the First, Second and Fourth Seals). The problem begins when we begin to interpret the redemption and the Bridal Chamber (which I call the Third and Fifth Seals).

Through a close reading of *The Gospel of Philip*, the sacrament of redemption gradually emerges as a rite performed in close conjunction with the other rites: *"Baptism includes the resurrection* Gs Phil 69:25
[and the] redemption; the redemption (takes place) in the bridal

chamber." From this passage, I decided to link the rite of redemption with the baptism and the resurrection. The resurrection, as *The Gospel of Philip* states, is a visionary ascent through the aeons. (See Gs Phil 56:18, 67:15, as well as Allog, Ap Paul, Gs Magd for examples of visionary ascents).

Meanwhile, another valuable text for Gnostic sacraments, *The Gospel of the Egyptians*, speaks of *"They who are worthy of (the) invocation, the renunciations of the five seals in the spring-baptism."* From this passage, I decided to link the redemption with the preliminary rites of the baptism, involving 'the renunciation' of the demons and 'the invocation' of the angels.

Gs Egypt 66:2

In the end, the redemption or Third Seal becomes a rite of *naming*, in which the demons and angels are named ('renounced', 'invoked') before the baptism, and afterwards they are named again in a visionary ascent through the aeons ('the resurrection').

Ironically, the seal which is mentioned the most, and yet, remains the most vague – is the Fifth Seal, the Bridal Chamber. At the expense of taxing the reader's attention, I have included in *The Hidden Passion* almost all the passages from the Gnostic and heresiological texts that mention the Bridal Chamber. These, it turns out, are extremely vague and often contradictory.

Interestingly, the vast majority which describe the Bridal Chamber as a vow of abstinence come from the Nag Hammadi corpus, while those that see it as a libertine 'love-feast' come from the accounts of the heresiologists. Of the original Gnostic texts, only *The Gospel of Judas* condemns abstinence (*"those who abstain, and the rest of the people of pollution and lawlessness and error..."*) while the vast majority support it. *The Pistis Sophia* goes so far as to condemn libertines (ch 147).

Gs Judas 40

To reflect this, I have represented both versions through the two chambers Magdalene enters: asceticism on the right, libertinism on the left. The final chamber, at the end of the hallway, offers 'a middle path' which actually has a fair amount of evidence to support it. And, I would like to believe that this was the practice current among many Gnostics, based on a sacramental interpretation of the *syzygy* of Christ and Sophia.

However, after a close reading of the Nag Hammadi Corpus, I am forced to accept that these Gnostics were, for the most part, *ascetic* – far more monastic and ascetic than popular interpreters of Gnosticism would have us believe. And that the rite of the Bridal Chamber was, for them, a vow of abstinence.

THE PASSION

When the time came to write the Passion of the Gnostic Christ, I was confronted by a bewildering variety of interpretations. After much reflection, I was able to reduce these down to four possible scenarios, which I then linked to the point-of-view of four characters. They are as follows:

– That neither Jesus nor the Christ suffered (Peter)
– That Jesus suffered but Christ did not (James)
– That Jesus did not suffer but Christ did (symbolically - John)
– That they both suffered (Jesus)

As with the case of the Bridal Chamber, where three chambers manifest its mystery to Magdalene in three different ways; so with the Passion, three apostles view the mystery of the crucifixion from three different perspectives. I leave it open to the reader to decide which of these mysteries resonates with the truth.

While I was writing the final chapter, the scenes began to flow past my eyes, much in the manner of a vision or a dream. And yet, I would not like to be unjustly accused of transforming Christ's Passion into an illusion, apparition or fantasy. (The heretical charge of *docetism* – that Christ suffered *in appearance only* – was frequently leveled at the Gnostics).

If one has truly stepped inside the Gnostic worldview (and, by extension, if one has entered into my novel), then the material world is an illusion created by Yaltabaoth to trap us in ignorance. The illusion, then, lies with treating the events of this world too literally, historically or realistically.

Instead, the images that we see here are based upon heavenly archetypes, which we must learn to discern and properly decipher. As *The Gospel of Philip* reminds us, *"The mysteries of truth are revealed,* Gs Phil 84:20
though in type and image." I believe that, when we approach these events creatively, with much meditation and reflection, then we can finally

...enter through the image Gs Phil 67:17
into truth.

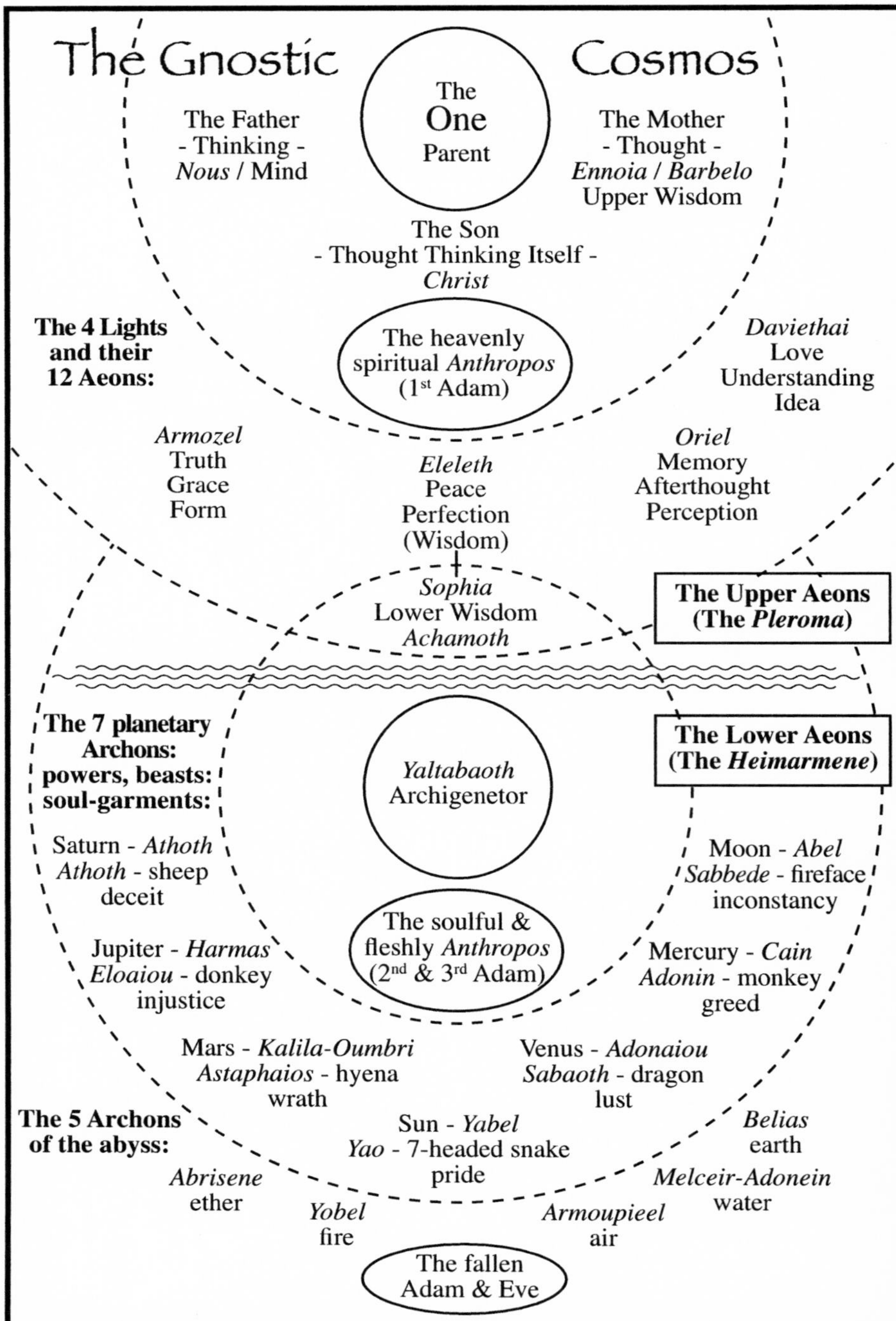
The Gnostic Cosmos
The One Parent
The Father
- Thinking -
Nous / Mind
The Mother
- Thought -
Ennoia / Barbelo
Upper Wisdom
The Son
- Thought Thinking Itself -
Christ
The heavenly spiritual Anthropos (1st Adam)
The 4 Lights and their 12 Aeons:
Daviethai
Love
Understanding
Idea
Armozel
Truth
Grace
Form
Eleleth
Peace
Perfection
(Wisdom)
Oriel
Memory
Afterthought
Perception
Sophia
Lower Wisdom
Achamoth
The Upper Aeons (The Pleroma)
The Lower Aeons (The Heimarmene)
The 7 planetary Archons: powers, beasts: soul-garments:
Yaltabaoth
Archigenetor
Saturn - Athoth
Athoth - sheep
deceit
Moon - Abel
Sabbede - fireface
inconstancy
The soulful & fleshly Anthropos (2nd & 3rd Adam)
Jupiter - Harmas
Eloaiou - donkey
injustice
Mercury - Cain
Adonin - monkey
greed
Mars - Kalila-Oumbri
Astaphaios - hyena
wrath
Venus - Adonaiou
Sabaoth - dragon
lust
Sun - Yabel
Yao - 7-headed snake
pride
The 5 Archons of the abyss:
Belias
earth
Abrisene
ether
Melceir-Adonein
water
Yobel
fire
Armoupieel
air
The fallen Adam & Eve

A GLOSSARY OF PROPER NAMES AND GNOSTIC TERMS

- **Achamoth -** The Lower Sophia. See Sophia.
- **Adam and Eve -** See Anthropos.
- **Aeons -** Also called 'extensions' or 'heavens'. The aeons are like concentric heavenly spheres, one within the next, and extending outward from a common centre. In the Upper Aeons, each aeon reflects the One to itself, preserving its unity while extending it outward. These aeons reflect the One to itself as images in the watery light or as names in the silence. The Upper Aeons are twelve in number (see Mind) and have no temporal or spatial measure. The Lower Aeons imitate the Upper Aeons, as images and names in matter, and have spatial and temporal measures (see the Lower Aeons). They are also twelve in number. The first seven are the seven visible heavens, each with a planet as a gateway. The last five make up the earth through the four elements mixed in the ether.
- **Allogenes -** Also called 'the Great Teacher'. Father of the Gennesaret monastery.
- **Andrew -** A disciple. Also called: 'the younger son of Jonah' (in contrast to his elder brother Cephas-Peter, who is 'the elder son of Jonah').
- **Androgyne -** A being of both male and female genders. See Consort, the One.
- **Annas -** Also called: 'the Elder', 'the Sadducee Elder'. He is father-in-law of Caiaphas and former High Priest of the Temple.
- **Anthropos -** Also called 'Man', 'First Man', 'Adam'. The One created the Anthropos in the Upper Aeons, as an image of itself that was androgynous and spiritual ('the First Adam'). When Yaltabaoth and his Archons saw the luminous image of the Anthropos in the Upper Aeons, they created an imitation, at first as an androgynous soul ('the Second Adam') and then as an androgynous body ('the Third Adam'). Yaltabaoth then divided the ensouled body of the androgynous Anthropos into male and female, Adam and Eve, but the spiritual Anthropos remained androgynous in the Upper Aeons. In *The Poimandres*, a different story of the creation is given, where the (masculine) Anthropos saw its reflection in the pool of (feminine) Nature and, out of love, fell into her embrace, becoming the material male and female.
- **Antipas -** See Herod-Antipas.
- **Archons -** Rulers. Also called: 'Planetary Rulers'. See Lower Aeons.
- **Archigenetor -** 'First Begetter'. See Yaltabaoth.
- **Archigenetor's Son -** See Yaltabaoth's Son.
- **Arsinoe -** A disciple. Also called Mary-Arsinoe. She is one of Jesus' younger siblings, along with Jude and the younger James.
- **Awake -** A state of being in the Upper Aeons. Also called: 'sober', 'standing (at rest)'. Opposite of 'sleeping', which is to exist in the Lower Aeons.

- **Barabbas -** The Blind Prophet of the Zealots. See also: Yaltabaoth's Son.
- **Barbelo -** The Upper Sophia. See Sophia.
- **Beasts -** The third type of men (see Types of men), who are materialistic, and continually distracted by the needs of the body and the passions of the soul. The Archons also have the forms of beasts, and rule over such men.
- **Bethanite -** See Mariam of Bethany
- **Bethsaidean -** See Cephas-Peter
- **Caiaphas -** Also called: 'the High Priest'. He is the present High Priest of the Temple, and the son-in-law of Annas.
- **Cananaean -** See Simon the Zealot
- **Cephas-Peter -** A disciple. Nicknamed Cephas, later called Peter. Birth name is Simon. Also called: 'the Bethsaidean', 'the elder son of Jonah' (in contrast to his younger brother Andrew, who is 'the younger son of Jonah').
- **Chief Archon -** See Yaltabaoth
- **Christ -** He is the reflection of the One, as its 'name' or 'image'. He was created through the union of the Father as *Nous* ('Thinking' or 'Mind') and the Mother as *Ennoia* ('Thought'), to become their Son as the One's reflection ('itself' in 'Thought-Thinking-itself'). As well, he was created through the union of the Father as 'the Silence' and the Mother as 'the Voice' to become the Son as 'the Word'. He was then 'anointed' as 'the Christ'. In the Upper Aeons, he is also called 'the first-born Son', 'the countenance of the Father', 'the only-begotten one' and 'the Fifth Light'. He is also the consort or *syzygy* of Sophia, but she did not consent to unite with him during the creation. During the baptism at the Jordan, he descended into Jesus. With Jesus, he became 'the Messiah', also called 'the Messiah of the Five Seals', 'the Anointed One', 'the saviour', 'the Lord', and 'the Illuminator'.
- **Chuza -** He is the Vizier of Herod-Antipas, and is married to Joanna.
- **Consent -** See Consort.
- **Consort -** Also called *'syzygy'*. In the Upper Aeons, each 'image of the One' (an angel or aeon) is androgynous, but with a male and female aspect (or 'name'). For example 'the Father' and 'the Mother' are the male and female aspects (or 'names') of the androgynous 'Parent'. These two become consorts when they consent to unite, and create a further extension of the One's unity (another angel or aeon, which is androgynous, but with male and female aspects or 'names'). For example, 'the Father' consented with his consort 'the Mother' to create 'the Son' (whose masculine aspect or name is Christ, while its feminine aspect or name is Sophia). Christ is the consort (or *syzygy*) of Sophia, but she did not consent to unite with him when she created the next extension of the aeons. The result was her bastard offspring Yaltabaoth, who created the twelve Archons. Subsequently, Yaltabaoth's archons raped Sophia to engender the Lower Aeons.
- **Daughter of the Herodians -** See Salome.
- **Dreaming -** A state of being in the Lower Aeons. Also called: 'sleeping', 'forgetful', 'drunk'. Opposite of 'awake', which is to exist in the Upper Aeons.
- **Drunk -** A state of being in the Lower Aeons. Also called: 'sleeping',

'forgetful', 'dreaming'. Opposite of 'sober', which is to exist in the Upper Aeons.

- **Elder** - See Annas.
- **Elect** - Also called: 'the shining ones', 'the pneumatic race', 'the children of Seth', 'the chosen ones', 'the imperishable seeds', 'whose names are written in the Book of the Living'. Those whose names and images appeared in the Upper Aeons during the foundation of the world, and who will return to the Upper Aeons at the end.
- **Ennoia** - 'Thought'. See the One and Sophia.
- **Enoch** - One of the three hermits or 'wise men'. A Hebrew sage.
- **Essenes** - A secessionist group of Judeans who claimed that they, and not the Sadducees, were the true sons of Zadok. Some withdrew to the desert and founded the Qumran community (where the Dead Sea scrolls were discovered).
- **False Messiah** - See Yaltabaoth's Son and Barabbas.
- **Fate** - See *Heimarmene.*
- **Fifth Light** - Christ. See Four Lights.
- **Four Lights** - The Upper Aeons are twelve in number (see Mind) and each aeon is associated with an angel (as well as with a state of mind). The twelve angels are divided into four groups of three each, and one angel heads the group as its archangel. These four archangels are called the Four Lights, and named *Armozel*, *Oriel*, *Daveithai* and *Eleleth*. On the earth, they find their images in the disciples Peter, Andrew, James and John. Christ, as head of all the angels, is sometime called the Fifth Light, which finds its image on earth as Jesus.
- **Fullness** - Also called 'the *Pleroma*'. See Upper Aeons.
- **Heimarmene** - Fate in the astrological sense. The Archons contributed matter and passions to the make up of the human body and soul. Meanwhile, the Archons themselves are the planetary rulers or gate-keepers. Thus, humans are subject, in body and in soul, to the influence of the Archons and their planetary movements. This is one's astrological fate or *Heimarmene.*
- **Hellenist** - See Judas-Thomas.
- **Herod the Great** - Father of Herod-Antipas. He ruled Israel at the time of Jesus' birth. Upon his death, his kingdom was divided among his sons Archelaus, Herod-Antipas and Philip.
- **Herod-Antipas** - the Tetrarch of Galilee and Perea. Also called 'Herod', 'Antipas', 'Tetrarch', 'Basileus', 'Archon'. The son of Herod the Great, he is married to Herodias, and is the step-father of Salome.
- **Herodias** - Wife of Herod-Antipas and mother of Salome.
- **Hylic race** - 'The material' race. See Types of men.
- **Iscariot** - See Judas-Thomas.
- **James (the elder)** - A disciple. Also called: 'the elder son of Zebedee' (in contrast to his younger brother John, who is 'the younger son of Zebedee'), 'the elder James' (in contrast to 'the younger James', who is the younger sibling of Jesus).
- **James (the younger)** - A disciple. Called 'the younger James' (in contrast

to 'the elder James'). He is one of Jesus' younger siblings, along with Jude and Mary-Arsinoe.

- **Jesus -** Also called: 'the Nazarene', 'the son of Nazareth', 'the Galilean', 'the son of Mary', 'the rabbi', 'the master'. Born Yeshua ben Yosef. Hidden name: *Yesseus Mazareus Yessedekeus*. He becomes the Messiah, also called 'the Messiah of the Five Seals', 'the Anointed One', 'the saviour'. During his baptism in the Jordan, the Christ enters him. See also: Christ.
- **Joanna -** A disciple. She is Salome's tutor and is married to Chuza.
- **John -** A disciple. Also called: 'the beloved disciple', 'the younger son of Zebedee' (in contrast to his elder brother James, who is 'the elder son of Zebedee'). Spiritual name: *Bonarges*.
- **John the Baptist -** Also called: 'the Last Prophet', 'the Baptizer', 'the Immerser', 'the Voice' and 'the Nazarite' (see Nazarite).
- **Judas-Thomas -** A disciple. At first called Judas, later Thomas. Also called: tauma, 'the twin', 'the Iscariot', 'the son of Kerioth', 'the Hellenist'. Spiritual name: *Didymos*.
- **Jude -** A disciple. He is one of Jesus' younger siblings, along with Mary-Arsinoe and James the younger.
- **Levi-Matthew -** A disciple. At first called Levi, later Matthew. Also called: 'the publican', 'the son of Sepphoris', 'the son of Alphaeus'.
- **Lower Aeons -** The aeons as manifest materially in space and time (see Aeons). These are twelve in number: seven are 'heavenly', 'celestial' or 'planetary', while five are 'earthly', 'sublunar' or 'of the abyss'. The seven consist of the seven planetary spheres encompassing the earth, and each has an Archon as its ruler or gate-keeper. Each Archon also has an adjunct or 'power' with the face of a beast. And each of these rules over a passion in the soul. Thus, from highest to lowest, the seven planetary aeons, Archons, powers, beasts and passions are as follows:

Saturn - *Athoth* - *Athoth* - sheep - deceit
Jupiter -*Harmas* - *Eloaiou* - donkey - injustice
Mars -*Kalila-Oumbri* - *Astaphaios* - hyena - wrath
Sun -*Yabel* - *Yao* - seven-headed serpent - pride
Venus - *Adonaiou* - *Sabaoth* - dragon - lust
Mercury - *Cain* - *Adonin* - monkey - greed
Moon - *Abel* - *Sabbede* - fire-face - inconstancy

Beneath the moon, five more Archons rule over five more spheres. These are the five 'sublunar' aeons 'of the abyss', which are composed of ether, fire, air, water and earth (the last four, as the elements, are intermixed). From highest to lowest, the Archons and aeons are as follows:

Abrisene - ether
Yobel - fire
Armoupieel - air
Melceir-Adonein - water
Belias - earth

Usually Yaltabaoth is associated with the sun, but he actually encompasses all the Archons and aeons in himself. Since the Archons

contributed matter and passions to the make up of the human body and soul, humans are subject to the Archons' influence. See: *Heimarmene.*
- **Mariam -** A disciple from Bethany. Also called the Bethanite. She is the sister of Martha and Lazarus.
- **Marsanes -** One of the three hermits or 'wise men'. A Greek ascetic.
- **Martha -** A disciple from Bethany. She is the sister of Mariam and Lazarus.
- **Mary -** See 'Virgin Mary' as well as 'Sophia'.
- **Mary-Arsinoe -** See Arsinoe.
- **Mary Magdalene -** A disciple. Also called: 'Miri', 'the Magdalene', 'the daughter of Magdala', 'the younger Mary' (in contrast to the Virgin, who is 'the elder Mary'). Gradually she becomes aware that Sophia has fallen into her. See also: Sophia.
- **Matthew -** See Levi-Matthew.
- **Melchizedek -** Also called 'the Great Teacher'. After the death of Allogenes, he becomes Father of the Gennesaret monastery.
- **Messiah -** The Hebrew word for Israel's 'anointed' king. For the Messiah of the Five Seals, see Christ.
- **Mind -** Also called *'Nous'* or 'Thinking'. See the One. In the Upper Aeons, the Mind has twelve aeons or aspects, which are twelve ways of thinking. In the Lower Aeons, these twelve aspects take the form of images in the twelve disciples, as follows: Peter - grace; Thomas - truth; Matthew - form; Andrew - afterthought; Jude - memory; young James - perception; elder James - understanding; Philip - love; Nathanael - idea; John - perfection; Simon - peace; Miri - wisdom.
- **Miri -** See Mary Magdalene.
- **Nathanael -** A disciple, usually paired with Philip.
- **Nazarite -** One who takes the Nazarite vow: abstaining from wine, hair-cutting and contact with the dead. Used as an epithet for John the Baptist. See John the Baptist.
- **Nous -** 'Thinking' or 'Mind'. See Mind and the One.
- **One -** The unity from which 'the all' came, and into which 'the all' will resolve. In the beginning, the One was 'the Parent' which divided into two aeons, as 'the Father' and 'the Mother' or as *'Nous'* ('Thinking' or 'Mind') and *'Ennoia'* (Thought) or as 'Silence' and 'Voice'. These two united to create the third aeon, as 'the Son' or as the One's reflection ('itself' in 'Thought-Thinking-itself') or as 'the Word'. The One continued to create the Upper Aeons in this manner, without any loss of its unity, until the twelfth aeon, called Sophia. Sophia then begot Yaltabaoth and the Lower Aeons.
- **Parent -** See the One.
- **Parousias -** Mankind will pass through three catastrophes, called the three *parousias* (or 'presences') before the end of time. The first is the Flood, and has already passed. The second is the Great Fire or Conflagration, and is imminent (though some texts see this as past, with Sodom and Gomorrah). The last is the Judgement, and will come at the end of time.
- **Pearl -** See *Pneuma.*

- **Peter** - See Cephas-Peter.
- **Pharisees** - A religious faction of Judeans who claimed that an oral law existed independently of the Torah's written laws, and was passed down through the generations. Typically, the Pharisees observed scrupulous laws of purity.
- **Philip** - A disciple, usually paired with Nathanael.
- **Pilate** - The Prefect and Procurator of Syria-Palestine (i.e. Phoenicia and Israel).
- **Pleroma** - Also called 'the Fullness'. See Upper Aeons.
- **Pneumatic Race** - 'The spirit-endowed' race. See Types of men.
- **Pneuma** - Literally: 'breath'. The particle of the divine hidden in men and women. Also called: spirit, divine spark, seed, dew drop, or pearl. It should not be confused with the soul, which is the seat of the passions.
- **Prunikos** - The Lower Wisdom, called 'the whore'. See Sophia.
- **Psychic Race** - 'The soul-endowed' race. See Types of men.
- **Publican** - See Levi-Matthew
- **Rest** - A state of being in the Upper Aeons. See Stand (at rest)
- **Sadducee Elder** - See Annas
- **Sadducees** - A religious faction of Judeans claiming descent from Zadok. They considered only the first five books of the Torah as authoritative. Typically, they were wealthy, privileged, and of the ruling class.
- **Salome** - Also called: 'daughter of the Herodians', 'Herod's daughter', 'the princess'. She is married to Philip, the brother of Herod-Antipas. Salome is the daughter of Herodias, whose husband, Herod-Antipas, is Salome's step-father. She is also the grand-daughter of Herod the Great.
- **Simon the Zealot** - A disciple. Also called: 'the Cananaean', 'the Zealot'.
- **Sophia** - Wisdom. As the Upper Sophia, or Sophia of the Upper Aeons, she is called *Barbelo*, 'the Virgin', 'the Mother', *'Ennoia'* ('Thought') 'the Voice' and is present in the Virgin Mary. As 'the Mother' she united with 'the Father' to create 'the Son' or Christ. As the Lower Sophia, or Sophia of the Lower Aeons, she is called *Achamoth* or *Prunikos*, 'the Whore', and is present in Miri. The Lower Sophia begot Yaltabaoth, her son, when she created an aeon without the consent of Christ, who is her consort or *syzygy*. The Lower Sophia is also Nature or Zoe ('Life'). The Hebrews called Sophia 'Hochmah', and she was worshipped in Phoenicia as Astarte. See also Mary Magdalene and Virgin Mary.
- **Sleeping** - A state of being in the Lower Aeons. Also called: 'dreaming', 'forgetful', 'drunk'. Opposite of 'awake', which is to exist in the Upper Aeons.
- **Sober** - A state of being in the Upper Aeons. Also called: 'awake', 'standing (at rest)'. Opposite of 'drunk', which is to exist in the Lower Aeons.
- **Son of Alphaeus** - See Levi-Matthew.
- **Son of Jonah (elder)** - See Cephas-Peter.
- **Son of Jonah (younger)** - See Andrew.
- **Son of Kerioth** - See Judas-Thomas.
- **Son of Mary** - See Jesus.

- **Son of Nazareth -** See Jesus.
- **Son of Sepphoris -** See Levi-Matthew.
- **Son of Zebedee (elder) -** See James.
- **Son of Zebedee (younger) -** See John.
- **Stand (at rest) -** To stand is to exist in the Upper Aeons. To 'stand at rest' is to achieve a state, here below in the Lower Aeons, which is equivalent to existence in the Upper Aeons: mindful, unmoved by passion, unbound by temporal or spatial measures. Also called: 'still', 'immobile', 'at rest', 'undistracted', 'sober', 'awake'.
- **Susanna -** A disciple.
- **Syzygy -** See Consort.
- **Tauma -** 'the twin' in Aramaic. See Judas-Thomas.
- **Thomas -** From *tauma*, 'the twin' in Aramaic. See Judas-Thomas.
- **Three parousias -** See Parousias
- **Three types of men -** See Types of men.
- **Twin -** See Judas-Thomas
- **Types of men -** Men and women are composed variously of spirit, soul and body, which come from different aeons. The spirit comes from the Upper Aeons while the soul and body come from the Lower Aeons (the soul is considered to be the seat of the passions, not the eternal soul). The spiritual type of man belongs to the Spiritual or *Pneumatic* race, and will return to the Upper Aeons. The soulful type of man belongs to the Soulful or *Psychic* race, and may rise to the Upper Aeons or fall to the Lower Aeons. The 'embodied' or fleshly type of man belongs to the Material or *Hylic* race, and will fall once more to the Lower Aeons. The Gnostics associated themselves with the *Pneumatic* race, while associating more orthodox Christians with the *Psychic* race. The remainder, who are more material, are considered 'beasts'. In the novel, Thomas is more the image of the Gnostics, while Peter is the image of the Christians.
- **Upper Aeons -** Also called: 'the *Pleroma*', 'the Fullness', 'the Silence', 'watery light', 'luminous waters'. For their creation, see: the One. For their arrangement, see: Mind. In general, see: Aeons.
- **Virgin Mary -** Also called: 'the Virgin', 'the elder Mary' (in contrast to Miri, who is 'the younger Mary'). See also: Sophia.
- **Yaltabaoth -** The Chief Archon, a lion-headed serpent. Also called 'the Archigenetor', 'the Arrogant One', 'YHWH'. He is the offspring of Sophia, and through her *pneuma* he begot the twelve Archons. They engendered the Lower Aeons, as well as the body and soul of the *Anthropos*, which became Adam and Eve.
- **Yaltabaoth's Son -** Also called 'the Archigenetor's Son'. He is the False Messiah or 'imitator', and descended into Barabbas. See Barabbas.
- **Zealot (the) -** See Simon the Zealot
- **Zealots -** A religious faction of Judeans who followed the revolutionary teachings of Judas the Galilean. Typically they resorted to violence and rebellion.
- **Zostrianos -** One of the three hermits or 'wise men'. A Persian Magus.

ACKNOWLEDGEMENTS

This work would not have been possible without the efforts of many scholars and translators, which I would like to acknowledge here.

To begin, *The Nag Hammadi Library in English*, edited by James M. Robinson, (HarperSanFrancisco), with the following translations:

The Prayer of the Apostle Paul, Dieter Mueller; *The Apocryphon of James*, Francis E. Williams; *The Gospel of Truth*, Harold W. Attridge, George W. MacRae; *The Treatise on the Resurrection*, Malcolm L. Peel; *The Tripartite Tractate*, Harold W. Attridge, Elaine H. Pagels, Dieter Mueller; *The Apocryphon of John*, Frederik Wisse; *The Gospel of Thomas*, Helmut Koestler, Thomas O. Lambdin; *The Gospel of Philip*, Wesley W. Isenberg; *The Hypostasis of the Archons*, Roger A. Bullard, Bentley Layton; *On the Origin of the World*, Hans-Gebhard Bethge, Bentley Layton; *Exegesis on the Soul*, William C. Robinson, Maddalena Scopello;

The Book of Thomas the Contender, John D. Turner; *The Gospel of the Egyptians*, Alexander Böhlig, Frederik Wisse; *Eugnostos the Blessed*, Douglas M. Parrott; *The Sophia of Jesus Christ*, Douglas M. Parrot; *The Dialogue of the Saviour*, Stephen Emmel, Helmut Koester, Elaine Pagels; *The Apocalypse of Paul*, George W. MacRae, William R. Murdock, Douglas M. Parrott; *The (First) Apocalypse of James*, William R. Schoedel, Douglas M. Parrott; *The (Second) Apocalypse of James*, Charles W. Hendrick, Douglas M. Parrott; *The Apocalypse of Adam*, George W. MacRae, Douglas M. Parrott; *The Acts of Peter and the Twelve Apostles*, Douglas M. Parrott, R. McL. Wilson; *The Thunder, Perfect Mind,* R. McL. Wilson, Douglas M. Parrott;

Authoritative Teaching, George W. MacRae, Douglas M. Parrott; *The Concept of our Great Power*, Francis E. Williams, Frederik Wisse, Douglas M. Parrott; *Plato, Republic 588A - 589B*, James Brashler, Howard M. Jackson, Douglas M. Parrott; *The Discourse on the Eighth and Ninth*, James Brashler, Peter A. Dirkse, Douglas M. Parrott; *The Prayer of Thanksgiving* and *Scribal Note*, James Brashler, Peter A. Dirkse, Douglas M. Parrott; *Asclepius 21 - 29*, James Brashler, Peter A. Dirkse, Douglas M. Parrott; *The Paraphrase of Shem*, Michel Roberge, Frederik Wisse; *The Second Treatise of the Great Seth*, Joseph A. Gibbons, Roger A. Bullard; *Apocalypse of Peter*, James Brashler, Roger A. Bullard;

The Teachings of Silvanus, Malcolm L. Peel, Jan Zandee; *The Three Steles of Seth*, James E. Goehring, James M. Robinson; *Zostrianos*, John H. Sieber; *The Letter of Peter to Philip*, Marvin W. Meyer, Frederik Wisse; *Melchizedek*, Birger A. Pearson, Søren Giversen; Marsanes, Birger A. Pearson; *The Interpretation of Knoweldge*, Elaine H. Pagels, John D. Turner; *A Valentinian Exposition*, with *On the Anointing, On Baptism A and B*, and *On the Eucharist A and B*, Elaine H. Pagels, John D. Turner;

Allogenes, Antoinette Clark Wire, John D. Turner, Orval S. Wintermute; *Hypsiphrone*, John D. Turner; *The Sentences of Sextus*, Frederik Wisse; *Fragments*, Frederik Wisse; *Trimorphic Protennoia*, John D. Turner; *The Gospel of Mary*, Karen L. King, George W. MacRae, R. McL. Wilson, Douglas M. Parrott; *The Act of Peter*, James Brashler, Douglas M. Parrott.

Comparative translations of the Nag Hammadi Texts were also consulted, including: *New Testament Apocrypha*, Wilhelm Schneemelcher, R. McL. Wilson, eds, (James Clarke & Co.); *The Gnostic Scriptures*, Bentley Layton (Doubleday); John D. Turner, (jdt.unl.edu website), *Gnosis*, Kurt Rudolf (HarperSanFrancisco), *The Gnostic Gospels of Jesus*, Marvin Meyer (HarperSanFrancisco); *et al.*

Other Gnostic text translations consulted include: *The Gospel of Judas*, Rodolphe Kasser, Marvin Meyer, Gregor Wurst, François Gaudard; *The Books of Jeu*, Carl Schmidt; *The Untitled Text in the Bruce Codex*, Carl Schmidt; *The Pistis Sophia*, G. R. S. Mead; *The Acts of John*, M.R. James; *The Hymn of the Pearl*, Bentley Layton, cf. Hans Jonas, Willis Barnstone, William Wright.

Hermetic text translations consulted include: *The Corpus Hermeticum* (incl. *The Poimandres*), *Asclepius*, Brian P. Copenhaver (Cambridge U. Press).

Translations of the Church Fathers include: Irenaeus of Lyon, *Against All Heresies*, A. Roberts, J. Donaldson, cf. Bentley Layton; Origen (Ophite Diagram) *Contra Celsum*, Henry Chadwick; Epiphanius of Salamis, *Against Heresies*, K. Holl, cf. Bentley Layton.

Translations of the Old and New Testaments of *The Bible* include: The King James version, cf. *The New Oxford Annotated Bible* (NRSV), various translators (Oxford U. Press).